What a remarkable book! I have always believed in penal substitution in the atoning death of Christ, but have not seen so much useful material brought together before. I was struck by the breadth of biblical evidence, especially the material on the Passover. The book is a remarkable combination of biblical evidence for penal substitution, its integration into the big themes of the Bible, examples from historical theology, its trinitarian context, and answers to current objections.

Peter Adam, Principal, Ridley College, Melbourne

If gospel people are to be clear on the nature of the gospel, then they need to have a clear understanding of penal substitution. This is a timely and magnificent book, which will inform heads and warm hearts about the amazing love of God for us. There is much loose talk in the church about the gospel – this book tells us so powerfully how truly wonderful it is.

Wallace Benn, Bishop of Lewes, and President,
Church of England Evangelical Council

For all who suspect that penal substitutionary atonement may not be a central biblical truth, think it a Johnny-come-lately doctrine, or judge it objectionable on other grounds, read this book! For all who gratefully believe that 'the Lord has laid on him the iniquity of us all', read this book – and let your heart sing!

Steve Brady, Principal, Moorlands College, and Trustee, The Keswick Convention

In every generation, the great truths of Christian faith need to be restated in a fresh way. We are indebted to the authors of this book for the masterly way in which they have lucidly articulated and defended the vital doctrine of the penal substitution of Christ. It is at the very heart of the gospel. Careful reading of this material will captivate the mind, warm the heart and fill the senses with a sense of wonder at what God has done out of love for his people. I warmly commend it.

Lindsay Brown, General Secretary, International Fellowship of Evangelical Students

This book is important not only because it deals so competently with what lies at the heart of Christ's cross work, but because it responds effectively to a new generation of people who are not listening very carefully to what either Scripture or history says. One of the delightful features of this book is reflected in the subtitle: the authors make no apology for their thesis, but underscore the *glory* of penal substitution. This book deserves the widespread circulation achieved by corresponding contributions a generation ago – the contributions of Leon Morris, Jim Packer and John Stott.

D. A. Carson, Research Professor of New Testament,
Trinity Evangelical Divinity School, Deerfield, Illinois

D1336033

As I was sitting on a log in the mountains of the Lebanon, my uncle explained to me, a fifteen-year-old, the gospel. It was the explanation of the cross that struck me and convinced me that I must trust Jesus as my Lord and Saviour. If he had loved me enough to pay the penalty for my sin, then I had to receive him. Since then I have sought to proclaim 'Christ and him crucified' to everyone I can. It is sad that *Pierced for our Transgressions* has had to be written to defend the very heart of the Christian message, but I am delighted that the authors have produced a warm, biblical, thorough and endearing defence of Jesus' great work on the cross. Whilst I would want to passionately argue that Jesus died for everyone, I commend this book and its great theme to all. As D. L. Moody said, 'The main thing is to keep the main thing the main thing.'

Roger Carswell, Evangelist

As secular society bullies the church into air-brushing out the harder elements of the gospel, evangelicals will find themselves tempted to downplay the central importance of penal substitution. If we do, we will lose the authentic, historic gospel for at least a generation. This brilliant book is a timely gift to God's people (not least to students) to help us hold firm. *Pierced for our Transgressions* is set to become one of the most important books for evangelicalism at this critical moment of time.

Richard Cunningham, Director, Universities and Colleges Christian Fellowship

The treatment of the biblical material is in itself worth the price of the book. A model of biblical-theological exposition. They expound the weightiest texts so concisely and so clearly – as they argue for the rugged truth about the rugged cross.

Dale Ralph Davis, Pastor, Woodland Presbyterian Church, Hattiesburg, Mississippi

The Bible historically has been understood to teach explicitly and implicitly that Christ died as a penal substitute for sinners. That's what this excellent volume teaches us, too. Carefully studying the primary biblical texts and then answering numerous objections, this book explains and defends the understanding that Christ died in our place, taking our penalty for us. From the biblical material to patristic quotations, from pastoral implications to present objections, this book is a responsible and comprehensive introduction. All the authors' careful work promises to make this book the new standard text on Christ's atoning work. Now, I can't wait to read it again, devotionally.

Mark Dever, Pastor, Capitol Hill Baptist Church, Washington, DC

This book is a serious and scholarly defence of one of the fundamentals of the Christian faith. Its exegesis of Scripture is as refreshing as it is thorough. Its defence of penal substitution against various criticisms is sharp, focused and helpful. It has enriched my understanding of Anglican theology and encouraged me in my faith. I recommend it to preachers, apologists and all serious Bible students – it is worth ten times whatever it will cost you!

John Dunnett, General Director, Church Pastoral Aid Society

A scholarly, detailed, heart-warming and satisfying response to those who deny the penal substitutionary atonement of Christ. The authors have well covered the biblical and historical ground, and opposing arguments are considered and answered. It is an accessible and most valuable addition to the strong defence of the vital Christian doctrine of propitiation. Let all who deny the doctrine respond to this book.

Brian H. Edwards, author of *The Divine Substitute*, and former President, FIEC

Agreement on the nature of the atonement has long been a defining feature of evangelical Christianity. Today, however, all is in crisis. For some time the writings of a number of scholars reared in evangelicalism have eroded, even denied, that the heart of the gospel is to be found in Christ's penal substitutionary death and his glorious resurrection. But now – inevitably – this view has begun to appear in books written by popular authors who are viewed as contemporary, cutting-edge leaders. Sadly, much that is said and written unwittingly repeats what was long ago rejected as unorthodox. In the past, those views irrevocably led – within a generation – to a rejection of evangelical faith; unchecked, they will inevitably do so again. The stakes could scarcely be higher – the very nature of the gospel itself. *Pierced for our Transgressions* is a courageous, timely, comprehensive and welcome study. It is biblically sensitive and pastorally astute, with the added strength of being aware of where similar false steps in the past eventually led. Here is a sure-footed guide to the message of the cross – and therefore to Christ himself, and ultimately to God the Trinity. It deserves widespread and careful reading.

Sinclair B. Ferguson, Pastor, First Presbyterian Church, Columbia, South Carolina

This is certainly one of the most comprehensive treatments available of the doctrine of penal substitutionary atonement. It presents exegesis, historical theology, and responses to contemporary debate, all in one volume. In all these areas, the book is excellent, both in its exposition and in its argument. It presents a cogent defence of the biblical and historic church doctrine, and in my view it devastates the criticisms of this position. The writing is clear and understandable to non-specialists, but its authors fully understand the technical issues, so that the book makes a real contribution to the academic discussion as well. I am delighted to see this book appear, and I hope that it gets a very wide readership.

John M. Frame, Professor of Systematic Theology and Philosophy, Reformed Theological Seminary, Orlando, Florida

The doctrine of the penal substitutionary atonement of Jesus Christ can be abandoned only by eviscerating the soteriological heart of historic Christianity. This teaching has deep roots in both the Catholic and Protestant theological traditions and deserves to be taken seriously in the church's proclamation of the doctrine of reconciliation today. This is an important scholarly contribution to a current doctrinal debate with enormous spiritual and pastoral implications.

Timothy George, Dean, Beeson Divinity School, and Executive Editor, *Christianity Today*

The authors have given us a wide-ranging and heart-warming treatment of penal substitution. They have a firm grasp of the biblical material, and are thoroughly aware of the current debates and scholarly issues involved. Above all they know the stakes are high, none other than the gospel itself and the health of Christ's church. It deserves to be widely used by serious Christians concerned to know both what the Bible teaches and what the church has preached from its earliest days concerning the cross of Christ.

Liam Goligher, author of *The Jesus Gospel*, and Pastor, Duke Street Church, Richmond-upon-Thames

A well-thumbed copy of *Pierced for our Transgressions* ought to rest on the bookshelf of every thoughtful Christian. This even-handed, masterful defence of penal substitutionary atonement is clear and convincing. Readers will quickly grasp the theology and the urgency of the issues, and will be especially grateful for the classic objection–response format of Part Two, which makes for easy reference. A crucial read.

R. Kent Hughes, Senior Pastor Emeritus, College Church, Wheaton, Illinois

Thoroughly researched and documented, cogently argued and presented with great clarity, this is a timely and much-needed restatement of the central biblical doctrine of penal substitution. Its great strength lies in its comprehensive exegesis of the biblical text itself, explaining the positive content and answering its opponents with gracious fairness, but penetrating force.

David Jackman, President, Proclamation Trust, London

This excellent study is sufficiently thorough to engage seriously with the key issues, and sufficiently accessible for those who might not regard themselves as 'theologians'. Its biblical survey, historical overview, pastoral focus and thoughtful reply to today's questions make it a vital contribution to our understanding of what Christ achieved on the cross. I particularly wish to encourage those who might not usually dip into such a substantial work to read this careful treatment of a central and glorious Christian doctrine. It will strengthen your understanding, warm your heart and increase your devotion to Christ.

Jonathan Lamb, International Director, Langham Preaching, and former Chair, Keswick Ministries and Word Alive

In God's mission to have a people that 'no one could number from every nation, from all tribes and peoples and languages', the penal substitution of his Son in our place, receiving in full the punishment of God's righteous indignation that should have been ours, is absolutely central and critical to the whole enterprise. So this new contribution really does help us rediscover the glory of penal substitution; showing us its biblical foundations, the way that it has been clearly taught by the church for 2,000 years and refuting contemporary objections to it. You will find this book a very useful resource, and an important one in contending for this key understanding of what Christ achieved at Calvary.

Andy Lines, General Secretary, Crosslinks

*Pierced for our Transgressions* is a treasure trove of information and analysis on the important, yet disputed doctrine of penal substitution. As a biblical scholar, I enthusiastically commend the authors for their careful exegesis of the biblical text. From this point on, critics of the biblical teaching must interact with the arguments of this book. Further, every Christian, whether aware of the debate or not, can greatly benefit from this comprehensive and penetrating treatment of this crucial doctrine.

Tremper Longman III, Robert H. Gundry Professor of Biblical Studies,
Westmont College, Santa Barbara, California

It is difficult to imagine a more important book than *Pierced for our Transgressions*, or a more helpful one. It is important because of its skilful and thorough defence of the doctrine of penal substitution against a growing chorus of objections – objections that threaten our very understanding of the gospel. It is helpful because of its clear and accessible style that illuminates the issues, whether you are a scholar, pastor or simply a Christian who loves the Saviour. I am deeply grateful to God, and to the authors, for this critical and timely book.

C. J. Mahaney, Sovereign Grace Ministries

I commend this book for its comprehensive and fair scrutiny of the many objections brought against the doctrine of penal substitution in recent years. Even those who, like me, would disagree with the authors' belief that a doctrine of particular redemption (or 'limited atonement') is a necessary part of this doctrine will be grateful for this useful contribution to the current debate with its careful demonstration of the weaknesses of so many of the common criticisms made of the doctrine.

I. Howard Marshall, Emeritus Professor of New Testament Exegesis,
University of Aberdeen

This is a valuable contribution to the defence of a biblical understanding of the atonement. The exposition of Scripture is solid and helpful. The historical section puts to the sword any notion that penal substitution is a modern doctrine, not found in the early church Fathers. The 'objection and response' format of the central chapters is an excellent way of responding to arguments that are widely used but often lack theological substance. Overall, this book will be of great service to the church, especially to those who have been influenced by recent popular works on the subject of the atonement that deny the biblical teaching on penal substitution. We are indebted to the authors of this volume.

Professor A. T. B. McGowan, Principal, Highland Theological College, Dingwall

At the very heart of the Christian faith is the penal substitutionary atonement of Christ. Those who deny this central doctrine to Christianity are in effect denying the faith once entrusted to the saints. Every generation needs a full defence of this biblical truth and the authors have provided us with an eminently winsome and forthright defence of this glorious doctrine.

Martin Morrison, Bishop, Church of England in South Africa

The authors of this work compel us to take seriously an objective view of the cross of Christ, one that is not simply dependent on how we feel and what the culture around us promotes. The truth of the matter is that God has sent his Son, the eternal Word and the creative Wisdom, in human form so that he could stand in our place, do what we could not and would not do and by his obedience undo the wrongdoing of Adam and Eve. It is this radical act of obedience, with the cross as its climax and fulfilment, that turns away God's anger from our wrongdoing, restores our relationship with the source of our being and makes us God's beloved. The atonement is, of course, multifaceted; Christ certainly defeated sin and conquered the powers of evil. He is an example to us as we carry our own crosses in following him, and the cross manifests the extent of God's love for us. There would, however, be no sanctification, no transformation of self or society, no working out of the social, economic and political implications of the cross unless the fundamental transaction between God and ourselves had been completed and the impasse caused by sin broken by our representative, substitute and champion. Thanks be to God.

Michael Nazir-Ali, Bishop of Rochester

Atonement is the central doctrine of the Christian faith, and penal substitution is the heart of this doctrine. It is wonderful to have a whole book on penal substitution.

Roger Nicole, Professor of Theology, Reformed Theological Seminary, Orlando, Florida

This is a very significant book. It addresses the subject of Christ's penal substitutionary death, which lies at the heart of the biblical gospel, but which has now come under serious threat in the current theological ferment. The authors have carefully and convincingly evaluated the biblical material on which the teaching of penal substitution has been based and reaffirmed it. They have set the doctrine within the theological framework of creation, sin, redemption and relationships within the Trinity, while adducing key witnesses from two millennia of church history in support. Every major objection to penal substitution has been considered, and courteously but firmly answered. This refreshing affirmation encourages us to praise God in wonder at Christ's atonement for us sinners. The authors have placed us in their debt. Their book deserves to be read widely.

Peter T. O'Brien, Senior Research Fellow in New Testament, Moore Theological College, Sydney

This extended declaration and defence of the penal substitutionary view of Christ's atoning death responds to a plethora of current criticisms, many of them in-house, with a thoroughness and effectiveness that is without parallel anywhere. The book's existence shows that a British evangelical theology which exegetically, systematically, apologetically and pastorally can take on the world is in process of coming to birth. I hail this treatise as an epoch-making *tour de force*, and hopefully a sign of many more good things to come.

J. I. Packer, Professor of Theology, Regent College, Vancouver

This book offers a formidable challenge to the caricatures and misunderstandings of penal substitution that flourish in many Christian circles today. It does so by providing a careful analysis of the relevant biblical material, an exhaustive engagement with the theological objections often raised, and a revelation of the historical pedigree of this doctrine that will surprise some. Such a thoroughly integrated approach to the topic is without precedent. My hope is that it will arouse opponents of this position to reassess their arguments and interact carefully with the case presented here. My prayer is that it will also reassure and strengthen Christians who have long believed that this teaching is at the heart of the gospel.

David Peterson, Principal, Oak Hill Theological College, London

As a preacher, I welcome this book defending the orthodox doctrine of Christ's substitutionary atonement. It is scholarly, but just the kind of scholarship we need: readable, relevant to the whole church, and thus serving the flock of God. Drawing together in one place clear biblical exegesis, careful theological argument, comprehensive historical research, but also real pastoral wisdom, the authors show us that all this matters *in real life*. Go wrong in doctrine here, and our churches will bear the pastoral consequences. That's why we all need to *rediscover the glory of penal substitution*.

William J. U. Philip, Minister, St George's-Tron, Glasgow

*Pierced for our Transgressions* is probably the most significant book on the doctrine of the cross since *The Cross of Christ*. It is timely and urgently needed. Let the exposition of this magnificent doctrine both inform your mind and warm your heart.

Mike Pilavachi, Founder and Director, Soul Survivor

In *Pierced for our Transgressions*, the authors do at least three things for all of us. First, they answer the challenge to the crucial doctrine of penal substitution in a clear, credible, loving and scholarly manner. Second, they do so simply and in an easy to understand manner. In my own situation this means that even those whose first language is not English will be able to follow the reasoning. Third, they focus our attention yet again on the very heart of the gospel, and in doing so not only encourage us as preachers but also give us confidence to stand by our message. This book is superb and, in my view, should always be near the preacher's desk.

Frank Retief, Presiding Bishop, Church of England in South Africa

The doctrine of penal substitution is often maligned and misunderstood today. *Pierced for our Transgressions* is the perfect antidote. The authors defend the doctrine with sparkling clarity and winsome logic. I thank God for this work in which penal substitution is biblically grounded, theologically articulated and historically vindicated. Nor could one object that the authors fail to consider alternative views. Every objection to penal substitution is considered and refuted. In this book we are summoned again to the heart of the gospel.

> Thomas R. Schreiner, James Buchanan Harrison Professor of New Testament, Southern Baptist Theological Seminary, Louisville, Kentucky

Some things are worth fighting for. The evangelical doctrine of penal substitution is one of them. Remove this strand of atonement theology from Christian proclamation and you fairly rip the heart out of the gospel drama. One does not have to agree with everything written here in order to appreciate that *Pierced for our Transgressions* is a methodical and reasoned response to the current debate. To be sure, as our authors point out, penal substitution is not the only way to understand what happens at the cross of Christ, nor must it be detached from a doctrine of creation; but to deny it altogether, as some are now doing, is just plain silly.

> Ian Stackhouse, author of *The Gospel-Driven Church*, and Pastor, Guildford Baptist Church

Not so much a defence of the doctrine of penal substitution, this book is more a magnificent counter-attack, lifting the siege against it. The authors' comprehensive survey of the evidence successfully calls the bluff of those whose aim is to airbrush the true nature of the atonement from the Bible and church history. Brilliant, passionate and unapologetic, such a response almost makes one grateful for the errorists.

> Jonathan Stephen, Principal, Evangelical Theological College of Wales, and Director, Affinity

*Pierced for our Transgressions* is a timely, masterful and accessible exploration of the doctrine of penal substitution. It is timely because this doctrine has been under siege in recent years. It is masterful because its handling of the biblical, doctrinal and historical material is impressive. It is accessible because it is written in a way that makes maximum use of scholarly resources without obscuring the issues. This is a much needed and very welcome addition to the doctrine of the atonement. May it be used far and wide to restore confidence in the message that Christ died for our sins. And may the Holy Spirit use it – as he did me – to fill you with a new passion for worshipping God and for sharing the gospel.

> Mark Stibbe, author, and Vicar, St Andrew's, Chorleywood, Hertfordshire

The glorious truth of penal substitution lies right at the heart of the authentic Christian faith once for all delivered to the saints. It needs to be reaffirmed in each generation. I am delighted at this well-argued, carefully researched, gracious and thorough defence of the doctrine.

> William Taylor, Rector, St Helen's, Bishopsgate, London

*Pierced for our Transgressions* is carefully argued and richly edifying. More than that, it is a book sorely needed in the current confusion about the meaning of Jesus' death for us. The authors bring together biblical, theological and historical material in a compelling way, with a clear concern to remain faithful to Scripture and communicate clearly in today's world. They combine deft description with judicious defence as they explore the most important lines of the contemporary critique of evangelical thought on this vital subject. Even in those few places where there is room for disagreement, there can be no doubt that their purpose is to challenge us to a more biblically directed understanding of the wonder of God's mercy to us in the cross of Jesus, and that must always be welcome. This book deserves a wide readership.

Mark D. Thompson, Academic Dean, and Head of the Department of Theology, Moore Theological College, Sydney

This book shows how the classical doctrine of the atonement is the most reasonable and honest way of making sense of the Bible, human sin and the character of God. As an evangelist, I gained renewed confidence to preach the glorious gospel of redemption. In this *tour de force* we are shown again why God's grace is so amazing.

Rico Tice, author of *Christianity Explored* and Associate Minister for Evangelism, All Souls, Langham Place, London

This is a significant book. At a time when some people seem determined to snuff out this doctrine from what is sung and taught – unwittingly assisted by others who circumvent the issue in the interests of church unity – there is a need for the vital doctrine of penal substitution to be clearly, comprehensively and compellingly explained. This book does the job admirably.

Stuart Townend, Songwriter

A person's attitude to the cross tells you much about their theology as a whole, as it is on Calvary that we see the divine response to the human predicament. Thus the perennial attempts throughout church history to relativize and even deny the propitiatory and substitutionary nature of Christ's sacrifice should not simply be understood as peripheral discussions; they indicate a constant tendency to revise the very essence of the Christian faith to conform to wider cultural mores and shibboleths. It is thus a great pleasure to commend a book such as this, which seeks to defend a biblical, orthodox understanding of the atonement and to reinforce the non-negotiable centrality of God's wrath against sin and his merciful grace towards humanity. Careful readers will find much here that will enable them to articulate with clarity and conviction this important gospel doctrine.

Carl R. Trueman, Professor of Historical Theology and Church History, and Dean of Faculty, Westminster Theological Seminary, Philadelphia, Pennsylvania

Thoroughly researched and well presented, *Pierced for our Transgressions* demonstrates the Scripture's unyielding insistence on the necessity for penal substitution as the only means of removing our guilt and enabling us to be presented faultless before a holy God.

Terry Virgo, Founder, New Frontiers

At the cross, when Jesus bore the penalty for our sins in our place, the grace of God paid the price his holiness required. This has been the message of the gospel down the ages because this is the message of the gospel as Scripture reveals it. I am deeply grateful for this book, which illumines these facts so well. It is a book faithful to Scripture, knowledgable of history, conversant with current debate and deeply committed to seeing the church flourish in our day.

David F. Wells, Andrew Mutch Distinguished Professor of Historical and Systematic Theology, Gordon-Conwell Theological Seminary, Hamilton, Massachusetts

Jeffery, Ovey and Sach have produced a careful and well-informed defence of the Christian doctrine of substitutionary atonement. It is a valuable contribution to the current debate.

Gordon Wenham, formerly Professor of Old Testament, University of Gloucestershire

The need for mission to be directed by a responsible reading of the Bible is essential. This book strives to put an essential doctrine – the penal substitutionary atonement of Christ, in the context of the major themes of Scripture. As an exercise in biblical theology it is very helpful, especially to those who would be using a chronological method of teaching the Bible in a cross-cultural situation. It also shows the importance of the study of church history as an exercise in the tradition of the interpretation of Scripture and in understanding the present. Whilst probably too academic for many mission contexts, it does provide Bible teachers with all they need to know in order to explain the importance of this doctrine and its relationship to other key doctrines of Scripture. As a resource for the missionary it is invaluable, providing the foundation for building up of the church worldwide. It will be up to the missionary to look for those contact points in the host culture that give an opening for the explanation of a vital aspect of the work of Christ.

Chris Wigram, National Director, OMF International (UK), and Chairman, Global Connections

The preaching of the cross has always been central to the life and growth of the church. Every generation has had to grapple with the question of why, if God is love, he cannot simply forgive us. This book tackles this question head on – is the cross morally abhorrent, or is it absolutely necessary? The good news that the church has to offer is that Christ willingly and joyfully gave himself up to death on the cross, bearing a punishment that only we deserved, and so securing our salvation and fellowship with God himself forever. This is why we sing and rejoice!

Michael Ramsden, European Director, RZIM Zacharias Trust, and Lecturer in Christian Apologetics, Wycliffe Hall, Oxford

# PIERCED FOR OUR TRANSGRESSIONS

He was pierced for our transgressions,
    he was crushed for our iniquities;
the punishment that brought us peace was upon him,
    and by his wounds we are healed.
Isaiah 53:5

ivp

# PIERCED FOR OUR TRANSGRESSIONS

Rediscovering the glory of
penal substitution

Steve Jeffery
Mike Ovey
Andrew Sach

Inter-Varsity Press
Norton Street, Nottingham NG7 3HR, England
Email: ivp@ivpbooks.com
Website: www.ivpbooks.com

First published 2007

British Library Cataloguing in Publication Data
A catalogue record for this book is available from the British Library.

ISBN 978-1-84474-178-6

Set in Monotype Garamond 11/13pt
Typeset in Great Britain by Servis Filmsetting Ltd, Manchester
Printed and bound in Great Britain by Ashford Colour Press Ltd, Gosport, Hampshire

Inter-Varsity Press publishes Christian books that are true to the Bible and that communicate the gospel, develop discipleship and strengthen the church for its mission in the world.

Inter-Varsity Press is closely linked with the Universities and Colleges Christian Fellowship, a student movement connecting Christian Unions in universities and colleges throughout Great Britain, and a member movement of the International Fellowship of Evangelical Students. Website: www.uccf.org.uk.

To Steve's wife, Nicole, and to Mike's wife, Heather, two women who love the Lord Jesus and live every day trusting in his blood.

And to Andrew's godson, Edward Grey, that he would grow up doing the same.

# CONTENTS

# FOREWORD

Out of the Jewish leadership of Jesus' day had risen teachers of the law who did not know what the law meant. Jesus found himself saying things like 'Are you the teacher of Israel and yet you do not understand these things?' (John 3:10 ESV). Some of the teachers had lost all sense of biblical proportion, 'straining out a gnat and swallowing a camel!' (Matt 23:24 ESV). And as they lost their bearings, they came under Jesus' most serious charge: 'You have made void the word of God' (Matt 15:6 ESV).

Emotionally, Jesus' response was a sinless combination of grief and anger. 'He looked around at them with anger, grieved at their hardness of heart' (Mark 3:5 ESV). Why both anger and grief?

The anger was because people were being hurt – eternally. These teachers were supposed to know what the word of God meant, but instead Jesus said they were 'like unmarked graves, and people walk over them without knowing it' (Luke 11:44 ESV). This made Jesus angry. Their job was to teach what God had said. Instead, they were blind guides and were leading others with them into the ditch. Jesus loved people. Therefore, he was angry with professional teachers who imperilled people with biblical blunders.

But Jesus was not only angry; he was 'grieved at their hardness of heart'. These were his kinsmen. These were the leaders of his people. These were the representatives of the Jerusalem he loved and wept over. 'Would that you . . . had known . . . the things that make for peace! But now they are hidden from your eyes' (Luke 19:42 ESV). The condition of their heart and the blindness of their eyes were a grief to Jesus.

This is how I feel today about teachers of Christ's people who deny and even belittle precious, life-saving, biblical truth. When a person says that God's 'punishing his Son for an offence he has not even committed' would be as evil as child abuse, I am angered and grieved. For if God did not punish his Son in my place, I am not saved from my greatest peril, the wrath of God.

In part, I write this foreword to defend my Father's wrath against me before I was adopted. He does not need my defence. But I believe he would be honoured by it. On behalf of my Father, then, I would like to bear witness to the truth that, before he adopted me, his terrible wrath rested upon me. Jesus said, 'Whoever believes in the Son has eternal life; whoever does not obey . . . *the wrath of God remains on him*' (John 3:36 ESV; italics added). Wrath remains on us as long as there is no faith in Jesus.

Paul puts it like this: We 'were by nature children of wrath, like the rest of mankind' (Eph. 2:3 ESV). My very nature made me worthy of wrath. My destiny was to endure 'flaming fire' and 'vengeance on those . . . who do not obey the gospel of our Lord Jesus . . . [and who] suffer the punishment of eternal destruction' (2 Thess. 1:8–9 ESV). I was not a son of God. God was not my Father. He was my judge and executioner. I was 'dead in . . . trespasses and sins', one of the 'sons of disobedience' (Eph. 2:1–2 ESV). And the sentence of my Judge was clear and terrifying: 'because of these things the *wrath of God* comes upon the sons of disobedience' (Eph. 5:6 ESV; italics added).

There was only one hope for me – that the infinite wisdom of God might make a way for the love of God to satisfy the wrath of God so that I might become a son of God.

This is exactly what happened, and I will sing of it forever. After saying that I was by nature a child of wrath, Paul says, 'But God, being rich in mercy, because of the great love with which he loved us, even when we were dead in our trespasses, made us alive together with Christ' (Eph. 2:4–5 ESV). What a grievous blindness when a teacher in the church writes that the term 'children of wrath' cannot mean 'actual objects of God's wrath . . . [because] in the same breath they are described as at the same time objects of God's love'. On the contrary. This is the very triumph of the love of God. This *is* the love of God – the 'great love with which he loved us'. It rescued me from his wrath and adopted me into sonship.

'But when the fullness of time had come, God sent forth his Son . . . to redeem those who were under the law, so that we might receive adoption as sons' (Gal. 4:4 ESV). God sent his Son to rescue me from his wrath and make me his child.

How did he do it? He did it in the way one writer slanderously calls 'cosmic child abuse'. God's Son bore God's curse in my place. 'Christ redeemed us from the curse of the law *by becoming a curse for us* – for it is written, "Cursed is everyone who is hanged on a tree"' (Gal. 3:13 ESV; italics added). If people in the twenty-first century find this greatest act of love 'morally dubious and a huge barrier to faith', it was not different in Paul's day. 'We preach Christ crucified, a *stumbling block* to Jews and *folly* to Gentiles' (1 Cor. 1:23 ESV; italics added).

But for those who are called by God and believe in Jesus, this is 'the power of God and the wisdom of God' (1 Cor. 1:24 ESV). This is my life. This is the only way God could become my Father. Now that his wrath no longer rests on me (John 3:36), he has sent the Spirit of sonship flooding into my heart crying Abba, Father (Rom. 8:15). *I thank you, heavenly Father, with all my heart, that you saved me from your wrath. I rejoice to measure your love for me by the magnitude of the wrath I deserved and the wonder of your mercy by putting Christ in my place.*

Those who try to rescue the love of God by minimizing the wrath of God, undermine not only the love of God, but also his demand that we love our enemies. It is breathtaking to hear one of them say, 'If the cross is a personal act of violence perpetrated by God towards humankind but borne by his Son, then it makes a mockery of Jesus' own teaching to love your enemies, and to refuse to repay evil with evil.' Those are deadly words, which, if they held sway, would take enemy love out of the world.

Why? Because Paul said that counting on the final wrath of God against his enemies is one of the crucial warrants for why we may not return evil for evil. It is precisely *because* we may trust the wisdom of God to apply his wrath justly that we must leave all vengeance to him and return good for evil. 'Never avenge yourselves, but leave it to the wrath of God, for it is written, "Vengeance is mine, I will repay, says the Lord." To the contrary, "if your enemy is hungry, feed him"' (Rom. 12:19–20 ESV). If God does not show wrath, sooner or later we shall take justice into our own hands. But God says, 'Don't. I will see to it.'

Every section of this book yields another reason to thank God for the labours of the authors and for IVP in Britain. I pray that the Lord will give the book success in the defence and honour of God, and that Jesus Christ will be treasured all the more fully when he is seen more clearly to be *Pierced for our Transgressions*.

John Piper
Pastor for Preaching and Vision
Bethlehem Baptist Church
Minneapolis, Minnesota

# ACKNOWLEDGMENTS

Like the apostle Paul, we thank our God and pray with joy for many who have been our partners in the gospel (Phil. 1:6). The completion of this book in its present form is testimony not only to their theological insights, but also to their gracious encouragement at those times when the project seemed very daunting. Particular mention must be made of Steve's wife, Nicole, who bore with extraordinary patience and grace the protracted absence of a distracted husband, and without whose support the project would have been impossible. In a similar vein, Mike is thankful for his wife Heather, and Andrew for his housemates Andrew Towner, Patrick McBain and Phil Allcock. Phil made a particular contribution to our understanding of the relationship between divine retribution and God's fatherly discipline, the subject of his BA dissertation.

We are grateful to God for those of a previous generation whose writings first taught us the glory of penal substitution, in particular Leon Morris, J. I. Packer and John Stott. We heard news of Leon Morris's death just as we were preparing the final version of chapter 2, in which his outstanding scholarly work plays a significant part. We dare to hope that he would have approved our attempt to take up the cause for which he contended with such boldness and godliness throughout his ministry.

David Field, Chris Green and Garry Williams, all on the faculty of Oak Hill College, London, have given substantially of their time and wisdom – there was a period when barely an afternoon went by without a knock on one of their study doors. Garry is engaged in ongoing research on the theology of the atonement, and our historical survey owes much to his Oxford DPhil dissertation. Wendy Bell, the librarian at Oak Hill, has assisted us many times and even showed genuine compassion when Andrew paid a rather substantial library fine for overdue books on Isaiah 53!

John Piper agreed to meet us during his sabbatical at Tyndale House, Cambridge, and greatly encouraged us with his concern to see the doctrine of penal substitution defended against criticisms from both sides of the Atlantic.

Tom Schreiner responded warmly to an email from complete strangers and has since become a valued friend. He made an essay of his available to us prior to publication, and has responded helpfully to many other enquiries along the way. He introduced us to Frank Thielman, who also sent us useful material. Ian Shaw and Brian Edwards allowed us to see the manuscript of their book *The Divine Substitute* before it went to press.

We thank God for Phil Duce, our editor at IVP, who has been patiently supportive throughout, and has spurred us on with his own personal commitment to the defence of the doctrine of penal substitution. Eldo Barkhuizen checked and corrected the manuscript with meticulous care.

Lyndon Drake and Chris Slater lent us their expertise in computing and graphic design respectively, enabling the launch of www.piercedforour transgressions.com

There are many others who have helped in different ways throughout the project – Tim Ambrose, Angus and Liz Barnard, Ken Campbell, Paul Clarke, Ros Clarke, Emma Desmond, Charles Dobbie, Matt Fuller, Greg Haslam, Marc Lloyd, Matthew Mason, Thomas Renz, James Robson, David Russell, Steve Smith, Dan Strange, Chris Thomson and Tom Watts. We are thankful to God for all of them.

Above all, of course, we praise our Saviour, the Lord Jesus Christ, for 'God made him who had no sin to be sin for us, so that in him we might become the righteousness of God' (2 Cor. 5:21).

Steve Jeffery
Mike Ovey
Andrew Sach

# THE AUTHORS

Steve Jeffery gained a degree in Materials Science and a doctorate in Experimental Physics at Oxford University before spending three years working at a church in South London. He is currently studying at Oak Hill Theological College in preparation for full-time Christian ministry. He is married to Nicole, and they have two children, Ben and Becki. When he's not teaching his son to play cricket or his daughter to make animal noises, he enjoys football and jazz piano.

Mike Ovey is Principal-elect and Lecturer in Doctrine and Apologetics at Oak Hill Theological College, and holds a PhD in trinitarian theology from King's College London. He once worked as a lawyer drafting government legislation, and subsequently served as a curate at All Saints, Crowborough, before teaching at Moore Theological College, Sydney. Married to Heather, they have three children, Charlie, Harry and Anastasia. His interests include Arsenal Football Club, really complicated whodunnits and strong coffee.

Andrew Sach graduated in Natural Sciences from St John's College, Cambridge, before completing a doctorate at the University of York exploring brain mechanisms involved in human hearing. He then spent three years in Christian ministry before embarking on theological studies at Oak Hill Theological College. He will soon be joining the staff of St Helen's, Bishopsgate, in central London, and is co-author of *Dig Deeper!* (IVP, 2005), a popular book on how to understand the Bible. His current obsessions include the BBC drama *Spooks*, a particularly tricky piano piece by Prokofiev (which he can't play) and his three godsons, Eden, Edward and Thomas.

# Part One: Making the Case

## 1. INTRODUCTION

### Setting the scene

The doctrine of penal substitution states that God gave himself in the person of his Son to suffer instead of us the death, punishment and curse due to fallen humanity as the penalty for sin.

This understanding of the cross of Christ stands at the very heart of the gospel. There is a captivating beauty in the sacrificial love of a God who gave *himself* for his people. It is this that first draws many believers to the Lord Jesus Christ, and this that will draw us to him when he returns on the last day to vindicate his name and welcome his people into his eternal kingdom. That the Lord Jesus Christ died *for us* – a shameful death, bearing our curse, enduring our pain, suffering the wrath of his own Father in our place – has been the wellspring of the hope of countless Christians throughout the ages.

It is therefore unsurprising that many have been deeply troubled in recent years to hear dissenting voices raised against this teaching. We fear that Christ will be robbed of his glory, that believers will be robbed of their assurance and that preachers will be robbed of their confidence in 'the old, old story' of the life-transforming power of the cross of Christ. The great Baptist preacher Charles Spurgeon foresaw the devastating consequences of losing penal substitution well over a century ago, in a sermon that now takes on an eerily prophetic tone.

> If ever there should come a wretched day when all our pulpits shall be full of modern thought, and the old doctrine of a substitutionary sacrifice shall be exploded, then will there remain no word of comfort for the guilty or hope for the despairing. Hushed will be for ever those silver notes which now console the living, and cheer the dying; a dumb spirit will possess this sullen world, and no voice of joy will break the blank silence of despair. The gospel speaks through the propitiation for sin, and if that be denied, it speaketh no more. Those who preach not the atonement exhibit a dumb and dummy gospel; a mouth it hath, but speaketh not; they that make it are like unto their idol . . .
>
> Would you have me silence the doctrine of the blood of sprinkling? Would any one of you attempt so horrible a deed? Shall we be censured if we continually proclaim the heaven-sent message of the blood of Jesus? Shall we speak with bated breath because some affected person shudders at the sound of the word '*blood*'? or some 'cultured' individual rebels at the old-fashioned thought of sacrifice? Nay, verily, we will sooner have our tongue cut out than cease to speak of the precious blood of Jesus Christ.[1]

Mercifully, that 'wretched day' has not quite arrived – at least not yet. For 'the old doctrine of a substitutionary sacrifice' has not been 'exploded'; it is still preached faithfully and fervently in churches all over the world. However, an increasing number of theologians and church leaders are calling it into question.

Where did these dissenting voices come from? Many of them can be traced to the rise of liberal theology in the middle of the nineteenth century. Liberalism had little time for the motifs of sacrifice, divine wrath and propitiation entailed in penal substitution. As Henri Blocher observes, 'Liberal Protestants . . . felt outraged at the doctrine and complained about a "blood" theology, in their eyes an ugly relic of primitive stages in man's religious evolution.'[2]

During the decades that followed, various alternative accounts of the atonement emerged, none of which left room for penal substitution, and some of which explicitly attacked it. Among the most prominent were John McLeod

---

1. C. H. Spurgeon, 'The Blood of Sprinking (part 1)', Sermon no. 1888 in *The Metropolitan Tabernacle Pulpit: Sermons Preached and Revised by C. H. Spurgeon during the Year 1886*, vol. 32 (London: Passmore & Alabaster), pp. 121–132 (p. 129), italics original.

2. Henri Blocher, 'The Sacrifice of Christ: The Current Theological Situation', *European Journal of Theology* 8.1 (1999), pp. 23–36 (p. 25).

Campbell's *The Nature of the Atonement* (1856), Horace Bushnell's *The Vicarious Sacrifice* (1866), R. C. Moberly's *Atonement and Personality* (1901) and Gustav Aulén's Christus Victor (1931).[3]

In the mid-twentieth century, the case against penal substitution was articulated most strongly by the biblical scholar C. H. Dodd.[4] In his commentaries on Romans and the letters of John,[5] Dodd argued against the traditional rendering 'propitiation' for the Greek *hilastērion* word group, thereby obscuring the references in Romans 3:25, 1 John 2:2 and 4:10 to the fact that Christ's death averted God's wrath from sinful people. Dodd's view was vigorously challenged by evangelicals such as Leon Morris and Roger Nicole, and was later opposed by popular preachers, particularly Martyn Lloyd-Jones, but nonetheless proved influential, not least because Dodd directed the committees that produced the New English Bible. His understanding of these texts was also reflected in the Revised Standard Version, produced in 1946.

In recent years this tide of criticism has intensified with the appearance of works such as Stephen Travis's *Christ and the Judgment of God* (1986); Eleonore Stump's essay 'Atonement According to Aquinas' (1988); Colin Gunton's *The Actuality of Atonement* (1988); Paul Fiddes' *Past Event and Present Salvation* (1989); Vernon White's *Atonement and Incarnation* (1991); Stephen Sykes's 'Outline of a Theology of Sacrifice' (1991) and *The Story of Atonement* (1997); Timothy Gorringe's *God's Just Vengeance* (1996); Tom Smail's *Once and*

---

3. John McLeod Campbell, *The Nature of the Atonement* (Cambridge: Macmillan, 1856); Horace Bushnell, *The Vicarious Sacrifice* (Alexander Strahan, 1866); R. C. Moberly, *Atonement and Personality* (London: John Murray, 1901); Gustav Aulén, Christus Victor: *An Historical Study of the Three Main Types of the Idea of the Atonement*, trans. A. G. Herbert (London: SPCK, 1945; first pub. 1931). This was not the first time that penal substitution had come under criticism. A notable example from the Reformation period is Faustus Socinus, the Unitarian theologian who attacked the doctrine in *De Iesu Christo Servatore*, in *Opera Omnia*, vols. 1–2 of *Bibliotheca Fratrum Polonorum Quos Unitarios Vocant*, 8 vols. (Irenopoli: post 1656), despite the positive case put forth by the Protestant Reformers.

4. This paragraph is indebted to John Stott's helpful outline of Dodd's position and his influence on biblical interpretation, in John R. W. Stott, *The Cross of Christ* (Leicester: IVP, 1986), pp. 170–172.

5. C. H. Dodd, *The Epistle of Paul to the Romans* (London: Hodder & Stoughton, 1932), pp. 54–55; *The Johannine Epistles* (London: Hodder & Stoughton, 1946), pp. 25–26, 112.

*for All* (1998); Joel Green and Mark Baker's *Recovering the Scandal of the Cross* (2000); J. Denney Weaver's *The Nonviolent Atonement* (2001); and Martin Davie's article 'Dead to Sin and Alive to God' (2001).[6] John Goldingay, then Principal of St John's College, Nottingham, edited *Atonement Today* (1995),[7] many of the contributors to which are wary or explicitly critical of penal substitution. John Carroll and Joel Green collaborated with Robert Van Voorst, Joel Marcus and Donald Senior to produce *The Death of Jesus in Early Christianity* (1995).[8]

In one sense, it is no surprise that the Bible's teaching should be criticized in this way, for foundational truths of the Christian faith always come under attack from time to time – witness the debates that have raged in the past over the Trinity, the deity of Christ, the bodily resurrection, and so on. The apostle Paul warned that 'the time will come when men will not put up with sound doctrine. Instead, to suit their own desires, they will gather around them a great number of teachers to say what their itching ears want to hear' (2 Tim. 4:3).

---

6. Stephen H. Travis, *Christ and the Judgment of God: Divine Retribution in the New Testament* (Basingstoke: Marshall, Morgan & Scott, 1986); Eleonore Stump, 'Atonement According to Aquinas', in Thomas V. Morris (ed.), *Philosophy and the Christian Faith* (Notre Dame: University of Notre Dame Press, 1988), pp. 61–91; Colin E. Gunton, *The Actuality of Atonement: A Study of Metaphor, Rationality and the Christian Tradition* (Edinburgh: T. & T. Clark, 1988); Paul S. Fiddes, *Past Event and Present Salvation: The Christian Idea of Atonement* (London: Darton, Longman & Todd, 1989); Vernon White, *Atonement and Incarnation* (Cambridge: Cambridge University Press, 1991); Stephen W. Sykes, 'Outline of a Theology of Sacrifice', in Stephen W. Sykes (ed.), *Sacrifice and Redemption: Durham Essays in Theology* (Cambridge: Cambridge University Press, 1991), pp. 282–298; *The Story of Atonement* (London: Darton, Longman & Todd, 1997); Timothy Gorringe, *God's Just Vengeance: Crime, Violence and the Rhetoric of Salvation* (Cambridge: Cambridge University Press, 1996); Tom Smail, *Once and for All: A Confession of the Cross* (London: Darton, Longman & Todd, 1998); Joel B. Green and Mark D. Baker, *Recovering the Scandal of the Cross: Atonement in New Testament and Contemporary Contexts* (Downers Grove: IVP, 2000); J. Denney Weaver, *The Nonviolent Atonement* (Grand Rapids: Eerdmans, 2001); Martin Davie, 'Dead to Sin and Alive to God', *Scottish Bulletin of Evangelical Theology* 19 (2001), pp. 158–194.

7. John Goldingay (ed.), *Atonement Today* (London: SPCK, 1995).

8. John T. Carroll and Joel B. Green, with Robert E. Van Voorst, Joel Marcus and Donald Senior, C. P., *The Death of Jesus in Early Christianity* (Peabody: Hendrickson, 1995).

The more disturbing thing is that some of the more recent critics of penal substitution regard themselves as evangelicals, and claim to be committed to the authority of Scripture. Moreover, whereas criticism of penal substitution was once confined largely to academic books and journals, it has now found its way into popular Christian books and magazines, creating confusion and alarm among Christians.

One of the most significant books of this kind is *The Lost Message of Jesus* by Steve Chalke and Alan Mann (2003).[9] Although not written explicitly as a critique of penal substitution, its description of the doctrine as 'a form of cosmic child abuse'[10] provoked considerable disquiet, not least because Steve Chalke is well known as the founding director of the Oasis Trust and a contributor to several popular Christian magazines. The Evangelical Alliance (EA) responded to the controversy by hosting a public debate in London in October 2004, attended by hundreds of Christians from both sides of the dispute. Both positions were aired but with little resolution. The following summer, the EA organized a symposium at the London School of Theology, attended by over a hundred evangelical scholars, pastors and laypeople. The EA's own research showed that the vast majority of those present affirmed penal substitution, but the controversy remains firmly on the evangelical agenda, and shows no sign of receding.[11]

Other criticisms of penal substitution at a popular level have come from Alan Mann in his *Atonement for a 'Sinless' Society* (2005), Stuart Murray Williams in his contributions to the public debates, and Brian McLaren, a leading figure in the 'Emerging Church' movement in the USA, in *The Story We Find Ourselves in* (2003).[12]

---

9. Steve Chalke and Alan Mann, *The Lost Message of Jesus* (Grand Rapids: Zondervan, 2003). See also Steve Chalke, 'Cross Purposes', *Christianity* (September 2004), pp. 44–48.

10. Chalke and Mann, *Lost Message of Jesus*, p. 182.

11. *Evangelical Alliance Atonement Symposium Statement*, 8 July 2005, www.eauk. org/ theology/atonement/atonement-statement.cfm (accessed 21 April 2006).

12. Alan Mann, *Atonement for a 'Sinless' Society: Engaging with an Emerging Culture* (Milton Keynes: Paternoster, 2005); Stuart Murray Williams, 'Stuart Murray Williams on the Lost Message of Jesus: A Speech at the Debate on Steve Chalke's Book *The Lost Message of Jesus*', http://www.anabaptistnetwork.com/node/233); Brian D. McLaren, *The Story We Find Ourselves in: Further Adventures of a New Kind of Christian* (San Francisco: Jossey-Bass, 2003).

In short, after rumbling away for a century and a half behind the closed doors of the liberal scholarly academy, criticisms of penal substitution have recently been voiced by several influential evangelical theologians and church leaders, provoking a storm of controversy within the Christian community.

## Responding to the challenge

Of course, advocates of penal substitution have not been silent during this time. Many have written in defence of the doctrine and the biblical and theological framework that underpins it.

One of the most significant contributions came from the pen of Leon Morris. His article 'The Use of *hilaskesthai* etc. in Biblical Greek' (1951) was a direct challenge to Dodd's attempt to reinterpret the vocabulary of 'propitiation' in the New Testament. Morris concludes that 'the word group under discussion has reference to the wrath of God, and expresses the great truth that the death of Christ is the means of turning that wrath away from sinners conclusively and finally'.[13] A few years later, he published *The Apostolic Preaching of the Cross* (1955), which discusses in detail the meaning in context of important New Testament vocabulary such as 'redemption', 'propitiation' and 'reconciliation', and clearly affirms the doctrine of penal substitution. He built on this foundation in *The Cross in the New Testament* (1965), which adopts a broader perspective, surveying all of the New Testament's teaching about the cross, and harvested the fruits of his academic work for a wider audience in *Glory in the Cross* (1966), *The Atonement* (1983) and *The Cross of Jesus* (1988).[14]

Unfortunately, Morris's writings have not had the impact they deserve, because critics of his position paid little attention. Indeed, one of the strangest things about modern challenges to penal substitution is the extent to which they continue to rely on interpretations of Scripture soundly refuted by Morris decades ago, without even attempting to reply to his case.

---

13. Leon Morris, 'The Use of *hilaskesthai* etc. in Biblical Greek', *Expository Times* 62 (1951), pp. 227–233 (p. 233).

14. Leon Morris, *The Apostolic Preaching of the Cross* (London: Tyndale, 1955); *The Cross in the New Testament* (Exeter: Paternoster, 1965); *Glory in the Cross: A Study in Atonement* (London: Hodder & Stoughton, 1966); *The Atonement: Its Meaning and Significance* (Leicester: IVP, 1983); *The Cross of Jesus* (Grand Rapids: Eerdmans; Exeter: Paternoster, 1988).

At around the same time that Morris was writing in Australia, scholars in America also mounted a solid defence of the doctrine. Roger Nicole focused his attention on the task of biblical exegesis, and wrote two significant articles refuting Dodd's reading of the disputed New Testament texts. John Murray, meanwhile, gave a resounding endorsement to the Reformed doctrine of salvation in his *Redemption Accomplished and Applied* (1955), as did Louis Berkhof in his *Systematic Theology* (1941).[15]

A few years later, back in the United Kingdom, J. I. Packer defended penal substitution in his 1973 Tyndale Biblical Theology Lecture entitled 'What Did the Cross Achieve? The Logic of Penal Substitution'. This was subsequently published in the *Tyndale Bulletin* before appearing as a short booklet and as a chapter in volume 1 of his *Collected Shorter Writings*. Packer's best-selling book *Knowing God* (1973) also outlines and defends penal substitution in a chapter entitled 'The Heart of the Gospel'.[16]

One of the most important affirmations of the doctrine in recent years is John Stott's *The Cross of Christ* (1986). It is breathtaking in its scope and remarkable in its attention to detail, displaying the author's firm grasp of Scripture and his profound reflection on a whole range of theological and pastoral issues. It has deservedly come to be regarded among evangelicals as one of the standard texts on the cross. Mark Meynell's *Cross Examined* (2001) covers similar ground more simply, and draws on the author's experience of communicating the gospel to university students. This book sets the cross in the broad context of the doctrine of salvation and the Christian life, and it covers

---

15. Roger Nicole, 'C. H. Dodd and the Doctrine of Propitiation', *Westminster Theological Journal* 17 (1955), pp. 117–157, repr. in *Standing Forth: Collected Writings of Roger Nicole* (Fearn: Christian Focus, 2002), pp. 343–396; '*Hilaskesthai* Revisited', *Evangelical Quarterly* 49 (1977), pp. 173–177; John Murray, *Redemption Accomplished and Applied* (Edinburgh: Banner of Truth, 1961; first pub. Grand Rapids: Eerdmans, 1955): page references in our work are to the Banner of Truth edn; Louis Berkhof, *Systematic Theology* (London: Banner of Truth, 1959; first pub. 1941).

16. J. I. Packer, 'What Did the Cross Achieve? The Logic of Penal Substitution', *Tyndale Bulletin* 25 (1974), pp. 3–45; also pub. as *What Did the Cross Achieve? The Logic of Penal Substitution* (Leicester: Theological Students' Fellowship); and as 'What Did the Cross Achieve? The Logic of Penal Substitution', in *Celebrating the Saving Work of God: Collected Shorter Writings of J. I. Packer* (Carlisle: Paternoster, 1998), pp. 85–123; J. I. Packer, *Knowing God* (London: Hodder & Stoughton, 1973).

a range of biblical, theological and pastoral themes in a highly accessible style.[17]

More scholarly works in support of penal substitution continue to be published. The French theologian Henri Blocher has contributed three important essays to the debate. 'The Sacrifice of Christ: The Current Theological Situation' (1999) and 'Biblical Metaphors and the Doctrine of the Atonement' (2004) contain insightful replies to some recent criticisms of the doctrine, and '*Agnus Victor*: The Atonement as Victory and Vicarious Punishment' (2002) is an incisive response to the claim that penal substitution is excluded by the biblical teaching that at the cross Christ triumphed over evil.[18]

In a similar vein, *Where Wrath and Mercy Meet* (2001) is a collection of papers edited by David Peterson, presented at a conference on the atonement held at Oak Hill Theological College, London, in 2000.[19] It contains essays on the atonement in the Old and New Testaments, theological studies relating the doctrine to creation, new creation, sin, guilt and punishment, and some reflections on preaching the atonement. It makes a strong case for penal substitution, and responds to several recent challenges. Critics of penal substitution have received it in a similar way to Leon Morris's work: its arguments have largely been ignored.

*The Glory of the Atonement* (2004) is another substantial scholarly contribution, written in appreciation of the ministry of Roger Nicole.[20] It contains studies of some relevant biblical material, as well as essays from historical and practical perspectives. Nicole himself contributed a 'Postscript on Penal Substitution', which by itself does a great deal to clarify the issues involved.

Other recent works include Dan Strange's 'The Many-Splendoured Cross' (2005), Ben Cooper's *Must God Punish Sin?* (2005) and Garry Williams's contri-

17. John R. W. Stott, *The Cross of Christ* (Leicester: IVP, 1986); Mark Meynell, *Cross Examined: The Life-Changing Power of the Death of Jesus* (Leicester: IVP, 2001).

18. Henri Blocher, 'The Sacrifice of Christ: The Current Theological Situation', *European Journal of Theology* 8.1 (1999), pp. 23–36; 'Biblical Metaphors and the Doctrine of the Atonement', *Journal of the Evangelical Theological Society* 47 (2004), pp. 629–645; '*Agnus Victor*: The Atonement as Victory and Vicarious Punishment', in John G. Stackhouse (ed.), *What Does It Mean to Be Saved* (Grand Rapids: Baker, 2002), pp. 67–91.

19. David Peterson (ed.), *Where Wrath and Mercy Meet: Proclaiming the Atonement Today* (Carlisle: Paternoster, 2001).

20. Charles E. Hill and Frank A. James III (eds.), *The Glory of the Atonement: Biblical, Historical and Practical Perspectives* (Downers Grove: IVP; Leicester: Apollos, 2004).

bution to the EA symposium on penal substitution, 'Justice, Law, and Guilt' (2005). D. A. Carson's assessment of the 'Emerging Church' movement, *Becoming Conversant with the Emerging Church* (2005), includes brief responses to the criticisms levelled against penal substitution by Brian McLaren and Steve Chalke. Thomas Schreiner defends penal substitution and responds to some alternative positions in *Four Views of the Atonement* (2006). Frank Thielman has contributed a chapter on the subject for *Central Themes in Biblical Theology: Mapping Unity in Diversity* (2007).[21] Finally, A. T. B. McGowan's 'The Atonement as Penal Substitution' (2006)[22] includes a revealing analysis of how penal substitution has become in recent years 'a major fault line within evangelical theology',[23] as well as an illuminating critique of Steve Chalke and Alan Mann's *The Lost Message of Jesus*.

At a more popular level, Ian J. Shaw and Brian H. Edwards's *The Divine Substitute* (2006) contains a helpful survey of the last two thousand years, highlighting various figures who were committed to penal substitution. Liam Goligher's *The Jesus Gospel: Recovering the Lost Message* (2006) presents the story of the Bible as a drama in three acts, demonstrating how penal substitution is woven into it. Paul Wells's *Cross Words* (2006) reflects on the events at Calvary from a range of perspectives, such as 'Scandal', 'Violence' and 'Penalty'. Robert Reymond's *The Lamb of God* (2006) traces the idea of sacrifice through

---

21. Dan Strange, 'The Many-Splendoured Cross: Atonement, Controversy, and Victory', *Foundations* (autumn 2005), pp. 5–22; Ben Cooper, *Must God Punish Sin?* (London: Latimer Trust, 2005); Garry J. Williams, 'Justice, Law, and Guilt: A Paper Given at the Evangelical Alliance Symposium on Penal Substitution' (2005), http://www.eauk.org/theology/atonement/upload/garry_williams.pdf (accessed 27 March 2006), forthcoming in *Journal of the Evangelical Theological Society*; D. A. Carson, *Becoming Conversant with the Emerging Church: Understanding a Movement and Its Implications* (Grand Rapids: Zondervan, 2005); Thomas R. Schreiner, 'The Penal Substitution View', in James Beilby and Paul Eddy (eds.), *Four Views of the Atonement* (Downers Grove: IVP, 2006), pp. 67–98; Frank Thielman, 'The Atonement', in Scott J. Hafemann and Paul R. House (eds.), *Central Themes in Biblical Theology: Mapping Unity in Diversity* (Nottingham: Apollos, 2007). We are grateful to Professors Schreiner and Thielman for making their manuscripts available to us prior to publication.

22. A. T. B. McGowan, 'The Atonement as Penal Substitution', in *Always Reforming: Explorations in Systematic Theology*, ed. A. T. B. McGowan (Leicester: IVP, 2006), pp. 183–210.

23. Ibid., p. 201.

the Bible, offering helpful treatments of Exodus 12, Leviticus 16 and Isaiah 53 in particular.[24]

Finally, Ben Cooper's little book *Just Love* (2005) is designed to be accessible to both Christians and unbelievers.[25] In a short space and an informal style, it explores the specific question of how a loving God can punish sin, and approaches penal substitution from the perspective of God's justice.

In view of all this material in support of penal substitution, one might reasonably ask whether another book is necessary. If the answers are all out there, why add yet another volume to the pile? This one is distinct in several ways. First, it seeks to bring together in one place a detailed examination of the key biblical passages, a consideration of the important theological and doctrinal issues, and a comprehensive survey of the teaching of the Christian church through the ages.

Secondly, while there are now some very helpful introductory books (*The Jesus Gospel, Cross Examined* or *Just Love* would be excellent for a young Christian) and some formidable academic essays, there is little in between. We have tried to steer such a course. We go beyond the introductory because our intention is not only to explain what penal substitution is, but also to defend it, and that means we must engage with hostile and sometimes complex counter-arguments. But at the same time we have avoided producing a weighty technical volume, because we want to be understood by ordinary Christians and not only by scholars. Our desire is to help Christians without formal theological training (or perhaps some who have such training but lack the time to chase up all the references in a library) to get to grips with the debate. We hope to make accessible to a wider audience some of the answers that already exist, but are tucked away in academic journals, unpublished dissertations or out-of-print books. In particular, many voices from the distant past have been forgotten, and yet the likes of Athanasius and John Calvin have much to teach us if we would listen to them.

---

24. Ian J. Shaw and Brian H. Edwards, *The Divine Substitute: The Atonement in the Bible and History* (Leominster: Day One, 2006); Liam Goligher, *The Jesus Gospel: Recovering the Lost Message* (Milton Keynes: Authentic Media, 2006); Paul Wells, *Cross Words: The Biblical Doctrine of the Atonement* (Fearn: Christian Focus, 2006); Robert L. Reymond, *The Lamb of God: The Bible's Unfolding Revelation of Sacrifice* (Fearn: Christian Focus, 2006). We are thankful to Ian Shaw and Brian Edwards for allowing us to see their material before it went to press.

25. Ben Cooper, *Just Love: Why God Must Punish Sin* (London: Good Book, 2005).

But the most pressing reason why this book is necessary is that the miscon-ceived criticisms of penal substitution show no sign of abating, and the result-ing confusion within the Christian community seems to be increasing rather than decreasing. As Carl Trueman remarked, 'The classical evangelical position on atonement has fallen out of favour over recent years, often rejected on the basis of a theologically caricatured and historically inadequate understanding of what exactly the position entails.'[26] In Part One of this book we set out the positive case for penal substitution, biblically, theologically, pastorally, histor-ically. In Part Two we outline every objection we have been able to find against penal substitution, where possible giving examples in the writings of contem-porary theologians, and respond to each in turn. This prosecution and defence format was once a popular way of doing theology, though less so today; cer-tainly none of the other current books on penal substitution has adopted this approach. We hope it will prove a useful resource for those who believe in penal substitution yet find themselves assailed by some of these objections. We hope also to challenge those who deny the doctrine by engaging some of their claims head on. For too long the opposing sides of the debate have talked past each other. We have structured Part Two to avoid that. These, then, are the distinc-tive features of our book.

In brief, we argue that penal substitution is clearly taught in Scripture, that it has a central place in Christian theology, that a neglect of the doctrine will have serious pastoral consequences, that it has an impeccable pedigree in the history of the Christian church, and that all of the objections raised against it can be comprehensively answered. It may be helpful if we begin by giving a brief synopsis of each chapter.

Chapter 2 sets out the biblical foundations for the doctrine of penal sub-stitution. This is the basis for all that follows, for if penal substitution is unbib-lical, it must be abandoned. We look in some detail at a number of important biblical passages that contribute to a penal substitutionary understanding of the atonement.

The aim of chapter 3 is to explore how penal substitution fits within the 'big picture' of Christian theology, showing how it relates to other important biblical themes such as the character of God, the doctrine of creation, the con-sequences of sin, and other biblical perspectives on the atonement. Penal sub-stitution is shown to have a central place; to exclude it would distort or undermine many other theological themes.

Chapter 4 reflects on some of the most significant pastoral implications of

---

26. Peterson, *Where Wrath and Mercy Meet*, back cover.

the doctrine of penal substitution. There are many other facets to the Bible's teaching on the cross, and each has implications for the Christian life. Here, however, we have focused specifically on those things that depend predominantly on penal substitution, and would be imperilled if the doctrine were denied.

Chapter 5 presents a historical survey of belief in penal substitution. We provide primary documentary evidence to show that leading figures of every era, from the church Fathers until the present day, have held to the doctrine. Of course this does not by itself compel us to believe it: history is no substitute for theology, and Scripture remains our sole and final authority. Yet it has been claimed that penal substitution is a relative newcomer to the theological scene and in particular that it was not taught in the early church. These claims have no historical foundation whatsoever, and we hope to lay them to rest.[27] As we set out to defend penal substitution, it is an encouragement to see a great cloud of witnesses who have gone before us down the same road. Moreover, those who want to deny the doctrine and yet own the label 'evangelical' would do well to recognize just how far they are departing from their heritage. Few if any of their forefathers would stand with them.

We begin Part Two with a more detailed rationale for why we have engaged the critics of penal substitution in the way we have (chapter 6). We have classified the possible objections to the doctrine under six headings, which give us chapters 7–12. Sometimes the objections stem from a misunderstanding of the Bible's teaching, sometimes they arise from misconceptions about penal substitution itself, but in every case they can be answered. Finally, we deal with a different species of objection in chapter 13.

It is our prayer that this book will help many people to grasp more fully the wisdom of God in conceiving so perfect a plan to save a fallen world, the love of God the Father in sending his Son, the love of God the Son in going willingly to his death for our sake, the justice of God, which was vindicated at Calvary as the sin of his people was paid for, and the confidence that we can have to approach such a God, imperfect as we are, on account of the One who was 'pierced for our transgressions' (Isa. 53:5).

---

27. We are particularly indebted to Garry Williams for providing us with a copy of his doctoral thesis, which provided many of the references for the earliest proponents of penal substitution (Garry J. Williams, 'A Critical Exposition of Hugo Grotius's Doctrine of the Atonement in *De Satisfactione Christi*' [unpub. doctoral thesis, University of Oxford, 1999]).

## 2. SEARCHING THE SCRIPTURES: THE BIBLICAL FOUNDATIONS OF PENAL SUBSTITUTION

### Introduction

The aim of this chapter is to show that the doctrine of penal substitution is clearly taught within the pages of Scripture. It is not a tangential inference drawn from a few obscure texts, but a central emphasis of some foundational passages in both the Old and New Testaments. If we accept, as Jesus did, that the words of the biblical authors are at the same time the word of God, then this will be absolutely decisive. If God himself affirms penal substitution, if it is part of the explanation that he himself has given for why he sent his Son into the world, then we dare not maintain otherwise. To be sure, there will always be some who rail against the doctrine, complaining that it is barbaric or unjust or foolish or whatever else. But Jesus' disciples are marked by their humble trust in all that God has said.

Of course the idea that Jesus died in the place of sinners, bearing the punishment of God's wrath due to them on account of their rebellion, is not the *only* thing the Bible teaches about the crucifixion. We find also, for example, that the cross was the means by which Jesus triumphed over evil powers (Col. 2:15), that it offers an inspiring example to those who suffer unjustly (1 Pet. 2:21–23), and that it brings about a decisive end to our old life of sin, that we might live as new people (Rom. 6:6). The biblical portrayal of the atonement has many facets. Our task here is simply to show that penal substitution is one of them, and has such prominence that it cannot be sidelined.

We shall proceed by examining a number of passages of Scripture, ranging in length from a few verses to several chapters. Of course, these are not the only places in the Bible where penal substitution is taught. We have selected a small number for the sake of simplicity and to allow space to explore each in some detail.

## Exodus 12

### Introduction

Exodus 12 narrates the events of the first Passover. God's people, who were slaves in Egypt, were given detailed instructions about the preparation of a meal of roast lamb 'along with bitter herbs, and bread made without yeast' (v. 8). They were to 'eat it in haste' (v. 11), for later that very night they would be led out of Egypt to freedom. At midnight God visited on the land of Egypt the last in a series of ten devastating plagues, killing every firstborn son of their oppressors, and thereby persuading Pharaoh finally to release the Israelites. But the judgment at midnight also lent special significance to the lamb eaten during the meal: it was the blood of this lamb, daubed on the doorposts of the Israelite houses, that meant they were spared from the plague – 'when I see the blood, I will pass over you' (Exod. 12:13).

We shall see in this chapter that the Passover lamb functioned as a penal substitute, dying in the place of the firstborn sons of the Israelites, in order that they might escape the wrath of God.

Before we look in more detail at the text of Exodus 12, it is as well that we appreciate the significance accorded to this chapter in the rest of the Bible. That penal substitution should be taught *here* of all places is to give the doctrine a high prominence. Moses' instructions to the Israelites in respect of the first Passover are couched in terms of a ritual that was to be repeated in the first month of every year (12:6; cf. v. 2), and whose meaning was to be taught from generation to generation:

'Obey these instructions as a lasting ordinance for you and your descendants. When you enter the land that the LORD will give you as he promised, observe this ceremony. And when your children ask you, "What does this ceremony mean to you?" then tell them, "It is the Passover sacrifice to the LORD, who passed over the houses of the Israelites in Egypt and spared our homes when he struck down the Egyptians."'
Then the people bowed down and worshipped. (Exod. 12:24–27)

The Old Testament recounts individual Passover celebrations that occurred at decisive moments in Israel's history – just before they set out from Sinai after Moses received the law; just before the conquest of Jericho, the first city to be conquered in the Promised Land; at the time of the national reforms by Josiah and Hezekiah; immediately after the return from exile (Num. 9:1–14; Josh. 5:10–11; 2 Kgs 23:21–23; 2 Chr. 30:1–5; 35:1–13; Ezra 6:19–21).

The significance of the Passover is apparent also from the wider salvation-historical context in which it is located. The most important turning point in the Bible story before this, apart from the creation of the world and the fall of humanity, was God's covenant promise to Abraham in Genesis 12:1–3, 7.[1] The substance of the promise was threefold: Abraham would have many descendants, a land to live in, and the blessing of relationship with God. The Abrahamic covenant, as it is often called, forms the theological backbone of the Old Testament. Moreover, in the New Testament, the apostle Paul teaches that now all who believe in Christ, Jew or Gentile, are Abraham's spiritual children (Rom. 4:16–17) and heirs of the promise (Gal. 3:14, 29). In other words, the promise is nothing less than 'the gospel in advance' (Gal. 3:8).

If we read the opening chapters of Exodus with this interpretive framework in place, we immediately recognize the Israelites' slavery in Egypt as a problem of unfulfilled covenant promise. Though as a people they had become very numerous (Exod. 1:7), fulfilling God's promise that Abraham would have many descendants, they did not yet enjoy a land of their own, nor were they free to enjoy a relationship with God.[2] God's salvation in Exodus thus lies at the heart of the fulfilment of his covenant promises (cf. Exod. 2:23–25; 6:2–8). The Passover lies at the heart of God's salvation in Exodus. And, as we shall see, penal substitution lies at the heart of the Passover.

It is helpful to think of the events of Exodus 11–12 in terms of two distinct, though related, acts of salvation. First, by means of the judgment of God there is a salvation from the tyranny of the Egyptians. Secondly, by means of the Passover sacrifice there is a salvation from the judgment of God.

---

1. This promise is repeated in Gen. 15 and 17. It was then made to Abraham's son Isaac in Gen. 26:2–5, and to Isaac's son Jacob in Gen. 28:13–15.

2. God's repeated demand that Pharaoh should 'Let my people go, so that they may worship me' (Exod. 7:16; 8:1, 20; 9:1, 13; 10:3 cf. 3:12; 4:23; 5:1; 10:7, 8, 11, 24, 31) implies that they were unable to worship God, i.e. enjoy the fullness of relationship with him, while in Egypt.

It is the plague on the firstborn that ultimately breaks the bondage of Pharaoh and thereby delivers Israel from the Egyptian tyranny.[3] This plague shares many elements in common with the previous nine: Moses warns Pharaoh of a plague, in accordance with God's instructions (Exod. 11:4–8);[4] God sends the plague, but makes a distinction between the Israelites and the Egyptians such that only the latter are affected (Exod. 11:7; cf. 8:23; 9:4, 26; 10:22–23); Pharaoh's heart is hardened, so he ultimately refuses to let the people go (Exod. 11:10).[5]

God promises that, when this final and most devastating plague finally comes, Pharaoh will let the people go, and moreover that they will escape with articles of silver and gold from their neighbours, whom the Lord will make favourably disposed towards them (Exod. 11:1–3; cf. 3:19–22). This is exactly what happens (Exod. 12:31–36). Thus God's judgment on Pharaoh is the means of Israel's liberation from Egypt.

In this way, the exodus is a paradigm for God's deliverance of his people from hostile powers. Just as the Lord set his people free from slavery to Pharaoh, their oppressor, so also the Lord Jesus Christ has set us free from slavery to sin, the world and the devil, those hostile powers that once held us in bondage (cf. Eph. 2:1–3; Col. 2:14–15; Heb. 2:14–15; Rev. 12).

However, there is a second act of salvation depicted in Exodus 12:1–28. These verses form a discrete section bracketed by two parallel statements: in verse 1 the Lord begins his instructions 'to Moses and Aaron', and in verse 28 we read that 'The Israelites did just what the LORD commanded Moses and Aaron.' If this section were removed from the narrative, it would leave behind a perfectly coherent account of the tenth plague, resembling the accounts of the other nine. This section introduces a significant new element. Here we learn how the Israelites were to be delivered not from Pharaoh, but from the judgment of the Lord. It is here that we find an unambiguous affirmation of penal substitution, and to this we now turn.

---

3. Indeed, Exod. 4:22–23 indicates that this was God's plan right from the outset.

4. The previous plagues occur in a repeating cycle of three. In the first of each cycle (plagues 1, 4 and 7), Moses is instructed to confront Pharaoh 'in the morning'; in the second (plagues 2, 5 and 8) he is to go to Pharaoh, but the time of day is unspecified; in the third (plagues 3, 6 and 9) no warning is given.

5. Sometimes the text says that Pharaoh hardened his own heart, which emphasizes his personal culpability (e.g. Exod. 8:15, 32; 9:34); on other occasions it states that the Lord hardened Pharaoh's heart, which emphasizes God's overarching sovereignty (e.g. Exod. 7:3; 9:12; 10:1, 20, 27; 11:10; 14:4, 8, 17; cf. 4:1; 9:16); elsewhere it says merely that Pharaoh's heart became hard (e.g. Exod. 7:13, 22).

## The Passover and penal substitution

The first nine plagues present no danger to the Israelites. God's judgment falls only upon the Egyptians, for as we saw above, God makes a distinction between them and his people. What is perhaps a little surprising is that in the tenth plague this distinction between Israel and Egypt is *conditional*. The firstborn of the Israelites are not automatically spared from death; a lamb must be slaughtered, and its blood applied to the door frame of the house. The clear implication is that the firstborn son of the Israelite families would die if this instruction were not followed, for the Lord had said, '*when I see the blood*, I will pass over you' (Exod. 12:13; italics added). Thus the lamb becomes a substitute for the firstborn son, dying in his place.

This one-to-one correspondence between the life of the son and the life of a lamb is re-emphasized in the ceremony of the consecration of the firstborn, which is presented alongside the Passover in the book of Exodus and is intended explicitly to evoke its memory:

> After the LORD brings you into the land of the Canaanites and gives it to you, as he promised on oath to you and your forefathers, you are to give over to the LORD the first offspring of every womb. All the firstborn males of your livestock belong to the LORD. Redeem with a lamb every firstborn donkey, but if you do not redeem it, break its neck. Redeem every firstborn among your sons. In days to come when your son asks you, 'What does this mean?' say to him, 'With a mighty hand the LORD brought us out of Egypt, out of the land of slavery. When Pharaoh stubbornly refused to let us go, the LORD killed every firstborn in Egypt, both man and animal. This is why I sacrifice to the LORD the first male offspring of every womb and redeem each of my firstborn sons.' And it will be like a sign on your hand and a symbol on your forehead that the LORD brought us out of Egypt with his mighty hand.
> (Exod. 13:11–16)

Thus the consecration of the firstborn served as an enduring reminder of the events of the first Passover, and specifically of the substitutionary element inherent within it.

It is not only the firstborn sons who are involved in the Passover, however. The fact that the whole family shares together in the symbolic meal implies a wider application. Indeed, the striking emphasis on the proportionality between the amount of meat needed and the size of the Israelite household is most likely intended to highlight this: 'If any household is too small for a whole lamb, they must share one with their nearest neighbour, having taken into account the number of people there are. You are to determine the amount of lamb needed in accordance with what each person will eat' (Exod. 12:4). This extended comment would seem somewhat superfluous if intended only as a piece of culinary etiquette to guard against wasting food. An enslaved people, about to flee on a long and arduous journey into the desert, would hardly need to be warned against that!

The substitutionary element in the Passover is therefore beyond dispute. Moreover, given that the plagues function unambiguously as instruments of divine judgment, *penal* substitution is plainly taught here. This might seem puzzling, for while it is obvious why God would decide to punish the Egyptians, why would he judge his people? This seems all the more surprising given that the plague on the firstborn is described specifically as 'judgment on all the gods of *Egypt*' (Exod. 12:12). According to Ezekiel 20:4–10, however, the Israelites participated in the idolatry of their Egyptian masters; they too were guilty, and were no less deserving of God's judgment. Only by God's gracious provision of a means of atonement, a substitutionary sacrifice, were they spared.[6]

### *The Passover and the death of Jesus*

The New Testament writers make a connection between Jesus' death and the Passover sacrifice. The implication is clear. Just as the firstborn sons of Israel were spared from God's judgment at midnight on account of the blood of a lamb slain in their place, so God's new covenant people will be spared from his judgment on the final day through the substitutionary death of the Lord Jesus Christ.

The Synoptic Gospels (Matthew, Mark and Luke) make this link in their depictions of the Last Supper, the meal Jesus shares with his disciples shortly before his death. The events leading up to this last time of fellowship Jesus shares with his disciples before his death are striking, and suggest meticulous preparation on Jesus' part:

> [Jesus] sent two of his disciples, telling them, 'Go into the city, and a man carrying a jar of water will meet you. Follow him. Say to the owner of the house he enters, "The Teacher asks: Where is my guest room, where I may eat the Passover with my

---

6.  T. D. Alexander concurs: 'Implicit . . . is the idea that Israelites were inherently no different from the male firstborn of the Egyptians. Without the atoning blood of the sacrifice they too would have been struck dead by the "destroyer"' (T. D. Alexander, 'The Passover Sacrifice', in Roger T. Beckwith and Martin J. Selman (eds.), *Sacrifice in the Bible* [Carlisle: Paternoster; Grand Rapids: Baker, 1995], pp. 1–24 [p. 17]).

disciples?" He will show you a large upper room, furnished and ready. Make preparations for us there.' (Mark 14:13–15)

Clearly, there is much significance attached to the meal they are about to enjoy together. Adopting the role of head of the family, it would have been expected that Jesus would follow the custom of introducing the various elements of the meal, including the bread and the wine, according to a traditional Passover liturgy.[7] However, Jesus departs from the usual formula, and instead says something quite astonishing:

> While they were eating, Jesus took bread, gave thanks and broke it, and gave it to his disciples, saying, 'Take it; this is my body.' Then he took the cup, gave thanks and offered it to them, and they all drank from it. 'This is my blood of the covenant, which is poured out for many,' he said to them. (Mark 14:22–24)

Jesus' references to his 'body', and in particular his 'blood . . . poured out', allude to his death, which he thus sets forth as the decisive fulfilment of the Passover festival.[8] Whereas the old Passover focused on the body and blood of a lamb, slain as a penal substitutionary sacrifice for the redemption of Israel, the Lord's Supper focuses on the body and blood of Christ, who gave himself as a penal substitutionary sacrifice for his people.[9]

---

7. By the time of Jesus, the original intention that the Passover should serve as a reminder of the redemption from Egypt (Exod. 12:14) had come to be expressed in a well-defined liturgy, which incorporated the recitation of Pss 113–118 and a series of questions and answers between the firstborn son and his father about the meaning of various elements in the meal. Evidence for this may be found in the Mishnah, the written collection of the oral traditions that had served as a guide to the interpretation of the Old Testament law from several hundred years before Christ (William L. Lane, *The Gospel of Mark*, New International Commentary on the New Testament [Grand Rapids: Eerdmans, 1974], pp. 501–502, 505–508).

8. Allusions to other Old Testament themes are also present here. The words 'blood of the covenant' (Mark 14:24) allude to the ratification of the covenant in Exod. 24:6–8, and also evoke the promise of the new covenant in Jer. 31:31–33. These sit alongside the clear references to the Passover; they do not displace them.

9. It seems strange at first that Mark, and indeed Matthew and Luke, should mention only bread and wine, and not the lamb that was doubtless also on the menu. Perhaps they intend to avoid confusion, since the Lamb is sitting at the table with them.

The Gospel of John presents us with a countdown to the Passover as Jesus' death approaches.[10] This begins 'six days before the Passover' (John 12:1) with Jesus in Bethany. There Jesus ominously interprets Mary's gesture of anointing his feet with perfume as a fitting preparation 'for my burial' (John 12:7). A few days later, Jesus is in Jerusalem with his disciples and we are told, 'It was just before the Passover Feast. Jesus knew that the time had come for him to leave this world and go to the Father' (John 13:1). Immediately after this, Jesus sits down for a meal with his disciples (v. 2), which is perhaps to be identified with the Last Supper, though John does not record this in the same detail as the Synoptics.

Allusions to the ongoing Passover celebrations continue during John's account of Jesus' trial (John 18:28, 39), and the crucifixion itself (John 19:14, 31, 42).[11] Finally, John attaches great importance to his eyewitness testimony

---

10. Earlier mentions of the Passover in John anticipate Jesus' death in their own way. The two references in John 2 (vv. 13, 23) bracket a narrative in which Jesus invites his Jewish opponents to 'Destroy this temple, and I will raise it again in three days' (v. 19), which John explains is a reference to his death (v. 21). In John 6:4, the Passover is mentioned in conjunction with the feeding of the five thousand, where Jesus speaks of eating his flesh and drinking his blood (vv. 51–56), an obvious reference to his death, reminiscent of his later words at the Last Supper as recorded by the Synoptics (see above).

11. John 19 mentions three times that Jesus died on the 'day of Preparation'. There is some disagreement over whether this refers to the preparation for the Sabbath (which began the next day, Mark 15:42; John 19:31) or the preparation for the Passover meal. Carson argues against the latter, for that would introduce a discrepancy with the chronology of the Synoptic Gospels, which testify that Jesus ate the Passover with his disciples on the day before he died. Carson points out that the Passover festival, being combined with the Feast of Unleavened Bread, would have lasted several days, and thus it is perfectly possible that the meal itself took place on the Thursday night, before the day of preparation for the Sabbath (D. A. Carson, *The Gospel According to John*, Pillar New Testament Commentary [Leicester: Apollos; Grand Rapids: Eerdmans, 1991], pp. 455–458, 603–604). The alternative is to follow R. T. France ('Chronological Aspects of "Gospel Harmony"', *Vox Evangelica* 16 [1986], pp. 33–59) in his suggestion that Jesus ate the Last Supper with his disciples 'a day in advance of the official date' (p. 54) for the Passover. In that case we would be free to interpret the day of preparation as the day before Passover. This makes Jesus' crucifixion simultaneous with the slaughter of the Passover lambs, and, if anything, strengthens the theological connection between them.

that Jesus' bones were not broken during the crucifixion (John 19:35–36), seeing this as a fulfilment of the injunction in Exodus 12:46 (cf. Num. 9:12) that the bones of the Passover lamb must remain unbroken.

The connection between Jesus' death and the Passover sacrifice is made also in 1 Peter 1:18–19, where we are told that 'it was not with perishable things such as silver or gold that you were redeemed from the empty way of life handed down to you from your forefathers, but with the precious blood of Christ, a lamb without blemish or defect'. Many of the Old Testament sacrifices specify the need for a lamb 'without defect',[12] but whenever *redemption* is mentioned, with its connotations of deliverance from slavery, the events of the exodus cannot be far from any Jewish reader's mind.[13] The fact that Peter specifies Jesus' blood as the means of rescue recalls the night of the first Passover, in which the blood of the lamb on the doorpost averted God's judgment.

Finally, the identification of Jesus with the Passover lamb could not be clearer in 1 Corinthians 5:7, where Paul says that 'Christ, our Passover lamb, has been sacrificed'. In the context, Paul is urging his readers that as people redeemed by the sacrificial death of Jesus, there is no place for immorality among them. Paul urges them to rid themselves of 'yeast' of corruption, drawing on the imagery of the first Passover in which the Israelites were to 'eat nothing containing yeast' (Exod. 13:3; cf. 12:8, 15, 18–20; 13:6–7).

In view of this evidence, it is indisputable that the New Testament writers saw in the sacrifice of the Passover lamb a foreshadowing of Jesus' redemptive death.

### Summary

At the first Passover, the Jewish people were delivered not only from the tyranny of Pharaoh, but also from the judgment of God on their idolatry. It was through the substitutionary death of a lamb, whose blood marked out the Israelite households, that their firstborn sons were spared. These events occurred at a key turning point in salvation history, and were integral to God's faithfulness to his covenant with Abraham. Moreover, the ongoing celebration of the Passover

---

12. E.g. Lev. 1:10; 3:6; 4:32; 5:15, 18; 6:6; 14:10; 22:21; 23:12; Num. 6:14.

13. Moreover, the same Greek verb translated 'redeemed' in 1 Pet. 1:18 is used in the LXX of Exod. 6:6, the crucial passage in which the Lord first announces his intention to deliver his people from Egypt. (The abbreviation 'LXX' refers to the Septuagint, the Greek translation of the Hebrew Old Testament produced around the second or third century BC.)

served to implant the notion of salvation through penal sacrifice in every faithful Israelite mind. The New Testament writers see Jesus' death as the fulfilment of the Passover: he suffered in the place of his people in order that they might be marked out by his blood and thus spared from God's wrath.

## Leviticus 16

### Introduction

To many Christians, Leviticus is a closed book. Its world of animal sacrifice and religious ritual seems so remote from ours. In reality, however, Leviticus has a huge amount to teach us, if only we would scratch below the surface. In particular we shall see that chapter 16, right at the heart of the book, informs our understanding of Jesus' death as our penal substitute.

Leviticus takes its place after the book of Exodus in the single unfolding biblical narrative that stretches from the Garden of Eden to the new heavens and new earth. In order to appreciate the teaching of Leviticus, we need to realize that Exodus raises a profound question: How can a holy God dwell in the midst of a sinful people?

God's presence with his people is affirmed repeatedly in Exodus. For example, they were guided by him during their wanderings in the desert: 'By day the LORD went ahead of them in a pillar of cloud to guide them on their way and by night in a pillar of fire to give them light, so that they could travel by day or night. Neither the pillar of cloud by day nor the pillar of fire by night left its place in front of the people' (Exod. 13:21–22).

It is similarly 'in a dense cloud' that the Lord comes to Moses on Sinai (Exod. 19:9; cf. 24:15–18). This is supremely a place of encounter, for here God's voice is heard, his character is revealed, his law is given, his covenant is established. Later in the book, God once again descends on Sinai in a cloud to proclaim his covenant name, Yahweh ('the LORD'), in response to Moses' request for a glimpse of his glory (Exod. 33:18; 34:5–7). The closing chapters of the book give detailed instructions for the construction of the Tent of Meeting, also known as the Tabernacle, and the cloud of God's glory comes to rest there (Exod. 40:34–38).

Yet the sinfulness of God's people renders his closeness problematic, even dangerous. Limits are to be put around Mount Sinai so that the people do not draw too close to the Lord (Exod. 19:12, 23). If they do, they will 'perish' (v. 21), for the Lord will 'break out against them' (v. 24). After the people's idolatry in worshipping the golden calf (Exod. 32) the situation has degenerated. The Lord says to Moses, 'Go up to the land flowing with milk and honey. But

I will not go with you, because you are a stiff-necked people and I might destroy you on the way' (Exod. 33:3; cf. v. 5). In other words, the continuing sinfulness of God's people makes it impossible for the holy God to dwell with them without endangering them. Even after God graciously renews his covenant and agrees to accompany the people after all (Exod. 34), the tension remains. In Leviticus it finds its resolution.[14]

The book of Leviticus teaches that the relationship between a holy God and a sinful people (or in terminology more characteristic of Leviticus, an *unclean* people) can be maintained by sacrifice.[15]

While not all of the sacrifices prescribed by Leviticus are intended to atone for sin,[16] the rituals of the Day of Atonement most certainly are. Their importance is highlighted by their central position in chapter 16 as the 'keystone of the structure'[17] of the book, and is recognized in the New Testament, which portrays Christ's once-for-all sacrifice as the fulfilment of the Day of Atonement rituals (Heb. 9–10).[18] The ceremonies of the Day of Atonement centred around two goats, one of which was sacrificed to the Lord, the other being sent into the desert as a 'scapegoat', or, more literally, a 'goat for Azazel' (Lev. 16:8; cf. v. 21). The purpose of these ceremonies was to make 'atonement' for the people of Israel (e.g. Lev. 16:17, 24, 30, 32–34). In the following pages we shall consider the meaning of the central idea of 'atonement' and the significance of the scapegoat before reflecting briefly on how the sacrificial system is portrayed in the Psalms and the Old Testament prophets.

---

14. At least temporarily: only in the death of Jesus is it finally resolved.

15. Leviticus does not primarily address the 'initiatory' question of how someone who has no relationship with God can begin one. The Israelites for whom the Levitical sacrifices were prescribed were already God's people. Yet their sin continued to imperil their relationship with God and, unless dealt with, would have occasioned his wrath, as we shall see below.

16. Accordingly, the New Testament employs the motif of sacrifice in other important ways: 'Through Jesus, therefore, let us continually offer to God a sacrifice of praise – the fruit of lips that confess his name' (Heb. 13:15); 'you also, like living stones, are being built into a spiritual house to be a holy priesthood, offering spiritual sacrifices acceptable to God through Jesus Christ' (1 Pet. 2:5); 'offer your bodies as living sacrifices, holy and pleasing to God' (Rom. 12:1).

17. J. E. Hartley, *Leviticus*, Word Biblical Commentary (Dallas: Word, 1992), p. xxxv.

18. David Peterson, 'Atonement in the New Testament', in David Peterson (ed.), *Where Wrath and Mercy Meet: Proclaiming the Atonement Today* (Carlisle: Paternoster, 2001), pp. 26–67 (pp. 51–52).

### The meaning of atonement

The Hebrew verb *kipper*, translated 'to make atonement', occurs sixteen times in Leviticus 16. Its meaning can be understood only by paying careful attention to the way in which the word is used, for a word can mean different things in different contexts. There are four possible meanings for *kipper*, none of which necessarily excludes the others.[19]

First, where God is the subject, *kipper* can mean *to forgive*. However, this cannot exhaust the meaning, for in some texts *kipper* is distinct from forgiveness, as a prerequisite to it (Lev. 4:20, 26, 31; 19:22; Num. 15:25).[20]

Secondly, *kipper* can be to do with *cleansing*, for example, in Leviticus 16:30, where the Lord says to Moses, 'on this day *atonement* will be made for you, to *cleanse* you. Then, before the LORD, you will be *clean* from all your sins' (italics added).

In Leviticus 16 both the altar and the tabernacle itself need to be cleansed because of their defilement by proximity to sinful people. Thus Aaron is instructed as follows:

> In this way he will make atonement [*kipper*] for the Most Holy Place because of the uncleanness and rebellion of the Israelites, whatever their sins have been. He is to do the same for the Tent of Meeting, which is among them in the midst of their uncleanness . . . Then he shall come out to the altar that is before the LORD and make atonement [*kipper*] for it . . . to cleanse it and consecrate it from the uncleanness of the Israelites. (Lev. 16:16, 18–19)

The fact that Leviticus prescribes cleansing and atonement for some things that we would not consider morally culpable, such as skin disease (Lev. 14:18–20, 29–31; cf. v. 3) and menstruation (Lev. 15:19–30), might be thought to weaken the connection with sin. But this is not necessarily so. The underlying point could be rather that uncleanness is an intrinsic problem for fallen human beings; simply as we exist, experiencing nothing more than is common to everyday human life, we find ourselves unable to approach a holy God.

The third possible meaning for *kipper* is *ransom*, suggested by its possible relationship with the noun *kōper*, which carries this meaning. Indeed, the

---

19. For a more detailed discussion, see David Peterson, 'Atonement in the Old Testament', in David Peterson (ed.), *Where Wrath and Mercy Meet: Proclaiming the Atonement Today* (Carlisle: Paternoster, 2001), pp. 1–25 (pp. 9–12); Leon Morris, *The Apostolic Preaching of the Cross* (London: Tyndale, 1955), pp. 160–178.

20. Peterson, 'Atonement in the Old Testament', p. 10.

connection is sometimes explicit, as for example in Exodus 30:11–16, where *kipper* and *kōper* occur together (cf. Num. 35:29–34).[21] But what is the ransom that is paid? Sometimes *kipper* is used to refer to a financial payment – money or something else of value, as for example in Exodus 30:15–16 (cf. Num. 31:50). However, the ransom can also be the life of an animal. Significantly, this meaning is found in Leviticus 17:11, immediately following the instructions for the Day of Atonement ceremonies, in what 'is a key text for explaining the significance of sacrificial blood within the Israelite cult'.[22] This verse explains God's prohibition against eating blood on the grounds that 'the life of a creature is in the blood, and I have given it to you to make atonement [*kipper*] for yourselves on the altar; it is the blood that makes atonement for one's life'.[23] The Hebrew phrase underlying the words 'to make atonement for yourselves' is exactly the same as that found in Exodus 30:15–16. There may also be an element of substitution implied in Leviticus 17:11 by the parallelism 'the life of the creature . . . for one's life', although this is uncertain.[24]

Finally, *kipper* can refer to the averting of God's wrath. This meaning is apparent in several Old Testament texts. For example, Numbers 25 describes an occasion when the Israelites committed sexual immorality with Moabite women and began to worship their gods. As a result, 'the LORD's anger burned against them' (v. 3), manifested in a plague. As Moses attempted to deal with the Israelites' outrageous behaviour by putting their ringleaders to death in accordance with the Lord's instructions (vv. 4–5), 'an Israelite man brought to his family a Midianite woman right before the eyes of Moses and the whole assembly of Israel while they were weeping at the entrance to the Tent of

---

21. Ibid., p. 11.

22. Ibid.

23. Some have argued, largely on the basis of this verse, that 'blood' in Scripture signifies life rather than death. However, in all of the Old Testament sacrifices, blood is obtained by killing an animal, and the life spoken of in Lev. 17:11 is that 'which ceases to exist when the blood is poured out' (Morris, *Apostolic Preaching of the Cross*, p. 113). For further discussion see pp. 112–128; Alan M. Stibbs, *The Meaning of the Word 'Blood' in Scripture* (London: Tyndale, 1948); John R. W. Stott, *The Cross of Christ* (Leicester: IVP, 1986), pp. 179–181.

24. Emile Nicole defends this substitutionary sense in 'Atonement in the Pentateuch', in C. E. Hill and F. A. James III (eds.), *The Glory of the Atonement* (Downers Grove: IVP; Leicester: Apollos, 2004), pp. 35–50, although there remains some doubt over whether the final clause should be translated 'makes atonement for one's life' or 'makes atonement by the life'.

Meeting' (v. 6). This shameless display of godlessness so enraged Phinehas, the priest, that 'he left the assembly, took a spear in his hand and followed the Israelite into the tent. He drove the spear through both of them – through the Israelite and into the woman's body' (vv. 7–8). According to the text, it was this, and not Moses' attempts to restore order, that turned aside God's wrath from the Israelites: '*Then* the plague against the Israelites was stopped' (v. 8; italics added). We might instinctively judge Phinehas' actions as excessive, but the Lord has nothing but praise for him:

> The LORD said to Moses, 'Phinehas son of Eleazar, the son of Aaron, the priest, has turned my anger away from the Israelites; for he was as zealous as I am for my honour among them, so that in my zeal I did not put an end to them. Therefore tell him I am making my covenant of peace with him. He and his descendants will have a covenant of a lasting priesthood, because he was zealous for the honour of his God and made atonement [*kipper*] for the Israelites.' (Num. 25: 10–13)

For our purposes, the important thing to note is that Phinehas is said to have 'turned [the Lord's] anger away from the Israelites' (v. 10), and 'made atonement [*kipper*] for the Israelites' (v. 13). Thus the connection between *kipper* and averting God's wrath is inescapable.

A similar example is found in Numbers 16:46, where the Lord sends a plague on the Israelites in response to their persistent grumbling (cf. v. 41). Moses urges Aaron to offer incense to the Lord and make atonement for the sin of the Israelites, turning aside the Lord's righteous wrath.

> Then Moses said to Aaron, 'Take your censer and put incense in it, along with fire from the altar, and hurry to the assembly to make atonement [*kipper*] for them. Wrath has come out from the LORD; the plague has started.' So Aaron did as Moses said, and ran into the midst of the assembly. The plague had already started among the people, but Aaron offered the incense and made atonement [*kipper*] for them. (Num. 16:46–47)

Here, as in Numbers 25, the connection between *kipper* and averting God's wrath at human sin is plain.

We have thus seen that *kipper* can relate to forgiveness, cleansing, ransom, and the averting of God's wrath. But which of these meanings are in view in Leviticus 16? The idea of forgiveness is prominent throughout and, as we saw above, the language of cleansing is also present (vv. 16, 19). The notion of ransom is also evident – specifically the substitutionary payment of the life of a sacrificial animal for a human life. But is the idea of averting God's wrath found in Leviticus 16? Indeed it is.

Leviticus 16:1 introduces the instructions for the Day of Atonement in the following way: 'The LORD spoke to Moses after the death of the two sons of Aaron who died when they approached the LORD.' This calls to mind the events of Leviticus 10:1–2, 'Aaron's sons Nadab and Abihu took their censers, put fire in them and added incense; and they offered unauthorized fire before the LORD, contrary to his command. So fire came out from the presence of the LORD and consumed them, and they died before the LORD.'

Nadab and Abihu attempted to approach God in an inappropriate way and their deaths underline that the problem of a sinful people sustaining a relationship with a holy God is serious indeed (cf. Lev. 10:3). A few verses later, it becomes clear that the deaths of Nadab and Abihu were a manifestation of God's wrath, as Moses warns Aaron and his stunned family about their conduct, lest something similar should happen again: 'Then Moses said to Aaron and his sons Eleazar and Ithamar, "Do not let your hair become unkempt, and do not tear your clothes, or you will die and *the LORD will be angry* with the whole community"' (v. 6; italics added).

The allusion to these events in Leviticus 16:1 is not an irrelevant detail. It is a conspicuous allusion to a previous, failed attempt to draw near to God, in which the improper conduct of Nadab and Abihu provoked God's wrath, and with which the instructions for the correct conduct of the Day of Atonement are contrasted. It thereby highlights the fact that God's wrath must be overcome in order to draw near to him, and that only by performing the sacrifices in the correct manner is this possible. Indeed, there is a striking parallel between the consuming fire that enveloped Nadab and Abihu in Leviticus 10:1–2 and the fire that 'consumed the burnt offering and the fat portions on the altar' (Lev. 9:24) during the successful sacrifice recorded a few moments earlier.

Some contemporary interpretations of the Levitical sacrificial system are deeply flawed at this point. For example, John Goldingay claims that 'the question of propitiating God's wrath . . . has little place in Leviticus itself. The word anger hardly appears. The languages of atonement-propitiation-expiation and of anger do not come together . . . Sacrifice does not directly relate to anger.'[25]

What he fails to appreciate is that God's wrath would be seen far more often if it were not for the successful operation of the sacrifices set forth by God to deal with it. It is precisely because sacrifice *does* relate directly to anger that we see anger so rarely! When the sacrificial system is abused, as in the case of

---

25. John Goldingay, 'Your Iniquities Have Made a Separation between You and Your God', in John Goldingay (ed.), *Atonement Today* (London: SPCK, 1995), pp. 39–53 (p. 51).

Nadab and Abihu, God's wrath is seen plainly.[26] By showing us what happens in such cases, Leviticus reveals the problem is being successfully dealt with the rest of the time.[27]

Consider the analogy of our drinking water. Most of the time it is perfectly safe to drink, but it would be wrong to infer from this that dirty water could never be a problem. On the contrary, our tap water is drinkable only because the purification systems are working properly. If pranksters were to break into the treatment plant and turn off some of the crucial machinery, or perhaps fool around with some dangerous chemicals, then not only would poison be on its way to our taps, but the intruders themselves would be in great peril.

In summary, it is evident that in Leviticus 16 the Hebrew verb *kipper*, normally translated 'he made atonement', refers to the propitiation of God's wrath through the offering of a substitutionary animal sacrifice, which cleansed the people from their sin.

### The scapegoat

The instructions for the ritual involving the scapegoat are found in Leviticus 16:20–22:

> When Aaron has finished making atonement for the Most Holy Place, the Tent of Meeting and the altar, he shall bring forward the live goat. He is to lay both hands on the head of the live goat and confess over it all the wickedness and rebellion of the Israelites – all their sins – and put them on the goat's head. He shall send the goat away into the desert in the care of a man appointed for the task. The goat will carry on itself all their sins to a solitary place; and the man shall release it in the desert.

---

26. In view of the fate of Aaron's sons, it is surprising to read Goldingay's claim that 'The idea of punishment belongs in the framework of law rather than the framework of worship' (John Goldingay, 'Old Testament Sacrifice and the Death of Christ', in ibid., pp. 3–20 [p. 10]). His dichotomy is undermined by the fact that it was for an unlawful act of worship that Nadab and Abihu met their end. His claim also comes to grief in Lev. 7:20–21, where serious penalties are prescribed for inappropriate participation in a fellowship offering.

27. Similarly, we cannot infer from the fact that God does not punish Christians that his wrath is not provoked by sin. Rather, God's gracious treatment of his children presupposes that his wrath has already been turned aside through the sacrifice of his Son.

By laying his hands on the head of the goat and confessing the sins of the people, Aaron, as the representative of all the Israelites, identified with the goat and symbolically transferred the people's sins to it.[28] Some have doubted that this act of identification implies substitution, but such an interpretation is inescapable. For when a person lives who otherwise would have died, and an animal dies that would otherwise have lived, substitution is necessarily entailed.

The goat is sent away to 'a solitary place' (literally, 'a land of cutting off', v. 22), where without doubt it would be expected to die.[29] But the goat's fate has a greater significance than this. Throughout Leviticus we find that to be excluded, or 'cut off', from the camp of Israel was to experience God's punishment for sin (e.g. Lev. 7:20–27; 17:4, 9–14; 18:29; 19:8; 20:3, 5–6, 17–18; 22:3; 23:29).[30] The clear implication is that the goat is depicted in Leviticus 16:22 as suffering this fate.

Such an understanding is also implied by a description of the animal as a 'scapegoat' in verses 8, 10 and 26. The meaning of the underlying Hebrew expression has been extensively debated.[31] Some suggest that 'Azazel' means 'a rocky precipice'; others that it means 'complete destruction'. A final proposal is that it is the name of a demon thought to inhabit the desert. This latter suggestion seems rather unlikely given that offerings to 'goat demons' are explicitly forbidden in the very next chapter (Lev. 17:7). It is hard to decide between the first two alternatives, but for the purpose of our discussion it matters little. A terrible fate is in view in either case, entailing both exclusion and the certain expectation of death.

As the goat is sent away from the people, it is said to 'carry on itself all their sins' (Lev. 16:22). The meaning of the underlying Hebrew phrase *nāśā'* *'awōn* depends in part on the subject of the verb.[32] For example, where God is

---

28. Gordon J. Wenham, *The Book of Leviticus*, New International Commentary on the Old Testament (Grand Rapids: Eerdmans, 1979), p. 223.

29. Peterson, 'Atonement in the Old Testament', p. 15. As Gordon Wenham points out, the idea of death is also suggested merely by the notion of exclusion from the camp: 'To be expelled from the camp of Israel . . . was to experience a living death' (Gordon J. Wenham, *Genesis 1–15*, Word Biblical Commentary [Nashville: Thomas Nelson, 1987], p. 90].

30. Cf. Wenham, *Leviticus*, p. 125. The references in Lev. 20:3, 5–6 are particularly striking, for here God himself threatens to 'cut off' those who sin.

31. This paragraph is largely indebted to Wenham, *Leviticus*, pp. 234–235.

32. J. Alan Groves, 'Atonement in Isaiah 53', in C. E. Hill and F. A. James III (eds.), *The*

the subject, it means 'to forgive sin' (e.g. Num. 14:18). Where a sinful person is the subject, it usually means that he bears his own guilt (e.g. Lev. 7:18). Leviticus 16:22 is a rather different case, for an animal is the subject of the verb, and the judicial fate of the Israelites is transferred to the animal in such a way that they do not bear it themselves. The natural reading in this case is that the animal bears the sin and guilt of the people *in their place* and they are thereby released from this burden.[33]

But there is more to be said. Noting that *nāśā' 'awōn* is often found alongside another Hebrew phrase, *sābal ḥēṭ'*, and indeed that the nouns and verbs in the two phrases are sometimes interchanged, yielding the combinations *nāśā' ḥēṭ'* and *sābal 'awōn* with the same meaning, Garry Williams discusses several texts where these phrases refer unambiguously to the bearing of *punishment*, and not of guilt alone (Gen. 4:13; Lev. 5:17; 24:14–16; Num. 5:31; 14:34; Lam. 5:7).[34] Given that wrath is prominent in the background of Leviticus 16 (vv. 1–2; see above), and the 'land of cutting off' is a place of death and punishment, this meaning is surely implied. Here also the scapegoat bears the punishment due to the people on account of their sin.

Thus the scapegoat is depicted in Leviticus 16 as bearing the sin, guilt and punishment of the people, and being condemned to death in their place.

### The sacrificial system in the Psalms and the Old Testament prophets

We have seen from Leviticus 16 that penal substitution is central to God's dealing with sin. However, it is sometimes claimed that the Psalms and Prophets present a different picture, speaking of sacrifice as unnecessary, even fundamentally flawed, and suggesting even that forgiveness is possible without it.

This claim is unfounded. The point made by the Prophets and Psalms is not that sacrifices are irrelevant or inherently defective. Rather, these writings condemn various *abuses* of the sacrificial system.

Sometimes the problem was *presumption*. The people seemed to think that so long as they continued to offer the occasional sacrifice, the moral demands

---

*Glory of the Atonement* (Downers Grove: IVP; Leicester: Apollos, 2004), pp. 61–89 (pp. 69–75); Garry J. Williams, 'The Cross and the Punishment of Sin', in David Peterson (ed.), *Where Wrath and Mercy Meet: Proclaiming the Atonement Today* (Carlisle: Paternoster, 2001), pp. 68–99 (pp. 69–81).

33. Williams, 'Cross and the Punishment of Sin', pp. 78–79; Peterson, 'Atonement in the Old Testament', pp. 14–15. A similar meaning is found in Isa. 53 (see below).

34. Williams, 'Cross and the Punishment of Sin', pp. 69–81.

of God's law could safely be overlooked. Such an attitude is condemned in Isaiah 1:11–17 and Jeremiah 7:21–24 (cf. 1 Sam. 15:22–23). It was no more acceptable for Israelites under the old covenant than it is for Christians under the new. The apostle James has little time for those who claim to have faith in Christ but live no differently from the world around them: 'Show me your faith without deeds, and I will show you my faith by what I do' (Jas 2:18; cf. Rom. 6:1–2).

Amos 5:21–26 draws attention to a second problem; namely *syncretism*, the attempt to combine the worship prescribed by the Lord with elements of paganism. The people of Israel were repeatedly guilty of this, at one point even bringing pagan statues into God's temple (e.g. 1 Kgs 16:30–33; 2 Kgs 17:1–20; 21:1–6). The Lord will not tolerate this: his people must worship him alone, and in the way he has stipulated.

At a superficial glance, Psalm 51:16 might be thought to signal the end of the sacrificial system; for David, at the end of a psalm in which he has sought God's forgiveness for his adultery with Bathsheba, confesses that

> You do not delight in sacrifice, or I would bring it;
> you do not take pleasure in burnt offerings.

However, earlier in the same psalm David petitions God to 'cleanse me with hyssop' (v. 7), a likely allusion to the provisions for ritual cleansing for skin disease in Leviticus 14. It is hardly possible that David would impugn the sacrificial system immediately after appealing to God on its basis. Indeed, it is almost certainly not *atoning* sacrifices that are rejected in verse 16. It is typical of lament psalms such as this that after an initial period of mourning they turn to expressions of rejoicing and sacrifices of *praise*. These are the sacrifices David eschews here, recognizing that 'in the case of a woman pregnant through adultery and a grieving family due to murder, a joyous feast is entirely inappropriate'.[35]

Of course, the Old Testament sacrifices were never intended to be God's final word on the subject of atonement. The book of Hebrews draws attention to several shortcomings of a sacrificial system that depended on a sinful priesthood and the blood of bulls and goats, 'which can never take away sins' (Heb. 10:11; cf. 7:26–28; 10:4). Old covenant believers, no less than New

---

35. Bruce K. Waltke, 'Atonement in Psalm 51', in C. E. Hill and F. A. James III (eds.), *The Glory of the Atonement* (Downers Grove: IVP; Leicester: Apollos, 2004), pp. 51–60 (p. 59). This paragraph is indebted to pp. 57–59 of his chapter.

Testament Christians, were saved by the atoning sacrifice of Christ (Heb. 9:15). The Old Testament sacrifices provided a window through which they looked in faith to their Messiah who was yet to come. When he did come, the penal substitutionary principles underlying the Old Testament sacrifices were not abandoned or repudiated: they were fulfilled.

### Summary

The book of Leviticus addresses the question 'How can a holy God dwell in the midst of a sinful people?' The answer for old covenant believers was a system of atoning sacrifices, with the Day of Atonement at its heart. Both the vocabulary of atonement and the fate of the scapegoat in Leviticus 16 depict the propitiation of God's wrath by the substitutionary death of an animal. This anticipated the work of Christ in the new covenant, where God's wrath against all his people was propitiated by the once-for-all substitutionary death of his Son.

## Isaiah 52:13 – 53:12

### Introduction

Isaiah 40–55 contains some of the best known and most loved passages in the Old Testament. Doubtless the most famous of all is the fourth of the so-called 'Servant Songs', a series of meditations on the ministry of an enigmatic figure known as the 'Servant of the LORD' (Isa. 42:1–4; 49:1–6; 50:4–9; 52:13 – 53:12). As we approach the final Servant Song in Isaiah 53, we are confronted with two decisive questions.[36] First, is penal substitution taught here? Secondly, does this mean Jesus' suffering, in fulfilment of the Servant's role, should be conceived of in penal and substitutionary terms?

Most Christians would instinctively answer both questions in the affirmative. It seems obvious on first reading of the text that the Servant is portrayed as a penal substitute, willingly taking upon himself the sin and punishment of others, suffering in their place in accordance with God's will and under God's hand. And surely the many New Testament allusions to this passage establish beyond doubt that Jesus and the apostles understood Jesus' death in the same way. In our view this is entirely correct. Yet in recent years challenges have been raised to this traditional interpretation, and responsible

---

36. For convenience we shall refer to the fourth Servant Song as 'Isaiah 53', even though it actually begins at Isa. 52:13.

exegesis requires we examine the text closely to see whether the objections can be sustained. In any case, it can be no bad thing to meditate again on a favourite passage of Scripture, however many times we have mined its riches before.

### Penal substitution in Isaiah 53

Penal substitution lies so obviously at the heart of Isaiah 53 that, intriguingly, it is defended as the correct interpretation of that chapter even by a scholar who finds the notion completely unacceptable. Otfried Hofius' careful study of the text leaves him in no doubt that this is what Isaiah teaches,[37] although he complains that 'the ideas of substitution or place-taking . . . are simply outrageous . . . In the legal realm personal guilt is nontransferable; the punishment to be borne by any given person can *under no circumstances* be substitutionarily taken over and atoned for by another person.'[38] Or again, 'What this song says about the Servant's substitutionary death is theologically incomprehensible as it stands and as it is meant . . . being freed up from sin and guilt through *human* substitution is theologically simply unthinkable!'[39] It can hardly be said that Hofius has found penal substitution in Isaiah 53 because he *likes* the idea, as if he is desperate to 'read in' a meaning that his religious instincts tell him ought to be there. Quite the reverse! He is compelled by the sheer weight of evidence to admit that this teaching is there, even when he would rather it were not.

One scholar who dissents from the penal substitutionary reading is R. N. Whybray. He argues that the Servant does not suffer *instead* of others, as their *substitute*, but *alongside* them, as their *representative*.[40] To use alternative terminology, Whybray argues it was a case not of '*exclusive* place-taking' but of '*inclusive* place-taking'. However, a careful examination of the text

---

37. Otfried Hofius, 'The Fourth Servant Song in the New Testament Letters', in B. Janowski and P. Stuhlmacher (eds.), *The Suffering Servant: Isaiah 53 in Jewish and Christian Sources*, trans. Daniel P. Bailey (Grand Rapids: Eerdmans, 2004), pp. 163–188 (pp. 163–172).

38. Ibid., p. 168; italics original.

39. Ibid., p. 172; italics original. We address Hofius' theological objection in chapter 10.

40. R. N. Whybray, *Thanksgiving for a Liberated Prophet: An Interpretation of Isaiah Chapter 53*, Journal for the Study of the Old Testament Supplement Series 4 (Sheffield: JSOT Press, 1978); see also Morna D. Hooker, 'Did the Use of Isaiah 53 to Interpret His Mission Begin with Jesus?', in William H. Bellinger, Jr., and William R. Farmer (eds.), *Jesus and the Suffering Servant* (Harrisburg: Trinity Press International, 1998), pp. 88–103 (p. 96).

establishes beyond doubt that the traditional reading of Isaiah 53 is correct, and exposes fatal flaws in Whybray's case. We shall consider seven noteworthy features of the text that clarify the substitutionary character of the Servant's suffering.

First, the Servant is explicitly said to suffer 'for' others. The substitutionary character of his suffering is highlighted by the repeated contrast in Isaiah 53:4–6 between *he, his* and *him* on the one hand, and *we, us, we all* and *us all* on the other. The original Hebrew text underlines this even more forcefully by an emphatic use of personal pronouns. A more literal English translation reveals something of the impact of this:

> Surely our sicknesses – *he* bore them,
>     and our pains – he suffered them.
> Yet *we* considered him as one stricken,
>     as one struck down by God and afflicted.
> But *he* was pierced for our transgressions,
>     and crushed for our iniquities.
> The punishment for our salvation lay upon him,
>     and by his wounds, healing came to us.
> We all have strayed like sheep
>     each of us has turned to his own way.
> But Yahweh has caused to fall on him
>     the iniquity of us all.[41]

A similar emphatic use of pronouns is found in verse 11, 'their iniquities – *he* will bear them', and in verse 12, 'for *he* – the sins of many, he bore them'. All of this serves to underline the simple fact that the Servant, who is distinct from God's people, suffered in their place, as their substitute.[42]

Whybray objects to this argument, following Orlinsky in claiming that the Hebrew preposition *min*, translated 'for' in Isaiah 53:5 ('he was pierced *for* our

---

41. This translation is based on that of Hofius, 'Fourth Servant Song', pp. 164–165. The italics indicate where an emphatic independent personal pronoun occurs in the Hebrew.

42. This observation also provides an important insight into the question of the identity of the Servant throughout Isa. 41–53. For although he is sometimes identified with Israel (e.g. Isa. 49:3), at other points a clear distinction between Israel and the Servant is evident (e.g. Isa. 49:5–6). Isa. 53 is clearly an instance where he is distinguished from Israel.

transgressions, he was crushed *for* our iniquities'), implies the Servant suffered *because of* the sins of the people. This, he says, does not imply substitution. As Morna Hooker explains in her analysis of Whybray's view, 'it could be said of the Jews who perished in the Holocaust, that they were wounded because of Hitler's transgressions, crushed as a result of his iniquities',[43] but this would not imply that they suffered *instead* of him. According to Whybray, if Isaiah had wanted to convey the idea of substitution, it would have been more natural instead to use a different Hebrew preposition, namely *bĕ*.[44]

Although Whybray is correct that *min* can mean 'because of',[45] he is mistaken to think that such a meaning undermines a substitutionary view of the Servant's suffering. If a child strays too close to a bonfire despite being warned of the danger, and his mother leaps forward to rescue him from danger and is burned herself, she suffers 'because of' his disobedience. Yet her suffering would be substitutionary – she suffers in his place, and the disobedient child is thereby spared. It would have been perfectly acceptable for Isaiah to convey the notion of substitution in this way, and as we have seen, his emphatic use of pronouns confirms this is what he has in mind. In any case, even if

---

43. Hooker, 'Use of Isaiah 53', pp. 96–97.

44. Whybray, *Thanksgiving for a Liberated Prophet*, pp. 61–62; cf. H. M. Orlinsky, 'The So-Called "Servant of the Lord" and "Suffering Servant" in Second Isaiah', in H. M. Orlinsky and N. H. Snaith (eds.), *Studies on the Second Part of the Book of Isaiah*, Supplements to Vetus Testamentum 14 (Leiden: Brill, 1976), pp. 1–133 (pp. 57–58). Hooker makes the same point about the Greek preposition *dia*, which is used to translate the Hebrew *min* in this passage in the LXX ('Use of Isaiah 53', p. 96). However, as David A. Sapp has shown, the LXX displays a theological bias, deliberately obscuring some references to the Servant's substitutionary and atoning ministry contained in the Hebrew text that the translators deemed unacceptable. These alterations indicate that the significance of the ministry of the Servant was clear to readers of Isaiah long before Christ was born, for the LXX was produced at least as far back as the second century BC. Sapp suggests that the unreliability of the LXX at this point might explain why the New Testament writers sometimes prefer to give their own translation from the Hebrew text of Isa. 53. See David A. Sapp, 'The LXX, 1QIsa, and MT Versions of Isaiah 53 and the Christian Doctrine of Atonement', in William H. Bellinger, Jr., and William R. Farmer (eds.), *Jesus and the Suffering Servant* (Harrisburg: Trinity Press International, 1998), pp. 170–192 (see especially pp. 187–189).

45. Ludwig Koehler and Walter Baumgartner, *The Hebrew and Aramaic Lexicon of the Old Testament*, Study Edn, vol. 1 (Leiden: Brill, 2001), p. 598.

Whybray were right that the preposition *bĕ* is required to sustain a substitutionary reading, he has apparently failed to notice that Isaiah uses this very preposition in the second half of the same verse: 'the punishment that brought us peace was upon him, and by [*bĕ*] his wounds we are healed' (v. 5).[46] The prophet was apparently determined that no doubt over the meaning of this text should remain.

Secondly, the suffering of the Servant brings great benefits to those for whom he suffers. Indeed, as Oswalt argues, this fits the context well: 'there is every reason to see this poem as expressing the means of salvation that is anticipated in chs. 49–52 and in which the people are invited to participate in chs. 54–55'.[47] The text of Isaiah 53 also makes this clear, especially in verse 5, where his punishment and our *peace*; his wounds and our *healing* are starkly juxtaposed. It is not just that the Servant shares in the people's fate, and experiences their suffering alongside them. Rather, he experiences the punishment due to them, and they do not. Indeed, the sufferings experienced by the Servant are not shared by Israel precisely *because* he experienced them in their place, as their substitute.

This second point exposes the flaw in another of Whybray's arguments. Whybray observes that Isaiah 53 was originally written to the exiles in Babylon, who were under God's judgment for their sin, 'suffering the consequences of defeat and banishment'.[48] Consequently, he argues, 'the Servant cannot be said to be suffering, or to have suffered, *in place* of the exiles in such a way that they escape the consequences of their sins'.[49] But according to Isaiah, this is precisely why the Servant suffered, and it necessarily demands the element of substitution. The suffering of an oppressed people is not alleviated merely by one more person joining them, just as the patients on a tuberculosis ward would not be helped by a well-meaning doctor infecting himself with the disease.

There is no reason to deny Whybray's general point that the Servant shared in Israel's suffering. Indeed, that is doubtless true. However, to make sense of what Isaiah is saying here, we must conclude there was some *additional* suffering

46. Brevard S. Childs, *Isaiah*, Old Testament Library (Louisville: Westminster John Knox, 2001), p. 415, citing W. Zimmerli, 'Zur Vorgeschichte von Jes 53', in *Studien zur alttestamentlichen Theologie und Prophetie* (Munich: Theologische Bücherei, 1974).

47. J. N. Oswalt, *The Book of Isaiah, Chapters 40–66*, New International Commentary on the Old Testament (Grand Rapids: Eerdmans, 1998), p. 385.

48. Whybray, *Thanksgiving for a Liberated Prophet*, p. 30.

49. Ibid.; italics original.

that was *exclusive* to the Servant; there was a penalty greater than the experience of life in exile that the Servant bore in order that his people might not. And this is exactly what we find. From beginning to end, the passage emphasizes the appalling horror of what the Servant endured – far beyond what has ever been borne by any other human being.

> His appearance was so disfigured beyond that of any man
>> and his form marred beyond human likeness . . .
> He was despised and rejected by men,
>> a man of sorrows, and familiar with suffering.
> Like one from whom men hide their faces
>> he was despised . . .
> we considered him stricken by God,
>> smitten by him, and afflicted . . .
> But he was pierced . . .
>> he was crushed . . .
> He was oppressed and afflicted . . .
> he was led like a lamb to the slaughter . . .
> By oppression and judgment he was taken away
> . . . he was cut off from the land of the living . . .
> he was stricken . . .
> he poured out his life unto death.
> (Isa. 52:14; 53:3–5, 7–8, 12)

What more could Isaiah possibly have said to emphasize the unimaginable, unparalleled anguish the Servant endured? David Peterson concludes rightly that 'the Servant is punished in a manner that exceeds the just punishment of the Babylonian exile'.[50]

Indeed, nowhere in Scripture do we find the suggestion that the exile was redemptive in itself. If exile were the extent of the Servant's experience, he could not have brought peace to God's people. It is blood sacrifice, not exile, that is the means God appointed for his sinful people to be reconciled to him.[51] It is thus significant that Isaiah refers to the Servant as 'a guilt offering' (Isa. 53:10), for it is only suffering of this kind – sacrificial suffering – that can atone for sin.[52]

---

50. Peterson, 'Atonement in the Old Testament', p. 21.

51. Oswalt, *Isaiah, Chapters 40–66*, p. 385.

52. See below for a further discussion of the Servant's suffering as a sin offering.

Thirdly, Isaiah emphasizes that the Servant suffered willingly and deliberately, not as a passive victim of the actions of others.[53] As Spieckermann notes, 'The change to the active voice in verse 4a from the passive language in the surrounding context is particularly important . . . In verses 4–5 this Servant makes it clear that taking sins upon himself is *his* act.'[54] The same emphasis on the Servant's active participation is clear from verse 12, where the Lord promises to exalt the Servant because of his own initiative in giving himself up to die:

> Therefore I will give him a portion among the great,
>> and he will divide the spoils with the strong,
> because *he poured out his life unto death*,
>> and was numbered with the transgressors.
> For *he bore the sin of many*,
>> and made intercession for the transgressors. (Italics added)

Fourthly, it is God himself who acts to lay the people's sin upon the Servant and to punish him. This is clear in Isaiah 53:6 from the emphatic placement of 'the LORD' in the Hebrew word order – 'the LORD has laid on him the iniquity of us all'. A similar grammatical construction is used in verse 10, which contains an even more explicit statement about the Lord's role in the Servant's suffering:

> It was *the LORD's will* to crush him and cause him to suffer,
>> and though the LORD makes his life a guilt offering,
> he will see his offspring and prolong his days,
>> and the will of the LORD will prosper in his hand. (Italics added)

It is instructive to reflect on how these two points – the Servant's willingness and the Lord's intention – fit together. It would be easy to empha-

---

53. This constitutes a further reason for rejecting the interpretation that the Servant suffered 'because of' the sins of the people in the same way that the Jews suffered at the Holocaust 'because of' the sins of Hitler (see earlier discussion). The Servant's willingness makes much more sense if his death itself achieves something positive, as it does on the penal substitutionary reading.

54. Hermann Spieckermann, 'The Conception and Prehistory of the Idea of Vicarious Suffering in the Old Testament', in B. Janowski and P. Stuhlmacher (eds.), *The Suffering Servant: Isaiah 53 in Jewish and Christian Sources*, trans. Daniel P. Bailey (Grand Rapids: Eerdmans, 2004), pp. 1–15 (p. 6; italics original).

size one to such a degree that the other is undermined, but Isaiah will not allow this. The Servant consented to, and actively participated in, this ministry of sin-bearing and substitutionary death, in accordance with the will of God to afflict him in the place of others. Isaiah carefully guards against the false idea that God inflicted punishment *against* the Servant's will; indeed, 'God's responsibility for the Servant's vicarious role is articulated explicitly only after the Servant's acceptance of suffering has been established in 53:4a.'[55] Spieckermann comments on 'the close unity of the wills of both of them'.[56] If we step back for a moment and reflect on the way that this text speaks of the ministry of Christ, then we find in this solidarity of purpose a wonderful testimony to the unity of Father and Son within the Trinity.[57]

Fifthly, the suffering Servant is himself sinless and righteous. Thus Isaiah 53:9 reads, 'He was assigned a grave with the wicked, and with the rich in his death, though *he had done no violence, nor was any deceit in his mouth*' (italics added). Similarly, in verse 11 the Lord pointedly describes him as 'my *righteous* servant' (italics added). But immediately this raises an urgent question: if he is innocent, why should he suffer in this way? Israel was in exile because they deserved it, but the Servant's experience was undeserved.

One possible answer is that Isaiah wanted to hold the Servant up as a victim of injustice. In terms of the way he was treated by sinful humanity, he certainly was a victim, but this cannot be the whole story. For as we saw previously 'it was the LORD's will to crush him and cause him to suffer' (v. 10; italics added), and we dare not charge God with injustice! Thus the juxtaposition of the Servant's innocence and God's determination that he should suffer focuses our question: for what sins might God justly visit this judicial sentence upon him? Clearly not his own.

---

55. Ibid., p. 7.

56. Ibid., p. 7. He helpfully adds, 'God's will or "pleasure" in afflicting the Servant is not sadism but rather the manifestation of his loving intention that the wiping out of guilt . . . through the Servant's suffering should succeed' (p. 8).

57. Interestingly, while it is clear throughout the chapter that the Servant is to be distinguished from the Lord, there is also evidence that he is himself accorded divine status. The Hebrew expression underlying the phrase 'raised and lifted up', used of the Servant in Isa. 52:13, appears in only three other places in the Old Testament. All of them are in Isaiah (6:1; 33:10; 57:15), and in every case they refer to the Lord. Thus 'Yahweh's own lips declared that the Servant was to be identified with Yahweh himself' (Groves, 'Atonement in Isaiah 53', p. 81; cf. p. 80).

The answer is found in the following verses, and constitutes the sixth important feature of this passage. Isaiah clarifies that the Servant suffered not for his own sin, but for the sins of others: 'he will bear their iniquities' (*sābal 'awōn*, v. 11); 'he bore the sin of many' (*nāśā' ḥēṭ'*, v. 12). God acted justly in condemning the Servant for the sins of others – sins the Servant willingly bore.[58]

We saw in our study of Leviticus 16 that in the Old Testament these phrases (and the reversed pairings of *nāśā' 'awōn* and *sābal ḥēṭ'*) speak of the bearing of punishment, not just guilt. In Leviticus 16 the scapegoat bore the punishment due to the people as their substitute to make atonement for them, but only in Isaiah 53 are these phrases used in this way of a *person*. Indeed, the prophet recognizes this, and explicitly highlights the extraordinary nature of what is being said. As Hofius observes, 'The opening section (52:13–15) speaks about things previously "never told" and "never heard" (v. 15b). But this is hardly to be limited to the Servant's unique fate: it relates directly to the substitution of existence that occurs in that fate.'[59] The uniqueness of the events is highlighted again a few verses later: 'what happened to the servant was so unusual that the voice that speaks as "we" in Isaiah 53:1–8 felt it essential to justify what had happened as Yahweh's doing – "Yahweh laid on him our guilt" (Is 53:6). The voice in Isaiah 53:10 is more explicit – "Yahweh desired [willed] to crush him." The point is made because something most unusual has happened.'[60] Furthermore, the Hebrew syntax of Isaiah 53:11–12 is unusual. Groves explains the peculiarities in some detail, and concludes that 'The unique syntax is well suited to indicate a unique meaning.'[61] These unusual features of Isaiah 53:11–12, along with this other evidence from the rest of the passage, lead us to the conclusion that 'he will bear their iniquities' (*sābal 'awōn*, Isa. 53:11) and 'he bore the sin of many' (*nāśā' ḥēṭ'*, Isa. 53:12) speak of the Servant as an atoning penal substitute for the people whose sins he bore.

---

58. Peter combines the same perspectives in his appropriation of Isa. 53. Jesus is a victim of human injustice, and as such is a model for those who suffer unjustly (1 Pet. 2:18–23). Yet Jesus' death is also located within the purposes of God, by whom he is justly condemned for sins imputed to him. Peter establishes the former point by alluding to Isa. 53:7, 9, and the latter by alluding to vv. 4–5, 12.

59. Hofius, 'Fourth Servant Song', p. 168.

60. Groves, 'Atonement in Isaiah 53', p. 81. Text in square brackets original.

61. Ibid., p. 86. Groves also highlights several other surprising features of Isa. 53:11–12, providing still further support for the view that the phrases *sābal 'awōn* and *nāśā' ḥēṭ'* mean something unusual here (pp. 80–86).

The seventh noteworthy feature of this passage is the phrase 'guilt offering' in Isaiah 53:10. The Hebrew word *'āšām* underlying this phrase unmistakeably refers to the 'guilt offering' described in Leviticus 5–7 as an atoning sacrifice for sin (Lev. 5:16, 18; 7:7). By using the same word here Isaiah plainly intends to ascribe the same significance to the suffering Servant. Isaiah 53:10 thus anticipates something that will become explicit in the New Testament: the animal sacrifices of Leviticus are ultimately fulfilled in the sacrificial death of a person.

R. N. Whybray objects to this reading on the grounds that it makes Isaiah 53:10 unique. 'Nowhere else in the OT is it stated that a man's life can be a guilt-offering, whether in a literal or a metaphorical sense.'[62] But this objection is emptied of all force by the fact that Isaiah himself, as we have seen, recognizes the uniqueness of what is here described. Taken to its logical conclusion, Whybray's objection would mean that the 'the lamb of God' could not be a *person*. The New Testament writers do not share this view (John 1:29, 36; cf. Rom. 3:25; 8:3; Heb. 9:26; 10:1–18; 1 John 2:2; 4:10).[63]

Plainly, Isaiah 53 teaches that God's Servant willingly took the place of his people, bearing the penalty for their sins in order that they might escape punishment. As Peterson rightly says, 'Those who deny the theme of penal substitution in this chapter appear to be guilty of special pleading.'[64]

### Isaiah 53 and the death of Jesus

Isaiah 53 is formally quoted seven times in the New Testament. Matthew 8:16–17 (quoting Isa. 53:4) explains an extraordinary evening in Capernaum, when Jesus exorcized many demons and

> healed all the sick . . . to fulfil what was spoken through the prophet Isaiah:

> 'He took up our infirmities
>     and carried our diseases.'

In Luke 22:37 Jesus quotes from Isaiah 53:12 ('And he was numbered with the transgressors'), explaining that this text 'is reaching its fulfilment' in the events leading up to his crucifixion.

---

62. R. N. Whybray, *Isaiah 40–66*, New Century Bible (London: Oliphants, 1975), p. 179.

63. Peterson, 'Atonement in the Old Testament', p. 22.

64. Ibid., p. 21.

John 12:38 quotes Isaiah 53:1 to explain why people refused to believe in Jesus even after they had seen him perform miraculous signs:

Lord, who has believed our message
  and to whom has the arm of the Lord been revealed?

Paul quotes the first half of this verse with a similar purpose in Romans 10:16.

Acts 8:32–33 records that the Ethiopian eunuch was reading from Isaiah 53:7–8 when Philip met him on the road from Jerusalem to Gaza. After quoting the central section of the text, Luke explains that 'Philip began with that very passage of Scripture and told him the good news about Jesus' (Acts 8:35).

Paul quotes from Isaiah 52:15 to justify his

ambition to preach the gospel where Christ was not known, so that I would not be building on someone else's foundation. Rather, as it is written:

'Those who were not told about him will see,
  and those who have not heard will understand.'
(Rom. 15:20–21)

By far the longest sustained passage of quotations and allusions to Isaiah 53 in the New Testament, however, occurs in 1 Peter 2:22–25:

'He committed no sin,
  and no deceit was found in his mouth.'

When they hurled their insults at him, he did not retaliate; when he suffered, he made no threats. Instead, he entrusted himself to him who judges justly. He himself bore our sins in his body on the tree, so that we might die to sins and live for righteousness; by his wounds you have been healed. For you were like sheep going astray, but now you have returned to the Shepherd and Overseer of your souls.

Some of the allusions and quotations are clearer in the original Greek and Hebrew, and it is therefore worth highlighting them briefly.[65] The first sentence

---

65. For further discussion see J. Ramsey Michaels, *1 Peter*, Word Biblical Commentary (Waco: Word, 1988), pp. 144–150.

of this passage (v. 22) is a quotation from Isaiah 53:9 ('though he had done no violence, / nor was any deceit in his mouth'). The description of Jesus' silence and submissiveness during the events leading to his death in 1 Peter 2:23 is reminiscent of the Servant in Isaiah 53:7 ('He was oppressed and afflicted, / yet he did not open his mouth; / he was led like a lamb to the slaughter, / and as a sheep before her shearers is silent, / so he did not open his mouth'). The statement in 1 Peter 2:24 that Christ 'bore our sins' echoes both Isaiah 53:4 ('he took up our infirmities') and Isaiah 53:12 ('he bore the sin of many'). The concluding words of 1 Peter 2:24 paraphrase Isaiah 53:5 ('by his wounds we are healed'). Finally, 1 Peter 2:25 quotes Isaiah 53:6 ('We all, like sheep, have gone astray').

In addition to these explicit quotations, there are many passing allusions and verbal parallels – the editors of *The Greek New Testament* note a total of thirty-four.[66] We have space for only a couple of examples. Peter Bolt suggests that Jesus' words during the Last Supper in Mark 14:24, 'This is my blood of the covenant, which is poured out for many', may reflect the Hebrew text of Isaiah 53:12, where we read that the Servant 'poured out his life unto death'.[67] Again, Bolt suggests that in Mark 9:31 and 10:45, where Jesus says he will be 'betrayed' (more literally, 'handed over', *paradidōmi*), there is an echo of the LXX of Isaiah 53:12, where the same Greek word is used twice in regard to the ministry of the Servant.

It is thus undeniable that the New Testament writers identify Jesus with the suffering Servant. What has been contested, however, is that the New Testament writers wish to invoke the penal substitutionary elements of the Servant's ministry. In an influential essay, Morna Hooker argued that in the first six passages noted above (Matt. 8:17; Luke 22:37; John 12:38; Acts 8:32–33; Rom. 10:16; 15:21) the writers do not appeal to Isaiah 53 to inform their understanding of the *meaning* of Christ's death at all.[68] In particular, they do

---

66. 'Index of Allusions and Verbal Parallels', in B. Aland, K. Aland, J. Karavidopoulos, C. M. Martini and B. M. Metzger (eds.), *The Greek New Testament*, 4th edn (Stuttgart: Deutsche Biblegesellschaft, 2001), pp. 891–901. See also R. T. France, 'The Servant of the Lord in the Teaching of Jesus', *Tyndale Bulletin* 19 (1968), pp. 26–52.

67. Peter G. Bolt, *The Cross from a Distance: Atonement in Mark's Gospel*, New Studies in Biblical Theology 18 (Downers Grove: Apollos, 2004), p. 105.

68. Hooker, 'Use of Isaiah 53', pp. 90–91. Morna Hooker's first work on this subject appeared in 1959 with the publication of *Jesus and the Servant: The Influence of the Servant Concept of Deutero-Isaiah in the New Testament* (London: SPCK, 1959). In her more recent work, she explains that her views have since changed slightly, though not in ways that impact our discussion (Hooker, 'Use of Isaiah 53', pp. 88, 101–103).

not pick up on Isaiah's penal substitutionary themes. For example, referring to Acts 8:32–33, she writes, 'There is nothing here about the sins and iniquities which are mentioned immediately before and immediately after these words in Isaiah 53.'[69] She rejects the idea that Luke, in quoting only a part of Isaiah 53, would have expected his readers to recall the surrounding context. On the contrary, she suggests, 'If he had been trying deliberately to avoid the theme of atonement, he could not have done better!'[70]

We might wonder how Hooker could integrate 1 Peter 2:22–25 with these conclusions, for here the apostle cites precisely those sections of Isaiah 53 that refer to the penal substitutionary character of the Servant's atoning work.[71] Hooker acknowledges that 'we have scattered phrases from vv. 9, 4, 12, 5, and 6 of Isaiah 53 . . . their source is clear'.[72] More than this, she acknowledges that although Peter's primary purpose is to exhort his readers to follow Christ's example of 'undeserved punishment', nonetheless 'having begun with the appeal to Christ's sufferings as an *example* to be followed, he progresses to the idea that they have atoning value'.[73]

Does she then concede that 1 Peter is the exception that overturns her theory? No. On the contrary, she claims that it is 'cheating a little' to attach so much significance to what she calls an '*allusion* to Isaiah 53'.[74] She then states that 'The importance we attach to [1 Pet. 2:22–25] will, of course, depend very largely on the answers we give to questions regarding the date and authorship of that epistle.'[75] With that, she turns aside from this line of argument altogether, and does not return to it at any point during the remaining eleven pages of the essay.

Hooker's attempt to sidestep the evidence of 1 Peter 2:22–25 is wholly inadequate. To begin with, her classification of the numerous references to Isaiah 53 as 'allusions' is hardly sufficient grounds for dismissing them out of hand.

---

69. Hooker, 'Use of Isaiah 53', p. 91.
70. Ibid. An alternative explanation of why the quotation from Isa. 53 is limited to these verses is offered by Mikeal C. Parsons, 'Isaiah 53 in Acts 8: A Reply to Professor Morna Hooker', in William H. Bellinger, Jr., and William R. Farmer (eds.), *Jesus and the Suffering Servant* (Harrisburg: Trinity Press International, 1998), pp. 104–119 (pp. 115–116).
71. See the discussion of 1 Peter later in this chapter.
72. Hooker, 'Use of Isaiah 53', p. 92.
73. Ibid.; italics original.
74. Ibid.; italics added.
75. Ibid., p. 93.

In fact, even she must admit that 'the allusion to Isaiah 53 is so clear as to be beyond reasonable doubt'.[76] To take them seriously is not 'cheating' in the slightest. In any case, it is hardly accurate to describe them as 'allusions', for as J. Ramsey Michaels observes, 1 Peter 2:22 'is an exact quotation of Isa 53:9b LXX', with the exception of minor changes to the first two words.[77] Given all this, Hooker's attempt to call into question the authenticity, and hence the authority, of 1 Peter reads as a rather feeble last resort to rescue her argument. Such an approach will find little sympathy among those with a high view of Scripture.

What of Hooker's assessment of the other six New Testament passages that quote Isaiah 53? It is sometimes suggested that the New Testament writers, following the Jewish method of *midrash*, paid little regard to the original context of Old Testament texts. Of course, many have argued that the New Testament writers, by typological trajectory or some other method, find fuller significance in a given passage than the original author may have perceived. But Hooker is claiming more than this. For her, their use of the text may be *unrelated* to the original contextual meaning.[78] Thus the quotation of a few verses from Isaiah 53 need not constitute an appropriation of the substitutionary theology expressed elsewhere in that chapter.

In fact, not only has the assumption that contemporary Jewish exegesis was non-contextual been shown to be suspect,[79] but Hooker's argument about the practice of the New Testament writers themselves collapses under close scrutiny. Against Hooker, it appears that the apostles often *expect* us to consult the original Old Testament context: indeed, their point may not even be clear otherwise. Consider for example the quotation of Exodus 12:46 in John 19:36, discussed above. John's point is not merely that Jesus' bones remained intact. He wants us to see the significance of this in terms of the wider context of Exodus 12; namely the events of the Passover.

---

76. Ibid., pp. 92–93.

77. Michaels, *1 Peter*, p. 144.

78. Contrast the position of Douglas Moo: 'The ... meaning discerned by New Testament authors in passage after passage of the Old Testament often extends beyond, but is always based on the meaning intended by the human author' (Douglas J. Moo, 'The Problem of *Sensus Plenior*', in D. A. Carson and John D. Woodbridge [eds.], *Hermeneutics, Authority, and Canon* [Grand Rapids: Baker, 1995], pp. 175–211 [p. 211]).

79. D. Instone-Brewer, *Techniques and Assumptions in Jewish Exegesis before 70 CE*, Texte und studien zum antiken Judentum 30 (Tübingen: Mohr Siebeck, 1992).

With respect to the quotation of Isaiah 53:4 in Matthew 8:17, D. A. Carson argues that the apparent 'discrepancy' arising from Matthew's application of a text about atonement to a situation about healing 'is resolved if Matthew holds that *Jesus' healing ministry is itself a function of his substitutionary death*, by which he lays the foundation for destroying sickness'.[80] This is exactly what we would expect, for sickness is one of the consequences of the curse on creation resulting from Adam's sin. In his atoning death Christ endured and exhausted this curse, preparing the way for the inauguration of a new creation through his resurrection.[81] Morna Hooker has no grounds for concluding that the quotation from Isaiah in Matthew 8:17 is 'Taken out of its original context, and used as a proof text'.[82]

To take another example, in Acts 8:35, having quoted the portion of Isaiah 53 the Ethiopian eunuch had been reading, Luke tells us that 'Philip began with that very passage of Scripture and told him the good news about Jesus'. Hooker's suggestion that Philip would not have used this passage as a springboard for explaining the *meaning* of Christ's death seems most unlikely. Indeed, Mikeal Parsons has highlighted a subtle yet potentially significant verbal parallel between Acts 8:35 and Luke 24:27, where Jesus met two of his disciples on the road to Emmaus, and 'beginning with Moses and all the Prophets . . . explained to them what was said in all the Scriptures concerning himself'.[83] In the context of Luke 24:25–27 it is specifically with reference to his death (and resurrection) that Jesus teaches from the Prophets. It is only natural to assume that Philip, presented with a similar opportunity, should do the same, and Luke's use of a similar phrase seems designed to draw attention to this.

These examples suggest that the Gospel writers are far more sophisticated than Hooker allows. It is most unlikely that they link Jesus with the Servant of Isaiah 53 without any intention of affirming the wider theological implications of such an association for the nature of Jesus' death. In any case, even if Hooker's analysis of the texts above could be substantiated, we have seen that 1 Peter 2:22–25 suffices by itself to overturn her conclusion. In view of all we have seen, we must conclude that the New Testament does indeed interpret

---

80. D. A. Carson, *Matthew: Chapters 1 through 12*, Expositor's Bible Commentary (Grand Rapids: Zondervan, 1995), p. 205; italics original.
81. For further discussion see chapter 3 in this volume.
82. Hooker, 'Use of Isaiah 53', p. 90.
83. Parsons, 'Isaiah 53 in Acts 8', pp. 116–118.

Jesus' atoning death in the light of the penal substitutionary death of Isaiah's suffering Servant.

### Summary

According to Isaiah 53, the Servant of the Lord is punished in the place of God's people, as their substitute, to make atonement between them and God. The New Testament uses this passage to speak of Christ's death in penal substitutionary terms.

## The Gospel of Mark

### Introduction

Any attempt to understand the significance of Jesus' death must reckon with the accounts of his ministry in the Gospels, and we have chosen to focus our discussion here on Mark. Constraints of space forbid us from discussing in detail the allusions to the Passover ceremony of Exodus 12 or the many references to Isaiah 53; some of these are discussed earlier in this chapter. Neither shall we reflect in detail on the teaching of the other Synoptic Gospels, Matthew and Luke. We trust that if penal substitution is affirmed in Mark's Gospel, neither Matthew nor Luke will deny it.

Our approach will be to look at two short but important passages: Mark 10:33–45, which culminates in Jesus' famous confession that 'even the Son of Man did not come to be served, but to serve, and to give his life as a ransom for many', and Mark 15:33–34, which narrates the crucifixion itself.

### A ransom for many

Mark 10:45 has traditionally been interpreted as an affirmation of penal substitution. In his death Jesus paid the ransom price of his life as a substitutionary payment in the place of others. William Lane defends just this position in his commentary: 'The Son of Man takes *the place* of the many and there happens to him what would have happened to them.'[84] Some believe that the use of the term *lytron*, translated here 'ransom', by itself implies this.[85] Others discern an allusion to Isaiah 53 and the substitutionary ministry of the suffering Servant.[86] But far and away the most compelling evidence comes

---

84. Lane, *Mark*, p. 384; italics original.

85. See further Morris, *Apostolic Preaching of the Cross*, pp. 11–16.

86. See e.g. France, 'Servant of the Lord'; especially pp. 32–37.

from an appreciation of some other themes woven into the surrounding context.[87]

The section of Mark stretching from Mark 8:31 to Mark 10:52 is organized around three predictions of Jesus' death (Mark 8:31; 9:31; 10:33–34). Lane notes a further structural pattern: 'The second and third major prophecies of the passion . . . are both followed by an exposure of the presumption of the disciples . . . and by Jesus' instruction concerning humility and service.'[88]

In Mark 10 the disciples' presumption takes the form of James and John's vying for the places of highest honour at Jesus' side in glory. Jesus attempts to deter them: '"You don't know what you are asking," Jesus said. "Can you drink the cup I drink or be baptized with the baptism I am baptized with?"' (v. 38). James and John persist, and the resulting dispute between the twelve disciples earns Jesus' gentle rebuke: 'whoever wants to become great among you must be your servant, and whoever wants to be first must be slave of all' (Mark 10:43–44). It is in this context that Jesus sets forth his death as the supreme example of selfless sacrifice: 'For even the Son of Man did not come to be served, but to serve, and to give his life as a ransom for many' (Mark 10:45).

Jesus' passing reference to 'the cup I drink' in verse 38 is more important that it might first appear. The metaphor recurs on Jesus' lips in the Garden of Gethsemane, where Jesus, 'deeply distressed and troubled' (Mark 14:33) and 'overwhelmed with sorrow to the point of death' (v. 34), pleads with his Father, 'Take this cup from me' (v. 36), while at the same time submitting to his Father's will that he should drink it. It is worth quoting in full some of the Old Testament texts that would have been in Jesus' mind here, in order that we might feel their impact:

> In the hand of the LORD is a cup
>     full of foaming wine mixed with spices;
> he pours it out, and all the wicked of the earth

---

87. It is unfortunate that Green and Baker deny that Mark 10:45 supports the notion that Jesus' death is a ransom paid to a God who is angry without considering these wider themes (Joel B. Green and Mark D. Baker, *Recovering the Scandal of the Cross: Atonement in New Testament and Contemporary Contexts* [Downers Grove: IVP, 2000], p. 42).

88. Lane, *Mark*, p. 378.

drink it down to its very dregs.
(Ps. 75:8)

Awake, awake!
    Rise up, O Jerusalem,
you who have drunk from the hand of the LORD
    the cup of his wrath,
you who have drained to its dregs
    the goblet that makes men stagger.
(Isa. 51:17)

This is what the LORD, the God of Israel, said to me: 'Take from my hand this cup
filled with the wine of my wrath and make all the nations to whom I send you drink
it. When they drink it, they will stagger and go mad because of the sword I will send
among them.' (Jer. 25:15–16; cf. vv. 17–28)

This is what the Sovereign Lord says:

'You will drink your sister's cup,
    a cup large and deep;
it will bring scorn and derision,
    for it holds so much.
You will be filled with drunkenness and sorrow,
    the cup of ruin and desolation,
the cup of your sister Samaria.
You will drink it and drain it dry;
        you will dash it to pieces
        and tear your breasts.'

I have spoken, declares the Sovereign LORD. (Ezek. 23:32–34)

You will be filled with shame instead of glory.
    Now it is your turn! Drink and be exposed!
The cup from the LORD's right hand is coming round to you,
    and disgrace will cover your glory.
(Hab. 2:16)

Thus the cup from which Jesus must drink is the cup of God's wrath, which
in the texts cited above is destined variously for 'the wicked of the earth' (Ps.
75:8), God's rebellious people in exile or the pagan nations who oppressed

them. Why, though, should *Jesus* drink it? Mark 10:45 provides the answer. He came 'to give his life as a ransom for many', to drink the cup destined for them in their place.[89]

Further evidence pointing in this direction emerges from a careful examination of the vocabulary of the third passion prediction, which as we saw is closely linked in Mark's structure with the ransom saying of Mark 10:33–34:

> 'We are going up to Jerusalem,' he said, 'and the Son of Man will be betrayed [literally 'handed over', *paradidōmi*] to the chief priests and teachers of the law. They will condemn him to death and will hand him [*paradidōmi*] over to the Gentiles, who will mock him and spit on him, flog him and kill him. Three days later he will rise.'

Mark uses the verb *paradidōmi* in several different contexts to refer to the hostile act of delivering someone over to an unpleasant fate. It describes how John the Baptist was 'handed over' to be imprisoned (Mark 1:14), how Jesus was 'handed over' by Judas Iscariot, his betrayer (Mark 3:19; 14:10–11, 18, 21, 41–44), how the disciples would be 'handed over' to be persecuted (Mark 13:9–12), and how Jesus was 'handed over' to Pilate (Mark 15:1, 10).

As well as these usual negative connotations, when it occurs in Mark 10:33 in combination with the destination 'to the Gentiles' (literally, 'to the nations'), the verb *paradidōmi* admits an extra shade of meaning. Some passages in the Old Testament depict being handed over to the nations as a manifestation of God's wrath in punishing sin. Thus Psalm 106:40–41 reads:

> Therefore the LORD was *angry* with his people
> > and abhorred his inheritance.
> He *handed them over* [LXX: *paradidōmi*] *to the nations,*
> > and their foes ruled over them. (Italics added)

Similar expressions occur in Ezra 9:7 and Ezekiel 31:11 and also in the Apocrypha (Baruch 4:6; 2 Maccabees 10:4; cf. 5:17–20; 7:38; 8:5; 13:11), where

---

89. The importance of Jesus' death as an example and pattern for discipleship is taught throughout Mark 8–10. Every disciple of Jesus must 'take up his cross' (Mark 8:34). It is within this framework that we should understand Jesus' comment that James and John would indeed 'drink the cup' (Mark 10:39) that he will drink. Jesus' point is that their sufferings will be patterned on his, not that they will be identical in every respect. Neither James nor John will die under God's wrath in the place of others. For further discussion see Bolt, *Cross from a Distance*, pp. 69–71.

the LXX uses *paradidōmi*, and a similar thought is expressed with a different verb in Leviticus 26:32–33, 38. Bolt concludes, therefore, that for Jesus to be handed over to the nations 'is tantamount to being delivered over to the wrath of God'.[90]

Why, though, should *Jesus* be handed over? Mark 10:45 provides the answer. He came 'to give his life as a ransom for many', to be handed over to God's wrath in their place.[91]

### The crucifixion

We turn now to the account of the crucifixion in Mark 15:33–34: 'At the sixth hour darkness came over the whole land until the ninth hour. And at the ninth hour Jesus cried out in a loud voice, *"Eloi, Eloi, lama sabachthani?"* – which means, "My God, my God, why have you forsaken me?" '

As we reflect on the terrible final moments of our Lord's earthly life, two elements of Mark's account call for closer scrutiny: the supernatural darkness at midday, and Jesus' cry of dereliction, a quotation from Psalm 22:1.

On numerous occasions in the Old Testament, darkness denotes God's wrath. This imagery is used in particular with reference to the Day of the Lord; for example, in Isaiah 13:9–11:[92]

See, the day of the Lord is coming –
a cruel day, with wrath and fierce anger –
to make the land desolate

---

90. Ibid., p. 58; much of the argument of this paragraph is indebted to his analysis (pp. 56–58).

91. Scot McKnight, though he does not deny that penal substitution is taught elsewhere in Scripture, argues that it cannot be meant in Mark 10:45 on the grounds that 'To be a substitute the ransom price would have to take the place of another ransom price . . . and that is not what is involved here' (Scot McKnight, *Jesus and His Death: Historiography, the Historical Jesus, and Atonement Theory* [Waco: Baylor University Press, 2005], p. 347). McKnight's point is that when a sum of money is paid in order to redeem a slave, that money does not become a slave – it is still money. Thus those who find substitution in this text are guilty of a category error.

McKnight is mistaken, however, for the ransom in this case is not money but a life given up in death. This is precisely a substitute, for this life given up in death does take the place of other lives, which would have been given up in death. The substitute (Christ's death) and the thing substituted for (our deaths) are drawn from the same category.

92. Cf. Joel 2:31; Amos 5:18–20; Zeph. 1:14–15.

and destroy the sinners within it.
The stars of heaven and their constellations
    will not show their light.
The rising sun will be darkened
    and the moon will not give its light.
I will punish the world for its evil,
    the wicked for their sins.
I will put an end to the arrogance of the haughty
    and will humble the pride of the ruthless.

Significantly, Mark himself quotes from these verses two chapters earlier, in Mark 13:24–25. The meaning of the darkness at the cross therefore seems unambiguous. God was angry. But angry with whom? One possibility is that his wrath was directed against those crucifying his Son. There may be some truth in this, but the juxtaposition of the darkness with Jesus' cry of abandonment suggests that another meaning is primary: God's judgment was falling on his Son as he died as a substitute, bearing the sins of his people.[93]

Mark presents one final piece of evidence. On the Mount of Olives just before his arrest, Jesus predicted that his disciples would shortly desert him:

'You will all fall away,' Jesus told them, 'for it is written:

  ' "I will strike the shepherd,
    and the sheep will be scattered." '
(Mark 14:27)

---

93. Some have attempted to evade this conclusion by suggesting that Jesus' quote from Ps. 22:1 was not intended to describe the experience of God-forsakenness; rather, his intention in speaking these words was to call to mind the whole psalm, particularly its concluding note of victory. But as Stott comments, this seems 'far-fetched. Why should Jesus have quoted from the psalm's beginning if in reality he was alluding to its end? . . . Would anybody have understood his purpose?' (Stott, *Cross of Christ*, p. 81. For further discussion see pp. 78–82). Others object to the idea that Jesus was forsaken by his Father because they fear this might entail a sundering of the Trinity. Certainly, care is needed here, and a theologically nuanced exposition would need to avoid suggesting that God the Father was no longer 'there' at Calvary (even in hell God is not absent in every sense, as we discuss in chapter 3). Rather, the language of 'abandonment' or 'forsakenness' is a metaphorical way of referring to divine judgment.

The remarkable thing about the text in Zechariah 13:7 from which Jesus quotes is that *God* is the agent of the shepherd's suffering. Jesus is categorical: the afflictions that lie ahead of him, in consequence of which his disciples will desert him, come from his Father's hand.[94]

### Summary

The cup Jesus must drink, the darkness at noon, the cry of dereliction, and Jesus' own prediction that he will be handed over to the Gentiles all testify that at the cross he suffers God's wrath. Why is this? He dies as our substitute, paying the ransom price of his death for our life. Thus Mark's Gospel teaches penal substitution.

## The Gospel of John

### Introduction

In the opening chapter of John's Gospel, John the Baptist declares Jesus to be 'the Lamb of God, who takes away the sin of the world' (John 1:29; cf. v. 36). Later in John's Gospel the link is made specifically between Jesus and the lamb sacrificed at the Passover. As we saw in our discussion of Exodus 12, this amounts to John's endorsement of the penal substitutionary categories found there to explain Jesus' death. We shall not say more on this here.

John's Gospel provides further evidence for this understanding of the atonement. We shall see, first, that Jesus' death saves us from God's wrath, and secondly that this happens by way of substitution.

### Deliverance from God's wrath

John 3:16 is perhaps the most famous verse in the Bible. Less well known is the text from Numbers 21:4–9 that John draws on in the immediate context. This passage describes an episode during the wilderness wanderings of the Israelites after the exodus from Egypt. The Israelites rebelled against God and against Moses, and the Lord responded in judgment: 'the LORD sent venomous

---

94. Indeed, while Zechariah 13:7 portrays God as speaking to his sword, telling it to 'strike the shepherd', Jesus, in a subtly modified quotation, underlines that God is behind the action: '*I* will strike the shepherd' (Cf. Joel Marcus, 'The Old Testament and the Death of Jesus: The Role of Scripture in the Gospel Passion Narratives', in John T. Carroll and Joel B. Green (eds.), *The Death of Jesus in Early Christianity* [Peabody: Hendrickson, 1995], pp. 205–233 [pp. 225–226]).

snakes among them; they bit the people and many Israelites died' (v. 6). The people acknowledged their sin, and pleaded with Moses to pray for them. Then, 'The LORD said to Moses, "Make a snake and put it up on a pole; anyone who is bitten can look at it and live." So Moses made a bronze snake and put it up on a pole. Then when anyone was bitten by a snake and looked at the bronze snake, he lived' (vv. 8–9). Thus the Lord rescued his people from a punishment he himself had imposed.

Jesus plainly has this episode in mind in John 3:14–18:

> Just as Moses lifted up the snake in the desert, so the Son of Man must be lifted up, that everyone who believes in him may have eternal life. For God so loved the world that he gave his one and only Son, that whoever believes in him shall not perish but have eternal life. For God did not send his Son into the world to condemn the world, but to save the world through him. Whoever believes in him is not condemned, but whoever does not believe stands condemned already because he has not believed in the name of God's one and only Son.

These verses draw a striking parallel between Moses lifting up 'the snake in the desert' and Jesus, 'the Son of Man', being 'lifted up' (v. 14) on the cross.[95] The Israelites stood under the sentence of death in the desert, but any who looked at the snake were granted life; similarly, according to Jesus, all humanity is liable to 'perish', but anyone who looks to him and 'believes in him' will be granted 'eternal life' (v. 16). But why the danger of perishing? In Numbers 21, the danger was God's judgment on their sin, and the same is true here. As Jesus says in John 3:18, 'whoever does not believe stands *condemned*' (italics added). Again, in the summary statement at the end of the chapter, we read, 'Whoever believes in the Son has eternal life, but whoever rejects the Son will not see life, for *God's wrath* remains on him' (v. 36; italics added). It is thus from wrath and condemnation that Jesus' death saves us.

We find the same pattern elsewhere in John's Gospel. Death is the penalty for sin, imposed as God's sentence of condemnation on sinful humanity (John 5:24; 8:21, 24), from which we are delivered through the death of Jesus, by believing in him (John 6:50–58; 8:51).

---

95. John uses this phrase repeatedly to refer to Jesus' death (John 12:32–34; cf. 8:28). It may be a play on words, combining a description of the physical act of crucifixion with a reference to Christ's exaltation. The phrase probably also alludes to Isa. 52:13, where it describes the suffering Servant.

### Salvation by substitution

How does Jesus' death effect salvation from God's wrath and condemnation? According to John 11:47–52, Jesus died as our substitute. John here records an exchange during a meeting of the Sanhedrin, the Jewish ruling council:

> Then the chief priests and the Pharisees called a meeting of the Sanhedrin. 'What are we accomplishing?' they asked. 'Here is this man performing many miraculous signs. If we let him go on like this, everyone will believe in him, and then the Romans will come and take away both our place and our nation.'
>
> Then one of them, named Caiaphas, who was high priest that year, spoke up, 'You know nothing at all! You do not realize that it is better for you that one man die for [*hyper*] the people than that the whole nation perish.'
>
> He did not say this on his own, but as high priest that year he prophesied that Jesus would die for [*hyper*] the Jewish nation, and not only for that nation but also for [*hyper*] the scattered children of God, to bring them together and make them one.

Whereas Caiaphas is making a political comment – he fears that the Sanhedrin's political importance will be diminished if Jesus' popularity continues to grow – John sees in his words a more profound truth, that he himself may not have intended. This is signalled by John's remark that Caiaphas 'did not say this on his own, but . . . prophesied' (v. 51). As Carson puts it, 'when Caiaphas spoke, God was also speaking, even if they were not saying the same things'.[96]

John reinterprets Caiaphas' words in the context of Jesus' redemptive ministry. This becomes clear when John says that Jesus died for all his people, 'to bring them together and make them one' (v. 52). This 'oneness' motif is found in John 10:16, and again in John 17:22–23, where it describes the goal of his saving work – the spiritual unity in Christ of all those redeemed by him.

The main point to which we wish to draw attention here, however, is the repeated emphasis on substitution. This is present first in Caiaphas' own words 'it is better . . . that one man die for [*hyper*] the people', meaning that it would be better for the one man to die rather than for the whole nation to die ('perish', v. 50). Clearly, the preposition *hyper* conveys a substitutionary sense on Caiaphas' lips.

Even if John thinks Caiaphas mistaken in his political focus, he has no quarrel with the substitutionary emphasis, for he twice repeats the preposition

---

96. Carson, *John*, p. 422. The fact that Caiaphas himself did not know what he was saying imparts considerable irony to his bold declaration 'You know nothing at all!' (John 11:49).

*hyper* in his reinterpretation of Caiaphas' words. Moreover, the idea that Jesus should die in the place of his people is so important to John that he reminds us of Caiaphas' words again later in the Gospel, shortly after Jesus' arrest: 'Caiaphas was the one who had advised the Jews that it would be good if one man died for [*hyper*] the people' (John 18:14).[97]

The same preposition *hyper* occurs in John 6:51, where a substitutionary meaning is also probable. This text occurs as part of the dialogue that follows the feeding of the five thousand, which Jesus interprets with reference to God's miraculous provision of manna from heaven to feed his people in the desert at the time of Moses. As the 'bread of life' (v. 35), Jesus explains that he is superior to the manna in the Old Testament: 'Your forefathers ate the manna in the desert, yet they died. But here is the bread that comes down from heaven, which a man may eat and not die. I am the living bread that came down from heaven. If anyone eats of this bread, he will live for ever' (vv. 49–51).

Thus we see that Jesus offers life to people who would otherwise face death. How? Jesus continues, 'This bread is my flesh which I give for [*hyper*] the life of the world' (v. 51). Jesus' statement that he will 'give' his 'flesh' is a transparent reference to his death, and this is confirmed by his mention of 'blood' in verses 53–55. Thus Jesus dies, and in consequence others, who would have died, live.

Another significant use of *hyper* comes in John 10:11, where Jesus, speaking of himself, says, 'The good shepherd lays down his life for [*hyper*] the sheep.' The statement is repeated in verse 15.

At first glance, this imagery may seem to speak about what the shepherd would be *prepared* to do if the circumstances required it. For example, if a wolf attacked the flock, then, unlike the hired hand, he would be willing to risk his own life to rescue the sheep (v. 12). However, in verse 17 Jesus goes further, pointing beyond what he would be prepared to do to what he *intends* to do; indeed, what he does deliberately: 'The reason my Father loves me is that I lay down my life – only to take it up again.' It seems Jesus has decided that the sheep are already in danger, and he is resolved to give up his life to save theirs. Again, this hints strongly at substitution.[98]

---

97. This is one of those significant moments when John interrupts the narrative to comment on events and underline a point of importance (cf. John 2:21; 6:64, 71; 7:5, 39; 11:13; 12:6, 33; 20:9).

98. Our claim is not that *hyper* always carries a substitutionary meaning in John, though this sense could perhaps be defended in some other instances (e.g. John 13:37–38;

### Summary

John presents belief in Jesus' death as the means by which we can be saved from God's wrath and condemnation. Without him we perish. How is this salvation possible? Caiaphas' prophecy that Jesus would die 'for [*hyper*] the scattered children of God' (John 11:52) in its context teaches clearly that Jesus' death was substitutionary, and John 6:51 and John 10:11, 15 suggest the same thing.

To 'perish' in John is to suffer the punishment for sin under God's just condemnation. It is penal. Jesus perished in the place of his people, that they might live. This is penal substitution.

## Romans

### Introduction

The book of Romans teaches the doctrine of penal substitution so plainly that the steady stream of attempts by some recent commentators and theologians to evade the obvious is both surprising and a little tiresome. Nonetheless, the traditional understanding, that the Lord Jesus Christ gave himself in the place of his people in order to propitiate the wrath of God to which all humanity is justly subject, has been reaffirmed in numerous places; notably the recent treatments by D. A. Carson and Simon Gathercole.[99] We shall focus on four key texts that each affirm penal substitution: Romans 3:21–26; 4:25; 5:8–10; 8:1–3. Before turning to the first of these, however, we need to understand something of the wider theological context into which these passages speak.

### The wrath of God in the book of Romans

According to the book of Romans, the universal sinfulness of fallen humanity provokes God's righteous anger. Paul speaks of this as a present experience,

---

15:13). Our case stands purely on the basis that such a meaning is attested in some key passages that speak of Jesus' death. In John 11:50–52 and John 18:14 this is certain; in John 6:51 and John 10:11, 14 it is highly probable.

99. D. A. Carson, 'Atonement in Romans 3:21–26', in C. E. Hill and F. A. James III (eds.), *The Glory of the Atonement* (Downers Grove: IVP; Leicester: Apollos, 2004), pp. 119–139; Simon J. Gathercole, 'Justified by Faith, Justified by His Blood: The Evidence of Romans 3:21–4:25', in D. A. Carson, P. T. O'Brien and M. A. Seifrid (eds.) *Justification and Variegated Nomism*, vol. 2: *The Paradoxes of Paul* (Grand Rapids: Baker, 2004), pp. 147–184.

for 'the wrath of God *is being revealed* from heaven against all the godlessness and wickedness of men' (Rom. 1:18; italics added), yet also warns of a future 'day of God's wrath, when his righteous judgment *will be revealed*' (Rom. 2:5; italics added). God's wrath is manifested, and will be manifested, as he acts in human history to punish sin.

Some, however, have attempted to evacuate from the language of God's wrath in Scripture any sense of his *personal* hostility to evil or his *active* involvement in its punishment. Rather, they propose 'God's wrath' denotes the outworking of natural principles of cause and effect built into the way the universe works. In support of this view, sometimes called the 'immanentist' view, one might appeal to Proverbs 26:27:

> If a man digs a pit, he will fall into it;
>> if a man rolls a stone, it will roll back on him.

Of course, this proverb is true in what it affirms. The problem comes when it is thought either to exhaust the Bible's teaching on God's wrath, or to exclude the possibility of God's active involvement.

C. H. Dodd, the most famous proponent of the immanentist position, proceeded in just such a direction when he claimed that 'wrath' in Romans refers not to 'a certain feeling or attitude of God towards us, but some process or effect in the realm of objective facts'.[100] The false dichotomy is striking: for Dodd, the idea that God's wrath operates in the natural world excludes the possibility of any sort of personal response to evil on God's part.

A careful study of Romans, particularly chapters 1–3, presents insurmountable problems for the immanentist reading. The notion that God's wrath is not personal and that he is not active in judgment is simply unsustainable.[101]

To begin with, Romans 1:18–32, the section of Romans most often cited in support of the immanentist reading, teaches that 'the wrath of God is being revealed *from heaven*' (v. 18; italics added). These last two words emphasize the

---

100. C. H. Dodd, *The Epistle of Paul to the Romans* (London: Hodder & Stoughton, 1932), p. 22; cf. pp. 20–23. See also A. T. Hanson, *The Wrath of the Lamb* (London: SPCK, 1957). Simon Gathercole interacts with other interpreters who espouse similar positions, notably Ulrich Wilckens and Klaus Koch ('Justified by Faith', pp. 169–175).

101. We discuss some further difficulties with the immanentist view in chapter 11. We confine ourselves here to problems that arise directly from the text of Romans.

divine origin of sin's destructive consequences. It is perhaps significant, though unsurprising, that 'Dodd does not expound the phrase [from heaven] at all in his commentary.'[102]

Romans 2 and 3 similarly lay stress on God's personal involvement. As Gathercole points out, Paul speaks of '*God's* righteous judgment' (Rom. 2:5; italics added), 'not the inevitable, direct consequences of behaviour'.[103] Moreover, 'this is reinforced by the next verse, 2:6, where the action belongs clearly to God, who is described as the executor of the judgment'.[104] Again, God's involvement is clearly seen in verse 16, where Paul speaks of 'the day when *God* will judge men's secrets through Jesus Christ' (italics added), in Romans 3:5, 'which highlights judgment as something which God "brings"', and in Romans 2:26, 3:7 and 3:19, which 'talk of God coming to a *verdict*',[105] thereby invoking the idea of God's deliberate decision rather than a process of cause and effect that excludes him.

The same conclusion follows from 'the pattern of death as the consequence of sin [that] is integral to Paul's thought (Rom 1:32; 5:12–14; 6:23; 7:5; 7:11)'.[106] This connection between sin and death does not bypass divine government. On the contrary, 'God ordained that the penalty for the sin is death (1:32) and he does in fact himself bring judgment upon sinners (2:1–11).'[107] On Romans 5:12–21, Gaffin comments, 'In the flow of the argument . . . there is a middle factor between sin and death: condemnation . . . Death is God's judicial reaction to sin, which is to say, death is penal. It is his active punitive response to sin "from the outside" so to speak, not simply his allowing death as the self-generating result of sin.'[108] Gaffin makes a similar point from Romans 8:

In Romans 8:20–21, fairly seen as commentary on Genesis 3:16–19, due to sin the entire creation has been 'subjected to frustration' (or 'futility') and 'bondage to decay.'

---

102. Gathercole, 'Justified by Faith', p. 171.

103. Ibid., p. 174.

104. Ibid.

105. Ibid., p. 175; italics original. As Gathercole notes, the idea expressed in Romans 3:5 that *Jesus* plays an active role in the judgment is expressed even more starkly in Rev. 6:16, which speaks of 'the wrath of the Lamb'.

106. Ibid.

107. Ibid.

108. Richard B. Gaffin, Jr., 'Atonement in the Pauline Corpus', in C. E. Hill and F. A. James III (eds.), *The Glory of the Atonement* (Downers Grove: IVP; Leicester: Apollos, 2004), pp. 140–162 (p. 151).

This is so not simply as a natural outworking of sin, its inherent entropy, but ultimately 'because of him [God] who subjected it' (Rom 8:20 ESV). Death, including those conditions now present in the creation that tend toward death, is God's calculated response to sin, his retributive curse on sin.[109]

Given this weight of evidence, it is simply impossible to maintain that 'God's wrath' in Romans (or indeed anywhere else) refers simply to the natural outworking of sin in human experience. It is rather his active, retributive response to sin, a judicial penalty, imposed in accordance with his personal, righteous hostility to everything that is evil.

Romans 1–3, with its sustained emphasis on God's wrath, forms the backdrop to the texts we examine below. Although there are some finer points of interpretation in these early chapters about which interpreters continue to debate (salvation-historical nuances to do with how we should understand Israel's experience under the law and so on), these do not detract from the central point. In Carson's words, 'the flow of argument that takes us from Romans 1:18–32 to Romans 3:9–20 leaves us no escape: individually and collectively, Jew and Gentile alike, we stand under the just wrath of God, because of our sin'.[110]

### Christ was set forth as a propitiation (Rom. 3:21–26)

We might paraphrase Romans 3:21–26 as follows. All people are sinners, whether Jew or Gentile, but all may be justified through faith in Jesus. For God, who in the past had left his people's sin unpunished, has now demonstrated his justice by punishing their sin in Christ. He was set forth as a 'sacrifice of atonement' (literally, 'a propitiation', v. 25), turning aside God's wrath by suffering it himself in the place of his people.

Romans 3:25–26 is so important that it is worth quoting in full:

> God presented him as a sacrifice of atonement, through faith in his blood. He did this to demonstrate his justice, because in his forbearance he had left the sins committed beforehand unpunished – he did it to demonstrate his justice at the present time, so as to be just and the one who justifies those who have faith in Jesus.

That these verses teach penal substitution can be demonstrated in several ways, any of which is sufficient to establish the point on its own.

---

109. Ibid., p. 152. The text in square brackets is original.
110. Carson, 'Atonement in Romans 3:21–26', p. 120.

First, we can learn much about the meaning of these verses merely by observing the position they occupy in the flow of Paul's argument. As Gathercole explains, 'when we come to Romans 3:20, all are under judgment, and doomed to face God's wrath. By the time we reach 3:27–31, however, Paul is talking of people being justified. How is it, then, that sin and wrath have been dealt with?'[111] Whatever else Romans 3:21–26 says, it must provide an answer to this question. Something has happened to remove God's wrath from those who deserve it. Already we are within a hair's breadth of penal substitution; to complete the argument, we need only to establish that it was by Christ's death in our place that this was accomplished.

This final element of the argument is found in verse 25, where Paul explicitly highlights Jesus' 'blood' as the means of redemption, and 'the parallelism of "blood" and "death" in Romans 5:8–9'[112] makes clear that Jesus' death is in view. Indeed, the mere fact that Jesus died, in the context of the thought-world of Romans, constitutes an argument for penal substitution. As we saw above, death in Romans is understood as the penalty for sin, imposed deliberately by God. The reference to blood therefore functions as a reference to this penalty, which can have been borne only by Christ in the place of his people.

Secondly, Paul has already established in Romans 1:32 that according to 'God's righteous decree' all of us 'deserve death'. Thus when we read in Romans 3:26 that God's wrath has been turned aside in a way that demonstrates his *justice*, we cannot conceivably imagine that the punishment for sin has been overlooked! God must punish sin, and in the death of Christ he has done so.

This mention of God's justice being vindicated in the death of Christ raises the question of what happened before Christ came. What was God doing about the sins of those people in the Old Testament who enjoyed his favour? Surely he cannot have been ignoring them, for as we have seen that would impugn his justice. Paul's answer, which constitutes a third reason for seeing penal substitution in these verses, is that God was delaying his judgment of those sins until they could be punished in Christ. This is implicit in the use of the Greek word *anochē*, translated 'forbearance' in verse 25. This word appears only once elsewhere in the New Testament, in Romans 2:4, where it refers to God's patience in delaying the 'day of God's wrath, when his righteous judgment will be

---

111. Gathercole, 'Justified by Faith', p. 175.
112. Ibid., p. 179.

revealed' (v. 5).[113] Paul's argument, of course, is that God's 'forbearance' (his delay in punishing sin) is no longer in force now that Christ has died, for God *has* punished sin in him.

The final detail of Romans 3:25–26 that supports the doctrine of penal substitution is Paul's use of the Greek word *hilastērion* (translated in the NIV as 'sacrifice of atonement'). This noun in fact derives from the Greek verb *hilaskomai*, 'to propitiate' (i.e. to placate or turn aside wrath). The use of the word in connection with Christ's death emphasizes that it was by Christ's death that God's wrath was turned aside from sinners.

This meaning of *hilastērion* has, however, been disputed, notably by C. H. Dodd. Although he agreed with the scholarly consensus that in classical and Hellenistic Greek literature the meaning 'propitiation' for *hilaskomai* and its cognates 'is overwhelmingly the more common',[114] Dodd denied that this was the meaning in the *Jewish* Greek literature that formed the linguistic background to the New Testament. He claimed rather that in the LXX the word carries the sense 'purge', 'forgive' or 'expiate', and that this is the meaning in the four occurrences in the New Testament (Rom. 3:25; 1 John 2:2; 4:10; Heb. 2:17).[115] Crucially, the translations Dodd prefers refer to what happens to sin, not what happens to God's wrath. Sin is purged, forgiven or expiated; wrath is propiti-

---

113. The fact that Rom. 2:4 refers to a delay in God's judgment is further strengthened by the fact that the only other occurrence in this letter of the word translated there as 'patience' (*makrothymia*) is in Rom. 9:22, where once again a delay in God's judgment is in view (Gathercole, 'Justified by Faith', p. 181).

114. Dodd, *Romans*, p. 54. Cf. C. H. Dodd, '*Hilaskesthai*, its Cognates, Derivatives and Synonyms, in the Septuagint', *Journal of Theological Studies* 32 (1931), pp. 352–360. For a representative survey of the meaning in pagan Greek literature see E. A. Sophocles, *Greek Lexicon of the Roman and Byzantine Periods from B.C. 146 to A. D. 1100* (Whitefish, MO: Kessinger, 2004); J. H. Moulton and G. Milligan, *The Vocabulary of the Greek Testament, Illustrated from the Papyri and Other Non-Literary Sources* (London: Hodder & Stoughton, 1930), p. 303; Walter Bauer, *A Greek-English Lexicon of the New Testament and Other Early Christian Literature*, 3rd ed., rev. and ed. F. W. Danker (Chicago: University of Chicago Press, 2000), pp. 473–474; Roger Nicole, 'C. H. Dodd and the Doctrine of Propitiation', *Westminster Theological Journal* 17 (1955), pp. 117–157; repr. in *Standing Forth: Collected Writings of Roger Nicole* (Fearn: Christian Focus, 2002), pp. 343–396 (p. 357; this and all subsequent page references are to the latter version).

115. See e.g. Dodd, *Romans*, pp. 54–55; C. H. Dodd, *The Johannine Epistles* (London: Hodder & Stoughton, 1946), pp. 25–26.

ated. In rejecting the language of propitiation, Dodd is implicitly denying that Jesus' death needs to reckon with God's wrath, which is perhaps unsurprising given his commitment to the immanentist position on that subject.

The most comprehensive replies to Dodd have come from Leon Morris and Roger Nicole.[116] Their critiques are extensive and devastating, and we need do little more than summarize their main points.

To begin with, Dodd's claim that the meaning of *hilaskomai* in Jewish Greek writings differs consistently from its classical and pagan meaning 'to propitiate' is incorrect. Such a meaning is found in the prominent Jewish writers Josephus and Philo, both of whom Dodd ignores.[117] The same meaning is attested in the Apocrypha (4 Maccabees 17:22) and in the early extrabiblical Christian texts 1 Clement and The Shepherd of Hermas.[118]

So much for *hilaskomai* in Jewish Greek literature. But what about the LXX? Again, Dodd is wrong. Morris and Nicole cite several examples of the use of *hilaskomai* in the LXX where the averting of God's wrath is plainly implied in the context (e.g. Exod. 32:14; cf. vv. 11–12; Num. 16:46; cf. v. 47; 25:13; cf. v. 11; Lam. 3:42; cf. v. 43; 2 Kgs 24:4; cf. 23:26; 24:20; Ps. 78:38; cf. v. 31).[119] In these places the word must mean 'propitiate'. 'Expiate', 'forgive' or 'purge' would be inadequate translations.

In summary, not only does *hilaskomai* mean propitiation in the vast majority of cases in pagan Greek literature; it also bears this meaning in the LXX and other Jewish Greek literature dating from immediately before and after the New Testament era. Of course, this does not mean that *hilaskomai* and its cognates *always* refer to propitiation, or that they refer to this exclusively (other

---

116. Morris, *Apostolic Preaching of the Cross*, especially pp. 155–174; Leon Morris, 'The Use of *hilaskesthai* etc. in Biblical Greek', *Expository Times* 62 (1951), pp. 227–233; Nicole, 'Dodd and the Doctrine of Propitiation'. These critiques demonstrate not only that Dodd misunderstands the meaning of *hilastērion* and its cognates, but also that the linguistic methods he employs to determine their meaning are fundamentally flawed.

117. For Josephus, see *Antiquities* 6.124. For Philo, see the many references cited by F. Büchsel, 'Hilaskomai, hilasmos', in G. Kittel (ed.), *Theological Dictionary of the New Testament*, vol. 3 (Grand Rapids: Eerdmans, 1965), pp. 301–318 (pp. 314–316).

118. 1 Clement 7:7; The Shepherd of Hermas, Vision 1, 2.1. See M. W. Holmes (ed.), *The Apostolic Fathers: Greek Texts with English Translation* (Grand Rapids: Baker, 1999), pp. 36–37, 336–337.

119. Morris, *Apostolic Preaching of the Cross*, pp. 157–158; Nicole, 'Dodd and the Doctrine of Propitiation', p. 359.

elements could also be present, as we discuss below). It certainly does not import into the biblical notion of propitiation all of the objectionable pagan connotations of sinful human beings seeking to appease the malice of a petulant deity. However, it does mean that propitiation would be a perfectly natural meaning even where the context does not explicitly speak of wrath, and that this meaning is simply avoidable when it does.

So what does *hilastērion* mean in Romans 3:25? Here is a case where the context settles the issue beyond doubt. As we have seen, God's wrath at human sin is prominent in Romans generally, central in the section that immediately precedes Romans 3:21–26, and absent from God's justified people in the section that immediately follows. It is by setting forth his Son as 'a sacrifice of atonement [*hilastērion*]' that God has turned his wrath aside, leaving his people justified before him. That *hilastērion* here means 'propitiation' could hardly be clearer.

The meaning 'propitiation' is also present in 1 John, where the cognate noun *hilasmos* appears twice. The first occurrence is in 1 John 2:2, which reads, 'He [Jesus] is the atoning sacrifice [*hilasmos*] for our sins'. The reference in the previous verse to Jesus as the 'one who speaks to the Father in our defence' (v. 1, literally, 'our advocate') reminds us that before the throne of God we are guilty. As Stott points out, the very mention of an advocate 'implies the displeasure of the One before whom he pleads our cause',[120] displeasure arising from our 'sin' (v. 1). Thus the implication of verse 2 is not only that our sins are purged, but also that this displeasure is removed – God's wrath is propitiated. The other occurrence of *hilasmos* is in 1 John 4:10. Here wrath is not explicit in the immediate context, but in view of the previous usage in the same letter there is every reason to think that propitiation is also meant here.[121]

The indisputable fact that *hilastērion* in Romans 3:25 refers to propitiation does not exclude additional shades of meaning. For example, many think that the word could refer to the 'mercy seat'; that is, the covering of the ark of the covenant, on which blood was sprinkled on the Day of Atonement. If it does, then Paul here in Romans is recalling the theological emphases of the Day of Atonement as part of his explanation for Christ's death, and as we saw in our discussion of Leviticus 16 the same propitiatory emphases are present there. Again, although we have emphasized that 'expiation' would be an inadequate translation by itself, there is no reason to exclude it: the same sacrifice can

---

120. Stott, *Cross of Christ*, p. 172.

121. The other New Testament occurrences of the *hilaskomai* word group are in Luke 18:13; Heb. 2:17; 9:5. See Morris, *Apostolic Preaching of the Cross*, pp. 202–205, for a discussion of Heb. 2:17.

simultaneously expiate sin and propitiate God's wrath at that sin.[122] N. T. Wright puts it well:

> Dealing with wrath or punishment is propitiation; with sin, expiation . . . Paul has declared that the wrath of God is revealed against all ungodliness and wickedness and that despite God's forbearance this will finally be meted out; that in 5:8, and in the whole promise of 8:1–30, those who are Christ's are rescued from wrath; and that the passage in which the reason for the change is stated is 3:25–26, where we find that God, though in forbearance allowing sins to go unpunished for a while, has now revealed that righteousness, that saving justice, that causes people to be declared 'righteous' even though they were sinners.
>
> The lexical history of the word *hilastērion* is sufficiently flexible to admit of particular nuances in different contexts. Paul's context here demands that the word not only retain its sacrificial overtones (the place and means of atonement), but that it carry the note of propitiation of divine wrath – with, of course, the corollary that sins are expiated.[123]

The undeniable teaching of Romans 3:21–26 is that the Lord Jesus Christ was set forth as a propitiation, to turn aside God's wrath from his people by suffering it in their place.

### Christ was handed over for our sins (Rom. 4:25)

After a chapter devoted to arguing that righteousness has always been through faith, Paul concludes with the climactic statement that Jesus 'was delivered over to death for our sins and was raised to life for our justification' (Rom. 4:25). This statement refers back to the work of Christ explained in Romans 3:21–26, and it is therefore unsurprising that here, too, we should find the doctrine of penal substitution.

The Greek text does not mention 'death' or 'life' explicitly; it says only that Jesus was 'handed over [*paradidōmi*] for our sins and raised for our justification'.

---

122. So Thomas R. Schreiner, *Romans*, Baker Exegetical Commentary on the New Testament (Grand Rapids: Baker, 1998), p. 192.

123. N. T. Wright, *The Letter to the Romans: Introduction, Commentary and Reflections*, in *The New Interpreter's Bible*, vol. 10 (Nashville: Abingdon, 2002), pp. 393–770 (p. 476). In view of this, it is somewhat surprising that N. T. Wright endorsed so positively Steve Chalke and Alan Mann's *The Lost Message of Jesus* (Grand Rapids: Zondervan, 2003), which strongly criticizes the propitiatory and penal ideas Wright expressed here. See Part Two for further discussion of *The Lost Message of Jesus*.

However, the idea of death is clearly implied. The same word occurs in Romans 8:32, where God 'did not spare his own Son, but gave him up [*paradidōmi*] for us all', and there the reference to the crucifixion is unambiguous.[124] As we have seen already, death in Romans is God's penalty for sin. Thus where Romans 4:25 says '*he* was delivered over to death for *our* sins' (italics added), penal substitution is plainly in view. This conclusion gains further support from the transparent allusion to the LXX of Isaiah 53:6, 12.[125]

### We shall be saved from God's wrath (Rom. 5:8–10)

Romans 5:8–10 contains two parallel statements, both of them reasoning from what was accomplished by Christ at the cross to what can be expected on the future day of judgment. In outline, the logic runs as follows: We were sinners; Christ's death (his 'blood') justified us; we shall be saved from God's wrath (vv. 8–9). We were God's enemies; Christ's death reconciled us; we shall be saved (v. 10).

This salvation 'from God's wrath' (v. 9) lies in the future, presumably because Paul has in mind the final 'day of God's wrath, when God's righteous judgment will be revealed' (Rom. 2:5). The outcome of that judgment is already settled in respect of believers, however, since our future salvation follows necessarily from what Christ has already achieved. How does Paul arrive at this conclusion? Surely from his conviction, already expounded in Romans 3:21–26 (and his use of the word 'blood' in Romans 5:9 alludes to that earlier discussion), that Christ's death propitiated God's wrath. Once again, the doctrine of penal substitution underpins the logic of Paul's argument.

### God condemned sin in Christ's flesh (Rom. 8:1–3)

Romans 8 begins with the well-known declaration that 'there is now no condemnation for those who are in Christ Jesus' (v. 1). The reason is that, according to verse 3, God has (literally) 'condemned sin in the flesh'; that is, in Jesus' flesh.[126] The same Greek word underlies 'condemnation' in verse 1

---

124. See further Gathercole, 'Justified by Faith', p. 182. The other four uses of *paradidōmi* in Romans (1:24, 26, 28; 6:17) do not refer to Jesus' experience at all, and are therefore irrelevant to the discussion.

125. Ibid.; cf. C. E. B. Cranfield, *A Critical and Exegetical Commentary on the Epistle to the Romans*, vol. 1, International Critical Commentary (Edinburgh: T. & T. Clark, 1975), pp. 251–252.

126. Commenting on this text, Wright observes 'that on the cross God punished (not Jesus, but) "sin"' (N. T. Wright, *The Climax of the Covenant: Christ and the Law in Pauline Theology* [Minneapolis: Fortress, 1993], p. 213). It is true that 'sin' is the object

and 'condemned' in verse 3; it is a judicial term referring to the act of passing (and possibly also executing) a sentence on one found guilty.[127] Douglas Moo captures the play on words present in the Greek original: 'Believers are no longer "condemned" (v. 1) because in Christ sin has been "condemned".'[128] This amounts to an explicit statement of the doctrine of penal substitution.

### Substitution and participation

In the theology of the Bible generally, and particularly in Paul's writings, there is a sense in which believers are 'caught up' in the death of Jesus, such that his death becomes theirs. In Romans this emphasis comes to prominence in chapter 6, where we are said to have 'died with Christ' (Rom. 6:8; cf. v. 2) and to have been 'crucified with him' (v. 6). A similar point is made elsewhere; for example, Colossians 2:20 and Galatians 2:20, and possibly in 1 Peter 4:1, where McCartney has argued that the reason why believers should consider themselves to have 'done with sin' is that they have participated in the sufferings of Christ.[129]

Some writers, however, have mistakenly supposed that this emphasis on what is often termed our 'participation' in Christ's death excludes the idea of substitution. Or to use other terminology, they claim Christ's death was a case of 'inclusive place-taking' (he shared in our experience), and this is incompatible with 'exclusive place-taking' (Christ experienced something in order that we might *not* share it).[130]

---

of the verb 'to condemn', but as Gathercole points out, Paul also specifies the location of that condemnation; namely, the flesh of Jesus ('Justified by Faith', p. 177).

127. Douglas J. Moo, *The Epistle to the Romans*, New International Commentary on the New Testament (Grand Rapids: Eerdmans, 1996), p. 477.

128. Ibid.

129. Dan G. McCartney, 'Atonement in James, Peter and Jude', in Charles E. Hill and Frank A. James III (eds.), *The Glory of the Atonement: Biblical Historical and Practical Perspectives* (Downers Grove: IVP; Leicester: Apollos, 2004), pp. 176–189 (pp. 183–184).

130. See e.g. Hooker, 'Use of Isaiah 53', pp. 101–103; James D. G. Dunn, *The Theology of Paul the Apostle* (Grand Rapids: Eerdmans, 1998), p. 223; Hofius, 'Fourth Servant Song', pp. 172–188. Hofius insists that Isa. 53 speaks of a substitutionary death of the Servant for others, in their place, and moreover grants that there is no reason to deny that the wording of Rom. 4:25 and 1 Cor. 15:3–5, which allude to that text,

These writers are right to affirm the place of participation, but wrong to think that this displaces substitution. The two perspectives sit alongside each other in Scripture. Thus the emphasis in Romans 6:8 and Colossians 2:20 that we have 'died with Christ' comes together with the earlier affirmations in both letters that it was through '*his* blood' (and not ours) that we have been justified and have peace with God (Rom. 3:25; 5:1, 9; Col. 1:20). Similarly, 1 Peter 4:1 does not overturn the substitutionary emphases of 1 Peter 2:24 and 3:18.[131]

### Summary

Romans 1–3 depicts all humanity under the wrath of God. In Romans 3:21–26 we discover that God has turned aside his wrath by setting forth his Son as a propitiation, to suffer the wrath due to his people in their place. Romans 4:25 recalls this conclusion, combining this with a reference to Isaiah 53. Romans 5:8–10 teaches that through Christ's death we have already been delivered from God's future wrath. Romans 8:1–3 declares that the condemnation due to us has been borne by the Lord Jesus Christ. The doctrine of penal substitution is woven into the fabric of these chapters, the pathway from wrath to redemption, from condemnation to justification and glory.

## Galatians 3:10–13

### Introduction

On three occasions the book of Acts uses the distinctive language of 'hanging . . . on a tree [*xylon*]' to describe the crucifixion (Acts 5:30; 10:39; cf. Acts 13:29), presumably intending to evoke the words of Deuteronomy 21:23, 'anyone who is hung on a tree [LXX: *xylon*] is under God's curse'. An obvious

---

could be taken to mean the same thing. However, somewhat bizarrely, he denies that this is Paul's intended meaning, on the grounds that Paul teaches that Jesus' death atones for sins. By the same argument, he concedes that the most obvious reading of Heb. 9:28, 1 Pet. 2:21–25 and 3:18 is that Christ died as a penal substitute in the way that Isa. 53 envisages. Once again, however, he excludes this meaning because of the atoning efficacy of Christ's work affirmed in these texts. His argument is thus grounded on the unspoken premise that atonement by definition excludes substitution. Quite why this should be so is not explained (Hofius, 'Fourth Servant Song', pp. 177–182).

131. We reflect further on this issue in chapter 10.

question arises. Why should Jesus, the sinless Messiah, be cursed by God? Galatians 3:10–13 supplies the answer.

The argument of these verses is simple. Jesus bore the curse that was due to others as their substitute, and thereby redeemed them from it: 'Christ redeemed us from the curse of the law by becoming a curse for us, for it is written: "Cursed is everyone who is hung on a tree"' (Gal. 3:13). It is hard to imagine a plainer statement of the doctrine of penal substitution.

Some readers may be aware, however, that Galatians 3:10–13 has become one of the key battlegrounds in the debate about the so-called 'New Perspective on Paul'. Our intention is not to conduct a comprehensive evaluation of the New Perspective – the issues are complex, and we could not hope to do justice to all the detailed arguments and counter-arguments in the short space available. We shall merely demonstrate that the doctrine of penal substitution remains secure, regardless of which path is taken with respect to the issues of recent controversy.

### The traditional view

The presenting issue in Galatians is the existence of false teachers, sometimes called 'Judaizers', who insisted that Gentile converts to Christianity must be circumcised (Gal. 2:3–4, 12; 5:1–3; cf. Acts 15:1).[132] In Galatians 3:10 Paul warns that these people, 'who rely on observing the law' (literally, those who are 'of works of [the] law'), 'are under a curse'. On this all interpreters of Galatians agree. The question is, *why* are these people under a curse? At this point interpreters differ.[133]

According to the traditional view, the Judaizers sought to maintain favour with God by their meritorious observance of the requirements of the Old Testament law. They 'put confidence in the flesh' (Phil. 3:4); 'they did not know

---

132. F. F. Bruce defends the view that Acts 15 provides the background for the Galatian controversy in *The Epistle to the Galatians*, New International Greek Testament Commentary (Exeter: Paternoster, 1982), p. 31.

133. Dunn mistakenly accuses proponents of 'the usual reading' (i.e. the traditional reading, as opposed to the New Perspective) of claiming that Paul says in Gal. 3:10 that everyone is under a curse (Dunn, *Theology of Paul*, p. 361). In fact even opponents of the New Perspective agree that Paul is referring here to the Judaizers (e.g. Moisés Silva, 'Faith Versus Works of Law in Galatians', in D. A. Carson, Peter T. O'Brien and Mark A. Seifrid (eds.), *Justification and Variegated Nomism*, vol. 2: *The Paradoxes of Paul* [Tübingen: Mohr Siebeck; Grand Rapids: Baker, 2004], pp. 217–248 [p. 226]). Where they differ is in saying that this is a specific instance of a wider problem; namely, the attempt to maintain favour with God through legal obedience.

the righteousness that comes from God and sought to establish their own' (Rom. 10:3); they failed to appreciate that we have been saved 'not because of righteous things we had done, but because of [God's] mercy' (Titus 3:5). In short, they were legalists, and their insistence on circumcision was a symptom of this.

The problem with such 'works-righteousness' as a means to salvation, says the traditional view, is that the law required *perfect* obedience. This is implied by the references to '*everything* written in the Book of the Law' (Gal. 3:10; italics added) and 'the *whole* law' (Gal. 5:3; italics added). Because of sin, no-one is able to keep the law perfectly, and thus all who seek to be justified by the law find themselves condemned by it and subject to its curse.

The predicament of the Judaizers in Galatians 3:10 has implications for all people. The Judaizers found themselves under a curse because in choosing the path of legal obedience they failed to appropriate the grace of God in the gospel of Christ (cf. Gal. 2:21). But if there were no gospel, all of us would be in their position. What means of salvation would there be except our own attempts to keep God's commandments? As we tried and failed, we too would find ourselves under the law's curse.[134]

This traditional understanding of Paul's view of the law is captured succinctly by Peter O'Brien: ' "Works of the law" are inadequate to save because no one fulfills *all* the demands of the law.'[135] Or again, here is Thomas Schreiner: 'Paul rejected the law as a way of salvation because of human inability to obey it. No one can be justified by the works of the law because no one can obey the law perfectly.'[136]

Given this universal human predicament, Galatians 3:13 constitutes a clear statement of penal substitution: 'Christ redeemed us from the curse of the law by becoming a curse for us, for it is written: "Cursed is everyone who is hung on a tree." ' Christ was cursed in our place, and we were thereby redeemed.

### The New Perspective
According to proponents of the New Perspective, Paul was not opposing the problem of legalism in Galatia. E. P. Sanders argued from a survey of

---

134. Cf. Rom. 3:19–20.

135. Peter T. O'Brien, 'Was Paul a Covenantal Nomist?', in D. A. Carson, Peter T. O'Brien and Mark A. Seifrid (eds.), *Justification and Variegated Nomism*, vol. 2: *The Paradoxes of Paul* (Tübingen: Mohr Siebeck; Grand Rapids: Baker, 2004), pp. 249–296 (p. 280); italics original.

136. Thomas R. Schreiner, *The Law and Its Fulfillment: A Pauline Theology of Law* (Grand Rapids: Baker, 1993), p. 44.

background literature that the idea of earning one's salvation through good works was nowhere to be found in the Judaism of Paul's day,[137] a claim that has since been hotly contested.[138] But if legalism was not the issue, what was Paul so concerned about? According to James Dunn, his quarrel was with those Jewish nationalists who, by their insistence on the ethnic 'boundary-markers' of circumcision and Jewish food laws, excluded the Gentiles from God's people. It is these boundary-markers that are in view whenever Paul speaks of 'observing the law' (or more literally, 'works of the law'; e.g. Gal. 2:16; 3:2, 5, 10). On Dunn's view, it is specifically the sin of nationalism that brings a curse, according to Galatians 3:10.[139]

If we narrow the referent of 'works of the law' in the way Dunn suggests, Galatians says nothing in criticism of law-keeping *in general*. Indeed, was not covenant obedience required of God's Old Testament people as a condition of God's blessing? Were not curses threatened for disobedience? Dunn disagrees with the traditional reading that the law was in principle unkeepable, for it included within itself the means by which sin could be atoned for; namely, the sacrificial system. Thus considered as a whole, that is, 'including the provision of atonement by covenant law . . . obedience was considered practicable'.[140]

However, if the law can be successfully kept, at least by some, the question arises whether some people might escape its curse. Does this mean not all require the redemption from the curse of which Galatians 3:13 speaks? Are there some who do not require Christ as their penal substitute?

---

137. E. P. Sanders, *Paul and Palestinian Judaism* (Philadelphia: Fortress, 1977).

138. See e.g. D. A. Carson, Peter T. O'Brien and Mark A. Seifrid (eds.), *Justification and Variegated Nomism*, vol. 1: *The Complexities of Second Temple Judaism* (Tübingen: Mohr Siebeck; Grand Rapids: Baker, 2001).

139. Dunn, *Theology of Paul*, pp. 361–362.

140. Ibid., p. 361. According to Mark A. Seifrid, righteousness is a forensic concept, distinct from covenant-keeping ('Paul's Use of Righteousness Language against its Hellenistic Background', in D. A. Carson, Peter T. O'Brien and Mark A. Seifrid (eds.), *Justification and Variegated Nomism*, vol. 2: *The Paradoxes of Paul* [Tübingen: Mohr Siebeck; Grand Rapids: Baker, 2004], pp. 39–74). One might argue, therefore, that whether or not someone can keep the covenant is immaterial, for it remains that 'there is no-one righteous' (Rom. 3:10); i.e. forensically speaking, all are guilty before God. While there may be merit in this line of argument, it does not speak well to Gal. 3:10–13, for the language of 'curse' is taken from a distinctly covenantal context in Deut. 27.

Two responses might be made. First, Paul seems to regard the law as impossible to keep. The 'for' that links the two halves of Galatians 3:10 implies as much, for why else would the curse inevitably follow from the attempt to keep the law?[141] Moreover, in Galatians 5:3, the idea that one would have to 'obey the whole law' seems to function as a threat, and this makes sense only if such obedience is impossible.

But why is obedience impossible, if the law contained the means of atonement? The answer is that the provisions of the sacrificial system were limited.[142] Sins of covenant-breaking in particular could not be atoned for, and yet these very sins were foreseen as inevitable for sinful people (Deut. 31:16–21; 1 Kgs 8:46; cf. 2 Chr. 6:36). Moreover, the sacrificial system itself eventually became corrupt, and therefore no longer functioned properly as a means of atonement.[143] The apostle Paul testified that through Christ 'everyone who believes is justified from everything you could not be justified from by the law of Moses' (Acts 13:39).[144] Given that one of the things beyond the scope of the atonement provided in the law was the covenant curse of Deuteronomy 27:26, cited in Galatians 3:10, Jesus' substitutionary death is absolutely necessary.

Secondly, the means of atonement that Dunn sees as present within the law are in fact anticipations of the work of Christ, and derive their efficacy from it (Heb. 9:15). Even if the Levitical sacrifices had been sufficient for some individuals (and it is doubtful they were), one could not legitimately conclude that those people had no need of a penal substitute; precisely because the Levitical sacrifices themselves depended on Christ's curse-bearing, substitutionary death.[145] Indeed, even considered purely within the Old Testament context, there are many aspects of the sacrificial system that plainly teach penal substitution, as we have already seen.

In addition, we need to remember where Galatians stands in salvation-history. Now that fulfilment has come in Christ, the sacrifices that once

---

141. O'Brien, 'Was Paul a Covenantal Nomist?', pp. 280–281.

142. E.g. the sacrificial system did not provide atonement for sins committed 'with a high hand' (Num. 15:28–31).

143. This explains the criticisms of the sacrificial system found in some of the later Old Testament prophets (e.g. Isa. 1:11–17; Jer. 7:21–24; Amos 5:21–26). See the above discussion of the sacrificial system in the Psalms and Old Testament prophets.

144. Of course, the sin of rejecting God's appointed means of atonement altogether is not atoned for under either the old or new covenants (cf. 1 Cor. 10:1–13; Heb. 3:1 – 4:13).

145. See our treatment of the Day of Atonement earlier in this chapter.

pointed forward to him have been rendered obsolete, and it is impossible to return to them. Consequently, if the Galatian Judaizers (or indeed anyone else) were to rely on law-keeping at this later stage in salvation-history, they would be required to attain God's perfect standards, for they would not be able to rely on the means of atonement located within the law itself. They would *now* need to attain sinless perfection, and this is impossible.[146]

In summary, there is no way of evading the conclusion that all people need Christ's substitutionary death to redeem them from the curse that would otherwise be due to them for their failure to meet the requirements of God's holy law.

### The curse as exile

According to N. T. Wright, another prominent proponent of the New Perspective, the curse of Deuteronomy 27:26, quoted in Galatians 3:10, was realized in Israel's history as they were taken into exile. Moreover the New Testament writers would have regarded this exile as still in force at the time of Jesus, not least on account of the Roman occupation.[147] Interestingly, although some dispute this claim, it does not divide people neatly along party lines. O'Brien, a prominent critic of the New Perspective, is in disagreement with Wright here,[148] but then so is Dunn, one of the New Perspective's foremost proponents.[149] On the other hand, Schreiner, who expressly renounces the New Perspective as a whole, agrees with this aspect of Wright's position. Schreiner points out that Joshua 23:14–16 and Deuteronomy 27:15–26 warn of exile, and that both Jeremiah 11 and Daniel 9 speak of the fulfilment of this warning. Indeed, Jeremiah 11:4 contains the idea of doing *all* God's commandments, a theme present in Deuteronomy 27:26, and in the LXX Jeremiah 11:3 uses the same word for 'curse' as that found in both Deuteronomy 27:26 and Galatians 3:10.[150]

It is into the broad context of salvation from exile that many of the Old Testament prophets speak,[151] and it is the exile that lies behind the vocabulary

---

146. Cf. A. Andrew Das, *Paul, the Law, and the Covenant* (Peabody: Hendrickson, 2001), pp. 43–44, 144.

147. N. T. Wright, *The New Testament and the People of God* (London: SPCK, 1992), pp. 268–272; Wright, *Climax of the Covenant*, pp. 137–156.

148. O'Brien, 'Was Paul a Covenantal Nomist?', pp. 285–286.

149. James D. G. Dunn, *The Epistle to the Galatians*, Black's New Testament Commentaries (London: A. & C. Black, 1993), pp. 171–172.

150. Schreiner, *Law and Its Fulfillment*, pp. 47–48.

151. Notably, even Isa. 53, with its emphatic affirmation of penal substitution, occurs in such a context.

of 'curse' in Galatians 3:10. When Paul refers to those Judaizers 'who rely on observing the law', he is speaking of those who want to identify themselves with this Old Israel, the nation in exile, and who thereby place themselves back in the position they were in before Christ's salvation appeared.

Within this framework, when Paul says 'Christ redeemed us from the curse of the law by becoming a curse for us' (Gal. 3:13), he means Christ suffered God's punishment of exile in the place of his people – and not merely physical exile, as we saw in our exposition of Isaiah 53, but the fullest experience of spiritual alienation in penal death to which physical exile points. In so doing, he redeemed them from this curse by exhausting it in his own body. This understanding of Galatians 3:10–13 plainly entails the doctrine of penal substitution.[152]

At first sight, though, the 'exile' reading might seem to imply that only Israel is saved by Christ's penal substitutionary death. But this is not the case, for several reasons. First, Paul is clear that Gentiles can join the true Israel by faith in Christ. Israel's history becomes their history, even to the extent that Abraham becomes their father: 'There is neither Jew nor Greek . . . If you belong to Christ, then you are Abraham's seed, and heirs according to the promise' (Gal. 3:28–29; cf. Rom. 4:12). Conversely, Jesus warned those Jews who rejected him that they could lay no spiritual claim to Abraham as their father, whatever their ethnic heritage may have been (John 8:39–41). The true Israel now comprises all people, Jew and Greek, who put their trust in the Messiah.

Secondly, we need to remember that the history of Israel takes place within a bigger narrative that begins with Adam, the father of all people.[153] Indeed,

---

152. N. T. Wright himself appears to affirm penal substitution in *Letter to the Romans*, p. 476, but in his more recent writings fails to make this link. E.g. in his popular-level commentary on Galatians, he views the cross as a symbol of Roman oppression (for crucifixion was a distinctively Roman form of execution), and therefore of exile, explaining that Christ shared in that experience. However, he stops short of affirming that God brought about the penal suffering both of Israel in exile and of Christ on the cross (N. T. Wright, *Paul for Everyone: Galatians and Thessalonians* [London: SPCK, 2002], p. 34).

153. Wright has controversially suggested that the history of Israel informs the structure of Rom. 3–8 (N. T. Wright, 'New Exodus, New Inheritance: The Narrative Substructure of Romans 3–8', in Sven K. Soderlund and N. T. Wright [eds.], *Romans and the People of God* [Grand Rapids: Eerdmans, 1999], pp. 26–35). If this whole section of Romans does have such a Jewish flavour, it is nonetheless notable that Paul discusses the sin of Adam at the very heart of it (Rom. 5:12–21). Interestingly, the difficulty of integrating the Adam material is one of the reasons

Israel's exile from the land for breaking God's law parallels Adam's expulsion from the Garden of Eden for breaking God's command . Thus the problem of curse and exclusion from God's presence is common to all humanity, not just Old Testament Israel. The fact that Israel *repeats* Adam's fall is the more tragic given that they ought to have been the solution to it: as Abraham's offspring they should have been a blessing to 'all peoples on earth' (Gen. 12:3), 'a light to the nations' (Isa. 51:4). Interestingly, having stated that Christ 'redeemed us from the curse of the law by becoming a curse for us' (Gal. 3:13), Paul goes on to explain that he fulfilled this very function, bringing 'the blessing given to Abraham . . . to the Gentiles' (v. 14). Both Jew and Greek alike are beneficiaries of his penal substitutionary death.

Finally, elsewhere within Galatians itself, the problem faced by Jewish people under the law is set in parallel with the problem faced by Gentiles. The slavery from which redemption was needed was to 'the basic principles of the world' (Gal. 4:3), which in verses 8–9 are identified as the idolatrous pagan influences of the Gentile Galatians' past.[154] However, in verse 5 Paul says it is the *law* from which we were redeemed. Paul appears to treat these two slaveries together, as one. This in turn implies an identity in the means of redemption: for Christ to bear 'the curse of the law' (Gal. 3:13) is also for him to bear the curse due to Gentiles for their idolatry.[155]

### Summary

Although Galatians 3:10–13 is the subject of much discussion among interpreters, the doctrine of penal substitution emerges plainly: Christ endured God's curse in the place of his people, that they might be redeemed.

## 1 Peter 2:21–25 and 3:18

### Introduction

1 Peter speaks frequently about the death of Jesus in categories drawn from

---

why Moo rejects Wright's proposal (Douglas J. Moo, 'Israel and the Law in Romans 5–11: Interaction with the New Perspective', in D. A. Carson, P. T. O'Brien and M. A. Seifrid (eds.), *Justification and Variegated Nomism*, vol. 2: *The Paradoxes of Paul* [Tübingen: Mohr Siebeck; Grand Rapids: Baker, 2004], pp. 185–216 [pp. 193–195]).

154. Bruce, *Galatians*, pp. 29–30.

155. Stephen Westerholm, *Perspectives Old and New on Paul: The 'Lutheran' Paul and His Critics* (Grand Rapids: Eerdmans, 2004), pp. 378–379.

the Old Testament. Perhaps this is unsurprising, given his claim that 'the Spirit of Christ . . . predicted the sufferings of Christ' (1 Pet. 1:11) in the writings of the Old Testament prophets (cf. v. 10).[156]

Consider for example 1 Peter 1:18–19, where Peter reminds his readers that they were 'redeemed [*lytroō*] . . . with the precious blood of Christ, a lamb without blemish or defect'. As we discussed previously, the idea of redemption through the blood of a lamb alludes unmistakably to the Passover. When Peter specifies that this redemption was 'not with . . . silver or gold', he distances himself from the financial connotations of *lytroō* in secular contexts, where the verb was customarily used to refer to a payment of money to release slaves or prisoners of war from bondage,[157] and at the same time alludes to Isaiah 52:3:

> You were sold for nothing,
> > and *without money* you will be redeemed. (Italics added)

This passage occurs in the immediate context of the fourth Servant Song in Isaiah 52:13 – 53:12, which teaches penal substitution explicitly, as we have seen.[158]

In what follows, we shall see that the Old Testament background is prominent in two further texts in 1 Peter that speak clearly about the penal substitutionary death of Christ.

### Christ bore our sins in his body (1 Pet. 2:21–25)

Immediately prior to these verses Peter has been encouraging his hearers to '[bear] up under the pain of unjust suffering' (1 Pet. 2:19), and to this end, he sets forth Jesus as an example to follow in verses 21–23a:[159]

> To this you were called, because Christ suffered for you, leaving you an example, that you should follow in his steps.

---

156. For further discussion of some Old Testament allusions in 1 Peter see Peterson, 'Atonement in the New Testament', pp. 55–60.

157. Morris, *Apostolic Preaching of the Cross*, pp. 11–15, 29.

158. In commenting on Mark 10:45, Green and Baker assert that Jesus does not 'speculate on who pays the ransom' (*Recovering the Scandal*, p. 42). But it would hardly be speculation on Jesus' part, since Peter, one of his disciples, is here explicit on the matter: the blood of Jesus is that currency more precious than silver or gold that he himself gave to procure our redemption.

159. Cf. 1 Pet. 4:12–19; 5:10.

'He committed no sin,
  and no deceit was found in his mouth.'

When they hurled their insults at him, he did not retaliate; when he suffered, he made
no threats.

The exemplary significance of Jesus' death cannot, however, account for
all of the teaching in the passage. Take for example verse 25, 'For you were like
sheep going astray, but now you have returned to the Shepherd and Overseer
of your souls.' This alludes to Isaiah 53:6 ('We all, like sheep, have gone astray'),
and presents Jesus not as an example whose sufferings we should imitate,
but as the Saviour ('Shepherd and Overseer') from whose sufferings we
benefit.

The 'for' at the start of verse 25 points us back to the preceding verse as the
basis for our reconciliation with God: 'He himself bore our sins in his body
on the tree, so that we might die to sins and live for righteousness; by his
wounds you have been healed' (v. 24). Here the doctrine of penal substitution
is clear.

The phrase 'he bore our sins' alludes to Isaiah 53:4 ('he took up our
infirmities') and Isaiah 53:12 ('he bore the sin of many'). We saw in our
discussion of Leviticus that the Hebrew phrase *nāśā' ḥēṭ'* which underlies
the words 'he bore the sin of many' in Isaiah 53:12 implies not just the
bearing of sin and guilt, but also the bearing of punishment. The echo of
Isaiah 53:5 in the phrase 'by his wounds you have been healed' highlights
the substitutionary nature of his death – he suffered in order that we might
not.

Peter drives this message home still further by stating that Jesus 'bore our
sins in his body *on the tree* [*xylon*]' (1 Pet. 2:24). As we saw in our discussion of
Galatians, this distinctive way of referring to the crucifixion evokes
Deuteronomy 21:23, 'anyone who is hung on a tree [LXX: *xylon*] is under God's
curse', and establishes that at the cross Christ bore God's curse in the place of
his people (cf. Gal. 3:13).[160]

Thus 1 Peter 2:21–25, having begun by setting forth Christ's suffering as an
example to encourage Christians who suffer unjustly, moves on the ultimate
grounds of our hope: the atoning efficacy of his death. Christ bore our sin,
guilt and punishment, suffering in our place under the curse of God, that we
might be saved.

---

160. For further discussion see the earlier section on Gal. 3:10–13.

### Christ died for sins once for all (1 Pet. 3:18)

There is a striking parallelism between the phrasing of 1 Peter 2:21 and 1 Peter 3:18 (both read, literally, 'For Christ also . . . died', *hoti kai Christos . . . epathen*). Not only are many themes common to both passages, but so is the flow of the argument: In chapter 3, Peter again moves from the exemplary value of Christ's sufferings (vv. 14, 17) to a statement about their unique atoning efficacy. Peter signals his departure from the exemplary significance of Jesus' death particularly strongly in v. 18 by inserting the words *hapax peri hamartiōn* ('for sins once for all'). In the context Peter's readers are explicitly *not* to suffer for sin (vv. 14, 17), whereas this is precisely what Jesus did, and moreover there is no sense in which Peter's readers can be said to have suffered 'once for all'. Without question, Peter intends us to reflect on Christ's death as more than an example.

The phrase *peri hamartiōn* ('for sins', or perhaps 'a sin offering'; cf. Heb. 10:6, 8, 18, 26; 13:11) also has the effect of setting Jesus' death in the context of the Levitical sacrificial system. Interestingly, the same phrase also appears in the LXX of Isaiah 53:10, which in view of the multitude of earlier allusions to Isaiah 53 is unlikely to be accidental.

The substitutionary nature of Christ's death 'for sins' is clear from the following phrase, 'the righteous for [*hyper*] the unrighteous'. The juxtaposition of Christ's innocence with our guilt and the fact that his death benefits the guilty ('to bring you to God') together point to a substitutionary meaning for the preposition *hyper*.[161] This conclusion is further strengthened by the fact that the only other occurrence of *hyper* in the letter is found in 1 Peter 2:21 ('Christ suffered for [*hyper*] you'), where a substitutionary meaning is signalled by allusions in the context to Isaiah 53.

Thus 1 Peter 3:18 presents the Lord Jesus Christ as a righteous substitute for his unrighteous people; he bore our sins and died a sacrificial death to reconcile us to God.

In closing, we note that there is a possible allusion to Christ's victory over evil powers in the verses immediately following 1 Peter 3:18. The meaning of this passage is much debated, and we do not propose to adjudicate. However, any note of victory here sits alongside the penal substitutionary teaching of verse 18 (and, for that matter, 1 Pet. 2:21–25); it does not displace it. Indeed, Christ's victory over evil powers is dependent on his penal substitutionary death, as we discuss in chapter 3.

---

161. These same factors are among those that demonstrate unequivocally that a substitutionary meaning is intended in Isa. 53.

## Summary

In these two passages, Peter draws extensively on the imagery of the Servant of Isaiah 53 to explain the penal substitutionary significance of Jesus' death. Particularly noteworthy is the way these themes flow so naturally from, while remaining distinct from, the focus on Christ's example as an encouragement to a suffering church. Persecuted Christians, and indeed all believers everywhere, have only one final refuge: the Lord Jesus Christ, punished in our place on Calvary's tree.

## Conclusion

The Bible speaks with a clear and united witness. Christ our Passover lamb has been sacrificed. The Servant was pierced for our transgressions. He died, as Caiaphas prophesied, in the place of the people. He was set forth as a propitiation for our sins. He became a curse for us, bearing our sins in his body on the tree, drinking for us the cup of God's wrath, giving his life as a ransom for many.

Our aim in this chapter has been to demonstrate that penal substitution is taught in Scripture. This cannot be denied. We have not yet explored how it integrates with other biblical themes such as the justice of God, the love of God, the truthfulness of God. Such is the task of the next chapter.

## 3. ASSEMBLING THE PIECES: THE THEOLOGICAL FRAMEWORK FOR PENAL SUBSTITUTION

### Setting the scene

#### *Fitting things together*

Imagine a jigsaw puzzle. Confronted with a large pile of pieces, you idly push them around, looking at each in turn. You pick one up, and as you look at it a friend comes alongside and tells you it has no place in the puzzle – it must have found its way into the box by mistake. You do not need that piece, he says. Throw it away!

You would be reluctant to follow such a suggestion immediately. What if your friend were wrong? You would not want to discard a piece you will need later. How would you respond? Surely the best approach would be to assemble the rest of the puzzle as far as you can. If there were no space for the piece in question, or if it became clear that the picture on it does not fit with everything else, then your friend's suspicions would be confirmed – the piece is superfluous and should be set aside. There would be no point in trying to force it in somewhere. It would only ruin everything else.

But if there were a gap of just the right shape, and the picture on your piece matched well with everything else, then it would have found a home. Indeed it *must* be included, otherwise the puzzle will always be incomplete, the gap will be a blemish, and if the piece is particularly central, the rest of the picture may not even make sense at all.

This chapter aims to do something like this with the big picture of Christian theology: to see what it looks like and how it fits together, and then to ask whether or not penal substitution has a place. Penal substitution is, for these purposes, like the jigsaw puzzle piece under suspicion. Is it foreign to the big picture of Christian theology, an intruder that does not belong? Or does it have a place – maybe even a central place – such that if we discard it the picture will always be incomplete, defective, distorted?

Our primary goal is to understand penal substitution more clearly by placing it in its proper theological context. But there is another purpose. Increasing numbers of people are claiming that penal substitution is a cuckoo in the nest. For some, it grew out of the Latin Church's ideas about penance. Others argue it came from medieval feudal ideas about honour. Still others suggest it arose out of the preoccupation with legal categories and law courts in Europe during the Reformation. The details may differ, but the critics agree that penal substitution is an alien intrusion. Moreover, they believe it represents values that contradict the Bible, and has therefore had disastrous results. Like real cuckoos, it presents a danger to the other birds that rightly belong in the nest. Clearly, this is a serious accusation, and it needs to be answered.

Our plan is as follows. First, we shall carefully explain the doctrine of penal substitution itself, to show what shape it has. Then we shall put together the rest of the jigsaw, integrating some of the biggest and most fundamental themes of Christian theology. At each stage, we shall ask whether penal substitution fits into the picture, and whether any other understanding of the cross could successfully take its place.

But before we do any of that, we need briefly to defend the jigsaw methodology on which our whole endeavour is based. Is it really possible to construct a big picture of Christian theology at all?

### Is a 'big picture' possible?
Some people claim it is impossible to assemble all the pieces of Christian theology into a single coherent 'big picture'. Now, certainly it is true that our finite minds cannot fully comprehend the infinite mind of God: we can never give a complete and exhaustive account of him, nor reach the point where there is nothing more about God to know. But does this mean we cannot understand Christian theology at all? In particular, does it mean we cannot understand even enough to see whether penal substitution fits in? This is a very important question, and we need to spend time looking at it.

There is a difference between understanding something *truly* and understanding something *exhaustively*.[1] The distinction is useful in many areas of life. Take the physical world for example. We can know truly that our computer turns on when we push a button, without knowing exhaustively the electronic processes behind it. The same distinction applies to relational knowledge. A child can know truly that her parent loves her, without knowing exhaustively the full intensity of what her parent feels.

We can never have genuinely exhaustive knowledge about anything, because everything in the universe is interrelated, and exhaustive knowledge of any single part would therefore require exhaustive knowledge of everything else. To know exhaustively why the wind blew a leaf in a particular direction would require exhaustive knowledge of the weather all over the world! Only God has this kind of knowledge.

We cannot know everything, and that should be a humbling realization. But it is a fallacy to conclude from this that we do not know *anything*. An awareness of our limitations does not prevent us from learning a great deal that is true about the physical world or about people with whom we form relationships. Whenever we show compassion to a friend who is going through a tough time, we are acting on the basis of our knowledge of them and how they are feeling. This mutual understanding is the basis of human relationship. It is not necessary to have an *exhaustive* grasp of our friend's emotional state in order to act appropriately towards her.

Let us now apply the distinction between true and exhaustive knowledge to our knowledge of God. There are some statements about God we would be confident to affirm as true, such as 'God is good. God is loving. God is holy. God is the uncreated Creator of all things.' These statements do not represent a claim to exhaustive knowledge about God's goodness, his love, his holiness or his work as Creator. But they nonetheless get us somewhere. For one thing, they entail that some other statements are not true, such as 'God is not good. God is not loving. God is not holy. God is not our Creator.' Moreover, the things we know are true about God have consequences, and by following their logic we can arrive at other truths. For example, the fact that God is the uncreated Creator of all things implies he has certain rights over his creation.

We can therefore approach the task of constructing the 'big picture' of Christian theology with a certain degree of confidence. We shall not be able to say everything there is to say about God, but there is nothing in principle that prevents us from saying something.

---

1.  See Francis Schaeffer, *The God Who Is There*, in *Trilogy* (Leicester: IVP, 1990), pp. 1–202 (p. 100).

This takes us to another question: On what basis are we to believe anything about God? *Why* should we believe God is good, or loving, or holy, or our Creator? The simple answer is that he has told us. It is worth reminding ourselves of this. It is not our instincts or our feelings or our most sophisticated thoughts that tell us the truth about God. Rather, as Hilary of Poitiers insisted in the fourth century, God is the best witness concerning himself.[2]

It might be asked why we should trust God's self-attestation. After all, we do not always believe what people say about themselves. Sometimes there is a problem of ignorance: the speaker does not know what he is talking about. Sometimes there is a problem of character: the speaker is knowledgable but untrustworthy, and may set out to deceive us. But with God neither of these applies. God is good and holy: he will not deceive us. And as our Creator he is perfectly wise: he knows himself and everything else exhaustively. His own self-revelation, found in the pages of Scripture, is therefore utterly reliable and immensely precious.

In summary, to attempt to draw the 'big picture' of Christian theology is simply to pay due attention to what God says about himself. We must not ignore our speaking God; instead, we must recognize that his wisdom is infinitely greater than ours, and root out any thinking that conflicts with his word. The task of this chapter is therefore to seek to honour God by listening to what he says.

### What is penal substitution?

If we are to determine whether penal substitution has a place within Christian theology, we must first sketch its basic contours.[3] We began chapter 1 with the following definition: The doctrine of penal substitution states that God gave himself in the person of his Son to suffer instead of us the death, punishment and curse due to fallen humanity as the penalty for sin. This summary can be

---

2. Hilary of Poitiers, *On the Trinity*, in *Nicene and Post-Nicene Fathers*, ser. II, vol. 9 (Grand Rapids: Eerdmans, 1976), pp. 40–233, bk. 1, sect. 18 (p. 45).

3. For further discussion see Roger Nicole, 'Postscript on Penal Substitution', in Charles E. Hill and Frank A. James III (eds.), *The Glory of the Atonement: Biblical Historical and Practical Perspectives* (Downers Grove: IVP; Leicester: Apollos, 2004), pp. 445–452; and J. I. Packer, 'What Did the Cross Achieve? The Logic of Penal Substitution', in *Celebrating the Saving Work of God: Collected Shorter Writings of J. I. Packer* (Carlisle: Paternoster, 1998), pp. 85–123.

expanded to give some sense of how the doctrine connects with other important biblical themes.

God the Father gave his Son to save rebellious, God-hating people, knowing that he would be despised and rejected by those he had made, that he would be a man of sorrows, and familiar with suffering. He spared sinful people from condemnation, death and punishment, but he did not spare his own beloved Son, with whom he was well pleased.

God the Son gave himself, willingly undertaking the task appointed for him by his Father. He veiled his glory in a human body, experienced every temptation we face without succumbing to any, and lived a perfect human life. Yet he took our sin and guilt upon himself and died a cursed death, suffering in his human nature the infinite torment of the wrath and fury of his Father. After three days he was vindicated in his resurrection before being exalted to his heavenly throne. From there he rules his kingdom, awaiting the day of his glorious appearing when every eye shall see him, every knee bow before him, and every tongue confess that Jesus Christ is Lord, to the glory of God the Father.

God the Holy Spirit, having been sent by the Father and the Son, now works in our hearts through the proclamation of the gospel to convict us of sin, righteousness and judgment, to draw us to Christ in repentance and faith, and so to unite us to Christ that we may share in every blessing he has won for us.

God the Holy Trinity thus turned aside his own righteous wrath against sinful humanity; endured and exhausted the curse of the law that stood against us; cleansed us of our sin and clothed us in Christ's righteousness; ransomed us from our slavery to sin, the world and the devil by paying our debt, cancelling the devil's power of accusation against us, and liberating us to live new lives empowered by the Spirit; triumphed over all evil powers by punishing evil in the person of the Son; and reconciled us with himself by removing the barrier of sin and enmity between us; in order that we may stand blameless and forgiven in his glorious presence, credited with the perfect righteousness of the Lord Jesus Christ, as adopted children of God, gazing upon his face for all eternity.

God vindicated his truthfulness by remaining faithful to his promise that sin will be punished; he manifested his justice by punishing sin and acquitting the righteous; he glorified his name by exalting his Son and placing all things under his feet; and he demonstrated his love by dying for sinners and reconciling to himself those who were once his enemies.

### Summary

The big picture outlined in the rest of this chapter touches on some familiar themes, of which three are particularly important. First, creation has been corrupted by human sin. God's good work of creation has been undone, a 'decreation'. What is needed therefore is a work of recreation. Secondly, God is absolutely truthful. He is faithful to his warnings of judgment and promises of salvation, and always acts consistently with his own righteous, holy, just character. He cannot merely overlook sin. Thirdly, God is absolutely good and loving towards all he has made. He has manifested this goodness and love supremely in the atonement.

As we consider these themes, we shall see again and again that penal substitution has a central place in Christian theology and is fundamental to the fulfilment of God's purposes for his creation.

## Creation

### Introduction

The doctrine of creation is foundational to any understanding of how God acts in the world, for it is here that he begins his actions in human history, here that he first speaks, here that his world comes into being.

It might seem that the doctrine of creation is quite some distance from the doctrine of penal substitution, but this is not really the case. Redemption (the broader theological category in which we claim that penal substitution is central) is often presented in Scripture as a *new creation* or an act of *recreation*, both in connection with the salvation of individuals and the restoration of the cosmos. For example, in 2 Corinthians 4:6, God's work of bringing individual people to new life is described as illumination – God 'made his light shine in our hearts' – and this is linked with his first command in the original creation, 'Let there be light' (Gen. 1:3). This connection between creation and coming to Christ continues in 2 Corinthians 5:17, where Paul writes, 'If anyone is in Christ, he is a new creation'. Turning to the wider created order, Revelation 21:1 speaks of 'a new heaven and a new earth', and Revelation 22:1–5 describes the new creation in terms reminiscent of the Garden of Eden. The doctrine of creation is plainly important for a right understanding of redemption.

### The original creation

We must therefore turn to the opening pages of Scripture. What does Genesis 1–2 tell us? We learn a lot about humanity, especially as the man and the woman move to centre stage in Genesis 2:20–25. But the principal actor in these two chapters is God, and as we read about his work of creation, we begin to understand something of who he is. Two themes emerge in particular.

First, God's word is effective. All of the works of creation are accomplished by divine fiat: God spoke, 'and it was so' (Gen. 1:7, 9, 11, 15, 24, 30). As

Gordon Wenham explains, 'It is a divine word of command that brings into existence what it expresses.'[4] God speaks into the non-existent void and brings the universe into being. It is not merely that his word corresponds with reality; rather, reality conforms to his word.

Secondly, God is good. Not only does he create a good universe (Gen. 1:10, 12, 18, 21, 25, 31), but he also blesses his creation (Gen. 1:22, 28; 2:3), and generously provides for it, giving his creatures everything they need (Gen. 1:29–30). God is a generous giver. He is good to his creation.

Taken together, the goodness of God and the effectiveness of his word point towards his *truthfulness*. God has the character to speak the truth because of his goodness, and he has the capacity to speak the truth, for his word always corresponds with reality. God is truthful, and can therefore be trusted.

At this point we note an intriguing feature of these chapters. There is one statement that has not yet come to pass by the end of Genesis chapter 2. It is found in 2:17, when God warns Adam, 'You must not eat from the tree of the knowledge of good and evil, for when you eat of it you will surely die.' Of course, there is a good reason why the promise of death had not come about. The promise was conditional, and the condition had not yet been met, for Adam had not at this point eaten from the forbidden tree. But given all that we have just seen about God's word, we know what we would expect to happen when he does. After all, Genesis 2:17 was spoken by the same God who spoke into being the heavens and the earth.

### The implications of creation

Genesis 1–2 has already taught us important things about God's character and God's word. But there is still more to learn from the biblical account of creation. Consider Revelation 4:11, one of the many other biblical passages that reflect on this theme:

> You are worthy, our Lord and God,
>     to receive glory and honour and power,
> for you created all things,
>     and by your will they were created
>     and have their being.

This verse points to three important truths.

---

4.  Gordon J. Wenham, *Genesis 1–15*, Word Biblical Commentary (Nashville: Thomas Nelson, 1987), p. 18.

First, God 'created all things'. Everything in the universe, from the finely woven intricacies of the tiniest cells to the immense bulk of far-distant stars, and even the vastness of space itself, owes its existence to God. Secondly, the creation exists by God's 'will'; that is, his intention. God is not oblivious to creation, or ignorant of what goes on in his universe. Far from it. God is intentionally and deliberately aware of everything and everyone. Thirdly, God continues to be involved in creation, sovereignly upholding and preserving all things, for it is by his will that all things 'were created and *have their being*' (italics added). Hebrews 1:3 confirms that 'The Son is . . . sustaining all things by his powerful word.' The entire cosmos depends upon God's will for its continued existence just as much as it did for its initial creation. While we type this, and while you read it, our fingers and your eyes continue to exist only because God upholds them. It is inadequate to imagine God as a cosmic clockmaker, first creating the universe, designing it to operate in a certain way, winding it up and then leaving it to tick along on its own. The fact that the universe continues to function as it does, and that certain actions have certain consequences, needs to be seen in the light of God's continued, intentional, active, sustaining involvement.

This last point is very important. For some have argued that God does not actively punish sin, but instead allows sinners to reap the 'natural' consequences of their actions. The idea here is that God does not *intentionally impose* these consequences: they are the natural outcome of events, a moral cause and effect analogous to physical cause and effect. Thus the husband who commits adultery suffers the consequence of collapsed trust in his marriage, and the man with a violent temper experiences the inevitable decay and loss of friendship. Within such a framework, it is claimed, we should not talk about God *intentionally* or *actively* punishing sin.

But this is a mistake, because it downplays an aspect of God's work in creation; namely, his continuing, intentional sustaining of all things. All 'natural' consequences, whether physical or moral, take place because God *continues* to will the existence of the universe and the causal relationships that occur within it. Since the moral consequences of sin are willed in this way, they have the character of divine punishment.[5]

We need to look at one final implication of God's work as Creator to complete this part of the picture: all things *belong* to God, for he made them. Psalm 24:1–2 makes this point clearly.[6]

---

5. We discuss this in more detail in chapter 11, sect. 3.

6. See too e.g. Pss 89:11; 95:3–5.

> The earth is the LORD's, and everything in it,
>    the world, and all who live in it;
> for he founded it upon the seas
>    and established it upon the waters.

The fact that God owns the universe implies in turn that he is the rightful ruler of creation. He has the authority to govern the world as he sees fit, and we are in no position to argue with him: 'Woe to him who quarrels with his Maker' (Isa. 45:9). As the legitimate ruler of the universe, God is able to establish an order in creation. He is at liberty to organize things in a certain way, and this is precisely what he has done. Having made Adam and Eve in his image (Gen. 1:26–27), God gave them a degree of authority over his creation, instructing them to 'rule over the fish of the sea and the birds of the air, over the livestock, over all the earth, and over all the creatures that move along the ground' (Gen. 1:26; see also v. 28). He then instructed them to 'fill the earth and subdue it' (v. 28), a mandate we begin to see worked out when Adam names the animals in Genesis 2:19–20, 'establishing man's place in the world, a little lower than the angels and a little higher than the animals'.[7]

However, human authority in the world is not absolute. It is still God's world, and our authority is limited, delegated, and subordinate to him. It is God who gave authority to Adam and Eve, and he who told them how to exercise it (Gen. 1:26, 28–30). They were not given authority over God, or authority independent of him. Moreover, there were boundaries: Adam was told he 'must not eat from the tree of the knowledge of good and evil' (Gen. 2:17). By keeping back one part of creation like this from Adam and Eve, God reminds them that their authority is not absolute. They were, and we are, accountable to him.

Taking all this together, the hierarchy God established in creation can be represented like this:

God

Humanity

The rest of creation

There are two things we should note about this order. First, it is good. This needs to be said because, tragically, humans often abuse positions of authority, and we may therefore be tempted to think of any hierarchy as inherently

---

7.  Wenham, *Genesis 1–15*, p. 68.

exploitative. But obviously we must not think of the God-created order in this way. God is holy and perfect, and the order established in Genesis 1–2 is described by God as 'very good' (Gen. 1:31).

Secondly, the relationship between God and humanity is loving and personal. This is evident in the way God blessed Adam and Eve (Gen. 1:28; cf. 5:2; 9:1), in his abundant provision for them (Gen. 1:29–30), and in God's gracious gift of marriage in response to Adam's need: 'The LORD God said, "It is not good for the man to be alone"' (Gen. 2:18).

There is no tension here between the loving, personal nature of relationship and the existence of rules to regulate it. God set clear boundaries for Adam and Eve – it was a 'legal' relationship in the sense that he set a law for them (Gen. 2:17) – but this did not undermine his love for them, nor the closeness of their personal relationship with him. There is no inherent conflict between a *personal* relationship and a *legal* relationship.

This needs to be underlined because modern culture sometimes perceives the two as incompatible, as if one excludes the other. Indeed, at the superficial level, this resonates with our experience. Few of us have a personal and loving relationship with the staff at the Inland Revenue or our local traffic warden.[8] Such relationships seem to be regulated purely by rules, and indeed this may be the best thing. A traffic warden will struggle to do his job if he enters into close friendships with all those whose cars are towed away! Indeed, a personal relationship in such cases might actually impede the operation of the rules of the relationship, and lead to unfair or preferential treatment. By contrast, other relationships seem at first glance to be entirely rule-free, such as when close friends are relaxing together, enjoying each other's company.

However, even the most intensely personal relationships *are* governed by rules, albeit sometimes unspoken ones. Take marriage, for example. Marriage involves formal promises between bride and groom, and it is expected that these be kept. Each partner must treat the other with faithfulness. That is a rule of marriage, and the consequences are serious if it is broken. A similar set of rules applies to friendships: we are expected not to treat our friends cruelly, nor to speak unkindly about them to others. If we disregard these rules, we shall soon have no friends left, precisely because the *personal* element of the relationship will have been violated. Thus rules can actually serve to protect personal, loving relationships.

---

8. Our apologies to readers engaged in these much-slandered professions, and to their friends and relatives, who *do* have a close loving relationship with them!

The biblical idea of *covenant*, so prominent in Scripture, embraces both personal and legal aspects. God's covenant with his people laid the foundation for a relationship in which they would be his 'treasured possession' (Exod. 19:5) or, as the apostle Peter would later paraphrase it, 'a people belonging to God' (1 Pet. 2:9). It was intensely personal. Yet it also carried obligations, as Deuteronomy 28–31 makes especially clear – there were blessings for obedience and curses for disobedience. In particular, the curse of expulsion from the Promised Land was threatened if the people of Israel turned from the Lord to other gods (Deut. 30:17–18).

We find the same harmony between rules and relationship in Jesus' insistence that 'If you love me, you will obey what I command' (John 14:15), and the apostle John's declaration that 'This is love for God: to obey his commands' (1 John 5:3; cf. Deut. 11:13; Josh. 22:5; John 14:23–24; 15:10). In short, the fact that our relationship with God is regulated by rules, or 'laws', does not make it any less personal. The two go together.

### Summary

God created a perfect world, bringing it into being by his truthful, powerful word. He placed people in it, delegating to them a certain degree of authority to rule over it, setting the boundaries for their conduct, and establishing with them a personal, loving relationship where he generously gave them everything they needed.

Our understanding of salvation must cohere with God's original purposes in creation. This means it must preserve the truth of God's word, and must restore our relationship with God to its original created goodness, where our obedience to God goes hand in hand with a personal, loving relationship with him.

We now turn to the next chapter of the biblical account of human history to discover how this perfect creation was marred by human sin.

## 'Decreation' – the undoing of creation

### Introduction

The catastrophe of Genesis 3 is often called 'the fall', but is perhaps better described as an act of 'decreation'. For this chapter records the *reversal* of many of God's plans for the original creation, the unravelling of what was once 'very good' (Gen. 1:31). This theme of reversal is clear especially in the encounter between the serpent and Eve in Genesis 3:1–6.[9]

---

9. For further commentary on this text see Wenham, *Genesis 1–15*, pp. 72–76.

### Denying God's truthfulness and goodness

The serpent is introduced as being 'crafty', and his behaviour bears this out, for he begins by questioning God's word: 'Did God really say, "You must not eat from any tree in the garden"?' (Gen. 3:1). Eve replies that 'God did say, "You must not eat fruit from the tree that is in the middle of the garden"' (v. 3), recalling God's warning in Genesis 2:17, whereupon the serpent persists with a more direct challenge, openly denying the truth of the warning: '"You will not surely die," the serpent said to the woman' (v. 4). In effect, the serpent is denying God's *truthfulness*: 'God has spoken, but it will not come to pass.'

But the serpent goes further. He also questions God's *goodness*. This is evident from his first question, where he insinuates that God's command is more restrictive than it actually is: 'Did God really say, "You must not eat from *any* tree in the garden"?' (Gen. 3:1; italics added). In fact, God had said no such thing; he had given Adam and Eve great liberty – '*you are free* to eat from any tree in the garden' (Gen. 2:16; italics added). Out of the great abundance of the Garden of Eden only the fruit from a single tree was withheld (v. 17). Eve appears to spot this tactic, and corrects the serpent's malicious slander: 'We may eat fruit from the trees in the garden' (Gen. 3:2). But then, tragically, she succumbs to the same error, first subtly *understating* God's generous provision (she does not repeat God's gracious reference to '*any* tree') and then subtly *overstating* the severity of God's restriction by claiming that God had forbidden them even to 'touch' (v. 3) the tree of the knowledge of good and evil. The serpent presses the point further, implying that God's law is selfish, even repressive: 'God knows that when you eat of it your eyes will be opened, and you will be like God, knowing good and evil' (v. 5). The implication of this is that there is something good that God has not given to humanity. It is a denial of God's generosity.

In view of this, Eve's decision to take the fruit (v. 6) reflects disbelief in God's truthfulness and his goodness, those characteristics so prominently revealed in his creation, as we saw above. Her rebellion is fundamentally an exercise of autonomy, in which she places her faith not in what God has revealed but in her own appraisal of the situation – 'When *the woman saw* that the fruit of the tree was good for food and pleasing to the eye, and also desirable for gaining wisdom, she took some and ate it' (v. 6; italics added). Needless to say, 'her husband, who was with her' (v. 6) was no less to blame.

The sin of Adam and Eve also overturns the order God has established in Genesis 1–2.[10] The serpent, an animal creature, should have been ruled by

---

10. Ibid., p. 75.

Adam and Eve, they themselves being subject to the rule of God. But in fact, Adam and Eve do the serpent's bidding, and in turn defy the one to whom they really owe obedience. Creation is turned upside down. This disbelieving disobedience is a decreating act, because it reverses and undoes the ordered network of relationships God created. This process can be represented like this:

| God | Sin | The rest of creation |
| Humanity | $\longrightarrow$ | Humanity |
| The rest of creation | Decreation | God |

This understanding of the fall as a decreation helps explain why God's salvation is described in Scripture as a *recreation* or a *new creation* (e.g. Isa. 65:17–19; 2 Cor. 5:17; Gal. 6:15). Once sin is seen as decreating, nothing less than another act by God, on the scale of creation, can set things right.

### Disbelief and 'false faith'

John Calvin famously commented that 'Unfaithfulness . . . was the root of the Fall.'[11] Adam and Eve displayed a lack of faith in what God had said. Yet from another perspective, Adam and Eve in Genesis 3 are people of great faith. They do believe someone and something. The problem is they believe in the wrong person and the wrong thing: they believe a creature rather than the Creator, and exchange the truth about God for a lie. There is belief – even belief in God – but it is belief in a falsehood about him. Francis Turretin, Calvin's seventeenth-century successor at Geneva, captures this idea when he speaks of Adam 'engendering a *false faith* from [Satan's] lies'.[12]

Several things can be said about this false faith. First, it is closely related to *idolatry*. Fundamental to idolatry in biblical terms is the idea of an exchange – swapping the true God for something else. Thus Jeremiah laments that 'my people have exchanged their Glory for worthless idols' (Jer. 2:11; cf. Ps. 106:20), and the apostle Paul comments that 'they exchanged the truth of God for a lie, and worshipped and served created things rather than the Creator' (Rom. 1:25; cf. v. 23).

That idolatrous exchange can occur in various ways. Someone might exchange the true God for an alternative 'deity', such as the pagan god Baal who proved so

---

11. John Calvin, *Institutes of the Christian Religion*, trans. F. L. Battles, vol. 1 (Philadelphia: Westminster, 1960), II.i.4, p. 245.

12. Francis Turretin, *Institutes of Elenctic Theology*, trans. G. M. Giger, vol. 1 (Phillipsburg: Presbyterian & Reformed, 1994), 9.VI.ix, p. 605; italics added.

tempting for God's people in Old Testament times.[13] Alternatively, someone might exchange the true God who genuinely blesses for something else supposed to bring blessing, such as sex or money (Eph. 5:5).[14] Or the exchange may amount to modifying God's character, airbrushing out attributes we deem problematic to make a more convenient God in our image. This last kind of idolatry is hardest to spot, because we can indulge in it while retaining Christian vocabulary. We continue to speak enthusiastically of 'God', and even about 'Christ' and 'the gospel', while all along we are operating with an imitation forged by our own sinful imaginations. When we suppress certain truths about God (e.g. his holy wrath against sin) or distort others (e.g. his love) to produce our own designer deity, then we are guilty of false faith, and are left with a 'counterfeit God'.[15]

Secondly, false faith is *delusional*. It undermines our ability to think rightly, particularly about God. Thus Paul writes of all humanity that 'their thinking became futile and their foolish hearts were darkened. Although they claimed to be wise, they became fools' (Rom. 1:21–22). Similarly, he writes to the church in Corinth that 'the god of this age has blinded the minds of unbelievers, so that they cannot see the light of the gospel of the glory of Christ' (2 Cor. 4:4; cf. Eph. 4:17–18). False faith impairs our rational faculties, so that we are no longer reliably able to discern truth from error. Once again this is bound up with idolatry, for to embrace an idol is to embrace a lie (e.g. Isa. 44:20). The delusional character of false faith means that the effects of sin cannot be reversed simply by presenting correct, rational arguments to unaided human minds. Such arguments would not be understood, much less rightly appraised, by fallen human reason.

Thirdly, false faith is a *willed commitment*. It goes beyond a merely rational impairment, so that we actually *desire* what is evil. Nowhere is this more clearly manifested than in our propensity to hide from the truth about God. As the Lord Jesus said in his conversation with Nicodemus, 'This is the verdict: Light has come into the world, but men loved darkness instead of light because their deeds were evil. Everyone who does evil hates the light, and will not come into the light for fear that his deeds will be exposed' (John 3:19–20).

---

13. See D. F. Payne, 'Baal', in *The New Bible Dictionary*, 3rd edn (Leicester: IVP, 1996), p. 108.

14. The early church Fathers made much of the idea of idolatry as a way of analysing and critiquing the religious world in which they lived. See e.g. Tertullian, *On Idolatry*, in *The Ante-Nicene Fathers*, vol. 3 (Grand Rapids: Eerdmans, 1968), pp. 61–76.

15. R. Keyes, 'The Idol Factory', in O. Guinness and J. Seel (eds.), *Breaking with the Idols of Our Age* (Chicago: Moody, 1992), pp. 29–48 (p. 33).

Or again, consider Paul's words:

> For the time will come when men will not put up with sound doctrine. Instead, to suit
> their own desires, they will gather around them a great number of teachers to say
> what their itching ears want to hear. They will turn their ears away from the truth and
> turn aside to myths. (2 Tim. 4:3–4)

The problem here is not that people are seeking God but cannot find him.
On the contrary, there is 'no-one who seeks God' (Rom. 3:11). We choose to
keep ourselves in the dark. In this sense, false faith is a kind of addiction, where
we are attached and committed to our idols. Patrick McCormick offers some
striking insights on this theme in his book *Sin as Addiction*:

> Denial, projection and delusion constitute the unholy trinity of addiction. In order to
> justify irrational thought and behaviour it is necessary to block out painful
> information, create and maintain an unreal world, and affix blame for all bad news on
> any source except the self or the addiction.[16]

It is little wonder that the Bible associates sin so strongly with helplessness:
it enslaves us (John 8:34); it blinds us (2 Cor. 4:3–4); it has dominion over us
(Col. 1:13); it holds us in death (Eph. 2:1). 'Sin, like addiction, seems to involve
a progressive enslavement to our compulsions.'[17] Indeed, it is an enslavement
to which God has given us over in judgment for our rebellion against him
(Rom. 1:18–22, 24, 26).

Fourthly, false faith is a *relational disaster*, for false faith is a commitment to
a fictional god, not the God revealed in Scripture. False faith refuses to accept
God's words as truthful and his commands as authoritative; it denies he is the
Creator and we are his creatures. In doing so, it refuses the possibility of a relationship with him. This becomes clear if we imagine what would happen in a
relationship between two human beings who behaved in this way. Imagine if a
new resident in a street introduces himself to Marian, his new neighbour: 'Hi!
My name's Chris.' Over a cup of tea, Chris explains that he enjoys rock but
cannot bear Gilbert and Sullivan. Somewhat bewilderingly, Marian decides to
call him 'Woody', and books tickets for them both to see a production of *The
Mikado*. Worse still, Marian refuses to accept that Chris (whom she persists in
calling 'Woody') does not like 'G and S', even when he takes considerable pains

---

16. Patrick McCormick, *Sin as Addiction* (New York: Paulist Press, 1989), p. 155.
17. Ibid., p. 161.

to reiterate his musical preferences. This is a light-hearted example, but in fact such a situation would be absurd, not to mention profoundly insulting. To treat someone like this would be to call him a liar, and to imply that he does not even know himself. To ignore someone's self-revelation in this way, and to substitute one's own fictional account of who he is, spells the end of the relationship.

There is real poignancy here, for the self-delusion inherent in false faith can readily lead us to deny that our relationship with the real God has collapsed. The Pharisees and teachers of the law in Mark 7 behaved like this. They were fastidious over their religious observances, as if to give the impression that God was foremost in their hearts, but Jesus exposed them as hypocrites: they had 'let go of the commands of God' and were 'holding on to the traditions of men' (v. 8). Similarly, Jesus' opponents in John 8 claimed to be sons of God (v. 41), but Jesus asserted that their real father was 'the devil' (v. 44).

Thus false faith alienates us from God. More than this, it alienates us from ourselves, for we know how to be truly human only when our humanity is located in a right relationship with our Creator – human beings alienated from God live inauthentic lives. This has implications for the rest of creation, for it was designed to flourish under the governance of true humanity (Ps. 8), and now that order has been disturbed.[18]

Fifthly, the idea of false faith reminds us that all people have faith in something. Social commentators are fond of speaking of 'people of all faiths and none', as if some people 'believe in something' while others do not. But the real dividing line within the human race is not between people who have faith and people who do not, but between people who have true faith and people whose faith is false, whether they believe in another god (like Baal), or a social cause (like multiculturalism), or a lifestyle (like hedonism).[19] Furthermore, the thing that determines whether a person's faith is true or false is not the sincerity with which it is held, but whether it corresponds to reality. Adam and Eve were, apparently, perfectly sincere in Genesis 3.

In summary, false faith is a universal condition of fallen humanity, whereby we exchange the truth about God for a lie, and the true God for an idol. It is

---

18. Cf. Heb. 2:8, 'At present we do not see everything subject to him'; i.e. to humankind, as God had intended in Ps. 8. The author of Hebrews goes on to point to Jesus as the perfect man who fulfilled this role in the way we failed to do.

19. The cause may or may not be bad in itself; the problem arises when it displaces the true God from the centre of our lives.

profoundly captivating – even addictive – such that we cannot by intellectual endeavour or sheer will power liberate ourselves. False faith ruins our relationships with God, with each other, and with the rest of the created order. To be saved from this hopeless condition we need a Saviour free from the captivity of false faith.

### False faith throughout the Bible

We have seen how Genesis 1–3 portrays human sin as an act of decreation, a denial of God's truthfulness and goodness. A similar pattern recurs at several points in the Bible. We have space to look at only two examples, one from the Old Testament, and one from the New.

We begin with the fall of Solomon in 1 Kings 11:1–13. The chapters leading up to this sad turn of events describe something of a golden age in the history of Israel – the temple of the Lord has been built, the nation enjoys great prosperity and foreign rulers have travelled to Jerusalem to marvel at the wisdom of God's anointed king (1 Kgs 2–10). 1 Kings 11:2 recalls God's command to the Israelites against intermarriage with people from pagan nations, 'because they will surely turn your hearts after their gods' (v. 2; cf. Exod. 34:16; Deut. 7:3–4; Josh. 23:12–13). This command raises issues of truthfulness and goodness in almost exactly the same way as did the command in Eden. Is God's word *good* for Israel? Or is God playing the divine spoilsport, the cosmic miser, who forbids certain pleasures just because he can. And is his word *true?* Will the consequences of marrying outside God's people really be so devastating, or is God just issuing idle threats?

1 Kings 11 underlines the truth of God's word, for Solomon 'had seven hundred wives of royal birth and three hundred concubines, *and his wives led him astray*' (v. 3; italics added). His 'heart' (vv. 4, 9) was turned away from the Lord to foreign gods. The chapter also emphasizes that the command was good for Solomon and other Israelites, in the sense that obedience would have preserved the most valuable thing they had: a relationship with their Creator. As Solomon flagrantly disregarded the word of the Lord, 'who had appeared to him twice' about precisely this issue (vv. 9, 10), he did tremendous damage to his relationship with God, and to the relationship between God and his people.

We turn now to the New Testament, and to people's reactions to Jesus, where the themes of disobedience and disbelief we saw in Genesis 3 take on a sharper focus. The issue hinges on the question of Jesus' identity: 'Who do you say I am?' (Mark 8:29; cf. John 20:30–31). Will we humbly accept God's self-disclosure, his word about himself? Or will we reject him in favour of idols?

John 3:36 outlines the possible consequences of our response to Christ: 'Whoever believes in the Son has eternal life, but whoever rejects the Son will not see life, for God's wrath remains on him.' This verse falls into two contrasting halves: the first, positive, relating to life; the other, negative, relating to God's wrath. On the positive side, eternal life rests on belief (*pisteuō*) in Jesus as God's Son. However, when we come to the negative side in the second half of the verse, the phrasing is not quite what we might expect. The most obvious opposite of 'believe' would be 'not believe'. But here, the contrasting idea is not unbelief but rejection (*apeitheō*), even 'disobedience' (ESV, RSV, NRSV). Failure to believe in Jesus is not merely a mental error akin to thinking that $2 + 2 = 5$; it is *ethically* unjustified, an act of rebellion. As D. A. Carson puts it, there are 'only two alternatives, genuine faith and defiant disobedience'.[20] In a similar vein, Paul warns that Jesus 'will punish those who do not know God and *do not obey* the gospel of our Lord Jesus' (2 Thess. 1:8; italics added).

God's nature as Trinity means that disobedience to and disbelief in God the Son also entails disobedience to and disbelief in the Father, for the Father's will is that people should believe the truth about Jesus (John 6:29). Indeed, 'He who does not honour the Son does not honour the Father, who sent him' (John 5:23). Thus to disbelieve what Jesus says about himself is an attack on the Father. Jesus insists his words come from the Father (John 14:10; 17:8, 14), the Father commands us to listen to the Son (Mark 9:7), and refusal to believe the words of the Son makes the Father out to be a liar (1 John 5:10). It is a denial of his truthfulness. The echoes of Genesis 3 are hard to miss.

### Summary

Central to the sin of Adam and Eve was a denial of God's goodness and truthfulness. By rejecting God's authority and following instead their own desires and the serpent's temptations, they inverted the proper ordering of relationships between God, humanity and the rest of creation, displacing God's word from its rightful place and placing false faith in Satan's lies.

The problem of our sin runs so deep that we cannot and will not save ourselves. Sin is decreational, and only the Creator can recreate his world. Yet he must do this in a manner that upholds the goodness and truth of his word.

---

20. D. A. Carson, *The Gospel According to John*, Pillar New Testament Commentary (Leicester: Apollos; Grand Rapids: Eerdmans, 1991), p. 214.

## The consequences of sin

### *Introduction*

We have considered the nature of human sin, and the negative consequences inherent within it, such as the harm done to a relationship when one party stops trusting in the words of another. However, sin has further consequences beyond itself, imposed by God as an additional punishment for wrongdoing committed against him. This is such an important strand in the biblical testimony that we need to deal with it separately.

We begin back in Genesis 3, this time looking at verses 14–24, in which God declares his response to the sin of Adam and Eve. Startlingly, whereas God in chapters 1–2 is repeatedly said to 'bless' his creation (1:22, 28; 2:3), he now curses it (3:14, 17). Although God's blessings of the first two chapters are not wholly withdrawn, they turn sour. For example, in 1:28 we are told, 'God blessed [Adam and Eve] and said to them, "Be fruitful and increase in number; fill the earth and subdue it. Rule over the fish of the sea and the birds of the air and over every living creature that moves on the ground."' Clearly, the gifts of childbearing and work are part of this blessed vocation. But now in Genesis 3, under the experience of God's curse, childbearing will be marked by pain (v. 16) and work will be characterized by 'painful toil' (vv. 17–19). Again, in Genesis 2:18–25 the gift of marriage is seen as an unequivocal blessing, but Genesis 3:16 explains that the relationship between man and woman will now be marred by conflict.[21] Most importantly, Genesis 1–2 was about the giving of life, whereas in Genesis 3:19 God pronounces the sentence of death.

It is important to note that God imposes all of these consequences of sin. The pain, toil, conflict and death of Genesis 3:14–19 do not come about mechanically or impersonally; rather, God acts to bring them about. It is impossible to avoid seeing these verses as a judicial sentence, a punishment imposed by a judge. The subject of death is particularly significant in the context of God's warning in Genesis 2:17, and merits special consideration.

### *The nature of death*

What is the nature of the 'death' threatened in Genesis 2:17? The most obvious answer is that it refers to physical death, for this is the way the term is used elsewhere in Genesis, not least in connection with the death of Adam

---

21. There is debate among commentators about the precise nature of Eve's 'desire' in Gen. 3:16, but the idea of conflict is inescapable (Wenham, *Genesis 1–15*, pp. 81–82).

himself in Genesis 5:5. Physical death is implied also in the imagery of Genesis 3:19, 'dust you are and to dust you will return'.

Having said that, there are good reasons for thinking that 'death' here is not limited to physical death. First, as Augustine noted back in the fourth century, physical death does not come immediately upon Adam and Eve, despite the warning of Genesis 2:17 that (literally) '*in the day* [*bĕyôm*] you eat of it you will surely die' (italics added).[22] Gordon Wenham draws attention to the use of a very similar Hebrew expression in 1 Kings 2:37 (repeated in v. 42), where King Solomon warns Shimei, 'The day you [disobey me], you can be sure you will die.'[23] When Shimei does disobey, he is executed forthwith. Adam's case in Genesis is strangely different, for by the reckoning of Genesis 5:4, he does not die physically for at least 800 years after eating the forbidden fruit.[24] This sort of consideration prompted Augustine to ask whether, in fulfilment of God's word, another kind of 'death' came upon Adam on the day itself (though he did not mean by this to deny that the physical death that eventually came was also part of the fulfilment).[25]

Genesis 3 has a penalty that comes into effect immediately; namely, exclusion from the loving presence of God: 'The LORD God banished [Adam] from the Garden of Eden to work the ground from which he had been taken' (v. 23). This banishment is closely connected to the idea of death, for the idea of leaving Eden to return to the ground from where he had come alludes to a similar statement four verses earlier:

By the sweat of your brow
   you will eat your food
until you return to the ground,
   since from it you were taken;

---

22. Augustine, *City of God*, trans. Henry Bettenson (London: Penguin, 1984), bk. 13, ch. 12.

23. All three texts (Gen. 2:17; 1 Kgs 2:37, 42) contain the same Hebrew phrase underlying the words 'in the day . . . you will surely die'.

24. We do not know Adam's age at the time of the fall, but we do know that it preceded the birth of his children; hence we arrive at this figure of 800 years. The extraordinarily long lifespans of those who lived before the flood only furthers our point – physical death is far from immediate.

25. A similar distinction between different kinds of death is found in Irenaeus, *Against Heresies*, in *The Ante-Nicene Fathers*, vol. 1 (Grand Rapids: Eerdmans, 1973), bk. 2, ch. 33, pp. 410–411, and bk. 5, ch. 27, p. 556.

for dust you are
and to dust you will return.
(v. 19)[26]

This connection between death and banishment is confirmed elsewhere in Scripture. Death implies exclusion from the presence of God. Thus, from the safety of the fish's belly, Jonah reflects on the fact that he nearly drowned: 'I said, "I have been banished from your sight"' (Jon. 2:4). Similarly, one of the things that most terrifies the psalmist about his impending mortality is that

No-one remembers you when he is dead.
Who praises you from his grave?
(Ps. 6:5)

But the Scriptures also make the same connection the other way round: exclusion from the presence of God implies death. Gordon Wenham concludes from Leviticus 13:45–46, Numbers 5:2–4 and 1 Samuel 15:35 that 'to be expelled from the camp of Israel or to be rejected by God was to experience a living death', observing that 'in both situations gestures of mourning were appropriate'.[27] Again, the exile of the Israelites to Babylon is depicted in terms of death in Ezekiel 37:1–11, even though they were physically alive. In all these cases, the important thing about 'exclusion' is not geographical separation – God is not absent in every sense from Babylon, for his lordship continues to be exercised there.[28] He is absent in the sense that fullness of his blessing is not to be found there.[29]

---

26. Geerhardus Vos, *Biblical Theology: Old and New Testaments* (Grand Rapids: Eerdmans, 1948), pp. 50–51. See pp. 47–51 for further discussion of the character of the 'death' mentioned in Gen. 2:17.

27. Wenham, *Genesis 1–15*, p. 90.

28. For a helpful discussion of the nature of God's 'presence' even in hell see Henri Blocher, 'Everlasting Punishment and the Problem of Evil', in N. M. De S. Cameron (ed.), *Universalism and the Doctrine of Hell* (Carlisle: Paternoster; Grand Rapids: Baker, 1992), pp. 283–312. See also Charles Quarles, 'The 'APO of 2 Thessalonians 1:9 and the Nature of Eternal Punishment', *Westminster Theological Journal* 59 (1997), pp. 201–211.

29. Of course, in the midst of many of the horrific experiences associated with the exile to Babylon, God's good hand was not completely withdrawn (see e.g. his gracious treatment of the exiles in the book of Daniel). The same is true of the

The idea that death is more than simply a biological phenomenon is particularly clear from Ephesians 2:1–2, where the apostle Paul reminds his readers that, before they knew Christ, they 'were *dead* in [their] transgressions and sins, in which [they] used to live' (italics added).[30] In other words, while biologically they were alive and well, they nonetheless experienced spiritual death. That is why it makes sense to say that believers have been 'made . . . alive' and 'raised . . . up' (Eph. 2:5–6), and that we have 'crossed over from death to life' (John 5:24). This is not to deny that Jesus promised his followers a future bodily resurrection from physical death (e.g. John 11:25–26 in the context of 11:38–45; 1 Cor. 15), just as his own death was bodily and physical (e.g. Luke 24:37–43). We are merely observing that there is a spiritual resurrection from a spiritual death also.

In summary, 'death' in Genesis 2:17 includes physical death, but is not restricted to this. The immediate context prompts us to look deeper, and we see that there is a spiritual death also, associated with banishment from God's loving presence and withdrawal of his blessing.

### Is death a punishment?

We have become so accustomed to the reality of death that to us it just seems to be part of the way things are, a 'natural process' that comes to us all. But we need to remember that it was not part of the way things were created in the beginning. Against the backdrop of Genesis 1–2 it is very *unnatural*. There would have been no death if Adam and Eve had obeyed God's word.

Thus when we come to the genealogy of Genesis 5, it may seem strange to us that the writer should bother to specify of every generation (except Enoch, v. 24) that 'he died'. It seems almost too obvious to need saying. Yet in the

---

expulsion from Eden – God is gracious to Adam and Eve in various ways, even after their sin. Yet the dominant note of blessing in these contexts is the prophetic hope of return from exile, the promise of a return to Eden where God's blessings are fully enjoyed. This hope is possible because even in exile God had not abandoned his people, but planned to send his Messiah to rescue them from their sin. The prophets make it clear that some were spared for this reason: God preserved a remnant who would inherit a better future (e.g. Isa. 11; Jer. 50:19–20; Mic. 2:12). As we shall see, hell is different. He has no plans to rescue from there. Even hope is absent (cf. 1 Thess. 4:13).

30. Literally, 'in which you used to *walk*', but the point is the same. Here are dead people walking about! The death referred to is not physical.

original context, death was still a surprise, an unwelcome intruder in God's perfect creation. The incessant repetition of 'and then he died . . . and then he died . . . and then he died' functions almost as a lament, a sad meditation on the tragedy resulting from the sin of Genesis 3. The apostle Paul, commenting on these events, puts it this way: 'sin entered the world through one man, and death through sin, and in this way death came to all men, because all sinned' (Rom. 5:12). The very fact of our mortality, then, is a penalty for sin. Indeed, 'the wages of sin is death' (Rom. 6:23).

Although all must die in the end, the Bible also portrays God judging individuals or groups of people for their sin by bringing upon them an *untimely* death. Many examples could be given. Consider the flood at the time of Noah, in which God acts to wipe humankind from the face of the earth as a response to the evil he found in their hearts (Gen. 6:5). Consider the devastating plagues God visited on the Egyptians at the time of the exodus, or how he later drowned the Egyptian army in its pursuit of the Israelites through the sea. If we are embarrassed by these mighty acts of judgment, or we think it somehow 'out of character' for God to act like this, then we are out of step with the biblical narrative. The plagues are intended by God specifically as acts of self-revelation (see in particular Exod. 7:3–5; 9:13–16), and it was God's defeat of the Egyptians, even more than the safe passage of the Israelites through the miraculously parted sea, that called forth praise from his people (Exod. 15:1–21). Consider the fate of those living in the Promised Land of Canaan when the Israelites invaded, being instructed by God, 'do not leave alive anything that breathes. Completely destroy them' (Deut. 20:16–17; cf. Josh. 11:14–15). Again, while many wince at what appears to be a divinely sanctioned genocide, there is no hint of apology or regret in the biblical account. That said, it is important to realize that the judgment comes as a proportionate and just recompense for evil deeds: the conquest of Canaan was delayed for four generations until the heinousness of the crimes of those who dwelt there justly merited it (see Gen. 15:16). The New Testament similarly thinks of death as something imposed in accordance with what we *deserve* (Rom. 1:32; cf. Rev. 2:23). It has moral, judicial content.

The character of death as punishment is clear also from many of the prophecies concerning the exile of Israel (building on the death–exile connection established above). It is in direct response to the people's idolatry that God threatens the deathly triad of sword, famine and plague (e.g. Jer. 14:12; Ezek. 5:12–17). Even the deportation to Babylon itself was penal (Ezra 9:13; Dan. 9:4–19; Neh. 9:6–37). This exclusion from the Promised Land was the climax of the covenant curses promised in the law of Moses (Deut. 28:64–68; 29:28) – God's punishment of a rebellious people.

It is impossible to escape the conclusion that death is God's punishment for sin.[31]

### Final judgment: 'the second death'

We have considered two ways in which the Bible speaks of death – a spiritual death entered into by Adam and Eve on the day of their disobedience and now experienced by unbelievers (cf. Eph. 2:1), and the physical death of the body. There is one other way in which Scripture employs the term; namely, to refer to the fate of those without Christ at the final judgment. In this sense, death is a synonym for the suffering experienced in hell. In the book of Revelation it is referred to as 'the second death' (Rev. 2:11; 20:6, 14; 21:8).

Jesus spoke of the same reality, distinct from physical death, when he urged his hearers, 'Do not be afraid of those who kill the body but cannot kill the soul. Rather, be afraid of the One who can destroy both soul and body in hell' (Matt. 10:28). Notice here that the punishment of hell comes directly from God's hand.

The theme of exclusion, which we have noted already in connection with the first two kinds of death, is also prominent in biblical depictions of hell. Consider Jesus' forewarning of the terrible words that some will hear him say on the last day: ' "I don't know you or where you come from. *Away from me*, all you evildoers!" There will be weeping there, and gnashing of teeth, when you see Abraham, Isaac and Jacob and all the prophets in the kingdom of God, but you yourselves *thrown out*' (Luke 13:27–28; italics added).[32]

### God's wrath

So far, we have looked at how God must punish sin in order to uphold his *truth-fulness*: he promised that sin would lead to death, and he is faithful to his word. However, this is not the only biblical perspective. Scripture also views God's response to sin from another angle. He is holy, and sin is a personal affront to him. It angers him. His wrath burns against sinners.

The language of God's wrath in response to sin pervades the Scriptures.[33] His judicial acts are not dispassionate, but reflect his personal hostility to evil.

---

31. This raises the question of why believers still die, since we are delivered from the consequences of sin by the death of Christ. We discuss this in the postscript to chapter 10, sect. 2.

32. See also Matt. 8:12; 13:40–42, 49–50; 22:13; 24:51; 25:30.

33. The number of references to God's 'wrath' or 'anger' is so large that we cannot begin to list them. We offer only a few examples.

We are told that Israel's idolatry in making and worshipping the golden calf 'aroused the LORD's wrath so that he was angry enough to destroy' the people (Deut. 9:8), and indeed many of them were killed by plague and sword (Exod. 32). Similarly, Moses interpreted the plague that claimed the lives of 14,700 Israelites following the sin of Korah in this way: 'Wrath has come out from the LORD' (Num. 16:46). Again, 'the LORD's anger burned against Uzzah because of his irreverent act' of touching the ark of God, and 'therefore God struck him down' (2 Sam. 6:7). The events of the exile, which we have considered in some detail above, are also depicted as a manifestation of God's anger (e.g. 2 Kgs 17:17–23; 2 Chr. 36:16; Jer. 32:29; Lam. 2:2–3).

In the New Testament we also find references to the immediate outworking of God's wrath; for example, in the striking down of Ananias and Sapphira in Acts 5. More frequently, the New Testament employs the language of God's wrath with reference to a future 'day of God's wrath, when his righteous judgment will be revealed' (Rom. 2:5; cf. 12:19; Col. 3:6; Eph. 5:6). The book of Revelation, which portrays in vivid detail the events of that last day, speaks of the Lord Jesus as the one who 'treads the winepress of the fury of the wrath of God Almighty' (Rev. 19:15), a winepress in which his enemies are 'trampled' until their 'blood flowed . . . rising as high as the horses' bridles for a distance of 1,600 stadia' (Rev. 14:20). These are not easy images, and we do not cite them glibly. The truth is, they stand as part of God's gracious self-revelation. We dare not ignore them.[34]

### Summary

Genesis 3 shows the far-reaching consequences of human sin. It provokes God to anger and calls forth his curse. Aspects of the created order that had been full of blessing (marriage, work, childbearing) are now marked by pain and frustration. Most devastatingly of all, sin has brought death into the world – not merely physical death but the spiritual death of being banished from God's loving presence. A grim picture indeed.

## Truth, goodness, justice and salvation

Sin, as an act of decreation, is a denial of God's truthfulness and justice. In judging sin, God acts to reaffirm both. Consider first his truthfulness. Once

---

34. Some have attempted to escape the reality of God's anger and retributive punishment. We find their arguments unpersuasive, and have engaged them specifically in chapter 10, sect. 2, and chapter 11, sects. 2 and 3.

Adam and Eve had eaten the forbidden fruit in Eden, it was inconceivable that God should withhold the penalty he had threatened in Genesis 2:17, for that would have been to validate the serpent's insinuation that God was a liar ('you will not surely die', Gen. 3:2). The same is true of the exile. When God expelled his people from the Promised Land through the agency of the Assyrian army in 2 Kings 17, he did neither more nor less than he had promised to do.

What about God's goodness? The prayers of both Ezra and Daniel after the exile affirm not only God's justice but also his righteousness and covenant faithfulness in having executed judgment (Neh. 9:32–33; cf. Dan. 9:13–15). Very significantly, it is precisely on the basis of this faithfulness that Daniel and Ezra humbly confess the sin of Israel and plead for forgiveness, for the same covenant that promised judgment also promised mercy (e.g. Deut. 30:3). If God were to go back on his promise to punish sin, then his promise of mercy would be undermined also. Both God's judgment and his mercy are bound up with his character as a truthful God, faithful to his promises.

In fact we can put the matter quite sharply in this way: for God to punish sin means he upholds his own goodness and truthfulness that were manifest in creation in the beginning. By contrast, for God to fail to punish sin would mean denying his own truthfulness and thus exacerbating the very problem of *decreation* to which he must respond.

Having outlined the problem that faces humanity, we can begin to discern the shape an adequate solution must take. The disastrous consequences of our false faith must be put right. Salvation must be an act of illumination, for we have exchanged the truth about God for a lie, worshipping idols instead of the true God. Salvation must be an act of liberation, for we are captive to the delusions of our false faith, and cannot save ourselves. Salvation must be an act of divine grace, God's work from beginning to end, for the desires of our hearts are set against God – we do not even *want* to save ourselves. Salvation must be an act of reconciliation, for we are alienated from God and hostile to him. Finally, salvation must be an act of conquest, for we are oppressed by the devil, and need someone to win the victory for us. All this must be accomplished in a way that upholds the truthfulness of God's word.

In fact, the need for God's word to be proved true also informs the situation from another angle. In Genesis 1–2 God expressed his intention to create a perfect world. But this world was ruined by human sin. God cannot allow this state of affairs to persist, for this would be to concede defeat, to admit his original purpose in creation had been frustrated, and to accept he could do nothing.

God's truthfulness therefore requires him simultaneously to punish sin, and yet also to restore creation in line with his original purposes. God cannot compromise either of these requirements, yet this seems to present a dilemma, as Athanasius recognized as early as the fourth century:

> It would, of course, have been unthinkable that God should go back upon His word and that man, having transgressed, should not die; but it was equally monstrous that beings which once had shared the nature of the Word should perish and turn back again into non-existence through corruption. It was unworthy of the goodness of God that creatures made by Him should be brought to nothing through the deceit wrought upon man by the devil . . . Yet, true though this is . . . it was unthinkable that God, the Father of Truth, should go back upon his word regarding death in order to ensure our continued existence. He could not falsify Himself; what, then, was God to do?[35]

God must find a way to restore his creation to its original goodness, without compromising his promise that sin will bring death. His truthfulness requires it. Any adequate account of salvation must therefore answer this question: How can God save sinful people from death while remaining faithful to his promise to punish sin?

## Relationships within the Trinity

### Introduction

As we have already seen, God is good towards his creation. Many passages of Scripture meditate on his character as a generous giver. From him comes 'every good and perfect gift' (Jas 1:17). Every creature looks to him for daily provision of food:

> When you give it to them,
>     they gather it up;
> when you open your hand,
>     they are satisfied with good things.
> (Ps. 104:28)

---

35. Athanasius, *On the Incarnation* (New York: St. Vladimir's Seminary Press, 1993), sects. 6–7, p. 32. For further discussion of Athanasius' understanding of Christ's atoning work see chapter 5.

These observations all belong to the doctrine of creation. When it comes to his work of redemption, God's generosity is seen in even brighter colours. Indeed, from one point of view it could be said that the generosity of God the Father is the basis for his redemptive work – God the Father '*gave* his one and only Son' (John 3:16; italics added). But how deep does this generosity go? Is God the generous, loving Giver all the way down? We can begin to answer this question by reflecting on relationships within the Trinity, where God's generosity is rooted.

### Generosity within the Trinity: the giving Father

One of the most poignant moments in the earthly life of Jesus is his prayer in the Garden of Gethsemane, where he pleads with his Father, 'If it is possible, may this cup be taken from me. Yet not as I will, but as you will' (Matt. 26:39). In spite of this plea, God the Father still sends his Son to the cross, and it is therefore perfectly proper to ask what kind of a father he must be.[36] To answer this we must respect the principle we outlined at the start of this chapter: God must be allowed to be his own witness. We must endeavour to understand the cross and the relationship between Jesus and his Father according to the teaching of Scripture. When we do so, we find that Jesus is utterly convinced of his Father's love for him, even though it was the Father's purpose that he should die at Calvary.

Let us begin with Jesus' teaching about his relationship with the Father in John 5.[37] Jesus has just healed a man on the Sabbath (vv. 8–9), provoking claims of Sabbath-breaking from his Jewish opponents (v. 16). Jesus begins his defence by explaining that, just as his Father works on the Sabbath, so he is entitled to do likewise (v. 17). His opponents are outraged, for they recognize the implicit claim to deity, and imagine that he has set himself up as a rival to God (v. 18).

To address this misunderstanding, Jesus must clarify and explain his relationship with his Father. He begins and ends this section of his speech by explaining that he never acts independently of his Father, but always at his Father's behest, doing his Father's will (vv. 19, 30). Within this framework, Jesus asserts that his Father loves him (v. 20), and goes on to explain that his Father shows this love by *giving to the Son*. This giving is marked in two critical

---

36. Here, of course, we touch on the charge that penal substitution amounts to 'cosmic child abuse' – a criticism we address specifically in chapter 9, sect. 2.

37. A helpful discussion of this passage is contained in D. A. Carson, *The Difficult Doctrine of the Love of God* (Leicester: IVP, 2000), pp. 35–49; and *John*, pp. 246–267.

ways: the Father gives to the Son 'life in himself' (v. 26) and 'authority to judge' (v. 27; cf. v. 22).

Let us explore each in turn. The point about 'life *in himself*' (v. 26; italics added) is that it is the kind of life God the Father has, as the parallel 'as . . . so' construction makes clear. The Father's 'life in himself' is his self-existence, the fact that he is uncreated and is without beginning or end. Clearly, this is something only God possesses, and so if Jesus enjoys it he must be fully divine. But Jesus says more than this. He says his Father has 'given' him such self-existence. This gift cannot be confined to the pages of history for the simple reason that self-existence has no beginning. It must be something the Father has given the Son *eternally*. Thus we are given a window on to Jesus' eternal relationship to his Father. As D. A. Carson rightly comments, 'The impartation of life-in-himself to the Son must be an act belonging to eternity, of a piece with the external Father/Son relationship, which is itself of a piece with the relationship between the Word and God, a relationship that existed "in the beginning" (1:1).'[38]

The gift of 'authority to judge' (v. 27) is different in this respect, for it relates to the created world, and has a definite beginning in time. The purpose of this gift is the Father's desire that the Son be honoured by those whom he has made (v. 23).

Jesus therefore defines his relationship with his Father, in both time and eternity, in terms of the Father's loving generosity. Jesus is crystal clear that his Father loves him, and this gives him confidence always to do his Father's will. This is all the more remarkable when we remember that Jesus repeatedly makes clear in John's Gospel that the Father's will for him is that he lay down his life at the cross (e.g. John 10:7–18). Although 'troubled' at the fate that awaits him, he actually prays to travel the course that leads to his death, knowing that this will bring glory to his Father (John 12:27–28).

Thus the picture starts to become clear. Jesus understands the cross as his Father's will for him, but does not perceive any conflict between this task and his Father's love for him. He knows that his Father's purposes are good. Indeed, the cross is the path by which Jesus will enter his heavenly glory – a glory for which his Father destined him. This emphasis emerges clearly in Philippians 2:6–11, and also in John 17:1, a prayer offered on the very evening

---

38. Carson, *John*, p. 257. Raymond E. Brown is less content with this interpretation, but overlooks that the fundamental relationship between Father and Son is precisely what Jesus needs to establish in John 5 (*The Gospel According to John*, Anchor Bible [London: Geoffrey Chapman, 1966], p. 215).

Jesus was betrayed. Jesus' confidence in his Father's plan meant he was res-olutely determined to die. As he pointed out to the disciples on the road to Emmaus, 'Did not the Christ *have to suffer these things* and then enter his glory?' (Luke 24:26; italics added) .

In summary, whether one looks in eternity or in time, the Father emerges as one who loves to give to his Son. In eternity he gives 'life in himself', and in time, by way of the crucifixion, he gives nothing less than authority over the whole world. We are accustomed to thinking of God's love towards *us*, and cer-tainly that is a marvellous thing. But we must not neglect to consider the sur-passing greatness of God's love for his Son. After all, his plan for the fullness of time is 'to bring all things in heaven and on earth together under one head, even Christ' (Eph. 1:10).

### Trinitarian relations and trinitarian actions

So far we have been thinking about the Father's love for the Son, and the way this is demonstrated in the Father's generous giving to the Son. This giving suggests an asymmetry in the trinitarian relationship. Father and Son are not mirror images of each other, for the Father gives and the Son receives, and these roles are irreversible. The church Fathers who defended the Nicene Creed in 325 recognized this asymmetry, repeatedly emphasizing that the Father and Son are not 'two brothers'.

This asymmetry emphatically does not imply that the Son is any less divine than the Father. As we have just seen, the Father gives to the Son 'life in himself' (John 5:26) – the same kind of life as he himself has. Rather, the Father–Son relationship stresses a real personal relationship, in which each party is dependent upon the other: there cannot be a 'father' unless there is also a 'son', and vice versa.[39] This kind of relationship, in which each person depends upon the other in this way, is sometimes called a *correlative relationship*. The two parties in the correlative relationship are mutually dependent, yet are not interchangeable. They are inseparable yet distinguishable.

This idea of the inseparability of the persons takes us to a principle known as *inseparable operation*. As Augustine of Hippo put it, 'the Father, and the Son, and the Holy Spirit, as they are indivisible, so [they] work indivisibly'.[40] The

---

39. Analogous reasoning applies to relationships involving the Spirit, though this need not concern us here.

40. Augustine, *On the Trinity*, in *Nicene and Post-Nicene Fathers*, ser. I, vol. 3 (Grand Rapids: Eerdmans, 1956), pp. 17–228, bk. 1, sect. 7 (p. 20). The idea of inseparable operation was not original to Augustine, though he made great use of it.

principle of inseparable operation highlights that the persons of the Trinity do not act without each other any more than they can exist without each other. Indeed, the basis for their inseparable operation is their mutual indwelling, as Jesus explains in John 14:10: 'Don't you believe that I am in the Father, and that the Father is in me? The words I say to you are not just my own. Rather, it is the Father, living in me, who is doing his work.'[41]

This is important, because it safeguards the claim that our salvation is the work of the triune God, not an action done by one of the persons of the Trinity acting independently, much less by one person acting against the others. If the principle of inseparable operation did not hold, there would be no guarantee that the saving work of the individual persons would be effective. For example, suppose the Son decided to act completely independently of the Father. How could he be sure his work would be acceptable to the Father? The Father might even choose to *oppose* his work, thereby compromising its effectiveness, jeopardizing our salvation and dividing the Trinity. The principle of inseparable operation establishes that the Trinity is not a collection of three deities who each does his own thing, but one God in three persons who always act together, with unity of purpose.

It is important to say that although the persons of the Trinity act inseparably, their actions remain distinguishable, just as the persons themselves are distinguishable.[42] Although each is involved in the work of the others, it does not mean they all perform exactly the same function. For example, it was the Son, and not the Father or the Spirit, who became a man at the incarnation. And it was the Spirit, and not the Father or the Son, who came upon the believers at Pentecost.

One significant implication of this is that a particular action can be done *by* one person of the Trinity (the subject of the action) *to* another (the object). We can properly talk, as Jesus does consistently throughout John's Gospel, of

---

41. We discuss the idea of mutual indwelling, or *perichoresis*, in more detail in chapter 11, sect. 1.

42. To deny this comes close to *Sabellianism* or *Modalism*, a heresy refuted by the early church Fathers in which Father and Son are treated as indistinguishable and fundamentally the same person. For examples of refutations see Tertullian, *Against Praxeas*, in *The Ante-Nicene Fathers*, vol. 3 (Grand Rapids: Eerdmans, 1968), pp. 597–627; and Hippolytus' refutation of Noetus in *The Refutation of All Heresies*, in *The Ante-Nicene Fathers*, vol. 5 (Grand Rapids: Eerdmans, 1968), bk. 9, pp. 125–139. A brief summary of this error may be found in Wayne Grudem, *Systematic Theology: An Introduction to Biblical Doctrine* (Leicester: IVP, 1994), p. 242.

the Father (subject) sending the Son (object). Equally, we can talk of the Son (subject) speaking or praying to his Father (object). To speak in this way does not 'divide' the Trinity. On the contrary, by observing the appropriate differences in the actions of the persons, it preserves the appropriate asymmetry between them and thereby preserves the oneness of the Trinity via their correlative relationships.

The Bible explicitly teaches that one person of the Trinity can be the subject of an action of which another is the object. For example, Scripture affirms plainly that the Father *loves* the Son (John 3:35; 5:20; 17:23); the Father *sent* the Son (John 6:39), *giving* him to redeem a sinful world (John 3:16; Rom. 8:32); the Father *raised* the Son from the dead (Gal. 1:1; Eph. 1:20; see also Acts 2:24; Rom. 6:4; 1 Cor. 6:14); the Father has *exalted* the Son (Phil. 2:9); and the Father *glorifies* the Son (John 17:1, 22, 24).[43] Similarly, there are many examples where the Son is the subject and the Father the object: the Son *loves* and *obeys* the Father (John 14:31); and the Son *glorifies* the Father (John 17:1). This kind of interaction is not restricted to the Father and the Son; there are several instances involving the Spirit. For example, both the Father and the Son *sent* the Spirit (John 3:34; 14:16, 26; 15:26; 16:7; Acts 1:4);[44] the Spirit *sent* the Son into the desert (Mark 1:12); and the Spirit *glorifies* the Son (John 16:14).

This is important in the present debate about penal substitution, because some have suggested that for the Son (subject) to propitiate his Father (object) would be to divide the Trinity.[45] But this is simply not true. The principle of inseparable operation underlines that the Father and the Son share a unity of will and purpose. Penal substitution does not imply that the

---

43. There are many more examples in which the Son is the *indirect object* of an action performed by the Father. E.g. the Father *shows* the Son all he does (John 5:20); the Father *gave* the Son work to do (John 17:4) and words to say (John 17:8); the Father has *given* believers to the Son (John 6:37, 39; 10:29; 17:6, 9, 24) and authority to the Son (John 17:2), and has *placed* everything in the hands of the Son (John 3:35).

44. For a concise and helpful overview of the division that arose in 1054 between the Eastern and Western churches in connection with this point, see Grudem, *Systematic Theology*, pp. 246–247.

45. This criticism has been made in recent years by Paul S. Fiddes, *Past Event and Present Salvation: The Christian Idea of Atonement* (London: Darton, Longman & Todd, 1989), p. 108; Joel B. Green and Mark D. Baker, *Recovering the Scandal of the Cross: Atonement in New Testament and Contemporary Contexts* (Downers Grove: IVP, 2000), p. 57; Tom Smail, *Once and for All: A Confession of the Cross* (London: Darton, Longman & Todd, 1998), pp. 86–87. We respond in more detail in chapter 11, sect. 1.

Father is unwillingly coerced into an attitude of forgiveness, or that the Son is unwillingly coerced into offering himself. When we say that the Son propitiates the Father, this is not to be understood as if the Son and the Father are acting against each other. They are fulfilling different roles in a plan to which both are equally committed, in pursuit of outcomes they both desire.

### Summary

The generosity of God we see in creation lies at the heart of his trinitarian character: God the Father *gives* to his Son. Jesus does not doubt this giving nature, even when his Father's will is for him to go to the cross. The divine persons exist in correlative relationships, and act inseparably. The asymmetry of these relationships allows one person to act upon another without compromising their trinitarian oneness.

We would expect these aspects of God's character – the giving nature of the Father, and the inseparability and asymmetry of their actions – to be reflected in God's work of redemption. To this we now turn.

## Redemption

### Introduction

In view of what we have seen of the 'giving' character of God the Father, it is perhaps unsurprising to discover that this theme is central to the doctrine of redemption. To begin with, the Father gives his Son to believers. This is especially clear in the narrative following the feeding of the five thousand in John 6. The crowd recall the manna from heaven, by which God miraculously fed their forefathers in the desert in the time of Moses. In reply to their request for a further miraculous sign, Jesus identifies himself as this 'bread', the gift from God the Father to his people:

> Jesus said to them, 'I tell you the truth, it is not Moses who has given you the bread from heaven, but it is my Father who gives you the true bread from heaven. For the bread of God is he who comes down from heaven and gives life to the world.'
> 'Sir,' they said, 'from now on give us this bread.'
> Then Jesus declared, 'I am the bread of life. He who comes to me will never go hungry, and he who believes in me will never be thirsty.' (John 6:32–35)

Later in John 6 another related truth emerges. Not only does the Father give the Son to believers, but he also gives believers to his Son (vv. 37–40).

In what follows, we shall explore these two aspects of the Father's giving in some detail. We begin with the gift of his Son to believers, both as the incarnate Son, the perfect man who did not sin, and also as the penal substitutionary sacrifice for sin. We pause to consider how penal substitution relates to the themes of God's truthfulness and justice, and then explore how it relates to three important consequences of the atonement: victory, reconciliation and ransom. We then turn to the second aspect of the Father's giving – the gift of believers to Jesus – and reflect on the way God unites us to Christ by faith.

### The gift of the incarnate Son

We are accustomed to seeing the incarnation of Jesus as a loving act of humility, as emphasized in Philippians 2:5–8:

> Your attitude should be the same as that of Christ Jesus:
>
> Who, being in very nature God,
> did not consider equality with God something to be grasped,
> but made himself nothing,
> taking the very nature of a servant,
> being made in human likeness.
> And being found in appearance as a man,
> he humbled himself
> and became obedient to death – even death on a cross!

To this important theme we must add another. The Son became incarnate in order to bring completion to creation. For God intended his creation to be ruled by a perfect human being, and without such a ruler creation is incomplete, lacking, defective. The sinless Lord Jesus Christ is the ruler creation needs, for he is truly, authentically human in the way all human beings are supposed to be.

This aspect of Jesus' work is sometimes called *recapitulation*, a term coined by Irenaeus of Lyons to denote the idea of going over something again to get it right.[46] It is somewhat analogous to how we might go back over a word we have written, printing the letters more boldly to make the word clearer or to correct a spelling mistake. Jesus was the perfect man, succeeding where Adam had so disastrously failed.[47]

---

46. See Irenaeus, *Against Heresies*, bk. 5, pp. 526–567 (especially ch. 21, pp. 125–139).

47. The importance of the incarnation exposes a fundamental flaw in the account of the atonement given by Gustaf Aulén in Christus Victor: *An Historical Study of the*

We find this idea in the apostle Paul's designation of Jesus as 'the second man', in contrast to 'the first man Adam' (1 Cor. 15:45–49; cf. Rom. 5:12–21). Jesus relived Adam's life and experienced Adam's temptation, but where Adam became a transgressor, Jesus remained righteous. From another perspective, Jesus was the second Israel, brought out of Egypt as a child just as was the Jewish nation in its infancy (such is the perspective of Matt. 2:15, quoting Hos. 11:1, which in turn reflects on the events of the exodus). Just as Israel endured a period of testing in the desert for forty years (see e.g. Deut. 8:2–3), so also Jesus 'was in the desert for forty days, being tempted by Satan' (Mark 1:13). Again, where Israel proved faithless, Jesus was faithful to God's covenant. From still another perspective, Jesus was the true Son of David (e.g. Mark 10:48), and thus in some ways he relived the life of the kings of Israel. Where they failed to lead God's people in loving obedience to God, Jesus triumphed gloriously.

It is worth reflecting in more detail on the wilderness temptations of Christ in Matthew 4, for here we find the counterpart to the events of Genesis 3 that plunged the human race into ruin. Satan adopts the same approach here as in the Garden of Eden, questioning the truthfulness of God's word. When Satan says to Jesus, '*If* you are the Son of God' (Matt. 4:6; italics added), he is casting doubt upon God's verdict on the matter, declared by the voice from heaven at

---

*Three Main Types of the Idea of the Atonement*, trans. A. G. Herbert (London: SPCK, 1945; first pub. 1931). Aulén objects to so-called 'Latin' views of the atonement, including penal substitution, claiming that 'in the payment of the required satisfaction . . . the continuity of Divine operation is lost; for the satisfaction is offered by Christ as man, as the sinless Man on behalf of the sinners' (p. 163). In Aulén's view, penal substitution is one of a number of unacceptable understandings of the atonement that represent God's atoning work as '*discontinuous*' (p. 22; italics original; see also pp. 102, 107, 147); that is to say, 'the Divine operation in the Atonement was regarded as *interrupted* by the compensation paid from the human side, from below' (p. 147; italics added). But this criticism amounts to a denial that God could atone for sin if he did so 'from the human side'; i.e. having assumed a human nature and become incarnate. In other words, Aulén ends up attacking not merely a particular view of the atonement, but the place of the incarnation! Such a position is untenable, for the New Testament affirms from beginning to end that it was the *incarnate* Son of God who atoned for our sins. The fact that Aulén believed that the victory was won by the Lord Jesus Christ, whom he affirmed was God *incarnate*, merely highlights the inconsistency of his argument.

Jesus' baptism: 'This is my Son' (Matt. 3:17). Jesus' response is not to deny God's word as Adam and Eve did, but to reassert it in a series of Old Testament quotations. He does not have false faith in Satan but true faith in his Father. And therefore, unsurprisingly, in the final temptation he spurns idolatry. He will not exchange the worship of God for the worship of Satan.

Jesus led the authentic human life in perfect obedience to the word of God and thus in perfect relationship to his Father. He alone succeeded where Adam, Israel and the kings of Israel had failed. As we look at the incarnate Christ we see humanity as it was intended to be, humanity free from the corruption wrought by the fall. Of course, Jesus possessed both a human and a divine nature, and his ability to perform a miracle such as the calming of the storm (Mark 4:35–41) doubtless owes much to his divinity. Yet might there also be something of perfect humanity discernable in this act? Adam was given dominion in the Garden of Eden, and was instructed to 'subdue' the earth (Gen. 1:28). Here we see Jesus subduing the very forces of nature: 'even the wind and the waves *obey* him!' (Mark 4:41; italics added). Humanity's rule over creation is finally fulfilled in Jesus, the perfect man (Heb. 2:5–9; cf. Ps. 8).

This consideration of the life of Jesus accomplishes two things. First, by contemplating the perfect standard, we are able to see just how far humanity has fallen from it, and thus how great the effects of decreation have been. Secondly, it highlights the biblical teaching that Jesus is the head of a new humanity. In his resurrection he became 'the firstborn from among the dead' (Col. 1:18), the 'firstfruits of those who have fallen asleep' (1 Cor. 15:20). This language indicates he is the first of many who will be transformed and glorified beyond the grave. A humanity made new constitutes the pinnacle of God's new creation. But at this stage we encounter an unresolved problem. The resurrection of Jesus is his vindication before God, and it makes sense that Jesus should be vindicated: he led a perfect human life. What is less clear is how believers, who will share in his resurrection, come to be vindicated. Obviously, his perfection is important in this; somehow his sinlessness enables him to deal with our sin. But we have not yet reached the piece in the jigsaw that adequately explains how.

### The promised gift

God's gift of his Son, the Lord Jesus, was promised many times in the Old Testament. As far back as Genesis 3:15 God declared the offspring of the woman would crush the head of the serpent. As the Old Testament progresses we encounter promises of a prophet like Moses (Deut. 18:15–18), a kingly figure 'like a Son of Man' (Dan. 7:13), 'a priest . . . in the order of Melchizedek' (Ps. 110:4) and so on. The New Testament insists that God's promises are fulfilled in Christ (2 Cor. 1:20) – that he is the focal point, so to speak, of the Old Testament revelation – and Jesus himself insisted that 'the Scriptures . . . testify about me' (John 5:39; cf. Luke 24:27).

The promises of the Old Testament anticipate many different aspects of the work of Christ. It is unsurprising that his work should be so multifaceted, for, as we have seen, the problems created by decreation and false faith are many. Interestingly, some of the Old Testament promises seem to require a human saviour (e.g. the promise of a king from the line of King David, 2 Sam. 7), whereas others anticipate the action of God himself (e.g. Ezek. 34:11). To combine these prophecies is to anticipate a redeemer who is both truly human and truly divine, without compromising either nature.

It is worth saying that God's promises are only valuable if he, the author, is true to the whole of his word. If his promises of salvation conflict with or overrule his warnings of judgment, then his truthfulness is called into question, and neither promise can be trusted. We can have confidence in God's promises of salvation only if they do not contradict other things he has said.

### The promised gift of a penal substitute

The scope of God's promises is truly breathtaking: victory over the serpent, liberation from slavery to sin, deliverance from our spiritual enemies, a new covenant in which we are reconciled to God and our hearts are changed. In the life, death, resurrection and ascension of Jesus we see these promises fulfilled. We rightly praise God for these aspects of Jesus' work, for they reflect his dealing with the captivating and alienating aspects of the problem of false faith.

But false faith also has an ethical dimension: it is morally wrong and deserves punishment. As we have seen, this is part of the fabric of God's dealings with his creation (Gen. 2:17), just as it was written into his covenant with Israel (e.g. Deut. 30:17–18; Josh. 23:15–16). Those words of God that threaten punishment cannot be unsaid. To deny them would make God a liar, and would thereby compound the problem of decreation rather than solve it.

In setting up the problem of sin in this way, the Bible has already defined certain contours of what would constitute an adequate solution. We would expect an all-wise God who seeks relationship with sinful people to have made provision for the penal consequences of sin, on which he himself had laid such emphasis in the Scriptures. We would expect an atonement that deals not only with our sin but also with his own wrath against us, the retributive punishment we deserve.

Wonderfully, God has promised to deal with the penal consequences of our sin. We have reviewed the biblical texts most pertinent to this at some length in chapter 2. There we looked at a number of passages, all of which either anticipate or reflect upon the death of Christ as a penal substitutionary sacrifice for sin (Exod. 12; Lev. 16; Isa. 52:13 – 53:12; Mark; John; Rom. 3:21–26; Gal. 3:10–13; 1 Pet., especially 2:24 and 3:18). We shall not repeat the detailed exegetical work here, but merely summarize two of the most important conclusions.

First, Jesus bore the penal consequences of sin when he died. As Isaiah puts it, 'the *punishment* that brought us peace was upon him' (53:5; italics added). Elsewhere it was clear that God's *wrath* was poured out on his Son; for example, in the powerful Old Testament imagery of 'the cup' picked up in Mark 14:36 (cf. Ps. 75:8; Isa. 51:17–23; Jer. 25:15–29; Ezek. 23:31–34). That Jesus should die at all hints at his bearing sin's curse, for death only entered human experience on account of sin (Rom. 5:12). But the passages we explored in chapter 2 go further. Jesus experienced more than just *physical* death. In his cry of dereliction there are echoes of exclusion, reminiscent of Adam and Eve's eviction from Eden or Israel's exile from the Promised Land.

Secondly, Jesus bore the consequences of our sin *in our place*, as a substitute. It was a case of 'exclusive place-taking'. That is, he did not merely share in the punishment we deserve; he bore it *instead* of us. Thus Isaiah testified, 'he was pierced for our transgressions' (53:5). He had no guilt of his own, being innocent, but our guilt was imputed to him, and for this he suffered and died. As 2 Corinthians 5:21 puts it, 'God made him who had no sin to be sin for us, so that in him we might become the righteousness of God.'

It is because Christ bore God's wrath in our place that he is able to save us from it. The apostle Paul speaks of 'Jesus, who rescues us from the coming wrath' (1 Thess. 1:10). Or again, 'Since we have now been justified by his blood, how much more shall we be saved from God's wrath through him!' (Rom. 5:9).

### Penal substitution and the justice and truthfulness of God

Penal substitution upholds the truthfulness and justice of God: it is the means by which he saves people for relationship with himself without going back on his word that sin has to be punished. In addition to the basic requirement that God should not be proved a liar, there are several reasons why this is important.

First, it preserves our understanding of God as a perfect being, all of whose attributes are in perfect harmony: love, goodness, justice, holiness, truthfulness and so on. It would be misleading to say something like 'At the cross God's mercy triumphed over his justice.' That would imply that a conflict existed between God's attributes, such that his mercy 'won' while his justice was frustrated. By contrast, penal substitution maintains God's mercy and his justice, his love and his truthfulness. All are perfectly fulfilled at the cross. The writer of Psalm 85 expresses this beautifully, declaring that when the Lord saves his people,

> Love and faithfulness meet together;
>     righteousness and peace kiss each other.
>
> (v. 10)

In more technical terms, penal substitution preserves what is often called the doctrine of God's *simplicity*. This does not mean that God is easy to understand! It refers to the truth that he is not composed of different 'parts', as though he could be dismantled somehow into separate components.[48] We cannot speak of God's love as though it were a 'part' of God, separate from his holiness. Rather, all of God's attributes are in harmony with each other: his holiness is a loving holiness, a merciful holiness; his justice is a truthful justice, a holy justice, and so on. Within this framework, none of God's attributes should be regarded as more 'central' or 'essential' than any of the others.

Secondly, penal substitution preserves the truth that justice is firmly rooted in the character of God. Imagine if justice were not grounded in this way, but could be set aside. What would God's new creation be like? Could there not be a Hitler, a Mao or a Stalin, unchanged and operating unpunished for eternity? It is hard to see why not. And if the life to come is not marked by righteousness, why bother striving for it now? What would be the point in working for personal holiness or social justice, if justice were to be abandoned on the Last Day? Indeed, in such a world, it would be difficult even to know what justice is. The moral categories of good and evil, right and wrong would be redundant.[49] Ironically, some recent critics of penal substitution have claimed it severs the link from the cross to social action. It should be clear that the very opposite is the case.[50]

Thirdly, in relating Christ's death to the important biblical themes of God's truthfulness and justice, penal substitution actually provides the basis of other dimensions of the atonement. It is frequently pointed out that the Bible speaks

---

48. For a more detailed discussion see Turretin, *Institutes*, vol. 1, 3.VII, pp. 191–194.

49. There are, of course, many in today's world who would hold exactly to this position, and deny absolute moral norms. Such are the consequences of abandoning the notion of absolute truth. But we would not expect to find such a stance among Christians.

50. For further discussion of the connection between penal substitution and social involvement see chapters 4 and 12.

of the cross in many different ways, but less common are attempts to fit them together. To this we now turn.

### Penal substitution and victory

We begin with the idea that Christ was victorious over evil powers in his death, resurrection and ascension. In recent years this emphasis has been particularly associated with the Swedish theologian Gustav Aulén, whose own position has become known as Christus Victor, after the book of the same name.[51] While Aulén is right to draw attention to the biblical theme of conquest (e.g. Eph. 4:8–10; Col. 2:15), he fails to explain adequately *how* the victory is won. This leads to a number of serious deficiencies in his work, not least an obscuring of the close biblical connection between victory and penal substitution.

Perhaps the greatest weapon in the devil's armoury is his power to accuse us before God, a point highlighted in a recent article by Henri Blocher.[52] Blocher refers to Zechariah 3, which depicts 'Joshua the high priest standing before the angel of the LORD, and Satan standing at his right side to accuse him' (v. 1). He continues:

> How is Satan's role as the Accuser related to his *power*? If Satan's opposition to the Lord were a matter of mere power, the rebel's finite resources would equal zero confronted with infinity. But the Accuser can appeal to justice. He may also indulge in slander, but his force resides in the rightness of his accusation. Joshua *is* unclean, unspeakably unclean . . . (Zech. 3:4). The righteous Judge of all the earth, who can do only right, cannot refuse to hear the charges the Accuser brings without denying himself. In other words, the weapon in the devil's hand is God's own law, God's holy and perfect law – hence the association in some passages of the law and inimical powers, which Aulén was not able to read aright.[53]

Satan appeals to God's justice, calling upon him to punish humanity as we deserve. Consequently, the defeat of the devil must involve the removal of our guilt, and it is in precisely this way that the New Testament presents it.

---

51. See also Gustav Aulén, *The Faith of the Christian Church* (Philadelphia: Muhlenberg, 1948).
52. Henri Blocher, '*Agnus Victor*: The Atonement as Victory and Vicarious Punishment', in John G. Stackhouse (ed.), *What Does It Mean to Be Saved?* (Grand Rapids: Baker, 2002), pp. 67–91. This chapter exposes a number of historical, biblical and theological shortcomings in Gustav Aulén's Christus Victor.
53. Ibid., p. 83; italics original.

Blocher demonstrates this in a discussion of three texts: Colossians 2:14–15, Revelation 12 and Hebrews 2:14:

> [Col. 2:14–15] connects [Christ's] triumph to the cross and precisely to the cancellation of the bond of our debt (as defined by the ordinances of the law) when Jesus was crucified . . . Then and there were the principalities and powers, the chief of whom is called Satan, 'disarmed.' The action concerns judicial claims. Since God can be expected to uphold the rules he has set, we can also expect that the cancellation was obtained through the payment of the legal debt. This appears to be confirmed by the many *ransom* sayings that state that the life or blood of Christ *was the price paid* to free human beings from bondage . . .
>
> Revelation 12 reflects the same understanding. How have the brothers overcome the devil and his host? Not by superior might but 'by the blood of the lamb' (Rev. 12:11). Satan was the Accuser, and he prevailed as long as he could point to their sins. But the blood of the Lamb was the price paid for the cancellation of their debt. The blood of the Lamb wiped out the guilt of their sins forever, and the devil was disarmed. Similarly, Hebrews 2:14 stresses that Jesus deprived the devil of his power . . . through his death, and we are told that 'he has died as a ransom to set them [those who are called] free from the sins committed under the first covenant' (Heb. 9:15), his blood obtaining the remission of their sins (Heb. 9:22; cf. 27–28).[54]

Thus the biblical connection between Satan's power and human guilt points to the importance of penal substitution as the means by which our guilt is removed and the devil is defeated. God's response to the devil's accusation against us is consistent with divine justice.

Moreover, as God works through the atonement to reverse the effects of the fall and restore creation to its proper order, he brings his just judgment on evil powers. This theme appears at several points in the New Testament. For example, in John 12:31, speaking of his impending death, Jesus declares, 'Now is the time for judgment on this world; now the prince of this world will be driven out.' He later teaches it is an aspect of the Spirit's work to 'convict the world of guilt . . . in regard to judgment, because the prince of this world now stands condemned' (John 16:8, 11). The legal concepts of guilt, conviction, judgment and condemnation are prominent in these passages. Christ's victory is a righteous victory, a just victory.

A similar motif is found in 1 John 3:8: 'The reason the Son of God appeared was to destroy the devil's work.' The context here is revealing. John

---

54. Ibid., pp. 86–88; italics and text in square brackets original.

has just told his readers that 'sin is lawlessness' (v. 4). He then announces that the Son of God has come to 'take away our sins' (v. 5), and insists that 'no-one who lives in him keeps on sinning' (v. 6). He then draws a strong contrast, encouraging his readers to imitate the 'righteous' (i.e. 'just', *dikaios*) life of Christ: 'He who does what is right is righteous, just as he is righteous' (v. 7). Thus Jesus' mission 'to destroy the devil's work' (v. 8) is concerned both with the eradication of sin and the reinstatement of righteousness and justice. Jesus destroys the work of the devil in believers by liberating them to live for righteousness and justice (cf. 1 Pet. 2:24).

1 John links forgiveness of sins not simply with love but also with justice: 'If we confess our sins, he is faithful and *just* to forgive us our sins and to cleanse us from all unrighteousness' (1 John 1:9; italics added). Of course, this is not to deny that the Bible elsewhere links forgiveness with God's love (e.g. Exod. 34:7; Num. 14:19; Neh. 9:17; Ps. 86:5). But here it is the justice of God that forms the grounds of our confidence before him.[55] This makes sense only with reference to penal substitution, for only if we are convinced that God has justly punished our sins in the person of his Son can we appeal to his justice as something that would acquit rather than condemn us.

Similarly, God's final eschatological victory over evil is praised precisely on the grounds that justice is executed:

After this I heard what sounded like the roar of a great multitude in heaven shouting:

'Hallelujah!
Salvation and glory and power belong to our God,
  for true and just are his judgments.

---

55. Gustav Aulén claims in Christus Victor that there is a strong discontinuity at this point between the Old and New Testaments. He asserts that 'in the Old Testament, in spite of strong tendencies in the opposite direction, even the idea of the Divine "mercy" and "grace" stands on a legalistic basis' (p. 95), within a framework where 'justice' (p. 96) is central. By contrast, the picture in the New Testament is radically different, for 'sovereign Divine Love has taken the initiative [and] broken through the order of justice and merit' (pp. 95–96). Such a statement is almost Marcionite (Marcion was a heretic who in the second century AD denied the status of the Old Testament as Christian Scripture). It must be noted in response that the apostle John does not depart from the Old Testament in the way Aulén suggests: in John's view God's atoning love is grounded on his justice.

He has condemned the great prostitute
   who corrupted the earth by her adulteries.
He has avenged on her the blood of his servants.'
(Rev. 19:1–2)

Indeed, to exclude the idea of justice from God's victory would be to represent God as immoral. It would be impossible to see God's victory as anything other than a naked exercise of power – God was able to conquer the devil because he is stronger. Satan's defeat cannot be seen as a good thing unless he *deserved* it, unless *justice* required it. The Bible presents it in exactly these moral categories.

In summary, Aulén was right that the Bible depicts the cross as God's victory over evil. However, in order to see that victory in its biblical fullness and richness we must take account of its relationship to God's justice. Penal substitution is at the heart of this, for it was as Christ bore in our place the penal suffering due to us for our sin that he removed Satan's power of accusation; thereby disarming him. Penal substitution recognizes that God must *punish* evil in order for his defeat of Satan to be fully consistent with his righteousness. It is ironic that this biblical theme, which Aulén criticized so strongly, is in fact necessary for a full appreciation of the victory motif he was so concerned to emphasize.

### Penal substitution and reconciliation

Taken by itself, the idea of 'reconciliation' does not necessarily imply a moral framework. In general, people may need to be reconciled as a result of a simple misunderstanding, with neither party being at fault. Alternatively, it may be that both sides have legitimate points to make and a compromise is required.

However, the Bible is more specific when it comes to reconciliation between humanity and God. Reconciliation is necessary because we have *sinned* against God. We are at fault; we are in the wrong. There is blame to be apportioned, and it rests entirely with us. Inevitably this raises the issue of justice.

This is clear in 2 Corinthians 5:19, where the apostle Paul explains that at the cross 'God was reconciling the world to himself in Christ, *not counting men's sins against them*' (italics added).[56] This final phrase casts the alienation between humanity and God in an ethical or legal light – it is our sin, with all its associations of false faith and breaking God's law, that erects the barrier to our

---

56. The context of v. 17, 'if anyone is in Christ, he is a new creation', reminds us that
    sin is decreational and that salvation must recreate.

reconciliation with God. Reconciliation is therefore inseparably connected to the issue of justice, for sin cannot simply be ignored.

The subsequent appeal to 'be reconciled to God' (v. 20) is then followed by an explanation of how this legal, ethical barrier has been overcome: 'God made him who had no sin to be sin for us, so that in him we might become the righteousness of God' (v. 21). This emphasis on the imputation of our guilt to Christ and his righteousness to us amounts to a statement of penal substitution. If we sideline it, we risk distorting the biblical picture of reconciliation.

To downplay the legal or ethical demands of reconciliation also risks undermining the depth and wonder of God's love. For the Bible draws attention to the uniqueness of God's love by emphasizing the sinfulness of those who experience it: 'God demonstrates his own love for us in this: While *we were still sinners*, Christ died for us . . . if, when *we were God's enemies*, we were reconciled to him through the death of his Son, how much more, having been reconciled, shall we be saved through his life!' (Rom. 5:8, 10; italics added).

The full extent of God's reconciling love is seen only as we put it in its moral context, recognizing that as sinners we deserve only punishment. But as soon as we admit that, we are thrown back on the question of how as sinners, deserving of punishment, we can be justly reconciled to a righteous God. These are questions only penal substitution can answer.

### Penal substitution and ransom

We may be accustomed to thinking of ransom in relation to the rescue of prisoners unwillingly enslaved, who have found themselves in captivity through no fault of their own, whose imprisonment is a violation of justice. But the biblical picture is different. The Bible depicts all humanity as willing slaves of sin, who have chosen the path of wickedness, and whose bondage is God's just sentence on their rebellion. This willing slavery is emphasized in Ephesians 2:3, where Paul reminds his readers that 'all of us also lived among them at one time, *gratifying* the cravings of our sinful nature and *following* its desires and thoughts' (italics added). Similarly, Jesus denounces his opponents with the shocking words 'You belong to your father, the devil, and you *want* to carry out your father's desire' (John 8:44; italics added). The biblical theme of ransom thus has an unmistakeable overtone of moral culpability; in our perversity we choose to submit to the wickedness that enslaves us, and we therefore stand guilty before God.

We must steer clear of the unbiblical idea that a ransom must be paid to the devil to secure our release. This mistaken path was taken by some in the early church,[57] and resurfaces on the lips of the evil witch in C. S. Lewis's *The Lion, the Witch and the Wardrobe*. She implies that Edmund's sin leaves him indebted to her, and that she is the one to whom payment is due: 'That human creature is mine. His life is forfeit to me. His blood is my property . . . unless I have blood as the Law says all Narnia will be overturned and perish in fire and water.'[58]

According to Scripture, it is to God we are under obligation: to *him* the ransom must be paid. This takes us inescapably to the doctrine of penal substitution, for our sin has left us subject to God's righteous wrath and we deserve his punishment. It was this price Christ set out to pay when he came to earth 'to give his life as a ransom for many' (Mark 10:45).

We have seen how penal substitution, and particularly its associated ideas of justice and punishment for sin, integrate with three other important biblical perspectives on the cross: victory, reconciliation and ransom. It is clear that to dispense with penal substitution would distort these other perspectives. More than this, if penal substitution were abandoned, the very elements of these other perspectives that are praised with such passion in Scripture – the justice of God's victory and the surpassing glory of his reconciling love – would have to go as well. Thus we should not see these perspectives on the cross as alternatives to penal substitution, but rather outworkings of it. Penal substitution underpins and enriches them.[59]

### The gift of believers to Jesus

We have considered the importance within the doctrine of the Trinity of the Father's character as a 'giver', and have seen how this relates to God's work of redemption as the Father 'gives' his Son to believers. There is, however, another important aspect to the Father's giving: he gives believers to his Son. This is reflected in the Old Testament in God's promise of a kingdom for his Son in Psalm 110 (cf. Heb. 1:13), and particularly in Psalm 2, where the Lord declares:

---

57. For further discussion see John R. W. Stott, *The Cross of Christ* (Leicester: IVP, 1986), pp. 112–114.

58. C. S. Lewis, *The Lion, the Witch and the Wardrobe* (London: Fontana, 1980; first pub. 1950), p. 129.

59. It is not our intention here to discuss the relationship between penal substitution and *every* other theme of theological importance. That would require a book much longer than this! One other particularly important relationship, that between penal substitution and new creation, is discussed in chapter 12, sect. 1.

You are my Son;
> today I have become your Father.

Ask of me,
> and I will make the nations your inheritance,
> the ends of the earth your possession.

(vv. 7–8)

Turning to the New Testament, the idea of the Father's gift of believers to his Son emerges particularly clearly in John 6. In this chapter, Jesus repeatedly emphasizes that coming to him and receiving life from him involve believing in him: 'I tell you the truth, he who believes has everlasting life' (v. 47; cf. vv. 29, 35–36, 40). But this raises a problem. As we saw previously, false faith is delusional: it corrupts our minds, making it impossible for us to believe the truth about God. How can anyone come to Jesus if believing in him is something we by nature cannot do?

Jesus' answer is that 'all that the Father *gives* me will come to me, and whoever comes to me I will never drive away . . . I shall lose none of all that he has *given* me' (vv. 37, 39; italics added). Positively, then, Jesus implies that belief is possible by God's intervention. He then expresses the same truth negatively: 'No-one can come to me unless the Father who sent me *draws him*' (v. 44; italics added; cf. v. 65).

Thus the faith required if we are to follow Jesus comes as a gift from God the Father, by which he draws his people to his Son, and without which discipleship is impossible.

In a similar vein, Ephesians 2:8 speaks of faith as a 'gift of God',[60] and 2 Corinthians 4 emphasizes it is God who dispelled the blindness of our unbelief (v. 4) and 'made his light shine in our hearts to give us the light of the knowledge of the glory of God in the face of Christ' (v. 6).

Jesus also alludes to the role of the Spirit in John 6:63, anticipating an important theme of John 14–16. These chapters repeatedly speak of the Spirit's ministry of imparting truth to those who follow Jesus (see especially John 14:15–16, 26; 15:26; 16:8–15), which again emphasizes the necessity for divine revelation to overcome the delusion of false faith. Similarly, Paul insists,

---

60. Grammatically, the 'gift of God' in Eph. 2:8 refers not to faith only but to the whole of salvation by grace 'through faith' (Peter T. O'Brien, *The Letter to the Ephesians*, Pillar New Testament Commentary [Leicester: Apollos; Grand Rapids: Eerdmans, 1999], p. 175). This merely furthers our point, for the whole of salvation, including our faith, is God's gift.

'no-one can say, "Jesus is Lord," except by the Holy Spirit' (1 Cor. 12:3). It is thus by the gift of his Spirit that God grants faith, thereby giving a believing people to his Son. The Spirit does not just work after we are converted, prompting us to holiness of life or endowing with particular gifts. He works our conversion. As Calvin comments, 'Faith is the principal work of the Holy Spirit.'[61]

In summary, God gives believers to his Son by working in rebellious hearts by his Spirit, thereby overcoming our false faith and granting us true knowledge of him and trust in him.[62]

### Union with Christ

Having considered the related themes of God's gift of his Son to believers, and God's gift of believers to his Son, we can turn to the crucial doctrine of *union with Christ*, which brings these two 'giving' themes together.

Union with Christ is a way of talking about the mutual indwelling of Christ and believers. The Christian has been 'united with him' (Rom. 6:5); he or she is indwelt by Christ (Col. 1:27) and is 'in' him (e.g. Rom. 8:1; 2 Cor. 5:17; Phil. 1:1). Jesus prayed in John 17 that believers would 'be one, Father, just as you are in me and I am in you. May they also be in us so that the world may believe that you have sent me' (v. 21). To be a believer is thus to experience an intimate relationship with God, in Christ, by his Spirit.

Union with Christ is important for the doctrine of penal substitution, for it is on the basis of this union that our guilt is justly imputed to him, and that we are credited with his righteousness and receive all the benefits of his perfect life, sacrificial death and glorious resurrection.[63] As Calvin puts it:

> First, we must understand that as long as Christ remains outside of us, and we are
> separated from him, all that he has suffered and done for the salvation of the human
> race remains useless and of no value to us. Therefore, to share with us what he has
> received from the Father, he had to become ours and to dwell within us . . . the Holy
> Spirit is the bond by which Christ effectually unites us to himself.[64]

---

61. Calvin, *Institutes*, vol. 1, III.i.4, p. 541.
62. The Bible teaches that the Spirit is sent both from the Father and the Son (John 15:26; 16:7). For a brief discussion see Grudem, *Systematic Theology*, pp. 246–247.
63. E.g. 1 Cor. 15:22; 2 Cor. 5:21; Eph. 1:6–7; Phil. 1:9; Col. 2:10.
64. Calvin, *Institutes*, vol. 1, III.i.1, pp. 537–538.

This means, of course, that when Christ received the punishment for our sins, he did not do so as an unrelated third party. He was justly punished for sins that became his on account of his union with sinners.[65] Similarly, when his righteousness was imputed to us, it required no 'legal fiction', for his righteousness truly became ours. This answers the objection of some critics who complain that penal substitution is unjust.[66]

### Summary

Penal substitution emerges as a central aspect of God's redeeming work in Christ, integrating fully with God's justice and truthfulness, and safeguarding God's simplicity by preserving the harmony of his attributes of justice and mercy, holiness and love. In so doing, it establishes that justice has a fundamental basis within the character of God.

Penal substitution coheres perfectly with other biblical understandings of the atonement. It sheds light on Christ's victory over evil powers, explaining in particular how the devil is stripped of his power to accuse. It is the basis of our reconciliation with God, for there was a moral enmity between us and God, and our guilt had to be overcome. In its emphasis that God gave his Son for his *enemies* (Rom. 5:10), penal substitution deepens our appreciation of God's love. Finally, it places the theme of ransom in the correct biblical perspective, underlining the fact that we are indebted not to the devil but to God, and it is to him that a ransom must be paid.

Penal substitution integrates perfectly with the doctrine of union with Christ. For as we are united to Christ by his Spirit through faith, our sin and guilt are imputed to Christ, and we are credited with his righteousness and receive all the other benefits of his atoning work.

---

65. More precisely, we would distinguish between the union between Christ and believers conceived in God's mind in eternity, and the union we enter into by the Spirit when we put our faith in Christ. Plainly, it is the former union that grounds the imputation of our sin to Christ at the point of the *accomplishment* of our redemption at Calvary, for only this was then in existence. However, our faith union by which the benefits of Christ are *applied* to us is not something wholly different, but an outworking of this former union.

66. See chapter 10, sect. 1.

## Conclusion

Penal substitution has a foundational place in Christian theology. It fits right at the centre of the jigsaw to complete a magnificent picture. Here is the story of a God whose word is good and true, who refuses to be unfaithful to himself. Here is the story of a gracious Father, who gave his Son to redeem a sinful and undeserving people. Here is the story of a just and righteous God, who will not pretend that evil is of no account. Here is the story of an all-wise God, who works in all things for the good of his people and to the glory of his name, and penal substitution lies right at its heart.

## 4. EXPLORING THE IMPLICATIONS: THE PASTORAL IMPORTANCE OF PENAL SUBSTITUTION

### Introduction

I am laid low in the dust;
    preserve my life according to your word.
I recounted my ways and you answered me;
    teach me your decrees.
Let me understand the teaching of your precepts;
    then I will meditate on your wonders.
My soul is weary with sorrow;
    strengthen me according to your word.
Keep me from deceitful ways;
    be gracious to me through your law.
I have chosen the way of truth;
    I have set my heart on your laws.
I hold fast to your statutes, O Lord;
    do not let me be put to shame.
I run in the path of your commands,
    for you have set my heart free.
(Ps. 119:25–32)

These verses from Psalm 119 illuminate the relationship between knowledge and transformation that lies at the heart of the Christian life. The psalmist comes before the Lord in weariness and sorrow, pleading with him to 'Let me understand the teaching of your precepts' (v. 27). Having been strengthened with this understanding, he meditates upon what he has discovered, sets his heart upon it, holds fast to it, and delights in the freedom of running in the path the Lord has set before him.

This dynamic relationship between understanding and action reminds us that the Christian life must be lived out as well as thought about. Doctrine is for life and godliness, not for ivory-tower speculations. This is not to diminish the significance of understanding the meaning of Scripture; on the contrary, a correct understanding of God's word is the psalmist's first concern as he brings his burdened soul before God (v. 27). But this is only the beginning of the journey, and he proceeds to reflect on what he has learned, with a view to putting it into practice.

We would be wise to ask ourselves in relation to every element of biblical doctrine, 'How should this impact my Christian life?' The implications may be very practical, concerned with the hands-on decisions of everyday life. Or they may be more emotional, affecting how we feel about our relationship with the Lord. Both of these are reflected in the psalm quoted above: the psalmist's sorrow is removed, and he is liberated to live in a new way. Both are vitally important for Christians as we encounter challenges day by day, and as our churches strive to shine the light of the gospel into a dark world.

The purpose of this chapter is to take tentative steps in this direction. Our aim is not to spell out the implications of every aspect of the cross for our Christian lives. That would be an impossible task in so few pages. Rather, the aim is to consider penal substitution in particular, and to reflect on some of the pastoral consequences that flow from it.

We shall see in chapter 12 that some have argued that penal substitution is devoid of ethical implications. Nothing could be further from the truth. The implications of penal substitution for the Christian life are profound, and a great deal is lost if it is denied.


## Assurance of God's love

The idea that 'God is love' is hardly controversial. As Don Carson observes, 'If people believe in God at all today, the overwhelming majority hold that this God – however he, she, or it may be understood – is a loving being

. . . Nowadays if you tell people that God loves them, they are unlikely to be surprised.'[1]

Yet this superficial consensus can mask deeper problems. For 'love' means very different things to different people, and it can be hard to separate the biblical wheat from the sentimental chaff. A moment's thought tells us that the half-baked Hollywood caricature needs to be kicked firmly into the long grass; the trouble is that we are not always sure what to put in its place. We are unclear in our own minds about what *God's* love is. What does it mean for an infinite God to love finite people? What should it feel like to know that God loves me? We are in danger of treating God's love like the foundations of a glorious cathedral: we build an enormous edifice upon it, but rarely trouble ourselves with what is going on underground, and when cracks start to appear higher up we discover to our horror that no-one has the key to the basement.

This lack of clarity about what God's love is leads to a diminished certainty that we have truly encountered it. The vague, nebulous idea of love so prevalent in our society is very fragile. It serves us well when the sun shines down on us, and life is easy, but it offers no defence against the savage onslaught of personal tragedy. It easily gives way to doubt and a feeling of forsakenness at the very moment it is most needed. This is a far cry from the strong, powerful love spoken of in Scripture. Consider Paul's prayer for the Ephesians: 'I pray that you, being rooted and established in love, may have power, together with all the saints, to grasp how wide and long and high and deep is the love of Christ, and to know this love that surpasses knowledge – that you may be filled to the measure of all the fulness of God' (Eph. 3:17–19).

Can any of us honestly say we know Christ's love in this way? Do we experience the tangible intensity of God's love for which Paul prayed? And if not, where should we look?

The New Testament repeatedly turns to the cross of Christ as the supreme demonstration of the love of God. The apostle John provides the most famous example: 'This is how we know what love is: Jesus Christ laid down his life for us . . . God is love . . . This is love: not that we loved God, but that he loved us and sent his Son as an atoning sacrifice for our sins' (1 John 3:16; 4:8, 10). We can begin to appreciate the contours of God's love by reflecting on the cost of the cross, the depth of our sinfulness, and the perfection of God's holiness.

One way in which Scripture emphasizes the cost of the cross is to contrast the indignity to which Christ descended on earth with the glory from which he

---

1.  D. A. Carson, *The Difficult Doctrine of the Love of God* (Leicester: IVP, 2000), pp. 9–10, 12.

came. God the Son, the immortal, self-existent Word of God, who from all eternity had dwelt in unapproachable light, took the nature of a servant, veiled in human flesh, made in human likeness. This Jesus suffered the indignity of accusation and condemnation and the shame of crucifixion. His was the tortured soul in Gethsemane, the torn flesh at Calvary. And as thick darkness enveloped the whole land, it was he who was pierced for our transgressions and crushed for our iniquities; his was the punishment that brought us peace; his were the wounds that wrought our healing.

The Lord Jesus Christ did not come into the world to meet with his friends. He came to die for his enemies. He came to a people who had rejected his law and killed his prophets, who were confident of their own righteousness and looked down on everybody else, trampling his courts in the hypocrisy of their self-righteous religious observances. He came to nations that had exchanged the truth of the living God for a lie, the glory of the immortal God for man-made images, and the fountain of living water for cracked and broken cisterns. He came to a world stained with violence, to a people whose hands were full of blood and whose righteous deeds were like filthy rags, to a complacent humanity who proclaimed 'Peace! Peace!' while they waged war with God.

This is the biblical portrait of the people for whom Christ died. We were objects of wrath, rightly facing the unmitigated, everlasting fury of an incensed God, but now in Christ we have found mercy. We have been brought from death to life, from corruption to glory. We were slaves to sin, the world and the devil, but are now adopted children of our heavenly Father. We were stained with the filth of a wicked life and tormented by the pain of a guilty conscience, but are now pardoned and forgiven, standing blameless before him as a pure bride, clothed in the clean, white robes of Christ's righteousness.

Now contemplate the blistering holiness of our God, the Holy One of Israel, the high and lofty One who inhabits eternity. His eyes are too pure to look on evil; his voice shakes the heavens; at his sight the angels in glory hide their faces. Who can dwell with this consuming fire, with this everlasting burning? Who can ascend the hill of the Lord? Who can stand in his holy place? Yet this God took pity on us, this God stooped down to us and lifted us up to enjoy the blessing of restored relationship with him, that we may gaze upon his face for all eternity.

What love it is, that this holy God should give his Son – his only Son, his beloved – to suffer and die in the place of rebels. He gave him, not hoping that he might be spared, but knowing that he would be despised, rejected and killed. And as he turned his face away from his Son in the blackness of Golgotha, he turned towards us – a people loaded with guilt, children given to corruption –

and fulfilled those precious words 'God so loved the world that he gave his only Son'.

A penal substitutionary understanding of the cross helps us to understand God's love, and to appreciate its intensity and beauty. Scripture magnifies God's love by its refusal to diminish our plight as sinners deserving of God's wrath, and by its uncompromising portrayal of the cross as the place where Christ bore that punishment in the place of his people. If we blunt the sharp edges of the cross, we dull the glittering diamond of God's love.

## Confidence in God's truthfulness

Living as a Christian means acknowledging the authority of God's word. For God is the Almighty Creator of all things, the One to whom we owe our very being, who sustains us and the entire universe moment by moment. The invitation to repent and believe in the Lord Jesus Christ is simultaneously a call to a complete reorientation of life, a summons to bow before this mighty God and lay before him all we have and are, and a command to do what he says. There are no hidden corners of our lives where God's word can be disregarded,

> for the word of God is living and active. Sharper than any double-edged sword, it penetrates even to dividing soul and spirit, joints and marrow; it judges the thoughts and attitudes of the heart. Nothing in all creation is hidden from God's sight. Everything is uncovered and laid bare before the eyes of him to whom we must give account. (Heb. 4:12–13)

Moreover, God's word perfectly reflects his will, so to obey *it* is to obey *him*. As he declares through the prophet Isaiah,

> this is the one I esteem:
>      he who is humble and contrite in spirit,
>      and trembles at my word.
> (Isa. 66:2)

God's authority is not that of an unconcerned dictator, and his words are not the arbitrary decrees of a distant autocrat. He cares for us, and his word is our perfect and sufficient guide through the troubles and perplexities of life.

Your word is a lamp to my feet
     and a light for my path.
(Ps. 119:105)

From the seemingly minor choices we make every day to the agonizing decisions we face at the turning points of our lives, there is nothing for which
God's word is inadequate as a source of wisdom and guidance, for 'all
Scripture is God-breathed and is useful for teaching, rebuking, correcting and
training in righteousness, so that the man of God may be thoroughly equipped
for *every* good work' (2 Tim. 3:16–17; italics added). God's word always shows
us what is best for us, 'blessed are they who keep his statutes and seek him with
all their heart' (Ps. 119:2), and the path of obedience is perfect freedom (Ps.
119:32; Jas 1:25). More than this, God's word is the spiritual food that sustains
us every moment of our lives in this God-denying world, the imperishable
seed by which we are born again to new life in Christ, and the 'pure spiritual
milk' that keeps us persevering in him (1 Pet. 2:2; cf. 1:23–25; Matt. 4:4).

How strange it is, then, that Christians often find it hard to obey God's
word, particularly when the stakes are high. Sometimes we feel convicted
about something we know is ungodly, but are reluctant to change. Perhaps we
are involved in a relationship that compromises our devotion to Christ.
Perhaps we are greedily storing up treasure for ourselves on earth rather than
delighting to give sacrificially to the work of the gospel and to those in need.
Or perhaps we indulge our minds in lustful thoughts, or our tongues in gossip
and slander. Whatever the details, obedience is always easier said than done,
and godliness is often costly.

The challenge presented by many of these situations is not really intellectual. We know perfectly well what the Bible says, we know that God's word
carries his authority, we know what we ought to do. But these decisions involve
our emotions as well as our understanding, and we wrestle with doubt about
whether God's path really is the best one. These decisions are not merely
'difficult', but are painful, and our emotional uncertainty provides a happy
hunting ground for the weakness of our sinful flesh.

What we need at times like this is a heartfelt conviction that God's word is
true, that righteousness really is the path to life. We need to be able to banish the
secret, sneaking suspicion that ungodliness may actually be better for us. Once
we have understood the Bible's teaching, and after we have reminded ourselves
it is the word of the Almighty God that addresses us from those pages, and as
we count the cost of pinning all of our hopes on the promises of God, we need
to *know* that his words are true. We need to *know* that he does not lie. We need
to *know* that if we follow his way, the harder way, he will prove faithful and true.

Once again, the truth of penal substitution can help us. For Jesus' death at Calvary demonstrates beyond doubt that God is truthful. This insight flows from Athanasius' fourth-century work *On the Incarnation*.[2] Athanasius explained that Adam's sin brought death and corruption into God's perfect world, which seemed to place God in a dilemma.[3] On the one hand, it would have been 'both monstrous and unfitting' for God to allow this corruption to continue,[4] since this would entail the undoing of his good work of creation, and would thereby bring dishonour upon God. But on the other hand, God had promised in Genesis 2:17 that Adam would die if he disobeyed the command not to eat from the tree of knowledge of good and evil, and 'it would . . . have been unthinkable that God should go back upon his word'.[5] To maintain his honour, God needed to find a way of reversing the corruption of creation without allowing his promise of Genesis 2:17 to become a lie.

Athanasius recognized that God's solution was to send his Son into the world, taking the nature of a man, to suffer in himself the curse of corruption and death promised by God in Genesis 2. The Lord Jesus Christ exhausted this curse, and by his resurrection inaugurated a new creation, uncorrupted by Adam's sin. In this way God maintained his honour as our Creator by rescuing his creation from corruption, but he did not compromise his truthfulness, for sin did indeed bring death as he had said – the death of his only Son in the place of his people.

Let us pause here for a moment, and try to imagine what human history must look like from God's perspective. If God could have gone back on *just one* of his promises, would it not have been this one – the promise of Genesis 2:17? For if he had allowed just this one word to fall to the ground, his Son would have been spared agony and torment beyond imagination. But the living God would not lie, and so God the Son gave himself at the cross in order to uphold his own truthfulness.

---

2. Athanasius, *On the Incarnation* (New York: St. Vladimir's Seminary Press, 1993). A more detailed discussion of Athanasius' work may be found in chapter 5. See also M. Ovey, 'The Cross, Creation and the Human Predicament', in David Peterson (ed.), *Where Wrath and Mercy Meet: Proclaiming the Atonement Today* (Carlisle: Paternoster, 2001), pp. 100–135.

3. Strictly speaking, of course, this is not a 'real' dilemma in the mind of God, for he planned the whole course of history before the creation of the world. But it certainly appears as a dilemma from our perspective, and to frame the issue in these terms helpfully highlights the challenge Adam's sin posed.

4. Athanasius, *On the Incarnation*, sect. 6, p. 32.

5. Ibid.

In this way, the cross of Christ establishes that all of God's word is true. If God refused to break his word in this most extreme of cases, we can trust him in every other situation. The torment of the cross stands as a monument to the unchanging truthfulness of God's word:

The word of the LORD is right and true;
   he is faithful in all he does.
(Ps. 33:4)

Strikingly, this is precisely what was in Jesus' mind when he was arrested. As Jesus contemplated the cross from the quietness of Gethsemane, knowing that very soon he would be 'betrayed into the hands of men', he confessed to Peter, James and John, 'My soul is overwhelmed with sorrow to the point of death' (Mark 14:34, 41). As he cried out in anguished prayer, 'his sweat was like drops of blood falling to the ground' (Luke 22:44), and he pleaded with his Father to spare him what was to come, begging him to 'take this cup from me' (Mark 14:36). But despite all this, when the soldiers arrived to arrest him, he offered no resistance, but insisted instead that '*the Scriptures must be fulfilled*' (v. 49; italics added). His argument was not that resistance was futile because there were so many soldiers, but that resistance was unthinkable because God's word must be upheld. He gave himself up to death to preserve the truth of the Scriptures.

What extraordinary lengths the Son of God will go to in order to preserve his truthfulness! He took upon himself the frail body of a man, experienced the pain of grief and betrayal, suffered the indignity of death by crucifixion, and worse, the horror of his Father's wrath, all because he would not lie.

Does this not make us feel differently about God's word? As we wrestle against our sinful desires, struggling to bring every thought into captivity to Christ, as we struggle with the complexities of life, knowing that God's word is a lamp to our feet, yet not feeling the warmth of that light as we struggle to make the long journey from head to heart, let us meditate on the glorious truth of penal substitution, as the sufferings of our Lord Jesus Christ cry out 'Truth! Truth!' as the final verdict on God's unchanging word.


## Passion for God's justice

We live in an unjust world. From the comfort of our sheltered lives in the modern West, we easily forget that in past ages, and even today in many parts of the world, our Christian brothers and sisters are systematically marginalized, even violently persecuted, on account of their faith. Although the gospel declares that in Christ 'there is neither Jew nor Greek, slave nor free, male nor female' (Gal. 3:28) there are many around the world who are cruelly discriminated against because of their race or sex, and it was not so long ago that Britain traded slaves. Indeed, we need only peel back the respectable veneer of our own culture to find instances of terrible injustice. Many are bullied in the workplace, others are subject to domestic violence, and all too often the abusers get away with it.

Christians have always been troubled by injustice. The history of the church is full of examples of people who simply refused to stand by and watch ungodliness carry all before it. William Wilberforce, whose relentless campaigning brought an end to the slave trade in Britain, was a committed Christian, and there have been many like him. Yet it is hard not to be overwhelmed by the sheer scale of the crisis. The problems sometimes seem so vast, and our efforts so tiny, that we feel powerless to make a difference. We get angry at injustice, we feel guilty at our comparative ease, but we do nothing because of the immensity of the problem.

It is here that penal substitution stirs us to action. First, it reminds us that God is concerned for justice. God saves sinners not by finding a loophole in his righteous law, but by fulfilling its demands. God has not dispensed with justice in overlooking our sins: he has demonstrated it in the death of his Son. God is passionately concerned about justice, so we must be too. It will not do for us to ignore oppression in the world as if it does not matter. The instincts that compel us, in our better moments, to do something about our messed-up world are entirely right, for they are in line with God's concerns. Penal substitution provides a moral foundation for working for justice.

Secondly, penal substitution reminds us that God will one day put an end to injustice, for the crucial conflict with evil has been fought and won. The whole creation will one day be liberated from evil, for at the cross Jesus endured and exhausted sin's curse. We can be absolutely confident that *God's programme* for social justice will succeed. This is a head-on challenge to the pessimistic attitude that shrinks from the challenge of social reform, conceding defeat in the face of apparently insuperable opposition. Penal substitution assures us that sin will not be triumphant, that justice will prevail.

Thirdly, penal substitution reminds us that the restoration of a righteous world cannot be achieved by mere human effort. It requires God's intervention. We could not drag ourselves from the mire of sin and death and restore our corrupt and ruined nature, and are certainly in no position to do so for others. Only our Creator can recreate his crooked and decaying world. Christians have a responsibility to stand against injustice in society, but we must never make the mistake of thinking that such efforts are the means by which God's creation will be restored. It is the gospel that is 'the power of God for salvation' (Rom. 1:16), and only this can ultimately transform the world.

## Realism about our sin

The Bible depicts sin in uncompromising terms. Sin is stubborn rebellion against God's rightful authority, flagrant transgression of his holy law, wanton perversion of his good creation. Sin despises the sacrifice of God the Son and grieves the Holy Spirit. Sin is adultery with a sinful world and unfaithfulness to our loving heavenly Father, the self-exalting self-destruction of a proud humanity that turns away from the source of life, breath and everything else, and in its foolishness claims to be wise. It is filth that defiles and stains. And the Bible tells us we are all guilty of it. Our very hearts are corrupt, our very human nature fallen.

The Bible is so brutally honest about human nature that it is tempting to soften some of the hard edges in an attempt to salvage our self-esteem. This is all the more tempting in a society that has rebranded many sins as valid lifestyle choices. It is hard to maintain a biblical perspective when we are bombarded daily with a very different view – that it can't be wrong to do what feels right, that we must be 'true to ourselves', that we are all basically good.

This attempt to retouch the biblical picture can be reinforced by the technique of comparison. We can come to believe in our hearts that as long as we are *less bad than others*, the 'little sins' that continue to pollute us are not so important. This self-deception can be very powerful, particularly if we are willing to cast the net wide enough to include the horrific catalogue of depravity that fills our TV screens every evening. We are not as bad as that! And so our self-confidence is boosted, the Bible's picture is blurred, and the sinfulness of sin is quietly downplayed, ignored and forgotten.

But this is a dangerous path. We may convince ourselves that our 'little sins' do not matter, but we are unlikely to extend the same courtesy to others – at least not indefinitely. There is a line (normally just beyond where we stand) that may not be crossed: 'I thank you that I am not like other men – robbers, evil-doers, adulterers – or even like this tax collector' (Luke 18:11). And so the path of optimism leads easily to judgmentalism and hypocrisy – for which the Lord Jesus reserved his most vigorous rebukes (see Matt. 23).

If the denial of sin is a dead end, what is the alternative? Must sin have the last word? Are we to gaze despondently at the biblical portrait of wretched, fallen humanity, hypnotized by our own wickedness? Not at all. Here again penal substitution provides the right perspective, a place from which we can honestly confront our sin without succumbing to despair.

Penal substitution vividly underscores the seriousness of sin. It reminds us that sin has brought a curse upon the whole creation, and that nothing short of a recreation can put it right. It reminds us that our sin brought God the Son down from his heavenly throne to live and die a God-forsaken death among us. Many Christian martyrs have faced death bravely, even joyfully, knowing the joy that awaited them in the loving arms of their Lord. But the death that Jesus faced, enduring the unspeakable wrath of his Father, brought him to his knees in abject terror in Gethsemane as he contemplated the wrath to come.[6] The cross stands as a memorial to the inexpressible horror of sin; it will not allow us to escape into self-deceiving optimism.

But at the same time, the cross banishes our despair by declaring God's comprehensive solution to our plight. Christ willingly bore our sins in his body. He cried out in the pain of abandonment to his Father's wrath and curse, and at the same moment exhausted that curse himself. And now by his resurrection he has opened the gates of the new creation so that all those who are in him share in his triumph: 'if anyone is in Christ, he is a new creation; the old has gone, the new has come!' (2 Cor. 5:21). We can stand alongside C. H. Spurgeon and contemplate our sin from the foot of the cross with utter realism, but without despair.

> Trembling sinner, look to Jesus, and thou art saved. Dost thou say, 'My sins are many'? His atonement is wondrous. Dost thou cry, 'My heart is hard'? Jesus can soften it. Dost thou exclaim, 'Alas, I am so unworthy'? Jesus loves the unworthy. Dost thou feel, 'I am so vile'? It is the vile Jesus came to save. Down with thee, sinner; down, down with thyself, and up with Christ, who hath suffered for thy sins upon Calvary's cross. Turn thine eye thither; see Jesus only. He suffers. He bleeds. He dies. He is buried. He rises again. He ascends on high. Trust Him, and thou art safe. Give up all other trusts, and rely on Jesus alone, alone on Jesus, and thou shalt pass from death unto life. This is the sure sign, the certain evidence of the Spirit's indwelling, of the Father's election, of the Son's redemption, when the soul is brought simply and wholly to rest and trust in Jesus Christ, who 'hath once suffered for sins, the Just for the unjust, that He might bring us to God.'[7]

---

6. See John R. W. Stott, *The Cross of Christ* (Leicester: IVP, 1986), pp. 74–78.

7. C. H. Spurgeon, 'Our Suffering Substitute: A Sermon on 1 Peter 3:18', originally pub. in *The Sword and The Trowel Magazine* (1895), http://www.members.aol.com/pilgrimpub/substute.htm (accessed 20 February 2006).

If we look upon our sin from this perspective, the justice of God, which once aroused in us fear of punishment, now becomes a source of joy and comfort. Without Christ's death in our place, God's justice could lead only to our condemnation. But now Christ has been punished in our place, his justice demands our liberation and acquittal – only an *unjust* judge could demand payment for the same sins twice. As Augustus Toplady sang:

> From whence this fear and unbelief?
> Hath not the Father put to grief
> His spotless Son for me?
> And will the righteous Judge of men
> Condemn me for that debt of sin
> Which, Lord, was charged on Thee?
>
> Complete atonement Thou hast made,
> And to the utmost Thou hast paid
> Whate'er Thy people owed;
> How then can wrath on me take place,
> If sheltered in Thy righteousness,
> And sprinkled with Thy blood?
>
> If Thou hast my discharge procured,
> And freely in my room endured
> The whole of wrath divine;
> Payment God cannot twice demand,
> First at my bleeding Surety's hand,
> And then again at mine.[8]

---

8. Augustus M. Toplady, 'From whence this fear and unbelief?' (1772). Taken from *Christian Hymns* (Bryntirion, Bridgend: Evangelical Movement of Wales, 1977).

## 5. SURVEYING THE HERITAGE: THE HISTORICAL PEDIGREE OF PENAL SUBSTITUTION

### Introduction: Why bother with church history?

'History', according to Henry Ford, 'is more or less bunk. It's tradition. We don't want tradition. We want to live in the present and the only history that is worth a tinker's damn is the history we make today.'[1] While few Christians would be quite so dismissive of the past, a chapter on the history of the doctrine of penal substitution nonetheless requires some explanation in a book supposedly devoted to a biblical and theological investigation of the subject. After all, we are interested in whether penal substitution is biblical, not whether it is traditional, and the accumulated testimony of all the theologians in the world means nothing against the authority of the Bible.

However, the simple fact is that we are not the first, and certainly not the wisest, generation to reflect on the teaching of Scripture. Although we do not look to previous generations as a source of authority, they are a valuable source of wisdom. Many of the great theologians of previous generations were figures of prodigious learning, who contended for their faith in the face of

---

1. Interview with Charles N. Wheeler in *Chicago Tribune*, 25 May 1916. Cited from *The Oxford Dictionary of Modern Quotations*, ed. Tony Augarde (Oxford: Oxford University Press, 1991), p. 82.

extreme persecution. It would be hard to ignore the opinions of such giants as Athanasius and Augustine if we could speak to them face to face; why should we ignore them simply because they are dead? We want to be as sure as possible that we have understood the Bible correctly, so it makes sense to see how the great figures of the past interpreted it.

The question of historical pedigree has acquired a further significance in recent years, for increasing numbers of people are suggesting penal substitution is a novel doctrine, invented around the time of the Reformation by a church that was (it is alleged) drifting ever further from the biblical faith of the early church Fathers.[2] This is a serious challenge. To put the matter bluntly, we *ought* to be worried if what we believe to be a foundational biblical truth remained entirely undiscovered from the days of the apostles right up until the middle of the sixteenth century. At the very least, such a discovery would undermine the idea that penal substitution is *clearly* taught in the Bible. On the other hand, it would be immensely reassuring to find that our understanding of the Bible has indeed been the consensus of Christian orthodoxy for almost two millennia.

This chapter discusses twenty-three people and organizations ranging from the Latin and Greek Fathers of the early church to major figures within modern evangelicalism. We give each a brief biographical introduction before plunging headlong into their original writings to see what they really said. In truth, they are a mixed bag. There are a few unquestionable heroes and martyrs, and a few with a blemish or two on their characters; there are preachers, theologians and historians; Baptists, Anglicans and Independents. We have included the Universities and Colleges Christian Fellowship and the Evangelical Alliance, as these organizations represent large numbers of evangelical Christians today. Obviously, this diverse array of characters would have disagreed with each other on a range of issues. However, this only strengthens the force of any consensus we find among them on the doctrine of penal substitution. For if we find theologians who wrote at different times, in different cultural settings, with very different concerns, who would have fought tooth and nail about a whole welter of theological questions, nevertheless standing shoulder to shoulder on *this* issue, we shall be all the more confident that we have reached the right conclusion about the teaching of Scripture.

We ought at this stage to explain what this chapter does not set out to do. We do not give a detailed, nuanced account of the particular theological

---

2. We note some proponents of this view in ch. 8, sect. 1.

emphases of each of these writers. That would take thousands of pages and would add little to the point in question – plenty of references are provided for people who want to dig deeper. Neither do we engage in debate about whether their views are right. As it happens, we agree with almost everything they say in the texts we cite (though occasionally we may have phrased things a little differently) but we have given our own biblical and theological exploration of penal substitution in chapters 2 and 3. Our aim here is much more limited: we shall simply demonstrate that all of these writers, without exception, believed the doctrine of penal substitution.

Turning to the texts themselves, it is worth noting that most of the early material does not come from extended treatments of the doctrine of salvation. This is largely because the major debates in those early centuries centred on the Trinity and the divinity of Jesus, and people are more inclined to spill ink on controversial topics than on matters of broad agreement. In particular, several of the texts date from the fourth century, when many theologians were preoccupied with a heresy associated with Arius, an Alexandrian church leader. Though it evolved gradually in its details, the consistent feature of Arianism was its denial of the full deity of Christ. It was decisively laid to rest at the Council of Constantinople in 381.

The fact that some of the texts were not written specifically to expound the doctrine of salvation does not make them irrelevant to our argument. On the contrary, if a writer makes a passing, but nonetheless explicit, reference to the doctrine of penal substitution in a work largely devoted to another subject, this probably indicates that penal substitution was both widely understood and fairly uncontroversial among his contemporaries. For it would have confused his readers if he had made a passing reference to an unknown doctrine, and it would have distracted attention from his point and undermined his argument if he had made a brief allusion to a subject of intense disagreement.

Finally, a brief word of explanation is in order about our choice of writers. We have tried to be fairly exhaustive up to and including Gregory the Great (c. 540–604), in order to refute the claim that penal substitution finds no support in the early church. From this point onwards we pick up the pace, providing a representative selection of contributions from the major eras of church history. Readers may feel swamped by the seemingly endless parade of ancient worthies in the first half of the chapter, for it will be a good few pages before we get past the Dark Ages. But we hope the effort will be worthwhile. In truth the weight of evidence is quite overwhelming, and it is worth reflecting on the extracts cited in the following pages in order to feel the full force of it. The myth of the 'late development' of penal substitution has persisted for quite long enough. It is time to lay it to rest for good.[3]

## Justin Martyr (c. 100–165)

Justin Martyr was born to Greek parents in Samaria during the early years of the second century. He was unimpressed by the Greek philosophy he studied as a young man, and was converted to Christ around 130 when an old man on a beach near Ephesus told him that the wisdom for which he was searching could be found only in the Old Testament prophets. Justin became a bold defender of the Christian faith, and was finally executed in Rome for refusing to sacrifice to the Roman gods. He was also one of the most significant Christian writers of the second century, exercising a strong influence over other early Christian theologians. He is particularly important for our historical survey because he takes us back to within a generation of the apostolic era – it is quite likely Justin would have spoken to people who had met the apostles.

Justin reveals his understanding of penal substitution in his *Dialogue with Trypho, a Jew*, his account of a conversation that took place around 130. At one point, Trypho concedes he is 'inclined . . . very strongly' to think that Jesus is the Christ promised in the Old Testament. He recognizes that the Old Testament teaches that the Christ must suffer, which obviously fits the life of Jesus. However, he cannot bring himself to believe that the Christ would be crucified, since the Old Testament law teaches that anyone crucified is under God's curse:

> Then Trypho remarked, 'Be assured that all our nation waits for Christ; and we
> admit that all the Scriptures which you have quoted refer to him. Moreover, I do
> also admit that the name of Jesus, by which the son of Nave (Nun) was called, has
> inclined me very strongly to adopt this view. But whether Christ should be so

---

3. Henri Blocher draws attention to other evidence that 'the doctrine of vicarious punishment was by no means absent' among the church Fathers in 'Biblical Metaphors and the Doctrine of the Atonement', *Journal of the Evangelical Theological Society* 47 (2004), pp. 629–645 (p. 630). Another recent overview of the teaching on the atonement throughout the history of the church may be found in Ian J. Shaw and Brian H. Edwards, *The Divine Substitute: The Atonement in the Bible and History* (Leominster: Day One, 2006).

shamefully crucified, this we are in doubt about. For whosoever is crucified is said in the law to be accursed, so that I am exceedingly incredulous on this point. It is quite clear, indeed, that the Scriptures announce that Christ had to suffer; but we wish to learn if you can prove it to us whether it was by the suffering cursed in the law.'[4]

Trypho apparently has Deuteronomy 21:23 in mind: 'Anyone who is hung on a tree is under God's curse'. Justin responds in three stages. He begins by answering Trypho's immediate concern, insisting that Christ was not cursed for his own sins: 'Though a curse lies in the law against persons who are crucified, yet no curse lies on the Christ of God, by whom all that have committed things worthy of a curse are saved.'[5]

Justin then asserts that God's curse rests on 'the whole human race', both Jews and Gentiles, for the Jews have failed to keep God's law, and the Gentiles have turned from God to idols:

> For the whole human race will be found to be under a curse. For it is written in the law of Moses, 'Cursed is every one that continueth not in all things that are written in the book of the law to do them.' And no one has accurately done all, nor will you venture to deny this; but some more and some less than others have observed the ordinances enjoined. But if those who are under this law appear to be under a curse for not having observed all the requirements, how much more shall all the nations appear to be under a curse who practice idolatry, who seduce youths, and commit other crimes?[6]

Finally, Justin reaches the crucial point of his argument, where he explains that the reason why Jesus was crucified is that the curse which rested on us for our sin was transferred to him:

> If, then, the Father of all wished His Christ for the whole human family to take upon Him the curses of all, knowing that, after He had been crucified and was dead, He would raise him up, why do you argue about Him, who submitted to suffer these things according to the Father's will, as if he were accursed, and do not rather bewail yourselves?[7]

---

4. Justin Martyr, *Dialogue with Trypho, a Jew*, in *Ante-Nicene Fathers*, vol. 1 (Grand Rapids: Eerdmans, repr. 1969), sect. lxxxix, p. 244.

5. Ibid., sect. xciv, p. 247.

6. Ibid., sect. xcv, p. 247.

7. Ibid.

In summary, Jesus took upon himself the curse of God that had rested upon 'the whole human family'. This explains why he was crucified even though he himself had committed no sin. It also amounts to a clear statement of penal substitution: although Christ was innocent, he bore the curse due to sinful humanity, enduring in his death the punishment due to us. Justin is a very early example of a writer who explained the doctrine on the basis of the 'curse' vocabulary of Galatians 3:13 and Deuteronomy 21:23. As we shall see, Eusebius of Caesarea and Hilary of Poitiers are among a number of later theologians who also took this approach.

## Eusebius of Caesarea (c. 275–339)

Eusebius of Caesarea was born in Palestine towards the end of the third century. He became bishop of Caesarea in Palestine around 314, and was a major figure in the Western Church in the early fourth century. Among other things, he played an important part in the Council of Nicea in 325, and was a trusted advisor to the Roman Emperor Constantine, who famously asked him to supervise the production of fifty copies of the Scriptures for use in churches in Constantinople, the new capital of the Roman Empire.[8] His many historical writings show a careful use of primary sources, as exemplified in his best-known work, his *Ecclesiastical History*. He is widely recognized today as an outstanding historian; indeed, Arnold Ehrhardt called him 'the first great Christian historian, perhaps the greatest of all'.[9]

Eusebius' belief in penal substitution emerges in his *Proof of the Gospel*, a two-part explanation and defence of the Christian faith for a pagan audience, probably written between 314 and 318.[10] Eusebius explains that Jesus shared our experience as human beings during his earthly life, and then goes on to outline the significance of his death:

> And the Lamb of God . . . was chastised on our behalf, and suffered a penalty He did not owe, but which we owed because of the multitude of our sins; and so He became

---

8. F. F. Bruce, *The Canon of Scripture* (Downers Grove: IVP, 1988), pp. 197–207.

9. A. A. T. Ehrhardt, *The Framework of the New Testament Stories* (Manchester: Manchester University Press, 1964), p. 64, citing with approval the opinion of Eduard Meyer. Also cited in Bruce, *Canon of Scripture*, p. 197, n. 1.

10. W. J. Ferrar, 'Introduction', in Eusebius of Caesarea, *Proof of the Gospel*, vol. 1, trans. and ed. W. J. Ferrar (London: SPCK; New York: Macmillan, 1920), pp. ix–xl (pp. xii–xiii).

the cause of the forgiveness of our sins, because He received death for us, and transferred to Himself the scourging, the insults, and the dishonour, which were due to us, and drew down upon Himself the appointed curse, being made a curse for us.[11]

This is an unequivocal statement of penal substitution. Like Justin Martyr, Eusebius employs the vocabulary of God's 'curse', taken from Galatians 3:13, arguing that Jesus was 'made a curse for us'. He also expresses the same truth in a different way, using the vocabulary of 'penalty' – Jesus 'suffered a penalty He did not owe, but which we owed because of the multitude of our sins'.

## Hilary of Poitiers (c. 300–368)

Hilary is less well known than some of the other church Fathers of the fourth century, perhaps because his writings are a little harder to understand, but he was nonetheless a significant figure. Like many of his day, his life was shaped by the controversies surrounding the Arian heresy. By the middle of the fourth century many senior posts in the church were held by Arians, and the emperor Constantius II pursued a policy of theological compromise in an effort to keep the peace. Hilary refused to fall in line with this approach, and his principled opposition led to his exile in 356. Hilary's theological works include his masterpiece *On the Trinity*, as well as numerous polemical works, a commentary on Matthew, and an exposition of the Psalms.

It is in the last of these that Hilary reveals his belief in penal substitution. Hilary read the Psalms Christologically, interpreting aspects of the life of King David as foreshadowings of the life of Christ. In particular, in his *Homily on Psalm 53 (54)*, he maintains that David's 'sufferings prophetically foretold the future sufferings of the Lord'.[12] This enables him to explain how we may be redeemed through the death of Christ without the need for the animal sacrifices of the Old Testament. Hilary begins by pointing out that God's curse rested upon everyone who broke the law, and that the Old Testament sacrifices

---

11. Eusebius of Caesarea, *Proof of the Gospel*, vol. 2, trans. and ed. W. J. Ferrar (London: SPCK; New York: Macmillan, 1920), bk. 10, ch. 1, p. 195.

12. Hilary of Poitiers, *Homily on Psalm 53 (54)*, in *Nicene and Post-Nicene Fathers*, ser. II, vol. 9 (Grand Rapids: Eerdmans, repr. 1976), sect. 1, p. 243. Hilary's numbering of the psalms differs from ours – his Ps. 53 is our Ps. 54. For convenience, we refer to the numbering as it appears in English Bibles.

were therefore absolutely essential to escape God's sentence of death. They 'did not involve an expression of free will',[13] in the sense that they were oblig-atory under the old covenant:

> The sacrifices of the Law . . . did not involve an expression of free will, because the sentence of a curse was pronounced on all who broke the Law. Whoever failed to sacrifice laid himself open to the curse. And it was always necessary to go through the whole sacrificial action because the addition of a curse to the commandment forbad any trifling with the obligation of offering.[14]

According to this logic, New Testament believers would seem to be in imminent danger of death, for we no longer offer the animal sacrifices required to avert God's curse. However, Hilary continues, New Testament believers have been redeemed from this curse by the Lord Jesus Christ: 'It was from this curse that our Lord Jesus Christ redeemed us, when, as the Apostle says: "Christ redeemed us from the curse of the law, being made a curse for us, for it is written: cursed is everyone that hangeth on a tree."'

We now reach the crucial point of Hilary's argument, where he explains on the basis of Psalm 54 how this redemption has been accomplished. He cites the words of verse 6, 'I will sacrifice unto thee freely',[15] as if they were spoken by the Lord Jesus Christ in reference to his own death, contrasting Christ's vol-untary self-sacrifice with the obligatory Old Testament animal sacrifices. He then argues that this free sacrifice of Christ makes it unnecessary for us to con-tinue the Old Testament sacrifices, for Christ suffered 'the death of the accursed' that would otherwise have come upon all of us for breaking God's law, and thereby broke the curse once and for all: 'Thus he offered himself to the death of the accursed that he might break the curse of the Law, offering himself voluntarily a victim to God the Father, in order that by means of a vol-untary victim the curse which attended the discontinuance of the regular victim might be removed.'[16]

In summary, then, Hilary argued that God's curse rests on all who break his law, that animal sacrifices were required under the old covenant

---

13. Hilary probably has Deut. 27:26 in mind here, particularly since this text is cited in Gal. 3:10 and Hilary quotes from Gal. 3:13 in the same paragraph of his exposition.

14. Hilary, *Homily*, sect. 13, p. 246.

15. Ibid.

16. Ibid.

to escape this curse, but that Christ has removed the curse by suffering the punishment of death in our place, thereby making further animal sacrifices unnecessary. This reflects a clear doctrine of penal substitution.

## Athanasius (c. 300–373)

Athanasius was born in Alexandria around 300. He was made bishop of Alexandria in 328, and is best known for his defence of orthodox Christianity against Arianism. Athanasius' resolute stance earned him many powerful enemies, and he was forced into exile four times between 335 and 365 for a total of more than fifteen years.[17] The echoes of Athanasius' clear thinking and uncompromising boldness are still felt to this day, for our modern Nicene Creed is based on the 381 Council of Constantinople, which in turn was strongly influenced by the 325 Council of Nicea in which Athanasius played an important part. There are few people to whom the Christian church owes a greater debt than Athanasius, for his uncompromising stand for biblical truth.

Athanasius wrote several works countering Arianism, two of which are of interest to us. The first, *Against the Arians*, was probably composed when he returned from his first period of exile in around 339, apparently in response to a request from his supporters to explain the beliefs that had landed him in such trouble. At one point, while alluding to the apostle John's explanation of why Christ came into the world in John 3:17, he states that Christ ('the Word') accomplished our salvation by suffering the judgment due to the guilty world: 'Formerly the world, as guilty, was under judgment from the Law; but now the Word has taken on Himself the judgment, and having suffered in the body for all, has bestowed salvation to all.'[18] This is a straightforward statement of the doctrine of penal substitution. According to Athanasius, the whole world is guilty of failing to keep God's law, but Christ took upon himself the judgment due to us, and suffered in our place for our salvation.

---

17. E. Ferguson (ed.), *Encyclopedia of Early Christianity* (Chicago: St. James, 1990); E. Fahlbush et al. (eds.), *The Encyclopedia of Christianity* (Grand Rapids: Eerdmans; Leiden: Brill, 1999).

18. Athanasius, *Against the Arians*, in *Nicene and Post-Nicene Fathers*, ser. II, vol. 4 (Grand Rapids: Eerdmans, repr. 1975), sect. 60, p. 341.

The second of Athanasius' works of concern to us is *On the Incarnation*. We shall examine this piece in more detail, because it will allow us to appreciate the central place that penal substitution occupied in his thought. Athanasius composed this treatise around 318 to answer the simple question 'Why did the Son of God become man?' His answer is that God's overarching purpose in the incarnation, within which all of his other purposes are subsumed, was the salvation of his people: 'He has been manifested in a human body for this reason only, out of the love and goodness of His Father, for the salvation of us men.'[19]

Athanasius begins his argument by emphasizing that sin corrupts us, undoing God's good work of creation and progressively destroying us. This corruption and destruction comes in fulfilment of Genesis 2:17, where God says to Adam, 'You must not eat from the tree of the knowledge of good and evil, for when you eat of it you will surely die.' Referring to the rebellion of Adam and Eve, he writes:

> But men, having turned from the contemplation of God to evil of their own
> devising, had come inevitably under the law of death. Instead of remaining in the
> state in which God had created them, they were in process of becoming corrupted
> entirely, and death had them completely under its dominion. For the transgression of
> the commandment was making them turn back again according to their nature; and
> as they had at the beginning come into being out of non-existence, so were they now
> on the way to returning, through corruption, to non-existence again.[20]

Athanasius then argues that this places God in a dilemma. On the one hand, it would be 'unworthy of the goodness of God' for him to allow his creation to be destroyed by the corruption of human sin. In particular, it would be 'monstrous' if this became the fate of human beings, since we were created in his image. On the other hand, God would also be dishonoured if he simply put a stop to this corruption, for that would compromise the truth of his promise in Genesis 2:17. He must, it seems, either be discredited as an incompetent Creator or exposed as a liar:

> It would, of course, have been unthinkable that God should go back upon His word
> and that man, having transgressed, should not die; but it was equally monstrous that

---

19. Athanasius, *On the Incarnation* (New York: St. Vladimir's Seminary Press, 1993), sect.
    1, p. 26.
20. Ibid., sect. 4, pp. 29–30.

beings which once had shared the nature of the Word should perish and turn back again into non-existence through corruption. It was unworthy of the goodness of God that creatures made by Him should be brought to nothing through the deceit wrought upon man by the devil . . . Yet, true though this is . . . it was unthinkable that God, the Father of Truth, should go back upon his word regarding death in order to ensure our continued existence. He could not falsify Himself; what, then, was God to do?[21]

It would not be enough, Athanasius continues, for human beings simply to repent of our sin, for this would not reverse our corruption, and would still leave God open to the charge of untruthfulness:

But repentance would not guard the Divine consistency, for, if death did not hold dominion over men, God would still remain untrue. Nor does repentance recall men from what is according to their nature; all that it does is to make them cease from sinning. Had it been a case of a trespass only, and not of a subsequent corruption, repentance would have been well enough; but when once transgression had begun men came under the power of the corruption proper to their nature and were bereft of the grace which belonged to them as creatures in the Image of God. No, repentance could not meet the case.[22]

Athanasius explains that only by the death and resurrection of the Son could God both remain true to his word and at the same time save his creation from corruption and death. In taking a human body and dying, the Son suffered the penalty for sin promised in Genesis 2:17, thus maintaining God's truthfulness. Since the Son has power to give life, he was then able to overcome death through his resurrection. Thus 'the renewal of creation has been wrought by the Self-same Word Who made it in the beginning'.[23] The Son of God could thus free humankind from the power of death, and bring us to new life:

Thus, taking a body like our own, because all our bodies were liable to the corruption of death, He surrendered His body to death in place of all, and offered it to the Father. This He did out of sheer love for us, so that in His death all might die, and the law of death thereby be abolished because, having fulfilled in His body that for

---

21. Ibid., sects. 6–7, pp. 32–33.
22. Ibid., sect. 7, p. 33.
23. Ibid., sect. 1, p. 26.

which it was appointed, it was thereafter voided of its power for men. This He did that He might turn again to incorruption men who had turned back to corruption, and make them alive through death by the appropriation of His body and by the grace of His resurrection. Thus He would make death to disappear from them as utterly as straw from fire.[24]

For Athanasius, then, Jesus' *death* was the purpose of the incarnation; the immortal Son of God needed to become man to die. In saying this death was 'in place of' us, Athanasius has already hinted at penal substitution. It becomes explicit in what follows:

The Word perceived that corruption could not be got rid of otherwise than through death; yet He Himself, as the Word, being immortal and the Father's Son, was such as could not die. For this reason, therefore, He assumed a body capable of death, in order that it, through belonging to the Word Who is above all, might become in dying a sufficient exchange for all, and, itself remaining incorruptible through His indwelling, might thereafter put an end to corruption for all others as well, by the grace of the resurrection. It was by surrendering to death the body which He had taken, as an offering and sacrifice free from every stain, that He forthwith abolished death for His human brethren by the offering of the equivalent. For naturally, since the Word of God was above all, when He offered His own temple and bodily instrument as a substitute for the life of all, He fulfilled in death all that was required.[25]

The substitutionary element here is obvious, for the human body of the incarnate Son became 'a sufficient *exchange* for all', and was 'a *substitute* for the life of all'. The penal element is clear from his insistence that the Son offered himself as a substitute 'in *death*', which, as we saw, he understands as punishment for sin in line with God's warning in Genesis 2:17. Therefore, although Christians still face death in a biological sense, death no longer has the character of punishment for sin; rather, it is the pathway to resurrection:

Have no fear then. Now that the common Saviour of all has died on our behalf, we who believe in Christ no longer die, as men died aforetime, in fulfilment of the threat of the law. That condemnation has come to an end; and now that, by the grace of the

---

24. Ibid., sect. 8, p. 34.
25. Ibid., sect. 9, p. 35.

resurrection, corruption has been banished and done away, we are loosed from our mortal bodies in God's good time for each, so that we may obtain thereby a better resurrection. Like seeds cast into the earth, we do not perish in our dissolution, but like them shall rise again, death having been brought to nought by the grace of the Saviour.[26]

Penal substitution is thus central to Athanasius' thought. First, it is inextricably linked to the purpose of the incarnation: God became man in order to save sinful humanity from the divine curse on creation that is God's *punishment* for sin, and Christ accomplished this by enduring and exhausting this curse in our place, as our *substitute*. Secondly, according to Athanasius, Christ's death has implications for the whole created order, for he bore a curse that rested on all creation and thus brought renewed life to the entire cosmos. Thirdly, Athanasius argues that this renewal is the solution to social and political evil, for the moral degeneration of society and the violence between nations are both consequences of the corruption Christ has reversed.[27] In summary, Athanasius not only affirmed the doctrine of penal substitution, but also placed it squarely at the centre of his theology as integral to the purpose of the incarnation, the restoration of human society and the renewal of creation.

## Gregory of Nazianzus (c. 330–390)

Gregory was born around 330, and was ordained in 361 by his father, then Bishop of Nazianzus. He was a lifelong friend of Basil of Caesarea and Gregory of Nyssa, alongside whom he mounted a stanch defence of the orthodox faith against Arianism. Gregory presided over the 381 Council of Constantinople, and thereby bequeathed a lasting legacy to the Christian church in the form of the Nicene Creed, which is based on its decrees. His most significant theological works are his five *Theological Orations*, which earned him the nickname 'The Theologian', and it is in the fourth of these that we discover his commitment to the doctrine of penal substitution.

In his fourth *Oration*, Gregory addresses several biblical texts his opponents had cited to argue that the Son was inferior to the Father. These apparently included Galatians 3:13 and 2 Corinthians 5:21, where Paul speaks of

---

26. Ibid., sect. 21, p. 50. See also sects. 27–29.
27. Ibid., sect. 5, pp. 30–31.

Christ 'becoming a curse' and being 'made . . . sin'. In reply, Gregory argues that the reason why Christ was cursed is that our sin was transferred to him:

> As for my sake He was called a curse, Who destroyed my curse; and sin, who taketh away the sin of the world; and became a new Adam to take the place of the old, just so He makes my disobedience His own as Head of the whole body. As long then as I am disobedient and rebellious, both by denial of God and by my passions, so long Christ also is called disobedient on my account.[28]

Gregory's argument here is that believers are united to Christ, the 'Head of the whole body', and that our sin is thereby transferred to him – 'he makes my disobedience his own'. This is the reason, Gregory argues, that Christ 'was called a curse . . . and sin': he took 'the sin of the world' upon himself and suffered the curse of God 'for my sake'. He was not *himself* a sinner, and was not cursed for his *own* sin, but for 'the sin of the world'. Thus Gregory believed in penal substitution.

### Ambrose of Milan (339–397)

Ambrose was born in Trier, Germany, and was made Bishop of Milan around 373. He spearheaded the effort to reverse the policy of compromise with Arianism favoured by the emperors during the preceding years, and persistently refused to allow the church to be dictated to by the secular authorities. His resolute opposition to doctrinal compromise and his bold leadership of the church led Tony Lane to describe him as 'the greatest Western Church leader of the fourth century'.[29] On one famous occasion, the emperor's mother led a group of Arians in an attempt to force Ambrose to allow Arian worship in one of the churches of Milan. Ambrose refused, and organized vigils to prevent the building being taken by force, openly declaring his willingness to die rather than allow the building to be used by the Arians. Ambrose is often credited with inventing the practice of congregational hymn-singing, supposedly something he introduced to lift the spirits of the congregation during this protracted dispute.

---

28. Gregory of Nazianzus, *The Fourth Theological Oration*, in *Nicene and Post-Nicene Fathers*, ser. II, vol. 7 (Grand Rapids: Eerdmans, repr. 1974), sect. v, p. 311.

29. Tony Lane, *The Lion Book of Christian Thought* (Oxford: Lion, 1984), p. 37.

Ambrose affirms the doctrine of penal substitution in his *Flight from the World*. He seeks to explain how we can be freed from the curse of death that came upon humankind as a result of the fall without compromising God's justice. His answer is that Jesus became a man so that he could take the curse of God upon himself, and that he died to fulfil God's sentence upon cursed humanity. In this way he established God's justice while at the same time securing forgiveness and life for us:

> And so then, Jesus took flesh that He might destroy the curse of sinful flesh, and He became for us a curse that a blessing might overwhelm a curse, uprightness might overwhelm sin, forgiveness might overwhelm the sentence, and life might overwhelm death. He also took up death that the sentence might be fulfilled and satisfaction might be given for the judgment, the curse placed on sinful flesh even to death. Therefore, nothing was done contrary to God's sentence when the terms of that sentence were fulfilled, for the curse was unto death but grace is after death.[30]

Ambrose's whole argument hinges on the doctrine of penal substitution, for the curse that rested upon sinful humanity was transferred to Christ, and he died to satisfy God's just sentence of death upon us.


## John Chrysostom (c. 350–407)

John was born in Syrian Antioch some time between 344 and 354. Baptized as a young man, he adopted the life of a hermit, living in a cave on a hill outside the city. This austere lifestyle made him so ill that he was forced to return in 378, and shortly after this he was ordained before ministering in Antioch for almost two decades. During this period John became widely known as an extraordinary preacher, a talent that later earned him the nickname 'Chrysostom', meaning 'Golden-mouthed'.

Towards the end of a sermon on 2 Corinthians 5:21, John illustrates his point with the analogy of a king who takes pity on a miserable, condemned criminal. The king gives his only son to receive the guilt and punishment of the criminal, and to be killed in his place, and then exalts the criminal to a

---

30. Ambrose of Milan, *Flight from the World*, in *The Fathers of the Church*, vol. 65, trans. M. P. McHugh (Washington, DC: Catholic University of America Press, 1972), ch. 7, sect. 44, pp. 314–315.

place of glorious dignity. Surely, he argues, that criminal would be over-whelmed with gratitude; he would do anything rather than further outrage the king who had treated him so kindly. John then applies the lesson to his Christian hearer. God's past mercies ought to produce in us not presumption but remorse:

> If one that was himself a king, beholding a robber and malefactor under punishment, gave his well-beloved son, his only-begotten and true, to be slain; and transferred the death and the guilt as well, from him to his son (who was himself of no such character), that he might both save the condemned man and clear him from his evil reputation; and then if, having subsequently promoted him to great dignity, he had yet, after thus saving him and advancing him to that glory unspeakable, been outraged by the person that had received such treatment: would not that man, if he had any sense, have chosen ten thousand deaths rather than appear guilty of so great ingratitude? This then let us also now consider with ourselves, and groan bitterly for the provocations we have offered our Benefactor; nor let us therefore presume, because though outraged He bears it with long-suffering; but rather for this very reason be full of remorse.[31]

Chrysostom's commitment to the doctrine of penal substitution is plain in his king-robber illustration: the guilt of sinful people was transferred to the innocent son, who died in their place in order that they might be saved from the punishment they deserved and be crowned with 'glory unspeakable'. It is particularly significant that Chrysostom is not setting out to expound the doctrine of penal substitution in this sermon: he simply assumes it as part of an illustration of a completely different point. The fact that he can allude to the doctrine in this incidental way shows that it must have been widely accepted and understood by his hearers, for he would hardly have chosen to illustrate his point with an analogy that was unfamiliar or controversial.

---

31. John Chrysostom, *Homilies on Second Corinthians*, in *Nicene and Post-Nicene Fathers*, ser. I, vol. 12 (Grand Rapids: Eerdmans, repr. 1969), Homily XI, sect. 6, p. 335.

## Augustine of Hippo (354–430)

Augustine is a towering figure in Christian theology, hailed as 'the single most influential theologian in the history of the Church in the West'.[32] He was born in Thagaste, North Africa, and converted in 384 under the influence of his mother Monica and Ambrose of Milan. Despite some reluctance on his part he was ordained in 391, and four years later was made Bishop of Hippo, a post he occupied until his death.

Augustine's literary output was considerable. His own account of his early life and conversion appear in his *Confessions*, which ranks together with his *City of God* among the great works of world literature. He wrote numerous other theological and polemical works, many in the context of a protracted dispute with Pelagius and his followers, against whom Augustine defended the doctrines of sin, grace and God's sovereignty.

In addition, Augustine wrote a number of polemics against Manicheism, a sect to which he had belonged before his conversion, and it is here we discover his commitment to penal substitution. The Manicheans rejected the Old Testament on the grounds of its supposed immorality, and in *Against Faustus the Manichean* Augustine tackles the view that Moses was guilty of blasphemy against Jesus. Faustus found the offending words in Deuteronomy 21:22–23, which reads, 'If a man guilty of a capital offence is put to death and his body is hung on a tree, you must not leave his body on the tree overnight. Be sure to bury him that same day, because anyone who is hung on a tree is under God's curse.'

Faustus recognizes that the apostle Paul quotes these words in connection with Jesus' crucifixion (Gal. 3:13), and concludes that Moses includes Jesus in the category of people cursed by God. He finds this idea appalling, because in his mind this means that Jesus must have been guilty of sin: 'We abhor Moses . . . for the awful curse he has pronounced upon Christ the Son of God, who for our salvation hung on the tree.'[33]

The only alternative, as far as Faustus can see, is that Moses made a mistake. Perhaps, Faustus wonders, Moses meant that every *sinner* who is hung on a tree is cursed, but not necessarily *everyone*, although this is not what Moses actually wrote. But even if this were a slip on Moses' part, in Faustus' view it would still be culpable: 'Moses was no prophet, and while cursing in

---

32. M. Walsh (ed.), *Dictionary of Christian Biography* (London: Continuum, 2001), p. 109.

33. Augustine, *Against Faustus*, in *Nicene and Post-Nicene Fathers*, ser. I, vol. 4 (Grand Rapids: Eerdmans, 1974), bk. 14, sect. 1, p. 207.

his usual manner, he fell ignorantly into the sin of blasphemy against God.'[34] In summary, Faustus argues that Moses is guilty of blasphemy, because he implied that Jesus was cursed by God and therefore charged the innocent Son of God with sin.

In order to answer this charge, Augustine must explain how Jesus can have been cursed by his Father without having been guilty of sin. He begins by drawing a distinction between two meanings of the word 'sin'. According to Augustine, sin can refer either to actual sinful actions or to the consequence of those actions: death. He argues that Christ was not guilty of sin in the first sense, for his entire life was free of every kind of sinful action. Rather, Christ bore sin in the second sense – that is, he suffered death, the consequence of sin:[35] 'So sin means both a bad action deserving punishment, and death the consequence of sin. Christ has no sin in the sense of deserving death, but He bore for our sakes sin in the sense of death as brought on human nature by sin.'[36]

According to Augustine, this is what Moses meant when he said Jesus was cursed. Christ suffered our death, without being guilty of any sinful deeds. In this way, Christ has delivered us from death by dying instead of us, because death itself was cursed, condemned and destroyed at the cross. Speaking of death, he writes, 'This is what hung on the tree; this is what was cursed by Moses. Thus was death condemned that its reign might cease, and cursed that it might be destroyed. By Christ's taking our sin in this sense, its condemnation is our deliverance, while to remain in subjection to sin is to be condemned.'[37]

Augustine is quick to draw out the implication of this line of thought. If death is the punishment due to us for our sin, and if Christ suffered death in our place, then this means that Christ suffered the punishment we deserved. He makes this explicit a few sentences later: 'Christ, though guiltless, took our punishment, that He might cancel our guilt, and do away with our punishment.'[38] A few paragraphs further on, he summarizes the argument:

> But as Christ endured death as man, and for man; so also, Son of God as
> He was, ever living in His own righteousness, but dying for our offences, He

---

34. Ibid.

35. Augustine explains his view that death is the punishment for sin in *City of God*, trans. Henry Bettenson (London: Penguin, 1984), bk. 13, pp. 510–526.

36. Augustine, *Against Faustus*, bk. 14, sect. 3, p. 208.

37. Ibid.

38. Ibid., sect. 4, p. 208.

submitted as man, and for man, to bear the curse which accompanies death. And as He died in the flesh which He took in bearing our punishment, so also, while ever blessed in His own righteousness, He was cursed for our offences, in the death which He suffered in bearing our punishment.[39]

This is a straightforward statement of penal substitution: the sinless Lord Jesus Christ bore the curse of death due to sinful humanity, and thereby 'suffered in bearing our punishment'.

Two features of Augustine's presentation are worth noting. First, he is clear that it is not enough merely to affirm in a vague way, 'Christ died to save us'; it also matters *how* Christ won our salvation. Even Faustus believes that 'Christ the Son of God . . . for our salvation hung on a tree,'[40] but this does not satisfy Augustine, who seeks to correct his misunderstanding of exactly what happened at the cross. The precise 'mechanism' of Christ's redemptive work is important.

Secondly, Augustine emphasizes the sinlessness of Christ, insisting that the fact that Christ was cursed by God does not imply he had done anything worthy of death. Indeed, perhaps because Augustine is so acutely sensitive to Faustus' criticisms and anxious to avoid the implication that Christ had sinned, he is unwilling even to suggest *our* guilt was transferred to Christ. He says that Christ bore our curse, died in our place, and suffered our punishment, but not that he bore our guilt (i.e. the culpability for our sinful actions). In this respect Augustine differs from many later writers, who distinguish between guilt *incurred* by a person for their own sins and guilt *imputed* to them from a third party, and who hold that Christ was guilty in the second sense, though not the first. In this way they follow such biblical texts as Isaiah 53:6 and 2 Corinthians 5:21 and argue that although Christ was sinless in himself, he was reckoned by God as being guilty for our sins, and punished for this reason. In our view these later writers are correct, and a slight tension remains in Augustine's theology: if Christ was not guilty before God even by imputation, then God *unjustly* punished an innocent man. However, even if Augustine's precise formulation leads him to inconsistency, it cannot be doubted that he believed Christ bore our punishment – the essence of penal substitution.

---

39. Ibid., sect. 6, p. 209.
40. Ibid. sect. 1, p. 207.

## Cyril of Alexandria (375–444)

Cyril was made Bishop of Alexandria in 412, taking over from his uncle. The arguments over the succession had been intense, and Cyril was immediately plunged into stormy political waters. Nonetheless, if anyone was up to the task, it was Cyril, for he was an outstanding theologian and a fierce debater, as demonstrated in his famous opposition to Nestorius at the Council of Ephesus in 431. Unsurprisingly, his vigorous approach to theological discussion was not universally popular, although few felt as strongly as Theodoret, Bishop of Cyrus, who greeted the news of Cyril's death somewhat unkindly: 'His survivors are indeed delighted at his departure. The dead, maybe, are sorry. There is some ground for alarm lest they should be so much annoyed at his company as to send him back to us.'[41] This is perhaps a little unfair, given the debt of gratitude the Christian church owes Cyril for his uncompromising stand for Nicene orthodoxy. But our concern here is in any case not to commend his character but to demonstrate his commitment to penal substitution. This emerges in the following passage from his *De adoratione et cultu in spiritu et veritate*, an exposition of the Old Testament law:

> The Only-begotten was made man, bore a body by nature at enmity with death, and became flesh, so that, enduring the death which was hanging over us as the result of our sin, he might abolish sin; and further, that he might put an end to the accusations of Satan, inasmuch as we have paid in Christ himself the penalties for the charges of sin against us: 'For he bore our sins, and was wounded because of us', according to the voice of the prophet. Or are we not healed by his wounds?[42]

Cyril plainly affirms the doctrine of penal substitution here. Christ was our substitute, 'For he bore our sins, and was wounded because of us'. As our substitute Christ suffered the penalty due to us, 'enduring the death which was hanging over us as the result of our sin'.

---

41. Theodoret, Letter 180, to Bishop Domnus of Antioch, cited in Lane, *Christian Thought*, p. 47.

42. Cyril of Alexandria, *De adoratione et cultu in spiritu et veritate*, iii, 100–102, in J. P. Migne (ed.), *Patrologiae Cursus Completus: Series Graeca*, vol. 68 (Paris, 1857–), pp. 293, 296; English trans. from Garry J. Williams, 'A Critical Exposition of Hugo Grotius's Doctrine of the Atonement in *De Satisfactione Christi*' (unpub. doctoral thesis, University of Oxford, 1999).

It is worth noting in passing that Cyril's explanation of the significance of Christ's death includes the idea of *participation* alongside subsitution. As our substitute, Christ was punished in our place, instead of us. Yet because we are united to Christ by faith – we are 'in him' – it is possible for Cyril to affirm that '*we* have paid in Christ himself the penalties for the charges of sin against us' (italics added). We discuss the idea of participation and its relationship to substitution in more detail in chapter 10, section 1. At this stage it is sufficient merely to observe that Cyril regards them as complementary, not contradictory, perspectives on the death of Christ.

## Gelasius of Cyzicus (fifth century)

Little is known about Gelasius of Cyzicus. He is sometimes referred to in later literature as Gelasius Cyzicenus, and was born sometime during the fifth century, probably in Cyzicus, where his father was a presbyter. For at least part of his life he lived in Bithynia, where around 475 he wrote his best-known work, *The Acts of the First Council of Nicea*, an account of the proceedings of the 325 Council of Nicea. It includes an account of the life and death of Christ, in which Gelasius affirms that Christ willingly suffered the punishment due to us for our sins to free us from death. Speaking of Christ, he writes:

> After a period of three years and at the beginning of the fourth he thus draws near to his bodily suffering, which he willingly undergoes on our behalf. For the punishment of the cross was due to us; but if we had all been crucified, we would have had no power to deliver ourselves from death, 'for death reigned from Adam until Moses, even over those who did not sin' (Rom. 5:14). There were many holy men, many prophets, many righteous men, but not one of them had the power to ransom himself from the authority of death; but he, the Saviour of all, came and received the punishments which were due to us into his sinless flesh, which was of us, in place of us, and on our behalf.[43]

A few sentences later, he asserts that this is what Christians had believed since the days of the apostles: 'This is the apostolic and approved faith of the church, which, transmitted from the beginning from the Lord himself through

---

43. Gelasius of Cyzicus, *Church History*, ii, 24, in *Die Griechischen Christlichen Schriftsteller der ersten drei Jahrhunderte*, vol. 28 (Leipzig: Preussische Akademie der Wissenschaften, 1897–), p. 100; English trans. from Williams, 'Critical Exposition'.

the apostles from one generation to another, the church sets on high and has held fast until even now, and will do for ever.'[44]

Gelasius provides no detailed theological justification for his views, and has no particular interest in defending the doctrine of penal substitution. Instead, writing as a historian, he simply states what had been the consensus since the earliest days of the church, without argument or explanation. On this evidence it seems likely the doctrine of penal substitution was widely understood and agreed upon by his contemporaries.

Unfortunately, Gelasius was somewhat lacking in integrity as a historian. He wrote *The Acts* to counter a group of heretics who denied that Christ had both a human and a divine nature and who appealed to the decrees of the Council of Nicea to support their views. Gelasius was unable to find a complete account of the proceedings of the Council, so he set about compiling his own from the sources available to him. In the process, however, he embellished the facts in an attempt to strengthen the case against his opponents. As a record of the Council, therefore, Gelasius' work is extremely unreliable.

However, it does not follow that there is no historical value to the material on penal substitution cited above, for this relates to the historic teaching of the church, not to the proceedings of the Council. The details of the proceedings were apparently not widely known in Gelasius' time, which is why Gelasius compiled his account in the first place.[45] Gelasius could therefore freely produce a distorted account of what went on behind the closed doors of Nicea 150 years previously without fear of contradiction. But it would have been an entirely different matter to misrepresent the teachings of the contemporary church and of every previous generation since the apostles. There must have been some truth in these claims, otherwise his opponents would have been queuing up to contradict him and he would have jeopardized the credibility of the rest of his argument. For this reason, Gelasius' testimony indicates at the very least that his contemporaries believed in penal substitution, and that they would have agreed with his assessment of the historical preva-

---

44. Ibid., p. 101; English trans. from Williams, 'Critical Exposition'.

45. Indeed, the details of what went on at the council were apparently not widely known even in the middle of the fourth century, for when Athanasius was asked about the proceedings of the council he replied directly rather than by referring to another account of the proceedings. See H. Wace and W. C. Piercy (eds.), *Dictionary of Christian Biography* (London: John Murray, 1911); and Athanasius, *Defence of the Nicene Definition*, in *Nicene and Post-Nicene Fathers*, ser. II, vol. 4 (Grand Rapids: Eerdmans, repr. 1975), ch. 1, sect. 2, p. 151.

lence of that doctrine. This is why Gelasius' testimony is important to us. Frankly, he has almost no significance as a theologian, and is a very unreliable guide to the Council of Nicea. But his comments about the death of Christ strongly suggest that the doctrine of penal substitution was common currency in the Western Church in the fifth century.

## Gregory the Great (c. 540–604)

Gregory was born in Rome, and excelled himself in his early training as a lawyer before abandoning his secular career and becoming a monk. He was made Pope in 590, and his extensive administrative skills were tested immediately as he laboured to provide relief from a plague then ravaging the city. It was Gregory who sent Augustine (of Canterbury, not to be confused with Augustine of Hippo) to preach the gospel in England, and he also has the somewhat dubious distinction of being the pope who elevated the doctrine of purgatory to the status of official dogma. Gregory's most significant literary work was his *Pastoral Rule*, which remained an influential guide to the training of bishops until well into the medieval period. Other surviving pieces from Gregory's pen include around 850 letters and his *Morals on the Book of Job*. It is in this latter work that his belief in penal substitution becomes clear.

Gregory sees the innocent sufferings of Job as a foreshadowing of the innocent sufferings of Christ. With this in mind, he cites God's words to Satan in Job 2:3 ('Thou movest me against him to afflict him without cause'), which were originally spoken about Job, as if they might also be spoken about the Lord Jesus Christ. Referring to Christ, he writes:

> And of him is it rightly added, *without cause*. For 'he was destroyed without cause,' who was at once weighed to the earth by the avenging of sin, and not defiled by the pollution of sin. He 'was destroyed without cause,' Who, being made incarnate, had no sins of His own, and yet being without offence took upon Himself the punishment of the carnal.[46]

Gregory repeatedly emphasizes Christ's innocence, and explains his suffering on the grounds that he 'took upon Himself the punishment of the carnal' (sinful humanity). This obviously reflects a penal substitutionary view of the atonement.

---

46. Gregory the Great, *Morals on the Book of Job*, vol. 1 (Oxford: John Henry Parker, 1844), bk. 3, sect. 14, p. 148; italics original.

## Thomas Aquinas (c. 1225–74)

Thomas Aquinas was born around 1225 near Monte Casino, Italy. He joined the Dominican order of friars in the early 1240s, despite the outrage of his family, who kidnapped and held him hostage for over a year in a failed attempt to persuade him to change his mind. After his release he studied for a short time in Cologne before moving to France and later to Italy, where he devoted much of his time to study and writing. Of course, it is among Roman Catholics that Aquinas exerts his strongest influence today. However, he wrote several hundred years before the Reformation, and his work has historical importance for Protestants also. He is certainly hard to ignore, for he was without question the greatest of all the medieval theologians.

Aquinas began work on his greatest theological project, the *Summa Theologiae*, in 1266. There he explains that God the Father gave up his Son to suffer in our place, while at the same time Christ suffered willingly:

> It is wicked and cruel to hand an innocent man over to suffering and death if it is against his will. Nor did God the Father so treat Christ in whom he inspired the will to suffer for us. *God's severity* is thus manifested; he was unwilling to remit sin without punishment, as the Apostle intimates when he says, *He did not spare even his own Son.* But it also illustrates God's goodness, for as man was unable to make sufficient satisfaction through any punishment he might himself suffer, God gave him one who would satisfy for him. Paul stresses this, saying, *He has delivered him for us all,* and, *God has established him [Christ] as a propitiation by his blood through faith.*[47]

Aquinas argues that God shows both his severity towards sin and his goodness to his people by paying himself a debt we could not pay. This debt was the punishment due to us for our sin against him, and he paid it by giving his Son 'as a propitiation'. The insistence that God in his justice must and will punish sin, and that Christ's death is a 'satisfaction' on our behalf, recurs throughout questions 48 to 50 of the *Summa Theologiae*. Here is another example:

> By sin man contracts a twofold obligation. First, he is bound in slavery to sin inasmuch as *everyone who commits sin is a slave of sin, and by whatever a man is overcome, of this also he is the slave.* Because, then, the devil had overcome man by inducing him to sin,

---

47. Thomas Aquinas, *Summa Theologiae*, vol. 54 (London: Eyre & Spottiswoode, 1965), 3a, quest. 47, art. 3, p. 63, citing Rom. 11:22; 8:32; 3:25. The italics and text in square brackets are original.

man was delivered into the bondage of the devil. Secondly, by sin man was held to the debt of punishment according to divine justice . . .

As therefore Christ's passion provided adequate, and more than adequate satisfaction for man's sin and debt, his passion was as it were the price of punishment by which we are freed from both obligations. Satisfaction offered for oneself or for another resembles the price whereby one ransoms himself from sin and from punishment . . . Now Christ offered satisfaction . . . by giving the greatest of all things, namely himself, for us. For that reason, the passion of Christ is said to be our ransom.[48]

Here Aquinas argues that our sin leaves us enslaved to the devil and indebted to God, and that Christ's 'passion was . . . the price of punishment by which we were freed'. Aquinas guards against the misunderstanding that the price of punishment was paid to the devil.[49] Rather, it was by paying the debt we owe to *God* that Christ rescued us from Satan's bondage. This amounts to a clear statement of penal substitution: God must punish sin to maintain his justice, but Christ suffered in our place and freed us from this debt.

## John Calvin (1509–64)

John Calvin was born in 1509 in Noyon, France, and was converted some time in the early 1530s. After a few years in France he moved to Switzerland, and during an unplanned visit to Geneva in 1536 was persuaded by some of the local leaders to remain there. Calvin's work in Geneva included writing and lecturing, besides his role as the pastor of the city's church. His preaching was extraordinary: he addressed large congregations several times a week, always without notes, with only the Hebrew or Greek text of Scripture in front of him. These sermons later formed the basis of many of his commentaries, which are still in print and reflect a profound reverence for and understanding of Scripture.

He brought all this biblical insight to bear in the production of his greatest work, the *Institutes of the Christian Religion*, the final edition of which was published in 1559. Originally intended as a doctrinal supplement to his commentaries, it is justly regarded as one of the foundations of Reformed theology. Calvin turns to the doctrine of penal substitution in the course of explaining

---

48. Ibid., quest. 48, art. 4, p. 85, citing John 8:34; 2 Pet. 2:19. Italics original.

49. Ibid., p. 87.

how 'The awareness of God's wrath makes us thankful for his loving act in Christ.'[50] He asks his reader to consider someone who is beginning to discover all that God has done for him:

> Suppose he learns, as Scripture teaches, that he was estranged from God through sin, is an heir of wrath, subject to the curse of eternal death, excluded from all hope of salvation, beyond every blessing of God, the slave of Satan, captive under the yoke of sin, destined finally for a dreadful destruction and already involved in it; and that at this point Christ interceded as his advocate, took upon himself and suffered the punishment that, from God's righteous judgment, threatened all sinners; that he purged with his blood those evils which had rendered sinners hateful to God; that by this expiation he made satisfaction and sacrifice duly to God the Father; that as intercessor he has appeased God's wrath; that on this foundation rests the peace of God with men; that by this bond his benevolence is maintained toward them. Will the man not then be even more moved by all these things which so vividly portray the greatness of the calamity from which he has been rescued?[51]

This passage contains a clear affirmation of the doctrine of penal substitution: 'Christ . . . took upon himself and suffered the punishment that . . . threatened all sinners.' The same idea is repeated later in the same chapter.[52] The context in which Calvin chooses to expound this doctrine speaks volumes about his intense pastoral concern – he regards Christ's penal substitutionary death as a magnificent demonstration of the love of God, the basis of our peace with God, and a reason for intense gratitude to him.[53]

## Francis Turretin (1623–87)

Francis Turretin was born in 1623 in Geneva, where he lived for most of his life. After studying theology as a young man, he combined the roles of pastor to the French and Italian congregations in Geneva with the post of professor of theology at the Academy of Geneva.

---

50. John Calvin, *Institutes of the Christian Religion*, trans. F. L. Battles, vol. 1 (Philadelphia: Westminster, 1960), II.xvi.2, p. 504. The original text is a section heading, and is in italics.

51. Ibid., p. 505.

52. Ibid., II.xvi.5–6, pp. 507–511.

53. Ibid., II.xvi.2, pp. 505–507.

Turretin is less well known today than the earlier continental reformers Luther and Calvin, and some have suggested he led Reformed theology back from the dazzling heights of the sixteenth century towards the speculative philosophical theology of the medieval period. However, a study of his writings quickly reveals the injustice of this accusation. Turretin's most significant work, his *Institutes of Elenctic Theology*, reflects a mastery of the biblical languages, a profound understanding of Scripture, and a deep conviction that God's revelation forms a coherent whole. It combines an exhaustive coverage of biblical themes, meticulous attention to detail, and a thoroughly logical, orderly arrangement of topics, which together make the *Institutes* a superb reference work. But above all Turretin is remarkable for the clarity of his explanations. There have been others who wrote with greater emotion and verve, but for sheer precision Turretin is without equal.

Turretin introduces each theological topic by carefully defining and answering the question under discussion, before launching into a fuller explanation and biblical defence of his position. In the section on Christ's work as our mediator, he addresses the question 'Did Christ truly and properly satisfy God's justice in our place?' and answers in the affirmative:

> The question concerns a penal satisfaction properly so called by which he not only fulfilled the will of God, but also his justice (Christ having taken upon himself our sins). This the Socinians deny; we affirm.
>
> Second . . . the question concerns a true and proper satisfaction made by the payment of a full price and which meritoriously obtains the liberation of the guilty on the ground of justice. This we preach from the word of God . . .
>
> Third . . . the question is whether he [Christ] died for us substitutively (i.e., in our place, that by being substituted in our place, he suffered the punishment due to us). We affirm that he did.[54]

According to Turretin, then, Christ took our sins upon himself and bore the punishment due to us in our place, thereby liberating us from guilt while maintaining God's justice. This is penal substitution.[55]

---

54. F. Turretin, *Institutes of Elenctic Theology*, vol. 2, trans. G. M. Giger (Phillipsburg: Presbyterian & Reformed, 1994), 14.XI.ii–iv, pp. 426–427. An 'elenctic' theology is one in which the author sets out to refute opposing positions in the course of articulating his own.

55. Turretin also affirms the doctrine of penal substitution in *The Atonement of Christ*, trans. J. R. Willson (Grand Rapids: Baker, 1978).

## John Bunyan (1628–88)

John Bunyan was born in humble circumstances in rural Bedfordshire, and received only a brief education before taking up his father's trade as a 'tinker' – a maker and repairer of metal pots. After a wild youth, a short period of military service and several years of intense spiritual struggle, he was converted, a story he later related in *Grace Abounding to the Chief of Sinners* (1666).

Soon after his conversion Bunyan began to preach the gospel in the surrounding towns, displaying extraordinary speaking gifts. However, he was not officially licensed as a clergyman in the established church, and after several skirmishes with the authorities was eventually sentenced to three months' imprisonment in 1661. The authorities offered to release him if he promised to stop preaching, but he persistently refused and therefore remained in prison for twelve years. During this time he wrote several books, including *Grace Abounding*, and when he emerged from prison in 1672 began a long and influential ministry lasting until his death in 1688, interrupted only by another six-month prison term in 1677.

Bunyan's most famous book, *Pilgrim's Progress*, was probably written during his imprisonment. It is a classic of English literature, and has probably been more widely read than any other Christian book apart from the Bible. It is saturated with allusions to Scripture and stems from the profound spiritual reflection of a great nonconformist hero. Bunyan remained faithful to Christ through many persecutions, and his call to perseverance has been an inspiration to many.

*Pilgrim's Progress* is an allegory, in which Bunyan pictures the Christian life as the tortuous journey of a man named 'Christian' through many difficulties and temptations. These trials are depicted as people or hazards on the journey, such as 'Evangelist', 'Mr Worldly Wiseman' and 'The Slough of Despond'. One of the clearest expressions of Bunyan's belief in penal substitution comes from an extended conversation between Christian and Hopeful.[56] Hopeful describes how he had learned from Faithful that he must 'obtain the righteousness of a man that never had sinned' in order to be acceptable before God.[57] Christian enquires whether Hopeful had asked Faithful who this man was, and Hopeful replies:

---

56. Bunyan's commitment to penal substitution also emerges elsewhere, such as in the conversation between Christiana and Mr Great-Heart in pt. 2 of the work (*The Pilgrim's Progress* [Oxford: Oxford University Press, this version first pub. 1966], pp. 174–175).

57. Ibid., p. 114.

Yes, and he told me it was the Lord Jesus, that dwelleth on the right hand of the most High: And thus, said he, you must be justified by him, even by trusting to what he hath done by himself in the days of his flesh, and suffered when he did hang on the Tree. I asked him further, How that man's righteousness could be of that efficacy, to justifie another before God? And he told me, He was the mighty God, and did what he did, and died the death also, not for himself, but for me; to whom his doings, and the worthiness of them, should be imputed, if I believed on him.[58]

According to Bunyan, then, the only way we can be justified before God is for the righteousness of Christ to be imputed to us, which requires in turn that he should suffer the death we deserved for our sins: 'He was the mighty God . . . and died the death also, not for himself, but for me.' Later in the same conversation, Hopeful says this about the Lord Jesus:

From all which I gathered, that I must look for righteousness in his person, and for satisfaction for my sins by his blood; that what he did in obedience to his Fathers [sic] Law, and in submitting to the penalty thereof, was not for himself, but for him that will accept it for his Salvation, and be thankful. And now was my heart full of joy, mine eyes full of tears, and mine affections running over with love, to the Name, People, and Ways of Jesus Christ.[59]

Here Bunyan states that Christ both fully obeyed his Father's law and also suffered (shed 'his blood') as the 'penalty' due to us for our failure to keep the law – a plain statement of the doctrine of penal substitution.

## John Owen (1616–83)

John Owen was a towering theological giant, arguably England's greatest ever theologian. He went to Oxford University at the tender age of twelve, and studied there for nine years until he was forced to leave because of his opposition to the High Church reforms of Archbishop Laud. He ministered at two churches in Essex in the 1640s, during which time he became a convinced advocate of Independent church government. His outstanding ability as a theologian began to attract attention from Parliament, and he was invited to preach there on several occasions. In 1651 the House of Commons appointed him Dean of Christ

---

58. Ibid., p. 115.
59. Ibid., p. 117.

Church, Oxford, and he was made Vice Chancellor of the university the follow-ing year.

Owen's writings stretch to a massive twenty-four volumes, including a stag-gering seven-volume commentary on the book of Hebrews. When reading Owen, one gets the sense that his argument is utterly comprehensive; he has left no stone unturned. As Andrew Thompson observed in his biography of Owen, he 'makes you feel when he has reached the end of his subject, that he has also exhausted it'.[60]

Owen explains the doctrine of penal substitution in one of his early works, *The Death of Death*,[61] described by J. I. Packer as 'his first masterpiece'.[62] Owen summarizes his position at the start of chapter 9: 'Christ so took and bare our sins, and had them so laid upon him, as that he underwent the punishment due unto them, and that in our stead: therefore, he made satisfaction to the justice of God for them.'[63]

Then, in his characteristic style, Owen breaks down this summary statement into its individual parts: 'First, That Christ took and bare our sins, God laying them on him. Secondly, That he so took them as to undergo the punishment due unto them. Thirdly, That he did this in our stead.'[64]

He then proceeds to expound each point in detail, proving his case with careful argument and numerous biblical references, before concluding that Christ's purpose was to liberate us. Christ's death 'could not possibly have any

---

60. A. Thomson, *John Owen: Prince of the Puritans* (Fearn: Christian Focus, 1996), p. 38. These words are also cited on the inside cover of *The Works of John Owen*, vol. 1 (London: Banner of Truth, repr. 1967), and by J. I. Packer, 'Introductory Essay', in *John Owen, The Death of Death in the Death of Christ* (London: Banner of Truth, 1959), p. 13. Thomson's biography was first published as *The Life of Dr Owen* in the nineteenth century, and is contained in *The Works of John Owen*, vol. 1 (London: Banner of Truth, repr. 1967).

61. The full title of this piece is typically and entertainingly Puritan, sacrificing conciseness for the sake of comprehensiveness: *The Death of Death in the Death of Christ: A Treatise of the Redemption and Reconciliation That Is in the Blood of Christ, with the Merit Thereof, and the Satisfaction Wrought Thereby.* It appears in vol. 10 of *The Works of John Owen* (London: Banner of Truth, repr. 1967), and was also published separately in 1959 as *The Death of Death in the Death of Christ* (London: Banner of Truth, 1959). Page references to both works are given in the following footnotes.

62. Packer, 'Introductory Essay', p. 22.

63. Owen, *Death of Death*, p. 168; *Works*, p. 280.

64. Ibid.

other end than that we might go free'.[65] Then, in case there should be any doubt about the exact nature of the punishment he endured, Owen makes his position clear: 'we affirm that our Saviour underwent the wrath of God which was due unto us'.[66] Again, he proceeds to clarify and demonstrate his case with a cascade of biblical quotations and arguments. It is hard to imagine a clearer affirmation of the doctrine of penal substitution.


## George Whitefield (1714–70)

George Whitefield was born in Gloucester in 1714, and was converted at Oxford University, where he met John and Charles Wesley. He was ordained in 1736, and immediately his preaching began to attract attention. The following year he went to America at the invitation of the Wesleys. On returning he found himself shunned by most of the English clergy, who 'were . . . scandalized by his preaching the doctrine of . . . the new birth, as a thing which many baptized persons greatly needed!'[67]

This was the great turning point of Whitefield's ministry. Finding the pulpits closed to him, he began to preach in the open air. The impact of this was felt all over Britain as extraordinary revivals broke out across the land. Whitefield's powerful voice enabled him to preach to vast crowds, estimated by some to number tens of thousands. He preached to people from every walk of life, from the illiterate coal miners of the Welsh valleys to the Countess of Huntingdon and other members of the aristocracy. His ministry lasted over three decades, and he visited America a total of seven times. He preached an estimated 18,000 sermons.

Whitefield often taught the doctrine of penal substitution in the context of the so-called 'covenant of works' that God made with Adam and Eve. In line with mainstream Reformed theology, Whitefield taught that God promised to bless Adam and Eve if they obeyed him, but warned that he would punish them if they disobeyed. When Adam and Eve sinned, they brought upon themselves the judgment of exclusion, pain and death that God had promised. From this point on, Adam and Eve were totally unable to restore their broken relationship with God, for they would not only need to live lives

---

65. Ibid., p. 170; *Works*, p. 282.

66. Ibid., p. 171; *Works*, p. 283.

67. J. C. Ryle, *Christian Leaders of the 18th Century* (London: Banner of Truth, repr. 1997), p. 36.

of perfect obedience, but also to satisfy God's justice by making reparation ('satisfaction') for the sins they had already committed, neither of which they were able to do. Thus, speaking of Adam and Eve, Whitefield asked:

> For what must they do? They were as much under a covenant of works as ever. And though, after their disobedience, they were without strength, yet they were obliged not only to do, but to continue to do all things, and that too in the most perfect manner, which the Lord had required of them: and not only so, but to make satisfaction to God's infinitely offended justice for the breach they had already been guilty of.[68]

Whitefield combines this understanding of the covenant of works with the historic Reformed doctrine of sin, insisting not only that all people follow Adam's example of rebellion against God, but also that Adam is our representative, and therefore his sin is imputed to us directly. Consequently, according to Whitefield, all humankind is alienated from God, unable to live the perfect lives we ought to live, unable to make satisfaction for sins already committed, and facing God's just wrath and condemnation.[69]

This, in Whitefield's view, is the desperate situation from which the Lord Jesus Christ rescued us. Christ fulfilled the two obligations that rested upon all humanity: he lived the perfect life we could not 'and thereby fulfilled the whole moral law in our stead', and died the death we dared not, being cursed for us and suffering in our place the punishment due to us:

> Here then opens the amazing scene of *divine philanthropy*; I mean, God's love to man: for, behold, what man could not do, Jesus Christ, the Son of his Father's love, undertakes to do for him . . . he obeyed, and thereby fulfilled the whole moral law in our stead; and also died a painful death upon the cross, and thereby became a curse for, or instead of, those whom the Father had given to him.[70]

Whitefield frequently articulated the gospel in this way. Here is another example:

---

68. George Whitefield, *Select Sermons of George Whitefield* (Edinburgh: Banner of Truth, 1958), pp. 119–120.

69. For a concise summary of Whitefield's understanding of the covenant of works see George Whitefield, 'Sermons preached by the Rev. George Whitefield in the High Church-Yard, Glasgow', in D. MacFarlan, *The Revivals of the Eighteenth Century* (Wheaton: Richard Owen Roberts, 1980), p. 20.

70. Whitefield, *Select Sermons*, p. 120; italics original.

God the Father entered into an eternal covenant with God the Son; he made Christ the head, the representative of the elect, as Adam was the head, the representative of all his seed. For these the Lord Jesus Christ undertook to fulfil the covenant of works. For these Jesus Christ died a painful, cursed, ignominious death; and by his obedience, and by his death, wrought out an everlasting righteousness for them.[71]

These extracts show the centrality of penal substitution in Whitefield's thought. The death Christ died and the perfectly obedient life he lived in our place are two intertwined strands by which the Lord Jesus rescues us from our state of hopeless condemnation before God and presents us as righteous – justified – before him: 'As God, he satisfied, at the same time that he obeyed and suffered as man; and being God and man in one person, he wrought out a full, perfect, and sufficient righteousness for all to whom it was to be imputed.'[72]

## Charles H. Spurgeon (1834–92)

Charles Spurgeon was born into a poor family near Colchester in 1834. He received little formal education, and was famously converted during a sermon by an unknown lay preacher in 1850 when a snowstorm forced him to take shelter one Sunday morning in a tiny Methodist chapel. Spurgeon's extraordinary preaching gifts soon became apparent, and after a short spell as the pastor of Waterbeach Baptist Church near Cambridge he was invited in 1854 to become the pastor of New Park Street Chapel in London. He made an immediate impact, drawing such large congregations that the building was expanded almost immediately to accommodate two thousand people. Even this proved insufficient, and in 1861 the Metropolitan Tabernacle was built with a capacity of six thousand to accommodate the vast crowds of people who came to hear him speak.

---

71. Whitefield, 'Sermons Preached', p. 9.
72. Whitefield, *Select Sermons*, p. 120. J. C. Ryle cites one of Whitefield's letters in which he expresses dissatisfaction with the accuracy of a published version of one of his sermons (Ryle, *Christian Leaders*, p. 50). However, Whitefield's concern here is that his style has been distorted, not that his theology has been misrepresented. Moreover, the doctrine of penal substitution is woven into the very fabric of Whitefield's understanding of the gospel: it is simply impossible to imagine that a careless or disingenuous transcriber imported it.

Spurgeon's sermons had an astonishing impact, and at the height of his popularity were published in newspapers all over the world. His incisive mind more than compensated for the deficiencies in his formal education, and his preaching is full of thoughtful exegesis, vigorous application, and bold engagement with contemporary ideas. Moreover, he had a keen social conscience, and founded an orphanage and several almshouses for the poor.

Besides all this, Spurgeon's literary output was vast. He wrote over 200 books and pamphlets, and 3,544 of his sermons are still in print. One example will suffice to demonstrate his belief in penal substitution. In a sermon entitled 'Sin laid on Jesus', Spurgeon interprets Isaiah 53:6 as a prophecy of the death of the Lord Jesus Christ, and draws out the implications of the fact that 'Jesus Christ voluntarily took [our] sin upon himself':[73]

> God cannot look where there is sin with any pleasure, and though as far as Jesus is personally concerned, he is the Father's beloved Son in whom he is well pleased; yet when he saw sin laid upon his Son, he made that Son cry, 'My God! my God! why hast thou forsaken me?' It was not possible that Jesus should enjoy the light of his Father's presence while he was made sin for us; consequently he went through a horror of great darkness, the root and source of which was the withdrawing of the conscious enjoyment of his Father's presence. More than that, not only was light withdrawn, but positive sorrow was inflicted. God must punish sin, and though the sin was not Christ's by his actually doing it, yet it was laid upon him, and therefore he was made a curse for us . . . God only knows the griefs to which the Son of God was put when the Lord made to meet upon him the iniquity of us all. To crown all there came death itself. Death is the punishment for sin, and whatever it may mean . . . in the sentence, 'In the day thou eatest thereof thou shalt surely die,' Christ felt.[74]

This is the characteristic clarity of Spurgeon, spelling out simply and clearly that 'God must punish sin', and that Christ suffered the punishment due to those whose sins were 'laid upon him'.

## D. Martyn Lloyd-Jones (1899–1981)

Martyn Lloyd-Jones was born in Cardiff, and trained as a doctor. He excelled

---

73. C. H. Spurgeon, *The Metropolitan Tabernacle Pulpit*, vol. 12 (London: Passmore & Alabaster, 1896), p. 316; original text in italics.
74. Ibid., pp. 317–318.

in this profession, becoming the assistant to a Harley Street physician, but abandoned a dazzling medical career to become a pastor. He spent twelve years in a small church in Aberavon, Wales, during which time the congregations experienced extraordinary growth. His preaching gifts attracted the attention of G. Campbell Morgan, who asked Lloyd-Jones to join him at London's Westminster Chapel as assistant pastor in 1939. When Morgan retired in 1943, Lloyd-Jones succeeded him as senior pastor, serving for almost thirty years until ill health curtailed his preaching in 1968.

Affectionately known as 'The Doctor', Lloyd-Jones was instrumental in the founding of London Theological Seminary in 1977, played a prominent role in the leadership of the Inter-Varsity Fellowship (now the Universities and Colleges Christian Fellowship), campaigned vigorously for doctrinal faithfulness among evangelicals, and wrote a number of books. But he is best known as a preacher, and was much loved for his warm Calvinist theology and 'penetrating spiritual analysis'.[75]

In 1955 he began his most famous series of sermons, preaching through the book of Romans to a packed Westminster Chapel every Friday evening for more than twelve years, and it is perhaps appropriate that we should turn here to hear him expound penal substitution. During this monumental series, Lloyd-Jones preached two sermons on Romans 3:25, the first of which was an explanation of the meaning of the word 'propitiation' found in the Authorized Version of that verse. He summarizes the verse in this way: 'This is a statement to the effect that God's wrath has been appeased and that God has been placated as the result of the work which our Lord did there by dying upon the Cross.'[76]

The following week, in the second sermon, he built on the previous week's exposition, and set out to answer the question 'In what sense is the Lord Jesus Christ the propitiatory sacrifice?' After examining several New Testament texts, he argues that the Old Testament sacrificial system provides the crucial background. He notes that 1 Peter 2:25 refers back to Isaiah 53:4 and summarizes the essence of these verses as follows: 'That means that not only have the sins been laid upon him, but that the wrath of God has been poured out upon him. The punishment that should have come to you and to me on account of our sinfulness and our sins came to him.'[77] This is penal substitution.

---

75. Walsh, *Dictionary*, p. 782.

76. D. M. Lloyd-Jones, *Romans: An Exposition of Chapters 3:20–4:25, Atonement and Justification* (London: Banner of Truth, 1970), p. 70.

77. Ibid., p. 90.

## John R. W. Stott (born 1921)

John Stott was born in London in 1921. His mother encouraged him from an
early age to pray and read the Bible, and took him to Sunday school at All Souls
church. He was converted as a schoolboy in 1938, and was ordained as an
Anglican clergyman in 1945. He took up his first post as Assistant Curate at All
Souls, and five years later was appointed Rector, moving in to the very room in
which he had attended Sunday School as a child. He immediately set out the priorities that were to shape his ministry: prayer, expository preaching, evangelism,
discipleship, and training for laypeople. The congregation at All Souls grew
steadily, and Stott emerged as a significant leader among British evangelicals.

In the years that followed, Stott was invited to take up an increasing number
of speaking engagements in Britain and overseas, and played a central role in
both the National Evangelical Anglican Congress and the Lausanne Congress
on World Evangelization. In 1970 Michael Baughen was appointed Vicar of All
Souls, allowing Stott to devote more time to his growing international ministry.
Stott continued to travel extensively, and founded the London Institute for
Contemporary Christianity in 1982. His encounters with Christians in the developing world led to a deep social concern and to the establishment of the
Langham Trust to allow pastors and scholars from the developing world to study
in Europe and America.

Stott is without doubt one of the leading figures in modern evangelicalism.
The historian Adrian Hastings described him as 'one of the most influential
figures in the Christian world'.[78] His preaching ministry continues despite his
advancing years, and he has published more than forty books, including several
New Testament commentaries in the popular 'Bible Speaks Today' series.

In 1986 he wrote *The Cross of Christ*, regarded by many as his most significant
work. Here he sets out a clear case for the doctrine of penal substitution. At
the start of chapter 6, entitled 'The Self-Substitution of God', he asks the question 'How then could God express simultaneously his holiness in judgment
and his love in pardon?'[79] His answer constitutes a summary of the whole
chapter:

> Only by providing a divine substitute for the sinner, so that the substitute would
> receive the judgment and the sinner the pardon. We sinners still of course have to

---

78. Cited by J. P. Greenman, 'Stott, John Robert Walmsley', in T. Larsen (ed.),
    *Biographical Dictionary of Evangelicals* (Leicester: IVP, 2003), p. 641.
79. John R. W. Stott, *The Cross of Christ* (Leicester: IVP, 1986), p. 134.

suffer some of the personal, psychological and social consequences of our sins, but the penal consequence, the deserved penalty of alienation from God, has been borne by Another in our place, so that we may be spared it.[80]

Stott then sets out to provide biblical justification for this conclusion, beginning with a careful examination of Old Testament teaching about sacrifice. He evaluates several attempts by various scholars to avoid the biblical idea of substitutionary *punishment*, but remains unconvinced by all of them. He then suggests that 'the essential question . . . concerns how the biblical authors themselves employ "sin-bearing" language'.[81] After several more pages of biblical exegesis, he concludes:

> The sinless one was 'made sin for us', which must mean that he bore the penalty of our sin instead of us, and he redeemed us from the law's curse by 'becoming a curse for us', which must mean that the curse of the law lying upon us for our disobedience was transferred to him, so that he bore it instead of us . . .
>
> When we review all this Old Testament material . . . and consider its New Testament application to the death of Christ, we are obliged to conclude that the cross was a substitutionary sacrifice. Christ died for us. Christ died instead of us.[82]

## J. I. Packer (born 1926)

James Packer was born into a working-class family in 1926, but succeeded in winning a prestigious scholarship to study at Oxford University, where he was converted in 1944. During this time he took on the role of librarian for the Christian Union, which brought him into contact with the writings of the Puritans. John Owen, in particular, had a profound impact on his theology. Apart from a short period as an Anglican curate, Packer has devoted much of his life to serving the church as a theologian. He taught at Tyndale Hall, Bristol, remaining there when it later became Trinity College, and was Warden of Latimer House, Oxford, for most of the 1960s. In 1979 he moved to Canada to take up the post of Professor of Theology at the newly established Regent College in Vancouver.

---

80. Ibid.
81. Ibid., p. 143.
82. Ibid., pp. 148–149, quoting 2 Cor. 5:21 and Gal. 3:13.

Packer is best known as an author. His first book, *'Fundamentalism' and the Word of God*, was published in 1958, and has been described by Roger Nicole as 'a veritable classic'.[83] It was an instant popular success, establishing Packer as a leading evangelical voice in Britain, and was followed by nearly forty other books, including *Knowing God*.

Packer also wrote many scholarly essays and articles, including *What Did the Cross Achieve?*, in which he defends the doctrine of penal substitution. This short piece first saw the light of day as the 1973 *Tyndale Biblical Theology Lecture*, and has since been published in several other places.[84] It is subtitled *The Logic of Penal Substitution*, and Packer's view on the subject is abundantly clear from the start:

> The task which I have set myself in this lecture is to focus and explicate a belief which, by and large, is a distinguishing mark of the worldwide evangelical fraternity: namely, the belief that Christ's death on the cross had the character of *penal substitution*, and that it was in virtue of this fact that it brought salvation to humankind.[85]

After some comments on the method he plans to adopt, he explores 'what it means to call Christ's death *substitutionary*' and 'what further meaning is added when Christ's substitutionary suffering is called *penal*' before giving a biblical defence of his position.[86] He concludes with a probing rhetorical question: 'Can we then justify ourselves in holding a view of the atonement into which penal substitution does not enter?'[87]

According to Packer, the answer is no.

The doctrine of penal substitution also has a prominent place in Packer's *Knowing God*, one of the best-known Christian books of recent years. It has

83. Roger Nicole, 'James I. Packer's Contribution to the Doctrine of the Inerrancy of Scripture', in D. Lewis and A. McGrath (eds.), *Doing Theology for the People of God* (Leicester: Apollos, 1996), p. 178.

84. J. I. Packer, 'What Did the Cross Achieve? The Logic of Penal Substitution', *Tyndale Bulletin* 25 (1974), pp. 3–45; *What Did the Cross Achieve? The Logic of Penal Substitution* (Leicester: Theological Students' Fellowship); 'What Did the Cross Achieve? The Logic of Penal Substitution', in *Celebrating the Saving Work of God: Collected Shorter Writings of J. I. Packer* (Carlisle: Paternoster, 1998), pp. 85–123. Subsequent references are given to the latter version, which was published most recently.

85. Packer, *Celebrating*, p. 85; italics original.

86. Ibid.; italics original.

87. Ibid., p. 123.

sold well over a million copies since its publication in 1973, and has been translated into more than a dozen different languages. It was hailed by John Stott as
'a spiritual classic of the 20th century',[88] and continues to sell in huge numbers
all over the world.

In chapter 18, entitled 'The Heart of the Gospel', Packer explains that 'the
idea of propitiation – that is, of averting God's anger by an offering – runs right
through the Bible'.[89] He distinguishes between the biblical doctrine and the
very different concept of propitiation found in pagan religions, which
amounted to 'manipulating your gods by cunning bribery' and 'the appeasing
of celestial bad tempers'.[90] He also argues against the conclusions of C. H.
Dodd and others, who

> revived the view of the sixteenth-century Unitarian Socinus, a view which had already
> been picked up in the late nineteen-hundreds by Albrecht Ritschl, a founder of
> German liberalism, to the effect that there is in God no such thing as anger
> occasioned by human sin, and consequently no need or possibility of propitiation.[91]

Against this backdrop, he sets out the biblical teaching that God's
anger 'is *righteous* anger – the *right* reaction of moral perfection in the
Creator towards moral perversity in the creature',[92] that 'Propitiation is the
work of God himself,'[93] and that 'Propitiation was made by the death
of Jesus Christ.'[94] He then explains how:

> With the other New Testament writers, Paul always points to the death of Jesus as the
> atoning event, and explains the atonement in terms of *representative substitution* – the
> innocent taking the place of the guilty, in the name and for the sake of the guilty,
> under the axe of God's judicial retribution.[95]

It becomes clear what Packer means by this terminology in the subsequent
paragraphs. Referring to Galatians 3:13, he writes, 'Christ bore the curse of the

---

88. Comment on the front cover of the twenty-fifth-anniversary edition.

89. J. I. Packer, *Knowing God*, 2nd edn (London: Hodder & Stoughton, 1993), p. 202.

90. Ibid.

91. Ibid., p. 204; italics original.

92. Ibid., p. 207.

93. Ibid.; the original text is in italics.

94. Ibid., p. 209; original text in italics.

95. Ibid., pp. 209–210; italics original.

law which was directed against us, so that we might not have to bear it. This is representative substitution.'[96]

Again, 'It was as a sacrifice for sinners, enduring the death penalty in their stead, that "one died for all" (2 Corinthians 5:14, 18–21). This is representative substitution.'[97]

Representative substitution is thus equivalent to penal substitution, and Packer joins the ranks of modern evangelical scholars who unequivocally affirm this doctrine.

## The Universities and Colleges Christian Fellowship (UCCF) Doctrinal Basis

The Universities and Colleges Christian Fellowship (UCCF) grew out of the Inter-Varsity Fellowship (IVF), formed in 1928 as a central association for the growing number of Christian Unions in universities all over Britain.[98] It is now closely linked with a publisher (IVP), is represented in approximately 260 universities and higher education institutions all over Britain, and employs more than 50 permanent staff. The UCCF exercises a vital and influential ministry, encouraging evangelism and discipleship among students.

The modern UCCF doctrinal basis includes the following statements:

d: Since the fall, the whole of humankind is sinful and guilty, so that everyone is subject to God's wrath and condemnation.

f: Sinful human beings are redeemed from the guilt, penalty and power of sin only through the sacrificial death once and for all time of their representative and substitute, Jesus Christ, the only mediator between them and God.[99]

These statements do not use the phrase 'penal substitution', but they do construe the atonement in exactly these terms. For the consequences of sin include 'God's wrath and condemnation', Christ died as our 'substitute' and through his death we are 'redeemed' from this 'penalty'.

---

96. Ibid., p. 210.

97. Ibid.

98. D. Johnson (ed.), *A Brief History of the International Fellowship of Evangelical Students* (Lausanne: International Fellowship of Evangelical Students, 1964).

99. www.uccf.org.uk/resources/general/doctrinalbasis/doctrinalbasis.php (accessed 20 June 2006).

The doctrinal bases of IFES and other national organizations affiliated to IFES, such as the InterVarsity Christian Fellowship in the USA, are similar in content, and imply penal substitution in the same unambiguous terms.[100]

This understanding is made explicit in a short booklet entitled *Evangelical Belief: An Explanation of the Doctrinal Basis of the Inter-Varsity Fellowship*, first published in 1935 'to enable the reader to appreciate more clearly how the IVF Doctrinal Basis is generally understood by those who subscribe to it'.[101] It explains the phrase 'sacrificial death' as follows: 'In other words, the apostles taught that the divine judgment due to men for their sins was voluntarily endured in their place by the Son of God come in human form.'[102]

## The Evangelical Alliance Basis of Faith

The Evangelical Alliance (EA) was founded in 1846, and held its first conference in the Freemasons' Hall, London, 'a somewhat incongruous setting'.[103] It seeks to promote evangelical unity in gospel proclamation and social action, a concern reflected in its motto, 'We are One Body in Christ'.[104]

In 1968 the EA doctrine commission published a report on evangelism entitled *On the Other Side*. In the process of outlining the commission's understanding of the gospel, the report affirms that Christ endured 'the judgement upon sin' and 'took upon Himself the penalty of our sin':

> The judgment upon sin has been endured for man by Christ. God in Christ has taken the initiative in dealing with our sin and with the judgment upon it. By voluntarily giving himself to die upon the cross Christ suffered the worst that sin can do, including separation from His Father. God laid upon him all the consequence of human wrong-doing and wrong relationships, and He took upon Himself the penalty of our sin. This understanding of the Atonement, which is both clear and prominent in the New Testament, lies at the heart of the various

---

100. The doctrinal bases of IVP USA and IFES may be found respectively at www.intervarsity.org/aboutus/doctrine.php and www.ifesworld.org/about/doctrine.asp.
101. *Evangelical Belief: An Explanation of the Doctrinal Basis of the Inter-Varsity Fellowship*, 4th edn (London: IVP, 1973), pp. 10–11.
102. Ibid., p. 39.
103. I. Randall and D. Hilborn, *One Body in Christ: The History and Significance of the Evangelical Alliance* (Carlisle: Paternoster, 2001), p. 45.
104. Ibid., p. 1.

Biblical descriptions of Christ's death – e.g. sacrifice, redemption, justification, reconciliation.[105]

This extract highlights the commission's view that penal substitution is clearly taught in Scripture: 'This understanding of the Atonement . . . is both clear and prominent in the New Testament.' Moreover, they see it as a matter of central importance: it 'lies at the heart of the various Biblical descriptions of Christ's death'. The doctrine of penal substitution, according to the EA commission, is neither debatable nor peripheral.

This understanding of the death of Christ is also reflected in the latest EA Basis of Faith, formally adopted in September 2005. It includes the following statements:

> We believe in . . .
> 4. The dignity of all people, made male and female in God's image to love, be holy and care for creation, yet corrupted by sin, which incurs divine wrath and judgement.
> 6. The atoning sacrifice of Christ on the cross: dying in our place, paying the price of sin and defeating evil, so reconciling us with God.[106]

Like the UCCF doctrinal basis, these statements clearly refer to penal substitution, although they do not use that exact phrase. For article 4 states that human sin 'incurs divine wrath and judgment', and article 6 states both that Christ died as our substitute, 'in our place', and that in doing so he paid 'the price of sin'. The obvious implication is that Christ endured in our place the judgment of God due to us. The previous basis of faith, adopted in 1970, contains equivalent statements that imply the same.[107] Interestingly, the preamble to this earlier Basis of Faith states that 'Evangelical Christians . . . here assert doctrines which they regard as *crucial to the understanding of the faith*,'[108] reflecting the view that the Christian faith cannot be properly understood if penal substitution is denied.

There is an important postscript to this story. The publication in 2003 of *The Lost Message of Jesus* by Steve Chalke and Alan Mann sparked a furore within British evangelicalism, due in part to the book's caricature of penal substitution

---

105.  *On the Other Side: The Report of the Evangelical Alliance's Commission on Evangelism* (London: Scripture Union, 1968), p. 65.
106.  www.eauk.org/about/basis-of-faith.cfm (accessed 18 April 2006).
107.  Randall and Hilborn, *One Body*, pp. 360–361.
108.  Ibid.; italics added.

as 'a form of cosmic child abuse'.[109] The EA responded to the controversy by hosting a public debate in London on 7 October 2004. In July the following year the EA hosted a three-day symposium at the London School of Theology to discuss the issues further. A number of speakers were invited, several of whom do not believe in penal substitution. These included Steve Chalke, Joel Green and Stuart Murray Williams, whose writings we discuss in Part Two. By the end of the conference it was clear that the overwhelming majority of the attendees (who numbered more than two hundred) believed in the traditional doctrine of penal substitution – the EA's own survey put the figure at 94%. The EA issued a statement at the end of the conference, stating that 'penal substitution was taken to be implicit in the Alliance Basis of Faith by those who drafted it in 1970',[109] and in February 2006 this understanding was reaffirmed in a statement issued by the board of the EA.[110]

## Conclusion

We have reached the end of our survey, and have demonstrated that the doctrine of penal substitution has been affirmed from the earliest days of the Christian church, and has continued to find a place in the mainstream of historic Christian theology throughout the last two thousand years. Moreover, our study of Athanasius has shown that penal substitution was not an unimportant doctrine among the church Fathers, relegated to the sidelines and overshadowed by other, more significant themes. On the contrary, for this major figure at least, penal substitution was considered central to the Christian faith and a foundational element of God's plan for the world.

We saw in chapter 2 that penal substitution is biblical. As we emphasized at the start of this chapter, that counts for much more than the fact that lots of people throughout church history have believed it. However, it is reassuring to find that our understanding of the biblical texts has a long and distinguished pedigree.

---

109. Steve Chalke and Alan Mann, *The Lost Message of Jesus* (Grand Rapids: Zondervan, 2003), p. 182.

110. www.eauk.org/contentmanager/content/press/statements/symposium.cfm (accessed 31 October 2005).

111. www.eauk.org/theology/atonement/upload/board%20atonement% 20statement.pdf (accessed 18 April 2006).

In one sense, of course, our survey has been embarrassingly limited. We have omitted such towering figures as Martin Luther, John Wesley and Jonathan Edwards; we have passed over many of the scholars who exercised a formative influence on modern evangelicalism, including Louis Berkhof, Charles Hodge, John Murray, Francis Schaeffer and Leon Morris; and we have neglected many respected leaders and thinkers of our own day, including Don Carson, Wayne Grudem and John Piper. All of these people have affirmed the doctrine of penal substitution.[111] However, even this list is far from exhaustive, and little would be gained at this stage by simply multiplying quotations. The point has been amply proven.

---

112. Louis Berkhof, *Systematic Theology* (London: Banner of Truth, 1959; first pub. 1941), pp. 373–383; D. A. Carson, 'Atonement in Romans 3:21–26', in C. E. Hill and F. A. James III (eds.), *The Glory of the Atonement* (Downers Grove: IVP; Apollos, 2004), pp. 119–139 (pp. 133–134); Jonathan Edwards, 'Concerning the Necessity and Reasonableness of the Christian Doctrine of Satisfaction for Sin', in *The Works of Jonathan Edwards*, vol. 2 (Edinburgh: Banner of Truth, repr. 1986), pp. 565–578; Wayne Grudem, *Systematic Theology: An Introduction to Biblical Doctrine* (Leicester: IVP, 1994), pp. 572–581; Charles Hodge, *Systematic Theology*, vol. 2 (London: James Clarke, 1960), pp. 480–543; Martin Luther, *A Commentary on St Paul's Epistle to the Galatians* (London: James Clarke, 1953), pp. 268–276; John Murray, *Redemption Accomplished and Applied* (Edinburgh: Banner of Truth, 1961; first pub. Grand Rapids: Eerdmans, 1955), pp. 29–33, 76–78 (page references in our work are to the Banner of Truth edn); Leon Morris, *The Apostolic Preaching of the Cross* (London: Tyndale, 1955), p. 173; *The Cross in the New Testament* (Exeter: Paternoster, 1965), pp. 404–419; John Piper, *The Pleasures of God*, rev. edn (Fearn: Christian Focus, 2001), pp. 157–178; *The Passion of Jesus Christ: Fifty Reasons Why He Came to Die* (Wheaton: Crossway, 2004), pp. 20–21; Francis Schaeffer, *The Finished Work of Christ* (Leicester: IVP, 1998), pp. 79–80; John Wesley, *Explanatory Notes Upon the New Testament* (London: Epworth, 1976), pp. 530–531, 688, 879–880. In their own historical survey, Shaw and Edwards mention some of the figures whom we have omitted, in particular Martin Luther, Jonathan Edwards, John Wesley and Charles Hodge (Shaw and Edwards, *Divine Substitute*).

# Part Two: Answering the Critics

## 6. INTRODUCTION TO THE DEBATE

### Setting the scene

Have you ever witnessed one of those frustrating discussions when everyone is talking enthusiastically, but nobody seems to be listening to anyone else? Perhaps you have watched such debates on TV, or heard them on the radio, or even been involved in them yourself. Everyone is discussing the same subject, and they dutifully pause to allow each other to speak, but they never really seem to engage with the other views around the table; they do not answer the questions put to them. It can be particularly infuriating if the questions being dodged are those to which *you* want an answer. You find yourself wondering whether there is any point to the dialogue at all – the various parties turn up, read their script, frown while everyone else reads theirs, and go home.

Sadly, this sort of spectacle is not unknown among Christians. We often talk past each other. Our attempts at 'conversation' are sometimes little different from these TV or radio discussions, where the aim is to give the impression of serious engagement without listening honestly to what the other side is saying or allowing our own position to be subjected to scrutiny.

This is happening with the doctrine of penal substitution. Since the 1980s a number of influential books critical of the traditional view have appeared, and now the trickle has grown into a river. We believe penal substitution is thoroughly biblical, but it would not be good enough simply to ignore our critics. We need to hear what they say, engage with their objections, and answer them in a thoughtful, coherent way. Such is the purpose of this second part of our book.

## Our approach

The following pages outline all of the major objections to the doctrine of penal substitution we have encountered. Some readers may find their needs best served by dipping into sections of particular interest; others may prefer to read the whole thing. Either way, the thematic arrangement of the material is designed to make it as useful as possible.

We begin each section by stating and explaining the objection in question. As far as possible we do so in the words of those who have raised it, to ensure we represent them fairly and feel the full force of their arguments rather than dealing only with watered-down caricatures. For completeness we also include a few other criticisms that we have encountered in face-to-face discussion, but not found in print.

Having outlined an objection, we respond to it, drawing on some of the material covered in the first part of the book. In each case we argue that the objection does not successfully undermine the doctrine of penal substitution. Sometimes this is because it rests on a misunderstanding of some other aspect of the Bible's teaching. In other cases it misunderstands the doctrine of penal substitution itself, and a right understanding is not susceptible to the criticism at all. In every case we try to present all the evidence, and invite readers to make up their own minds.

On the whole, we engage with the work of recent critics. This is not because their objections have not arisen before; indeed some have surfaced again and again in different guises throughout history. Occasionally, we mention the historical background where it helps to clarify or illuminate the objection, but our chief intention is to engage with the most contemporary writing. Little is lost by this approach, because in general recent critics make their case just as well as their ancient counterparts. Some older critiques of penal substitution are included in the bibliography for those who wish to pursue them further.

Certain writers appear frequently in the following pages. We have not singled them out deliberately: it is simply that they have made more than one type of criticism, and our thematic arrangement of material means each is addressed separately in its own section. It is for this reason only that the same names recur.

## Why do it this way?

We are aware that polemic of this sort makes some uneasy. No-one enjoys disagreement, and it feels particularly awkward among Christians. Are we not being too confrontational? Stirring up controversy?

We discuss Christian unity and the place of disagreement in more detail in chapter 7, section 5, but a few preliminary comments by way of clarification and rationale are appropriate here. First, we are not on a theological witch-hunt or a personal crusade against individuals with whom we disagree. We are sometimes forceful in our opposition to certain things they have said, but this does not amount to hostility towards them as people (we hope that in this we are following Jesus' example).

Secondly, the very fact that these questions have been raised means controversy is upon us, whether we like it or not. Indeed, it is the critics of penal substitution who have been most forthright in their call for further debate. For example, at a public meeting attended by several hundred people in London in October 2004,[1] Stuart Murray Williams insisted that 'we will need to look again at many deeply held convictions'[2] about what happened at the cross. Criticisms of penal substitution are becoming increasingly widespread and influential. We can either bury our heads in the sand and hope the dissenting voices will grow silent of their own accord, or we can take the trouble to listen to them and then to respond.

We hope this second part of the book will benefit people starting from a range of different positions. Some will have believed in penal substitution for a long time (even if they did not call it by that name), but perhaps feel unsettled by the barrage of recent objections to it, or at least ill-equipped to answer them. Others are doubtless suspicious of the doctrine, or may have experienced increasing reservations in recent years. Still others may be genuinely undecided, and want to hear both sides of the story so they can make up their own minds. Our prayer is that what we have written will be helpful to all these people and more besides. One thing is certain: it helps nobody if one side of the debate simply opts out of the dialogue. Without discussion, progress is sure to be slow, if not impossible.

---

1. See www.eauk.org/theology/atonement/the-lost-message-of-jesus.cfm (accessed 17 April 2006).
2. Stuart Murray Williams, 'Stuart Murray Williams on the Lost Message of Jesus: A Speech at the Debate on Steve Chalke's Book *The Lost Message of Jesus*', http://www.anabaptistnetwork.com/node/233 (accessed 8 February 2006).

## Introduction

Five criticisms have been made about the relationship of penal substitution to the Bible and to other biblical themes. The first observes merely that there is more to say about the atonement than is encapsulated in the doctrine of penal substitution. The second goes further, arguing that penal substitution is less important than other perspectives on the cross. The third objection comes from a different perspective, criticizing penal substitution for focusing only on Jesus' death and failing to give due prominence to his life and resurrection. The fourth objection makes the strongest claim, arguing that penal substitution is simply not taught in the Bible at all. The fifth accepts that Christians will always have different views about what the Bible teaches, but protests that penal substitution is not important enough to be a source of division.

## 1. 'Penal substitution is not the only model of the atonement'

### Objection
Some object that the Bible says much about the atonement besides the doctrine of penal substitution. An exclusive emphasis on penal substitution, they suggest, distorts the Bible's teaching, for it forces other valid biblical

perspectives on the atonement to the sidelines or even leaves them out of the picture altogether.

For example, Joel Green and Mark Baker claim that 'today penal substitution is viewed by many as the one correct approach to explaining the saving significance of the cross',[1] and that 'for many American Christians "penal substitutionary atonement" interprets the significance of Jesus' death fully, completely, without remainder'.[2] They explain why they find this problematic: 'Penal substitution . . . is unbiblical not just because it distorts or leaves out biblical concepts but also because of its attempt at having one image or more serve as an all-encompassing theory, the only correct and needed explanation of the atonement.'[3]

Alan Mann harbours a similar concern that we should not privilege any single understanding of the atonement. He insists 'that no one soteriological model is meaningful and sufficient for expressing all plights, all conflicts that need resolution. The story of salvation, therefore, is not a narrative with a single plot.'[4]

Alan Mann rejects penal substitution in *The Lost Message of Jesus*, written jointly with Steve Chalke, although he does not do so explicitly in his more recent work, *Atonement for a 'Sinless' Society*, from which the above quotation is taken. Nonetheless, his misgivings about the doctrine are evident from the context in which the above quotation appears: on the previous page he emphasizes the inadequacy of 'a story of atonement that orientates itself purely and simply around the wrath of God, directed toward the self for sins committed against a divine law, which is absorbed by an innocent (Jesus)'.[5] Thus when he claims 'that no one soteriological model is meaningful and sufficient',[6] he is urging in particular that penal substitution is not enough. Other facets of the atonement must be communicated to the modern world.

---

1. Joel B. Green and Mark D. Baker, *Recovering the Scandal of the Cross: Atonement in New Testament and Contemporary Contexts* (Downers Grove: IVP, 2000), p. 150.

2. Ibid., p. 13.

3. Ibid., p. 148.

4. Alan Mann, *Atonement for a 'Sinless' Society: Engaging with an Emerging Culture* (Milton Keynes: Paternoster, 2005), p. 99.

5. Ibid., p. 98.

6. Ibid., p. 99.

*Response*

We agree that a comprehensive doctrine of the atonement must include other themes besides penal substitution. But then again, we have never read a proponent of penal substitution who claims that penal substitution is the *only* motif connected with the atonement in the Scriptures. Green and Baker fail to document a single case, and one wonders therefore whether they are not shooting at a non-existent target. Certainly, if any Christian were to hold that penal substitution is an exhaustive explanation of Jesus' death, we would join with Joel Green and Mark Baker in urging them to reflect on a richer tapestry of biblical themes.

However, the observation that there are other facets to the biblical teaching on the atonement does not answer the question of whether or not penal substitution should have a central place among them. This takes us to our next objection.


## 2. 'Penal substitution is not central to the atonement'

*Objection*

The previous objection is a plea to allow other aspects of the Bible's teaching on the atonement to sit alongside penal substitution. This objection urges that these other perspectives are *more important* than penal substitution, or even that penal substitution is a peripheral idea.

*Response*

It is generally agreed that some biblical doctrines are more in some sense important than others. Few would argue that the question of whether or not we should wear hats in church (a topic that sometimes arises in connection with 1 Cor. 11:1–16) is as significant as the question of how someone can be saved. In order to address the objection before us, we need to find a way of assessing the relative importance of different doctrines, so we can then evaluate the place of penal substitution.

It can be helpful to speak in terms of relative centrality, provided we are very clear about what we mean. We suggest than some doctrines are more central than others *in the sense that they are more closely related to a greater number of other biblical doctrines*. The jigsaw-puzzle analogy from chapter 3 can help us here. Pieces at the centre of a jigsaw are in direct contact with a greater number of other pieces than those at the corners. Removing a central piece will therefore disrupt more elements of the picture than omitting one of the corners. Similarly, some areas of Christian doctrine are intimately related to lots of other important themes (the question of how someone is saved, for example, or the nature of God as Trinity), whereas others are less strongly integrated into the big picture (such as whether or not we should wear hats in church). A useful way to assess the centrality of a given biblical doctrine is to ask ourselves how much distortion is introduced into other parts of the picture if we remove it.

It is clear from our discussion in chapter 3 that many biblical doctrines would be compromised if we were to remove penal substitution from the picture. We have seen that the doctrine of penal substitution is necessary to safeguard the justice and holiness of God, for to deny it is to suggest that God is content simply to overlook evil whenever he forgives someone. To discard penal substitution would also jeopardize God's truthfulness, for he has promised that sin will lead to death. Moreover, other aspects of the atonement cease to make sense if penal substitution is denied. We argued in chapter 3 that penal substitution is essential to Christ's victory over evil powers (something that Gustav Aulén's Christus Victor theory fatally missed), to his restoration of the relationships between sinners and God (reconciliation) and to the liberation he brings from captivity to sin and Satan (redemption or ransom). Far from being viable *alternatives* to penal substitution, they are outworkings of it. As the hub from which all of these other doctrines fan out, penal substitution is surely central.

To take another example, it is impossible to understand how the atoning death of Jesus could usher in the new creation and bring new life to the corrupt and degenerating cosmos if he did not endure and exhaust the divine curse on the old creation. The renewal of the cosmos by means of Jesus' death is explicable only by reference to penal substitution.[7]

Of course, none of this implies that the other biblical perspectives on the atonement are either untrue or insignificant. It does establish that penal substitution is absolutely central, and much else would simply fall apart without it.

---

7. See M. Ovey, 'The Cross, Creation and the Human Predicament', in David Peterson (ed.), *Where Wrath and Mercy Meet: Proclaiming the Atonement Today* (Carlisle: Paternoster, 2001), pp. 100–135.

## 3. 'Penal substitution diminishes the significance of Jesus' life and resurrection'

### *Objection*

It is often suggested that penal substitution diminishes the significance of Jesus' life and resurrection. For example, Stuart Murray Williams claims that 'If penal substitution is correct, neither the life of Jesus nor his resurrection have much significance.'[8] Joel Green and Mark Baker allege that according to Charles Hodge's understanding of penal substitution, 'Jesus' resurrection is not really necessary'.[9]

In a similar vein, Tom Smail claims that Jesus' resurrection cannot be readily incorporated into a penal substitutionary doctrine of the atonement:

> The penal model as such does not quite know what to make of the resurrection . . .
> The resurrection is seen only as the sign of the Father's acceptance of [Christ's]
> sacrifice, his affirmation of the sufficiency of what has been done to secure our
> pardon, and as a rather disconnected promise of life after death to those who belong
> to Christ.[10]

Paul Fiddes contends that proponents of penal substitution find it hard to integrate the life of Jesus into their doctrine of salvation: 'Protestant theologians who followed Calvin were intrigued by the place which Christ's active obedience had within the scheme of salvation, but as long as they held to a theory of penal substitution they remained perplexed and confused about it'[11] (by 'active obedience' theologians mean Jesus' obedience to his Father during his earthly life).

### *Response*

These objections betray grave misunderstandings of the doctrine of penal substitution. The great majority of Reformed theologians have always insisted

---

8. Stuart Murray Williams, 'Stuart Murray Williams on the Lost Message of Jesus: A Speech at the Debate on Steve Chalke's Book *The Lost Message of Jesus*', http://www.anabaptistnetwork.com/node/233 (accessed 8 February 2006).

9. Green and Baker, *Recovering the Scandal*, p. 148.

10. Tom Smail, *Once and for All: A Confession of the Cross* (London: Darton, Longman & Todd, 1998), p. 96.

11. Paul S. Fiddes, *Past Event and Present Salvation: The Christian Idea of Atonement* (London: Darton, Longman & Todd, 1989), p. 100.

that Christ's entire life on earth was part of his atoning work, for he lived in perfect obedience to the law of God, which was binding upon us but which we failed to keep. This integrates perfectly with the doctrine of penal substitution. The righteousness of Jesus' life was imputed (credited, or reckoned) to us, so that we might be justified, or declared righteous by God, and stand pure and blameless before him. Our sin, on the other hand, was imputed to Christ, and he was punished in our place. This is explained in any standard introduction to Reformed theology.[12] Fiddes' claim that 'Protestant theologians who followed Calvin . . . remained perplexed and confused' about Christ's active obedience is simply wrong.

Similarly, penal substitution is entirely at home with the resurrection of Jesus. The resurrection is seen by proponents of penal substitution as 'Christ's justification';[13] 'the culminating proof that Christ was a teacher sent from God (the sign of Jonah), and that he was the Son of God (Rom. 1:4)';[14] 'the supreme attestation of the fact of immortality';[15] an 'open demonstration'[16] of his victory over death, the pledge of our new birth in him;[17] the promise of the perfection of our resurrection bodies;[18] the beginning of the end for the old created order and the first fruits of the new creation;[19] and a motivation and

---

12. See e.g. John Calvin, *Institutes of the Christian Religion*, trans. F. L. Battles, vol. 1 (Philadelphia: Westminster, 1960), II.xvi.5, pp. 507–510; Francis Turretin, *Institutes of Elenctic Theology*, trans. G. M. Giger, vol. 2 (Phillipsburg: Presbyterian & Reformed, 1994), 14.XIII, pp. 445–455; Louis Berkhof, *Systematic Theology* (London: Banner of Truth, 1959; first pub. 1941), pp. 379–381; and Wayne Grudem, *Systematic Theology: An Introduction to Biblical Doctrine* (Leicester: IVP, 1994), pp. 570–571.

13. Richard B. Gaffin, Jr., *Resurrection and Redemption: A Study in Paul's Soteriology*, 2nd edn (Phillipsburg: Presbyterian & Reformed, 1987), p. 124. Gaffin's discussion here is particularly illuminating.

14. Berkhof, *Systematic Theology*, p. 349; see also Calvin, *Institutes*, vol. 1, II.xvi.13, pp. 520–522.

15. Berkhof, *Systematic Theology*, p. 349.

16. Athanasius, *On the Incarnation* (New York: St. Vladimir's Seminary Press, 1993), sect. 30, p. 60. See also sect. 26, pp. 56–57.

17. Grudem, *Systematic Theology*, pp. 614–615; Calvin, *Institutes*, vol. 1, II.xvi.13, pp. 520–522.

18. Grudem, *Systematic Theology*, pp. 615–616.

19. Athanasius, *On the Incarnation*, sect. 32, pp. 63–64; Ovey, 'Cross, Creation', pp. 100–135.

empowerment to godliness in the light of Christ's impending return.[20] These theological themes are integrated into a coherent theological framework in which penal substitution plays an indispensable part. In summary, the claim that penal substitution diminishes the significance of Jesus' life and resurrection is simply not true.

## 4. 'Penal substitution is not taught in the Bible'

### Objection
Critics frequently claim that the biblical texts traditionally cited in support of penal substitution do not really teach it at all. Some have argued that the sacrificial language of Leviticus does not relate to God's anger at sin, or that the 'suffering servant' in Isaiah 53 is not depicted as an atoning substitutionary sacrifice for sin, or that the Greek word traditionally translated 'propitiation' in Romans 3:25 and elsewhere does not imply that the death of Christ averted the wrath of God. Thus John Carroll and Joel Green claim that 'Paul uses an almost inexhaustible series of metaphors to represent the significance of Jesus' death, and penal substitution (at least as popularly defined) is not one of them.'[21]

These objections have one thing in common: they seek to demonstrate that penal substitution and related theological themes are not taught in Scripture.

### Response
This is an extremely serious objection, for if penal substitution is not biblical, it is not true. The only way it can be addressed is by a careful study of the texts in question, and we have attempted to provide such an analysis in chapter 2. There seems little point in repeating our conclusions here: we invite readers to scrutinize our exegesis of the texts and to draw their own conclusions.[22]

---

20. Grudem, *Systematic Theology*, p. 616; Calvin, *Institutes*, vol. 1, II.xvi.13, pp. 520–522.

21. John T. Carroll and Joel B. Green, with Robert E. Van Voorst, Joel Marcus and Donald Senior, C. P., *The Death of Jesus in Early Christianity* (Peabody: Hendrickson, 1995), p. 263.

22. The same response applies to the claim that penal substitution is merely a metaphor, and should not be confused 'with the actuality of atonement' (Green and Baker, *Recovering the Scandal*, p. 65). The heart of the issue is the same: whether or not the doctrine of penal substitution is taught in Scripture. For an illuminating discussion of the relationship between biblical doctrines and what some critics of

However, before leaving this objection, we note the irony that some of those who criticize penal substitution for being unbiblical expound the atonement in terms that have absolutely no scriptural basis at all! The French theologian Henri Blocher notes this feature of several chapters of *Atonement Today*, a volume of essays edited by John Goldingay:

> Even more distressing, we notice a strong liking for vague language and rudimentary metaphors. Stephen Travis sums up the teaching of 2 Corinthians 5.21 in these terms: 'The essential point is that Christ has experienced the sinner's estrangement from God, he has absorbed and thereby taken away sin, so that we might be brought into a right relationship with God.' Why 'experience' when Paul says 'death' (v. 14f)? Why 'estrangement' when Paul thinks in terms of 'imputation' (*logizomenos*, v. 19)? Why that verb 'absorb' that suggests a material substance to be destroyed by physical or chemical means? How did Christ 'absorb' sin? How did that supposed 'absorption' cancel the spiritual reality of sin? It is striking that this crude metaphor occurs no fewer than seven times in *Atonement Today*. And *it is not even biblical!*[23]

In fact, the curious notion that Christ 'absorbed' sin is surprisingly common among critics of penal substitution. Steve Chalke and Alan Mann write that 'Jesus . . . *absorbed* all the pain, all the suffering caused by the breakdown in our relationship with God.'[24] Indeed, just a couple of pages previously they explain the cross in even more idiosyncratic terms, declaring that 'Jesus, as he hung on the cross, *soaked up* all the forces of hate, rejection, pain and alienation all around him.'[25] These formulations of the atonement find little, if any, support in the Bible.

---

penal substitution call 'metaphors' see Henri Blocher, 'Biblical Metaphors and the Doctrine of the Atonement', *Journal of the Evangelical Theological Society* 47 (2004), pp. 629–645. We offer a few further comments on this topic, in relation to the claim that God's anger in the Bible is only metaphorical, in chapter 11, sect. 2.

23. Henri Blocher, 'The Sacrifice of Christ: The Current Theological Situation', *European Journal of Theology* 8.1 (1999), pp. 23–36 (p. 31), quoting from Stephen H. Travis, 'Christ as Bearer of Divine Judgement in Paul's Thought about the Atonement', in John Goldingay (ed.), *Atonement Today* (London: SPCK, 1995), pp. 21–38 (p. 26); italics original. As Blocher (p. 35, n. 59) notes, this 'crude metaphor' occurs five times in Stephen Travis's chapter (Travis, 'Christ as Bearer of Divine Judgement', pp. 26, 37, 38) and twice in John Goldingay's opening chapter ('Old Testament Sacrifice and the Death of Christ', p. 18).

24. Steve Chalke and Alan Mann, *The Lost Message of Jesus* (Grand Rapids: Zondervan, 2003), p. 181; italics added.

25. Ibid., p. 179; italics added.

## 5. 'Penal substitution is not important enough to be a source of division'

### Objection

The Bible teaches clearly that some issues should not be allowed to become a source of division between believers. We should 'make every effort to keep the unity of the Spirit through the bond of peace' (Eph. 4:2–3) and avoid 'passing judgment on disputable matters' (Rom. 14:1). Accordingly, James and the other apostles in Jerusalem resolved that they 'should not make it difficult for the Gentiles who are turning to God' (Acts 15:19) by requiring them to be circumcised, and Paul urged the Corinthians to curtail their freedom about what foods they ate in order to avoid being a 'stumbling-block' to other Christians with a 'weak conscience' (1 Cor. 8; 10:14 – 11:1). Is it not possible that penal substitution might be another issue of this kind, where differences must be acknowledged but need not cause schism?

### Response

We are sympathetic to this objection. Often those who raise it are driven by a godly desire to preserve our unity in the truth. All division is painful, unnecessary division is dishonouring to God, and endless infighting does not help the church's mission. However, the Bible teaches that there are some issues on which division is both necessary and inevitable (e.g. Gal. 1:8–9; 1 Cor. 5:11; 16:22; 2 Tim. 3:1–5; Titus 3:9–10; 2 John 9–11). We must therefore consider whether penal substitution is an issue of this kind.

Penal substitution lies at the heart of the gospel. As difficult as it may be, we can no more afford to sidestep this issue for the sake of unity than we can lay aside disagreements on the deity of Christ. This is of a different order to debates about the nature of church leadership or speaking in tongues. It is possible (and desirable) for Christians to retain unity in the gospel if they differ on those subjects. But when the gospel itself is the thing being debated, there is nothing around which to unite.

It seems that opponents of penal substitution are agreed on the magnitude of the issue. They contend that penal substitution is an unbiblical view of the cross without support in the historic church. They claim that penal substitution undermines the doctrine of the Trinity, without which Christianity would not be Christianity at all. More than that, they insist that penal substitution portrays God as an unjust tyrant, a vindictive child abuser, and a hypocrite who pays no regard to Jesus' foundational teaching about love. Finally, they have argued that penal substitution has disastrous pastoral consequences, that it has been used to justify violence against women and children, and that it is stifling the mission of the church in the world. All of these accusations have been made in recent years, and all are documented in this book.

These charges are extremely serious. We cannot pretend that critics of penal substitution are raising a minor point of dispute: they are accusing us of propagating a theological novelty, imposing our twisted modern world views on God's holy word, unwittingly encouraging and justifying sadistic acts of violence, and worshipping a malevolent, hypocritical deity who bears no resemblance whatsoever to the loving God of the Bible. Disagreements over penal substitution are fundamental; they cannot be ignored.

Of course, this does not mean Christian churches and organizations ought to divide at the first sign of disagreement on this issue. On the contrary, Christian love requires patient listening and discussion. However, if those who impugn penal substitution refuse to reconsider their position, there comes a time when we have no alternative but to part company. For the critics are right in this: differences over penal substitution ultimately lead us to worship a different God and to believe a different gospel.

# 8. PENAL SUBSTITUTION AND CULTURE

## Introduction

A number of objections concern the relationship of penal substitution to human culture. The first claims that the doctrine owes more to certain human ideas about guilt, justice, punishment and related concepts than to biblical teaching, and has therefore thrived in cultures where those ideas have been prominent. The second objection asserts the corollary of this; namely, that penal substitution either does not make sense or is deeply unattractive in cultures where these ideas are not prevalent. The final objection pertains to an alleged inadequacy of biblical language and concepts to communicate to the modern world.

## 1. 'Penal substitution is the product of human culture, not biblical teaching'

### Objection

Some critics argue that penal substitution does not arise from the Bible; instead, various human cultural norms have been imposed on Scripture, thereby distorting its teaching and leading to an unbiblical doctrine of the atonement.

Thus Paul Fiddes claims, 'penal substitution relies . . . upon a retributive view of penalty, and in this it is heavily conditioned by its social context',[1] and 'requires the addition of an Anselmian view of debt repayment and a Roman view of criminal law'.[2]

Joel Green and Mark Baker take a similar view, claiming that the popularity of penal substitution in the West is due in part to our individualism and our concern with moral guilt:

> One important reason for the ascendency of penal substitutionary atonement in the West has been our particular view of justice, with its orientation toward guilt and innocence on the one hand, and toward autobiography on the other. In the criminal-justice system, the question of guilt is paramount, together with the infliction of punishment upon the person or entity found guilty of having transgressed the law.[3]

Stuart Murray Williams proposes that the doctrine can be traced back to the conversion of Constantine, when Christianity became 'the imperial religion':[4] 'Penal substitution . . . is rooted in the Christendom system, in imperial and coercive Christianity, in a church colluding with the powers rather than offering a prophetic challenge or an alternative vision of justice and peace.'[5]

The view that penal substitution depends on certain cultural frameworks often goes hand in hand with the claim that it is not found in periods of history when these frameworks were absent. For example, Paul Fiddes claims that penal substitution was 'developed in the Reformation period (following earlier hints, especially in Augustine)',[6] and holds John Calvin largely responsible.[7] L. W. Grensted concedes that 'the beginning of a tendency' towards penal substitution was present in the more distant past (specifically the writings of

---

1. Paul S. Fiddes, *Past Event and Present Salvation: The Christian Idea of Atonement* (London: Darton, Longman & Todd, 1989), p. 102; see also p. 96.

2. Ibid., p. 98.

3. Joel B. Green and Mark D. Baker, *Recovering the Scandal of the Cross: Atonement in New Testament and Contemporary Contexts* (Downers Grove: IVP, 2000), p. 24; see also pp. 28–29, 169.

4. Stuart Murray Williams, 'Stuart Murray Williams on the Lost Message of Jesus: A Speech at the Debate on Steve Chalke's Book *The Lost Message of Jesus*', http://www.anabaptistnetwork.com/node/233 (accessed 8 February 2006).

5. Ibid.

6. Fiddes, *Past Event and Present Salvation*, p. 89.

7. Ibid., p. 70.

Gregory the Great, pope from 590 to 604), but concludes that 'before the Reformation only a few hints of a Penal theory can be found'.[8]

### Response

The claim that penal substitution is a relatively late doctrinal development is unsustainable in view of the historical survey we have presented in chapter 5, and we dare to hope that this myth might be laid to rest once and for all. The fact that penal substitution has been taught in many different social and political settings throughout the last two millennia also casts considerable doubt on the contention that the acceptance of the doctrine depends on a particular set of cultural norms.

Having said this, it is obvious that culture has *some* impact on our understanding of the Bible's teaching. The biblical doctrine of penal substitution incorporates ideas such as justice, guilt, forgiveness and penalty that have also found their way into other societies and legal systems. The prevailing world view will not necessarily *determine* what Christians believe, for Christians have often been those who swim strongly against the tide. Nevertheless, it may be *easier* for Christians to take on board biblical ideas shared by their contemporaries. This fits the common experience of missionaries that the gospel encounters different levels of acceptance in different cultures.

The key question, however, is not whether ideas found in penal substitution are also present within contemporary culture, but whether they are found in Scripture. There is obviously a danger of reading our cultural frameworks into the biblical text, but in the end this can be avoided only by sensitive exegesis and careful theology. Nor should we underestimate the extent to which Judaeo-Christian assumptions have influenced the culture of the Western world. It is wholly unsurprising that some Western notions of justice overlap those found in the Bible, for the simple reason that the Bible informed those notions in the first place. Nor is it surprising to find this common ground shrinking as biblical ideas become increasingly devalued in the Western mind.

---

8. L. W. Grensted, *A Short History of the Doctrine of the Atonement* (Manchester: Manchester University Press; London: Longmans, Green, 1920), pp. 99, 191. J. F. Bethune-Baker makes a similar claim. He surveys the theology of the early church as far as Augustine of Hippo and is adamant that during this period 'the sufferings of Christ were not regarded as an exchange or substitution of penalty, or a punishment inflicted on him by the Father for our sins' (J. F. Bethune-Baker, *An Introduction to the Early History of Christian Doctrine* [London: Methuen, 1903; repr. 1933], p. 352).

In summary, the correspondence or lack of it between a given doctrine and human cultural ideas is entirely irrelevant to the question of whether that doctrine is biblical. What counts is whether it is taught in Scripture.

## 2. 'Penal substitution is unable to address the real needs of human culture'

### Objection

Some critics claim that the doctrine of penal substitution fails to address the needs of the modern world, either because it does not address our problems, or because it is simply incomprehensible to us.

Joel Green and Mark Baker relate this to the previous objection: if penal substitution depends on a certain cultural framework, then it will have been shaped by the perceived needs of that culture, and is unlikely to appeal to people with a radically different world view: 'If, at least to a significant degree, penal substitutionary atonement has been a "cultural product" of life in the West, is it any surprise that proclamation of the gospel grounded in this theory has tended to fall on deaf ears in other social worlds?'[9]

Indeed, according to Green and Baker, 'in many societies . . . penal substitution is simply unintelligible'.[10] Consequently, 'the challenge before us is how to articulate the message of the cross in ways that are culturally relevant *and* that remain faithful to the biblical witness'.[11]

Steve Chalke and Alan Mann express a related concern; namely, that some of the necessary theological background for penal substitution – the doctrine of sin in particular – fails to attract people to Christ today: 'People are desperate for a message that they can buy into, that they can see will make a difference to them and to the world in which they live. The truth is that you can't engender a sense of lostness or need into people simply by pointing out that they are "sinners". It just doesn't work.'[12]

Paul Fiddes warns similarly that the social changes since the Reformation might render penal substitution incomprehensible to the modern mind.

---

9. Green and Baker, *Recovering the Scandal*, p. 29; see also pp. 32, 203.

10. Ibid., p. 148.

11. Ibid., p. 211; italics original. Green and Baker give the example of Norman Kraus, a missionary who worked for several years in Japan (pp. 153–170).

12. Steve Chalke and Alan Mann, *The Lost Message of Jesus* (Grand Rapids: Zondervan, 2003), pp. 117–118; see also pp. 97–98.

Calvin assumes that when law . . . is broken punishment must always be inflicted. As a matter of fact this no longer seems as self-evident to us today as it did in past ages . . . Indeed every preacher ought to ask himself whether a theory of penal substitution can even be understood in a society where it is no longer possible to use such words as 'Christ suffered the death penalty for us'.[13]

Finally, Alan Mann laments what he sees as our 'tendency to over simplicity in narrating the meaninglessness and insufficiencies that traumatize people'.[14] He claims that 'our soteriologies need to take with great seriousness the human condition from which salvation is needed',[15] and criticizes penal substitution for failing to do this:

A story of atonement that orientates itself purely and simply around the wrath of God, directed toward the self for sins committed against a divine law, which is absorbed by an innocent (Jesus), not only fails to map onto the story of the post-industrialized 'sinless' self in any meaningful way – it also fails to map onto significant chunks of the New Testament.[16]

In summary, it is claimed that penal substitution will not gain acceptance in large parts of the modern world, either because it fails to address our perceived needs or because it cannot be understood.

### Response

As we recognized in response to the previous objection, it is true that penal substitution may be less readily grasped in cultures where some of the foundational ideas on which it depends are absent or opposed. However, this does not make it 'unintelligible';[17] it just means that the task of explanation may be more difficult.

Indeed, if we really believed that cultural differences presented an insurmountable barrier to understanding, then we should have to avoid discussing monotheism when speaking to Hindus, or banish talk of the Holy Spirit when in dialogue with scientific materialists. This would obviously be ridiculous; we

---

13. Fiddes, *Past Event and Present Salvation*, pp. 102–103.
14. Alan Mann, *Atonement for a 'Sinless' Society: Engaging with an Emerging Culture* (Milton Keynes: Paternoster, 2005), p. 97.
15. Ibid.
16. Ibid., p. 98.
17. Green and Baker, *Recovering the Scandal*, p. 148.

would end up never trying to communicate anything our hearers did not already know. The lack of common ground with other people does not require that we abandon distinctive ideas; only that we work harder to explain them.

It is true that the prevailing social mood may explain why some societies find penal substitution unattractive. But there is a deeper problem here. The Bible offers a disturbing explanation for why people of every culture find it hard to understand aspects of the gospel, or may even find it repulsive. While they know in their hearts that there is a God and that they should acknowledge him, they 'suppress the truth' with the result that 'their thinking became futile and their foolish hearts were darkened' (Rom. 1:18, 21; cf. Eph. 4:17–18). Jesus explained likewise that it was not for lack of revelation that people rejected him, for the light had come, but 'men loved darkness instead of light because their deeds were evil' (John 3:19). Indeed, the world's yearning for what Chalke and Mann call 'a message that they can buy into'[18] is a call for a god in our image, on our terms – what the Bible calls 'idolatry'. The perceived needs of a sinful world will rarely coincide with its real needs: the dazzling glory of the gospel will appear dim to blinded eyes (2 Cor. 4:4), and its logic will seem incoherent to those who 'cannot understand' the things of the Spirit of God (1 Cor. 2:14). None of this provides a justification for changing our message.

Indeed, in first-century Corinth many Jews found the cross a 'stumbling block' and many Greeks judged it 'foolishness'; only those called by God saw it as 'Christ the power of God and the wisdom of God' (1 Cor. 1:23–24). But this did not deter the apostle Paul. Knowing that his message was inherently objectionable to his culture, and indeed to human nature, his strategy was simply to preach the gospel God had entrusted to him. For us also, the fundamental question is not whether penal substitution is attractive, or easy to understand, but whether it is part of the gospel with which God has entrusted us. Green and Baker challenge us to be 'culturally relevant *and . . .* faithful to the biblical witness'.[19] If they mean merely that we must find new ways to explain the unchanging biblical gospel, then we approve wholeheartedly. But if they mean we are at liberty to downplay aspects of the message in order that our world might more readily accept it, then we cannot agree. Our fallible notions about what is culturally acceptable must never be allowed to undermine the word of God.

We can take comfort from the fact that penal substitution has been believed by countless Christians from a vast range of different cultural backgrounds

---

18. Chalke and Mann, *Lost Message of Jesus*, p. 117.

19. Green and Baker, *Recovering the Scandal*, p. 211; italics original.

across nearly two thousand years of church history. No cultural barrier is insurmountable, and frankly it is blasphemous to suggest that the gospel of God is now somehow inadequate.

### 3. 'Penal substitution relies on biblical words, metaphors and concepts that are outdated and misunderstood in our culture'

#### Objection

Some critics warn that the biblical writers communicated using words and images drawn from their own social worlds that simply do not mean to us today what they did to their hearers then. Certain biblical terms are thus liable to be misunderstood. Joel Green and Mark Baker give an example, suggesting that 'Sharply put, to speak of "sacrifice" today may be to use the same terms as those used in the first-century world, but spoken in the context of modern-day America those words can hardly mean the same thing.'[20]

The solution to this kind of problem, according to Green and Baker, is to use 'metaphors and language that draw on the shared experience and vocabulary of people of that time and place'.[21] Thus they advocate that the *language* used to communicate the gospel be changed to reflect the evolving meaning of words.

On other occasions Green and Baker appear to go further, arguing that the actual *concepts* upon which penal substitution depends are no longer at home in our world. Thus, speaking of penal substitution, they claim that 'what we now take to be the traditional view of the atonement employs language *and depends on a model of divine-human interaction* that is alien to the lives of huge numbers of those to whom the church's mission is directed'.[22]

Green and Baker's response to this perceived problem is to abandon the offending theological concepts. This emerges in their discussion of the ministry of Normal Kraus, a missionary to Japan. They applaud 'his cultural sensitivity', which 'allowed him both to recognize the *inappropriateness* of teaching a Western penal substitutionary theory of the atonement and to discover an approach to which people could relate'.[23] Notice here that Green and Baker approve Kraus's alteration to the 'penal substitutionary *theory*' itself, not merely the language and metaphors used to express it.

---

20. Ibid., p. 111.
21. Ibid., p. 151.
22. Ibid., p. 114; italics added.
23. Ibid., p. 168; italics added; see also p. 140.

In summary, this objection claims that both the biblical concepts connected with penal substitution and the words used to convey them have become outdated, and that they must be changed to communicate the gospel to our modern culture.

### Response

We must distinguish between two different strands to this objection. The first claims that the meaning of language has changed since the Bible was written, so different words must now be used to convey the same concepts. We agree entirely. For one thing, few Christians understand the languages in which the Bible was originally written, and the use of an English translation immediately recognizes that different words must be used to convey the same concepts. Moreover, language never stands still, and the meaning of words changes with time.[24] Since much of the language used in the Bible in connection with penal substitution relates to sacrificial rituals absent from the modern world, considerable care must be taken to avoid misunderstanding. There may simply be no single word in twenty-first-century English that conveys exactly the same as any of the various Hebrew words for 'sacrifice' in 1,000 BC. All of this means simply that we must use terms with care, and if necessary take time to explain them.

However, there is a second and more serious strand to this objection; namely, the claim that the *concepts* connected with penal substitution are outdated and incomprehensible to the modern mind, and must therefore be abandoned. This must be firmly resisted. There may well be cultures where people are unfamiliar with, or even hostile to, important biblical concepts, and those concepts will therefore be hard to explain. But the solution is not to change the concepts: we must instead find new ways, and possibly different words, to express them. Modifying the message to suit the hearers is a commonplace among political spin doctors, for whom (all too often) the message itself is dispensable, and what really matters is getting into office. But the Lord of all creation is not up for election, and his word is not open for negotiation. As we concluded in the previous section, our task as Christ's servants is to preach the unchanging gospel, not to implement modifications as we see fit. Without doubt 'the time will come when men will not put up with sound doctrine. Instead, to suit their own desires, they will gather around them a great number of teachers to say what their itching ears want to hear' (2 Tim. 4:3). But woe to those false teachers who scratch where they itch.

---

24. D. A. Carson, *Exegetical Fallacies* (Grand Rapids: Baker, 1984), pp. 32–36.

## Introduction

This set of objections concerns the relationship between penal substitution and violence. The first argues that sacrificial motifs found in penal substitution are imposed on the Bible from unbiblical cultural or religious world views. The second and third reject the violence involved in penal substitution as unworthy of a loving God and inconsistent with Jesus' message. The final objection claims that penal substitution is an instance of 'the myth of redemptive violence', which is an ineffective response to evil.

## 1. 'Penal substitution rests on unbiblical ideas of sacrifice'

### Objection

Some critics claim that advocates of penal substitution misinterpret the sacrificial themes found in the Bible, particularly in the Old Testament, imposing upon them ideas foreign to biblical thought and thereby distorting the Bible's teaching. This is a specific instance of an earlier objection that penal substitution is dependent on unbiblical cultural presuppositions, but it contains particular emphases in connection with the theme of sacrifice and is best addressed separately.

The ancient pagan religions are often blamed for giving rise to the sacrificial ideas found in penal substitution. This is reflected in C. H. Dodd's view that the Greek word *hilastērion* should not be translated 'propitiation' in Romans 3:25. Dodd claims that such a translation would be 'misleading, for it suggests the placating of an angry God, and although this would be in accord with pagan usage, it is foreign to biblical usage'.[1] J. I. Packer summarizes the essential features of pagan religious systems in his defence of penal substitution:

> There are various gods, none enjoying absolute dominion, but each with some power to make life easier or harder for you. Their temper is uniformly uncertain; they take offence at the smallest things, or get jealous because they feel you are paying too much attention to other gods and other people, and not enough to themselves, and then they take it out on you by manipulating circumstances to your hurt. The only course at that point is to humour and mollify them by an offering. The rule with offerings is the bigger the better, for the gods are inclined to hold out for something sizeable . . . Human sacrifice, in particular, is expensive but effective. Thus pagan religion appears as a callous commercialism, a matter of managing and manipulating your gods by cunning bribery . . . the appeasing of celestial bad tempers.[2]

Thus the central theme of this objection is that penal substitution relies on sacrificial ideas imported from paganism, which are entirely absent from the Bible.

### Response

It is easy to understand why people might be repelled by penal substitution if they imagined it entails a view of propitiation like that outlined above. However, the Bible's teaching on propitiation is wholly different. Those who fail to recognize this are guilty of serious misunderstanding at both the historical and theological level.

From the historical point of view, it is important to recognize that the Old Testament rituals that form much of the biblical background to the New Testament teaching about Christ's sacrificial death were radically different from many of the pagan practices of other ancient Near Eastern peoples. God's people received detailed, lengthy descriptions of precisely how to conduct their

---

1. C. H. Dodd, *The Epistle of Paul to the Romans* (London: Hodder & Stoughton, 1932), p. 55. We examine Dodd's claims in more detail in chapter 2.

2. J. I. Packer, *Knowing God*, 2nd edn (London: Hodder & Stoughton, 1993), pp. 201–202.

sacrifices (see especially Lev. 1–7; also Exod. 29–30; Num. 15, 28–29), and were explicitly forbidden from imitating many of the rituals of other nations (e.g. Deut. 12:4, 31; 18:9; Lev. 18; 2 Kgs 17:15–17; 21:2; 2 Chr. 33:2), particularly the appalling practice of child sacrifice (Deut. 12:31; 2 Kgs 17:17; 2 Chr. 28:3; 33:6; Jer. 7:31; 19:5; Ezek. 20:31). The mere fact that the other nations also performed sacrifices should therefore not be allowed to obscure the huge differences between those practices and the Old Testament sacrificial system.

From a theological point of view, the biblical understanding of sacrifice is poles apart from pagan sacrificial ideas. John Stott outlines three fundamental features of the biblical idea of sacrifice that place clear blue water between Christianity and paganism. First, God's anger is not the volatile and erratic caprice of pagan deities: 'It is never unpredictable, but always predictable, because it is provoked by evil and by evil alone. The wrath of God . . . is his steady, unrelenting, unremitting, uncompromising antagonism to evil in all its forms and manifestations.'[3] Secondly, the propitiation is not made by us, but by God himself, who took 'the initiative . . . in his sheer mercy and grace'.[4] Thirdly, the propitiatory sacrifice 'was neither an animal, nor a vegetable, nor a mineral . . . but a person. And the person God offered was not someone else . . . No, he offered himself. In giving his Son, he was giving himself.'[5]

In summary, the character of God's wrath, the identity of the offerer and the nature of the offering are so utterly different from paganism that it is simply impossible to maintain that the biblical doctrine of penal substitution rests on pagan ideas of sacrifice.[6] To reject penal substitution on the ground of a supposed dependence on paganism is to dismiss a grotesque caricature of the biblical picture.


## 2. 'The violence involved in penal substitution amounts to "cosmic child abuse"'

### Objection

This objection probes the claim made by proponents of penal substitution that God the Son suffered violent punishment and death in our place, and that

---

3. John R. W. Stott, *The Cross of Christ* (Leicester: IVP, 1986), p. 173.

4. Ibid.

5. Ibid., p. 174.

6. The same clear differences between pagan and Christian sacrificial ideas are clear in Packer, *Knowing God*, pp. 201–224.

this penalty was imposed by God the Father. It protests that that this amounts to the infliction of extreme physical pain on an innocent victim, which has appalling parallels in the worst cases of child abuse.

This claim has gained prominence since the publication of Steve Chalke and Alan Mann's book, *The Lost Message of Jesus*. They raise the issue thus: 'How . . . have we come to believe that at the cross this God of love suddenly decides to vent his anger and wrath on his own Son? The fact is that the cross isn't a form of cosmic child abuse – a vengeful Father, punishing his Son for an offence he has not even committed.'[7]

Chalke and Mann are not the only people to make this criticism.[8] In his contribution to *Atonement Today*, a collection of essays edited by John Goldingay, Colin Greene claims that 'when substitution is understood in a punitive and exclusive sense . . . Christ becomes . . . the whipping-boy who appeases the wrath of God'.[9]

## Response

This objection is so charged with emotion that it is helpful to begin by defusing the rhetoric. There are two possible ways in which those who raise the criticism may want to be understood. On the one hand, they may be suggesting that the doctrine of penal substitution would mean the death of Jesus *really was*

---

7. Steve Chalke and Alan Mann, *The Lost Message of Jesus* (Grand Rapids: Zondervan, 2003), p. 182. Joel Green and Mark Baker also claim that penal substitution 'has been construed' in this way (Joel B. Green and Mark D. Baker, *Recovering the Scandal of the Cross: Atonement in New Testament and Contemporary Contexts* [Downers Grove: IVP, 2000], p. 32).

8. The 'child abuse' epithet also appears in Brian D. McLaren, *The Story We Find Ourselves in: Further Adventures of a New Kind of Christian* (San Francisco: Jossey-Bass, 2003), pp. 102ff., cited in D. A. Carson, *Becoming Conversant with the Emerging Church* (Grand Rapids: Zondervan, 2005), pp. 166–168; Joanne Carlson Brown and Rebecca Parker, 'For God So Loved the World', in Joanne Carlson Brown and Carole R. Bohn (eds.), *Christianity, Patriarchy, and Abuse: A Feminist Critique* (New York: Pilgrim, 1989), pp. 1–30 (p. 26); and Rita Nakashima Brock, 'And a Little Child Will Lead Us: Christology and Child Abuse', in Joanne Carlson Brown and Carole R. Bohn (eds.), *Christianity, Patriarchy, and Abuse: A Feminist Critique* (New York: Pilgrim, 1989), pp. 42–61 (pp. 51–53).

9. Colin Greene, 'Is the Message of the Cross Good News for the Twentieth Century?', in John Goldingay (ed.), *Atonement Today* (London: SPCK, 1995), pp. 222–239 (p. 232).

akin to child abuse, with all the appalling images and associations that term implies. On the other hand, the term 'child abuse' might have been chosen merely as a convenient (if pejorative) shorthand for the idea that God the Father wanted his Son to suffer; that he was involved in some way. This notion itself is thought objectionable, quite apart from the emotionally charged connotations of the term used to describe it.

These two objections are really quite different, and must be dealt with separately. The first is simply wrong: penal substitution emphatically does not imply that Jesus' death *really was* a form of child abuse. It differs in at least two fundamental respects.

First, according to the doctrine of penal substitution, Jesus *willingly* went to his death, in the full knowledge of what would be entailed. This is abundantly clear in the Gospels. For example, when Peter tried to deter Jesus from taking the path of suffering and death, Jesus denounced him with the words 'Get behind me, Satan!' (Mark 8:33). Moreover, Jesus explicitly insisted that nothing compelled him to suffer and die against his will: 'I lay down my life – only to take it up again. No-one takes it from me, but I lay it down of my own accord' (John 10:17–18).[10] By contrast, child abuse involves inflicting pain upon an unwilling victim, or exploiting a person who is unable to understand fully what is happening.

Secondly, according to the doctrine of penal substitution, Jesus died to bring glory to himself (e.g. John 17:1; Phil. 2:8–9; Heb. 2:9; Rev. 5:12) and to save his people (e.g. Rom. 5:8; 1 Cor. 15:3; 1 Tim. 2:6; 1 Pet. 3:18), as well as to glorify his Father. By contrast, child abuse is carried out solely for the gratification of the abuser.

For these two reasons, whatever else may be true about the violence of Jesus' death, it was not an instance of child abuse. Child abuse is carried out against the will of the victim for the sole gratification of the abuser; Jesus willingly went to his death to save his people and glorify his name. The label is misleading, disturbing – even blasphemous – and should be abandoned.

However, some critics may concede that the designation 'child abuse' is not strictly accurate: they use it merely as a shorthand for the idea that the Father willingly caused his Son to suffer. In objecting to this, they are challenging something fundamental to penal substitution.

Perhaps before attempting a fuller response, we should simply let the prophet Isaiah speak. In a famous passage, frequently applied to the Lord Jesus in the New Testament (see further in chapter 2), he says, 'it was the LORD's will

---

10. See also Matt. 20:28; Mark 10:45; John 10:15; Gal. 1:4; 2:20; Eph. 5:25; 1 Tim. 2:6.

to crush him and cause him to suffer' (Isa. 53:10). We can reject this idea only by rejecting the word of God.

It should be recognized, though, that *any* view of the atonement that upholds God's sovereignty – that is, his control over his creation – also implies that in some sense God *caused* Jesus' suffering and death. After all, he sent his Son to earth in the full knowledge of what would happen to him, and even with the intention that things should work out that way. Those who would deny this necessarily impugn not only penal substitution but also the doctrine of God's sovereignty. This is such an important theme that is it worth taking a little time to establish what the Bible actually teaches about it.

The best place to begin is with the apostles' accounts of Jesus' death in the book of Acts. Acts 2 records the speech of the apostle Peter on the day of Pentecost. Peter gives a brief description of Jesus' death that unambiguously affirms God was in full control of the event: 'This man was handed over to you by God's set purpose and foreknowledge; and you, with the help of wicked men, put him to death by nailing him to the cross' (Acts 2:23).

Notice that Peter affirms both that God had 'foreknowledge' of Jesus' crucifixion, and also that it was his 'purpose' to bring it about.

Peter makes the same point during his speech to the crowd at the temple in Jerusalem, recorded in Acts 3:11–26. Speaking of Jesus' death, Peter says, 'This is how God fulfilled what he had foretold through all the prophets, saying that his Christ would suffer' (v. 18). Peter explicitly teaches here that God had foretold the death of Jesus through his prophets in the Old Testament, and that he had then brought about the fulfilment of these promises at Calvary, again demonstrating his firm conviction that God was in complete control of the death of Jesus.

Finally, a similar understanding is evident in Acts 4, which records the disciples' meeting just after Peter and John's release from prison. They prayed together, recounting the mighty deeds of God culminating in the events that had led up to Jesus' death. The important words are found in verses 27–28: 'Indeed Herod and Pontius Pilate met together with the Gentiles and the people of Israel in this city to conspire against your holy servant Jesus, whom you anointed. They did what your power and will had decided beforehand should happen.'

These verses clearly reveal that Peter, John and the other disciples believed God had 'decided beforehand' that Christ would die. They do not teach only that God *knew* what would happen; they specify that he *caused* the conspiracy against Jesus – his '*power and will had decided beforehand*' what would come to pass. Human agents were also involved, just as in Acts 2:23, but this is not seen as undermining God's activity: God was working through these wicked men to accomplish his purposes.

Clearly, then, the New Testament apostles teach that God foresaw, planned and was in full control of the death of Christ. This was evident already in numerous Old Testament prophecies that either announced God's intention to send a suffering messiah or foretold his coming (e.g. Gen. 3:15; Pss 22; 69; Isa. 53:1–12; Zech. 12:10; 13:7). It is impossible to deny the divine authority of these prophecies, both because of the authority the prophets claimed for themselves[11] and because of the reverence with which Jesus himself regarded the Old Testament Scriptures.[12] Moreover, it is impossible to deny that these prophecies relate to Jesus' death, because this is how Jesus and the apostles understood them.[13]

In short, there is simply no way of avoiding the Bible's clear, repeated and unambiguous teaching that God was in control of Jesus' death, just as it presents him as sovereign over every other event in the entire universe.[14] God did not merely foresee Jesus' death; much less was he a passive bystander. The fact that penal substitution affirms this constitutes an argument in *favour* of this understanding of the atonement, not an argument against it.[15]

---

11. There are innumerable occasions in the Old Testament where the prophets claim to speak with the authority of God. A tiny sample of the total might include Isa. 1:10; Jer. 1:2, 4; Ezek. 1:1–3; Hos. 1:1; 4:1; Joel 1:1; Jon. 1:1 etc.

12. E.g. Matt. 5:17–19; 15:4; 22:31–32; Mark 12:10–11; Luke 4:21; John 10:35; 13:18; 17:12; 19:28.

13. The Old and New Testaments are intertwined in so many ways that it is impossible to represent the relationship merely by citing a string of biblical references. However, for our present purpose it is useful to highlight the instances where Jesus or the apostles explicitly refer to a specific Old Testament text in relation to Jesus' death. This list would include Matt. 27:46; Mark 15:34 (Ps. 22:1); John 13:18 (Pss 41:9; 55:12–15); John 19:28–29 (Pss 22:15; 69:21); John 19:32–37 (Exod. 12:46; Ps. 22:16; Zech. 12:10); Acts 1:16–20 (Pss 69:25; 109:8–15); 1 Pet. 2:22–25; (Isa. 53:3–9); Heb. 2:14; 1 John 3:8 (Gen. 3:15).

14. The biblical evidence for this point is overwhelming. See e.g. John M. Frame, *No Other God* (Phillipsburg: Presbyterian & Reformed, 2001), pp. 57–87.

15. This aspect of the Bible's teaching raises the challenging question of how God's sovereignty over evil can be reconciled with his goodness. It is clear that neither God's sovereignty nor his goodness can be denied, but beyond this the question becomes daunting indeed. On the philosophical side of this subject, D. A. Carson, *Divine Sovereignty and Human Responsibility: Biblical Perspectives in Tension* (London: Marshall, Morgan & Scott, 1981), is useful; on the pastoral side, the same author's *How Long, O Lord?* (Leicester: IVP, 1990) is very helpful. On the related question of

In summary, there is no justification whatsoever for labelling penal substitution as 'child abuse', nor for objecting to the biblical idea that God the Father willed his Son to suffer.

## 3. 'The retributive violence involved in penal substitution contradicts Jesus' message of peace and love'

### Objection

Some critics point to Jesus' teaching that we should love our enemies, offering them inexhaustible forgiveness without seeking retribution (Matt. 5:38–39, 43–48; 18:21–22; cf. Lev. 19:18). By contrast, they argue, penal substitution implies that God requires punishment before offering forgiveness, and therefore depicts him as a hypocrite, setting standards for us that he fails to meet himself. It is simply unbelievable that God would act in such a way, they claim, much less that he would treat his own Son more harshly than he urges us to treat each other.[16]

Stuart Murray Williams summarizes this objection, stating simply that 'penal substitution is inherently violent and contravenes central aspects of the message of Jesus'.[17]

Steve Chalke and Alan Mann make the point more forcefully: 'If the cross is a personal act of violence perpetrated by God towards humankind but borne by his Son, then it makes a mockery of Jesus' own teaching to love your enemies and to refuse to repay evil with evil.'[18]

---

the origin of evil in a world created by a good God, Henri Blocher, *Evil and the Cross: Christian Thought and the Problem of Evil*, trans. D. G. Preston (Leicester: Apollos, 1990), is highly recommended.

16. This criticism has a long pedigree. As Garry Williams noted in a recent defence of penal substitution, Faustus Socinus made it as long ago as 1578 (Faustus Socinus, *De Iesu Christo Servatore*, iii. 2, in *Opera Omnia*, vols. 1–2 of *Bibliotheca Fratrum Polonorum Quos Unitarios Vocant*, 8 vols. [Irenopoli: post 1656], vol. 2, pp. 115–246; see Garry J. Williams, 'Justice, Law, and Guilt: A Paper Given at the Evangelical Alliance Symposium on Penal Substitution' [2005], http://www.eauk.org/theology/atonement/upload/garry_williams.pdf [accessed 27 March 2006], p. 2).

17. Stuart Murray Williams, 'Stuart Murray Williams on the Lost Message of Jesus: A Speech at the Debate on Steve Chalke's Book *The Lost Message of Jesus*', http://www.anabaptistnetwork.com/node/233 (accessed 8 February 2006).

18. Chalke and Mann, *Lost Message of Jesus*, pp. 182–183.

Paul Fiddes pursues the idea of hypocrisy. He points to the ethical values of the Kingdom of God, where unconditional forgiveness is possible and punishment may simply be set aside:

> Jesus . . . set aside the Old Testament law of retribution which called for a just equivalence in punishment . . . he is giving a picture of what it can, in some circumstances, mean to love in the kingdom of God. There are no limits to love, and it may even be the loving thing in some situations to offer no resistance to an aggressor. On other occasions love for neighbour may demand that we resist. The point is that love lays down the limits; there is no such thing in the Kingdom of God as offended honour that must be satisfied. If our love may involve setting aside a penalty, can God act any differently?[19]

In summary, this objection claims that penal substitution is inconsistent with the way Jesus taught his followers to deal with evil. Jesus taught unconditional forgiveness; penal substitution requires retribution.

### Response

At first sight, this objection appears compelling, for it is true that both the character of God and the conduct of Jesus are laid down in Scripture as examples for us to follow. Peter cites God's words in Leviticus, 'Be holy, *because I am holy*' (1 Pet. 1:16; cf. Lev. 11:44–45; 19:2; 20:7; italics added), Paul urges us to 'be imitators of God' (Eph. 5:1) and Jesus presented his life as the supreme model for us to follow: 'If anyone would come after me, he must deny himself and take up his cross and follow me' (Mark 8:34). Penal substitution may seem to undermine this pattern by suggesting there are some things in which God is an unworthy example, for he himself fails to abide by the standards he sets for us.

However, the objection fails to recognize that the Bible does not urge us to imitate all of God's actions or every aspect of his character. We are urged to avoid some things precisely because God uniquely has the right to them. To put it another way, while we are often commanded to imitate God (e.g. Eph. 5:1–2), we are occasionally urged not to.

A moment's thought shows that this is a very familiar idea. For example, the first and second commandments (Exod. 20:1–6; Deut. 5:6–10) forbid a person from setting himself up as a deity to be worshipped. But these commandments do not imply there is something bad about being worshipped as such; merely

---

19. Paul S. Fiddes, *Past Event and Present Salvation: The Christian Idea of Atonement* (London: Darton, Longman & Todd, 1989), p. 103.

that this is God's prerogative, and his alone, 'For this is what the LORD says . . . "I am the LORD, and there is no other"' (Isa. 45:18). We would be distinctly unwise in this instance to follow God's example, as Herod discovered to his cost (Acts 12:21–23).

The principle that we should not *always* imitate God applies to exacting retribution against people for their sinful actions.[20] According to Scripture, this is something God may do, but individuals must not. We should not take revenge, not because retribution is inherently wrong, but because it rests with God. Paul teaches this in Romans 12:17–19: 'Do not repay anyone evil for evil. Be careful to do what is right in the eyes of everybody. If it is possible, as far as it depends on you, live at peace with everyone. Do not take revenge, my friends, but leave room for God's wrath, for it is written: "It is mine to avenge; I will repay," says the Lord.'

The first part of this passage teaches that individual Christians should not take revenge when evil is committed against them, which accords with Jesus' teaching in Matthew 5:38–39. But, crucially, the reason for this is not that in doing so we imitate God, who also does not punish wickedness. On the contrary, Romans 12:17–19 says we must not take revenge, because God *will* do so. It is wrong for us to punish sins committed against us, but it is not wrong for God to punish sins committed against him.[21] In fact his justice demands it.

Thus a right understanding of the Bible's teaching silences a criticism of penal substitution that at first seemed to enjoy biblical support.

## 4. 'The violence inherent in penal substitution is an example of "the myth of redemptive violence", which can never overcome evil'

### Objection
This criticism refers to what Walter Wink has called 'the myth of redemptive violence'.[22] According to this analysis, penal substitution amounts to an attempt to overcome violence with violence, which merely increases and compounds the problem.

---

20. This argument is indebted to Williams, 'Justice, Law, and Guilt', pp. 2–3.
21. The following section, Rom. 13:1–7, explains that there are certain circumstances where God has delegated the responsibility of punishing wickedness to 'the governing authorities' (v. 1) as 'God's servants' (v. 6), but individual believers do not have this prerogative.
22. Walter Wink, *Engaging the Powers: Discernment and Resistance in a World of Domination* (Minneapolis: Fortress, 1992).

Steve Chalke and Alan Mann provide an example of this objection:

> Jesus was determined to tackle what Walter Wink has described as *the myth of redemptive violence* – the belief that liberation, strength, protection and sustained freedom can only come from the power that violence gives to a person or a nation . . .
>
> All we know is that whenever aggression is met with aggression, the beast of violence is fed and grows stronger . . .
>
> The ultimate weakness of violence . . . is that whenever it is employed, at whatever level – personal, community, national or global – it is a descending spiral. It begets the very thing it seeks to destroy.[23]

Similar criticisms have been made by Stuart Murray Williams, who also draws on Wink's work.[24] The central claim here is that penal substitution simply *cannot* work. It would constitute an attempt by God to overcome the violence inherent in human sin – our violence against each other, and our violent opposition to God – by yet another act of violence. Penal substitution, it is claimed, simply adds one more act of brutality to the appalling catalogue of bloodshed that extends through human history.

### Response

Since this objection relies heavily on the work of Walter Wink, it is helpful to begin there. Wink's critique of penal substitution[25] is dependent in turn on the work of René Girard.[26] However, Girard's work is thoroughly unbiblical at key points. It displays a deficient understanding of the Old Testament sacrificial system, seeing sacrifice as a symptom of a violent and socially dysfunctional society rather than as God's appointed means to atone for the sin of his

---

23. Chalke and Mann, *Lost Message of Jesus*, pp. 125–126, 127, 129; italics original.

24. Stuart Murray Williams, 'Penal Substitution and the Myth of Redemptive Violence', paper given at the Evangelical Alliance Symposium on Penal Substitution (2005), http://www.eauk.org/theology/atonement/upload/stuartmurraywilliams.pdf (accessed 8 February 2006).

25. Wink, *Engaging the Powers*, ch. 7, especially pp. 148–149.

26. René Girard, *Violence and the Sacred* (Baltimore: Johns Hopkins University Press, 1977); *The Scapegoat* (Baltimore: Johns Hopkins University Press, 1986); *Things Hidden since the Foundation of the World*, trans. Stephen Bann and Michael Metteer (Stanford: Stanford University Press, 1987). Wink, *Engaging the Powers*, pp. 144–155.

people.[27] It exemplifies many of the misunderstandings we address elsewhere, such as the view that God is not angered by sin and therefore does not require atonement, or the idea that according to penal substitution God is required to punish sin by a law outside himself, rather than by his own holy and righteous character.[28] Girard also describes 'religion', including the religion of God's Old Testament people, as 'organized violence in the service of social tranquillity',[29] and displays a disturbing readiness to dismiss numerous passages of the Old Testament as 'legendary'.[30]

Perhaps this last point is the most surprising. According to Wink, Girard believes that 'in the Hebrew Bible, with only a few exceptions that are all legendary, whenever God acts to punish, God does so through human beings attacking each other'.[31] By this reckoning, these 'few . . . legendary' passages would have to include the flood in the time of Noah (Gen. 6–8), the biblical accounts of the plagues in Egypt (Exod. 8–12), the death of Aaron's sons Nadab and Abihu (Lev. 10; cf. Num. 3:4), the plagues among the Israelites in the wilderness and on numerous other occasions (e.g. Num. 11:33–35; 25:1–9; 2 Sam. 24:15–25; 1 Chr. 21), the rebellion of Korah and his men and the subsequent plague in the Israelite camp (Num. 16), and the destruction of the Assyrian army (Isa. 37:33–38; 2 Kgs 19:32–37).

If Girard's analysis were applied to the New Testament, the historical accounts of the silencing of Zechariah (Luke 1:20–22), the deaths of Ananias, Sapphira and Herod (Acts 5:1–11; 13:23), and the blindness of Elymas (Acts 13:8–11) would all be rejected as 'legendary'. Moreover, according to his own principle, he would presumably have to dissent from Paul's explanation of why some had died in the church at Corinth (1 Cor. 11:29–32). How he would understand the numerous explicit warnings of the final judgment is far from clear. What is clear is that Girard's analysis cannot be reconciled with an evangelical doctrine of Scripture.

Although Wink does 'offer a few criticisms'[32] of Girard's work, he does not distance himself from the points outlined above. Indeed, he adds the surprising claim that the apostle Paul was 'unable'[33] to understand correctly the

---

27. Wink, *Engaging the Powers*, pp. 144–147.
28. Ibid., p. 149. See chapter 11 for a response to these objections.
29. Ibid., p. 146.
30. Ibid., p. 147.
31. Ibid.
32. Ibid., p. 144.
33. Ibid., p. 154.

sacrificial nature of Jesus' death, and that 'Christianity has suffered from this confusion ever since'.[34] These misunderstandings are not incidental to Wink's case: they form central elements in his critique of penal substitution as an instance of 'the myth of redemptive violence'.

With these observations in mind, although Walter Wink's work has met with warm approval in some parts of the academic establishment,[35] it is surprising to find his conclusions appropriated by those who would profess to be evangelicals, such as Steve Chalke, Alan Mann and Stuart Murray Williams.

Having outlined serious flaws in the work that forms the background to this objection, we turn to the substance of the criticism itself. The objection entails more than that violence is morally reprehensible, and hence unworthy of God. Certainly, the death of Jesus did involve sinful acts by other human beings, such as the violence of the Roman soldiers and the Jewish Sanhedrin, and the cowardice of Pontius Pilate (Mark 14:65; 15:1–20), which the Bible views as reprehensible (e.g. Acts 7:52). However, at the same time, God chose to use these wicked deeds to accomplish his righteous purposes.[36]

At the heart of this objection is the claim that violence cannot solve the problem of violence; instead, it compounds the problem by adding another evil to the list of those it seeks to conquer. To this we respond in three ways.

First, Jesus was fully aware that a violent death awaited him in Jerusalem, and deliberately set himself on that course. He explained to his disciples on the way there that 'the Son of Man will be betrayed to the chief priests and teachers of the law. They will condemn him to death and will hand him over to the Gentiles, who will mock him and spit on him, flog him and kill him' (Mark 10:33–34). If the above critics were right, then Jesus made a terrible mistake. He should have taken steps to avoid such violence (and the Gospels are clear he had every opportunity to do so),[37] knowing that, in Steve Chalke and Alan Mann's words, 'violence . . . *whenever* it is employed . . . begets the very thing it seeks to destroy'.[38]

Second, the entire Old Testament sacrificial system was violent, but nonetheless had redemptive benefit. Moreover, in Numbers 25 the violent

---

34. Ibid.

35. The warm reception in these quarters is evident from the numerous glowing reviews on the inside cover of *Engaging the Powers*.

36. For a brief but helpful discussion see Blocher, *Evil and the Cross*, pp. 102–104.

37. E.g. he could have heeded Peter's warnings to avoid the Jewish capital (Matt. 16:21–22); instead, he rebuked Peter and did the opposite.

38. Chalke and Mann, *Lost Message of Jesus*, p. 129; italics added.

execution of Zimri by Phinehas was not only rewarded with 'a covenant of a lasting priesthood, because he was zealous for the honour of his God' (v. 13), but is also specifically identified as the means by which thousands of Israelites were spared from the ongoing effects of a plague.

Thirdly, there are important differences between the death of Jesus and other acts of violence perpetrated by sinful human beings against each other and against God. Because of these differences, penal substitution is not simply a case of adding one more act of violence to the list. For example, Jesus laid down his life willingly (John 10:17), whereas the violence perpetrated by sinful people involves acting against the will of those harmed by it.[39] Again, human violence is usually motivated by selfishness – we pursue our own good even when it causes harm to others. By contrast, it was a selfless act of God the Father to give his Son, motivated by his love for us (John 3:16) and his desire for his Son's glory (John 17:1, 5). Still again, human violence is a violation of justice, whereas the Bible declares that the death of Christ was ultimately the supreme demonstration of God's justice (e.g. Rom. 3:25–26).

There is one final problem with this objection. Even those who reject penal substitution on the grounds of the above objection must concede that the death of Jesus, with his flogging, the crown of thorns, and the appalling suffering of death by crucifixion, was extremely violent. Few would deny that in some sense it was also redemptive. The so-called '*myth* of redemptive violence' is, in the case of Jesus' death, no myth at all.

---

39. This point is discussed in more detail in chapter 11, sect. 1, where we consider how the persons of the Trinity acted together in accomplishing our redemption, such that there was a unity of purpose between them.

## Introduction

In this chapter we examine five objections that are related to the justice of penal substitution. The first objection challenges the idea that guilt and punishment can justly be transferred from one person to another. The second asserts that the very idea of retributive punishment is unbiblical, and is often stated in conjunction with the claim that biblical justice is concerned instead with restoring relationships. The third claims that the understanding of justice presupposed in penal substitution implies that God does not actually forgive sin. The fourth alleges that penal substitution does not work, because the punishment suffered by Christ was not equivalent to the punishment owed by us. Finally, the fifth claims that penal substitution leads to universalism, the unbiblical idea that all people will finally be saved and thus escape hell.

## 1. 'It is unjust to punish an innocent person, even if he is willing to be punished'

### *Objection*
Stuart Murray Williams states this objection concisely. He insists that

'punishing an innocent man – even a willing victim – is fundamentally unjust'.[1]

Tom Smail outlines the objection in more detail in his contribution to *Atonement Today*, a collection of essays edited by John Goldingay:

> By what right or justice can punishment be imposed on anybody except the person who has committed the offence? Is the bearing of punishment not one of those things that cannot be done by one person for another, where the protest on behalf of inalienable individual responsibility made by Ezekiel, echoed by Socinus, must be allowed to stand? Even though I, who am innocent of the offence, should be willing to bear the punishment you have incurred in committing the offence, it would be an unjust judge that would permit let alone organize such an illegitimate transfer.[2]

Smail says it is not enough that an innocent party is *willing* to be punished for another. Justice requires that only guilty people should be punished. Thus 'the penal substitution theory . . . must answer the question: How can it be just to punish a righteous man for the sins of many unrighteous people?'[3]

In Smail's view, there is an indissoluble connection between guilt and the person who incurs it, and between punishment and the person who deserves it: 'Guilt and punishment are not like fines, things that can be incurred by one person and settled by another. Intrinsically by their very nature, and morally by every rule of justice, they are inseparably attached to the person who, by what he or she does and is, has incurred them.'[4]

Colin Greene makes a similar claim in the same volume. He asks, 'Is it not the case that sins are so identified with their perpetrators that they cannot simply be transferred from one person to another as if by legal fiat?'[5]

---

1. Stuart Murray Williams, 'Stuart Murray Williams on the Lost Message of Jesus: A Speech at the Debate on Steve Chalke's Book *The Lost Message of Jesus*', http://www.anabaptistnetwork.com/node/233 (accessed 8 February 2006).

2. Tom Smail, 'Can One Man Die for the People?', John Goldingay (ed.), *Atonement Today* (London: SPCK, 1995), pp. 73–92 (p. 85).

3. Tom Smail, *Once and for All: A Confession of the Cross* (London: Darton, Longman & Todd, 1998), p. 97.

4. Smail, 'Can One Man Die?', p. 78. A similar argument is found in Smail, *Once and for All*, p. 98.

5. Colin Greene, 'Is the Message of the Cross Good News for the Twentieth Century?', in John Goldingay (ed.), *Atonement Today* (London: SPCK, 1995), pp. 222–239 (p. 231).

In summary, the objection is that guilt and punishment simply cannot be incurred by one person and transferred to another. People who sin, and only people who sin, are guilty, and only they should be punished.

### *Response*

We should begin by noting that the biblical writers do not share the concerns of Tom Smail, Colin Greene and Stuart Murray Williams. The apostle Peter, for example, testifies that God 'judges justly' (1 Pet. 2:23) and then in the very next verse affirms that Christ 'bore our sins' (v. 24).[6] Again, the apostle Paul declares that putting forth Christ as a propitiation for our sins was a demonstration of God's justice, not a violation of it (Rom. 3:25). Right at the outset, then, we must say that it is unbiblical to charge penal substitution with injustice. Nonetheless, it will be fruitful to spend a little time considering *why* penal substitution is not unjust.

Smail is correct when he asserts that the *willingness* of Christ's suffering is not a satisfactory explanation by itself. The reason is obvious. If an innocent person suffers the punishment for a crime for which he bears no guilt, then it makes no difference whether or not he does so willingly. It is a miscarriage of justice, pure and simple. The Bible roundly condemns such a thing when it comes to human courts, and it would seem strange if Christ did not adhere to the same standards himself:

> Acquitting the guilty and condemning the innocent –
> the Lord detests them both.
> (Prov. 17:15)[7]

To see why penal substitution is not a travesty of justice of exactly this kind, we need to recall the doctrine of union with Christ we discussed in chapter 3. The believer is not separate from Christ, an unrelated third party. He is in us, and we are in him, indwelt by his Spirit. It is easy to understate the significance

---

6. In the context of 1 Peter, of course, the manner in which Jesus went to his death is held up as an example for those who suffer unjustly (1 Pet. 2:18–21). Indeed, Jesus did suffer injustice at the hands of men, for as an innocent man he ought not to have been found guilty by Pilate's court, nor to have been sentenced to crucifixion. By contrast God acted justly in punishing him, for he saw him as guilty by virtue of his union with those whose sins he bore. We discuss this further below.

7. Numerous other biblical texts make the same point. See e.g. Exod. 23:7; Deut. 25:1; 1 Kgs 8:31–32; Ps. 15:5; Isa. 5:22–23; 29:20–21.

of our union with Christ, for it is not visible but spiritual – it exists by faith. But this is not at all to imply that it is not *real*. The 'spiritual' in 'spiritual union' means it is God's Holy Spirit who creates the union between Christ and believers; it does not imply that this union has no real consequences. Our justification, our adoption as God's children, and our present reigning with Christ in the heavenly places (Rom. 3:26–28; 5:1; Eph. 1:3–5; 2:6) are all real, even though spiritual and invisible, being perceived in the present only by faith.

The doctrine of penal substitution thus does not propose a transfer of guilt between unrelated persons. It asserts that guilt is transferred to Christ from those who are united to him.[8] In fact, 'transfer' may not even be the best term, since it could imply a separation between distinct persons. Instead, it may be better to say our sins were 'imputed' (i.e. 'reckoned', or 'credited', to use the vocabulary of Rom. 4 and Gal. 3) to Christ,[9] while his righteousness was imputed to us.[10] That Christ bore our sins *willingly* merely furthers the point:

---

8. Things become a little complex when we think about timing. Someone is united to Christ and receives the gift of his Spirit when he or she becomes a Christian. However, our sin must have been imputed to Christ back in the first century, at the time of the crucifixion. This is not a problem for a God who is outside time. He decrees that Christ should bear the sins of his elect, contemplating in advance their spiritual union with him, which makes this exchange efficacious and just. In God's mind the accomplishment of redemption at Calvary and its application to individual believers at their conversion are a unity, and it matters little that they are not simultaneous from our perspective. The apostle Paul seems to conflate the two: Were we raised with Christ (Eph. 2:6) at the time of Christ's resurrection, or at the time of our conversion? Were we justified when Christ died ('by his blood', Rom. 5:9) or when we believed in his death ('through faith', Rom. 5:1). It is not accidental that these questions are hard to answer! Paul does not allow us to separate the two perspectives too sharply, since they are so closely interrelated. We discuss these things further in relation to the doctrine of particular redemption in chapter 10, sect. 5.

9. See also 2 Cor. 5:19.

10. Some advocates of the 'New Perspective on Paul', a recent movement among some New Testament scholars, have questioned the historical understanding that justification involves the imputation of Christ's righteousness. A defence of the traditional view is beyond the scope of this book, but interested readers are referred to one of the following: John Piper, *Counted Righteous in Christ: Should we Abandon the Imputation of Christ's Righteousness?* (Leicester: IVP, 2003); D. A. Carson, Peter T. O'Brien and Mark A. Seifrid (eds.), *Justification and Variegated Nomism*, vol. 2: *The Paradoxes of Paul* (Tübingen: Mohr Siebeck; Grand Rapids: Baker, 2004);

he was not forced or coerced into this union with us, but entered into it voluntarily. Luther uses the analogy of a marriage between two people, one of them a debtor. The other knows that legal union will bring debt upon himself, but in love nonetheless willingly enters into the marriage.[11] The analogy is not perfect, for Christ does not merely share our debt, offering to pay it *with* us. Rather, he pays it *for* us. Nonetheless, marriage is intended to be illustrative of the costly love of Christ shown in the way in which he entered into such a union with his people (cf. Eph. 5:25).

Union with Christ explains how the innocent could be justly punished – he is judged for others' sins, which, by virtue of their union with him, become his. Conversely, it explains also how the guilty can be justly acquitted – believers are one with the innocent Lord Jesus Christ, and so his life of perfect righteousness is rightly imputed to us. The apostle Paul captures both sides of the exchange in a single verse: 'God made him who had no sin to be sin for us so that *in him* we might become the righteousness of God' (2 Cor. 5:21; italics added).

Sometimes people use the terminology of Christ dying as our *representative* in an attempt to give a coherent account of the atonement that incorporates the truth of faith union. Whatever Christ did as our representative, we also did by virtue of being 'in him'. Thus, in this sense, *we* died on the cross (2 Cor. 5:14).

However, representation and substitution are not mutually exclusive categories. On the contrary, each requires and implies the other. Representation explains the justice of imputing our guilt to Christ and his righteousness to us. Substitution, on the other hand, explains how this can be maintained without God punishing us *in ourselves*, for it was not us but Christ who was flogged, mocked, spat upon and crucified. While in the *representative* sense, our sins brought God's wrath upon Jesus, in the *substitutionary* sense we in our own persons did not experience his wrath. In the former sense, we were 'in him'. In the latter sense he was 'for' or 'instead of' us. Again, 2 Corinthians 5:21, cited above, combines both perspectives. John Owen puts it like this:

> [God] might punish the elect either in their own persons, or in their surety standing in their room and stead [as their substitute]; and when he is punished, they also are

---

Simon J. Gathercole, *Where Is Boasting? Early Jewish Soteriology and Paul's Response in Romans 1–5* (Grand Rapids: Eerdmans, 2002).

11. Martin Luther, *The Freedom of a Christian*, in *Three Treatises*, trans. W. A. Lambert, rev. H. J. Grimm (Philadelphia: Fortress, 1970), p. 286.

punished [in their representative]: for in this point of view the federal head and those represented by him are not considered as distinct, but as one; for although they are not one in respect of personal unity, they are, however, one, – that is, one body in mystical union, yea, *one mystical Christ*; – namely, the surety is the head, those represented by him the members; and when the head is punished, the members also are punished.[12]

It is clear, then, that representation and substitution are not alternatives. We are not at liberty to pick and choose between them. On the contrary, they are twin aspects of a single, coherent, integrated understanding of Christian theology. Failure to appreciate one will inevitably lead to misunderstanding and eventual rejection of the other.

We are now in a position to answer the objection that penal substitution entails unjustly punishing an innocent person. This rests on the claim that our guilt cannot be imputed to Christ, which is in turn grounded on the assumption that we are entirely separate and distinct from him. But the reality is that believers are united to Christ by his Spirit. The imputation of our guilt to Christ does not violate justice, because he willingly consents to a real, spiritual identification with his people. In short, this objection to penal substitution arises from a failure to understand the significance of union with Christ.

But why is this objection so pervasive? One possible reason is that union with Christ is seldom taught in our churches, and penal substitution has often been expounded without reference to it. Another possibility is that we have been unduly influenced by the individualism of contemporary society. Could it be this that leads critics of penal substitution to insist that sin and guilt can never be transferred between persons, and blinds them to the Bible's teaching to the contrary? It is surely ironic that some who make such criticisms also suggest that penal substitution is a product of our culture (e.g. Stuart Murray Williams). If anything, the shoe is on the other foot. It is their objection and not the doctrine of penal substitution that is the product of our individualistic age.

Indeed, the theme of corporate moral responsibility is far more pervasive in Scripture than is commonly realized. Apart from our union with Christ by faith, the most obvious example is the solidarity of all humanity with the first man, Adam. The apostle Paul draws a direct comparison in Romans 5:12–21

---

12. John Owen, *A Dissertation on Divine Justice*, in William H. Goold (ed.), *The Works of John Owen*, vol. 10 (London: Banner of Truth, 1967), pp. 481–624 (p. 598; italics original).

between the union of redeemed humanity with Christ and the union of fallen humanity with Adam. It is on the basis of the latter that the guilt and corruption of original sin is imputed to us.[13]

There are numerous other examples of corporate responsibility in Scripture.[14] For example, in Joshua 7, thirty-six Israelite soldiers lose their lives in battle on account of the sin of Achan, and his family members are then executed with him. In 2 Samuel 21:1–14, seven of Saul's sons are executed for their father's sin. In both cases, careful exegesis reveals that the deaths had the Lord's approval.[15] Similarly, there are many examples where people receive

---

13. The fact that we are all constituted sinners in Adam has never been denied within mainstream orthodoxy. However, there has been, and still is, debate about how Adam's sin comes to affect us. Calvin taught that we inherit from Adam a corrupted nature: 'We have . . . all sinned, because we are all imbued with natural corruption, and for this reason are wicked and perverse' (John Calvin, *The Epistles of Paul to the Romans and Thessalonians*, trans. Ross Mackenzie, eds. David W. Torrance and Thomas F. Torrance [Grand Rapids: Eerdmans, 1995], p. 112). However, the idea that we all sin, each in our own way, after Adam's likeness cannot adequately explain why Rom. 5 repeatedly speaks of our condemnation as a direct result of one sin (vv. 15–19). Consequently, others go further than Calvin and seek to explain how we could be implicated in Adam's sin itself. For Federalists, this happens because God has appointed Adam as our legal, covenantal representative (see e.g. John Murray, *The Imputation of Adam's Sin* [Grand Rapids: Eerdmans, 1959; repr. Phillipsburg: Presbyterian & Reformed, 1992]). For proponents of Realism, there exists some kind of metaphysical unity between Adam and all humanity (e.g. Augustine, *City of God*, trans. Henry Bettenson [London: Penguin, 1984], bks. 13 and 14; William G. T. Shedd, *Dogmatic Theology* [New York: Charles Scribner's Sons, 1889], pp. 168–257). Jonathan Edwards combines both Federalist and Realist elements (Jonathan Edwards, *The Great Christian Doctrine of Original Sin Defended*, in C. A. Holbrook [ed.], *The Works of Jonathan Edwards*, vol. 3, corrected edn [Yale: Yale University Press, 1997], pp. 102–437 [especially pp. 389–412]; Oliver D. Crisp, 'On the Theological Pedigree of Jonathan Edwards's Doctrine of Imputation', *Scottish Journal of Theology* 56 [2003], pp. 308–327).

14. A table listing over forty examples may be found in Joel S. Kaminsky, *Corporate Responsibility in the Hebrew Bible*, Journal for the Study of the Old Testament Supplement Series 196 (Sheffield: Sheffield Academic Press, 1995), pp. 190–191. See also Exod. 20:5–6; Deut. 5:9–10.

15. In Josh. 7, the executions are carried out as a result of Joshua praying to the Lord concerning the military defeat (vv. 6–12), and after the deaths 'the LORD turned

blessings from God because of the righteousness of others, such as the sparing of Mephibosheth because of the oath between David and Jonathan (2 Sam. 21:7; cf. 1 Sam. 18:3; 20:8, 17, 42; 23:18) and the reprieve granted to all Israel because of the humility and righteousness of King Josiah (2 Kgs 22:19–20). Human courts are explicitly prohibited from taking such relationships into account: 'Fathers shall not be put to death for their children, nor children put to death for their fathers; each is to die for his own sin' (Deut. 24:16). But it is evident from the above examples that this prohibition does not apply to God. Indeed, we are familiar with the idea that God's judgment extends further than ours. For example, God will judge the secrets of our hearts (Rom. 2:16; Heb. 4:12), but no human court should attempt to do so.

The above examples of solidarity do not in every respect mirror our union with Christ. Nonetheless, they reflect biblical ideas of corporate responsibility that fundamentally challenge the individualistic assumptions underlying this objection.

It is true that Jeremiah 31:29–30 and Ezekiel 18 appear to deny that individuals will bear the responsibility for the actions of anyone but themselves. We have two options. The first is to pit these verses against those above and concede that Scripture fundamentally contradicts itself. Those who share Jesus' high view of Scripture will be unwilling to take this course.[16] The second option is to affirm that both sets of texts are true, but that they apply in *different circumstances*. Jeremiah and Ezekiel wrote to people in exile who were suffering for the sins of an earlier generation. In this context, the prophets' assurances that the solidarity that bound the present generation to their forefathers' guilt could be broken functioned as an encouragement to repentance (see especially Ezek. 18:30–32). At the same time, the prophets' words implied that the present generation had no-one but themselves to blame. The fact that they continued to suffer God's displeasure was their own fault, and not the fault of their fathers. The specificity of the situation warns us against generalizing in such a way that would overturn the teaching of all those passages that teach

---

from his fierce anger' (v. 26). In 2 Sam. 21, the executions are carried out as a result of David seeking the Lord's face concerning the cause of a famine (v. 1), and afterwards 'God answered prayer on behalf of the land' (v. 14).

16. It is no more acceptable to suggest, as some do, that the theme of corporate responsibility in the early history of Israel reflects the dubious practices of a primitive religious system, gradually displaced by the prophets as the Hebrew mindset evolved out of its ancient prejudices and embraced the liberating notion of individual responsibility.

corporate responsibility. It is notable that Ezekiel himself, from the southern tribe of Judah, symbolically bears the guilt of the northern tribes of Israel in Ezekiel 4:4–5. That is, he symbolically suffers for the guilt of others. Thus there is a notion of shared guilt in the same biblical book as we find an emphasis on individual responsibility.[17]

In some ways, though, these Old Testament cases of shared or transferred punishment are the icing on the cake: they are not essential to our case. Even if Ezekiel were denying that, in the normal course of events, guilt can be transferred between human beings, that would still not preclude the imputation of our guilt to Christ. That is a unique case, for only he is said to be 'in us' and we 'in him'.

Before we conclude this section, it is worth reflecting on some of the consequences of denying that our guilt could be imputed to Christ. The theological and pastoral casualties are severe.

First, if our guilt was not imputed to Christ, the very fact that he died at all is an appalling injustice. The Bible teaches that death is the penalty for sin, and that it came upon humanity because of the sin of Adam.[18] Christ had no sin of his own for which he deserved to die, and therefore, if he bore the guilt of no-one else, he should not have died at all. Since God is sovereign over all of human history, including the death of Christ, we would be forced to hold God responsible for this injustice![19] Plainly this is a dead end. The only way to explain how Christ could have died at all without compromising God's justice is to say that our sin and guilt was imputed to him. Although Christ was sinless *in himself* (he bore no guilt for his own deeds), he nonetheless did bear the guilt of *our* sins. It is ironic that this criticism of penal substitution, which claims to be concerned to uphold God's justice, actually ends up undermining it.

Secondly, if our guilt has not been imputed to Christ, then it remains on us, and we are still guilty. God would therefore either have to condemn all humanity without exception or ignore the sin of some people in order to save them. But both of these options are clearly unbiblical. The first is wrong because the

---

17. Joel Kaminsky discusses these issues in more detail in *Corporate Responsibility*, pp. 139–189. See also Francis Turretin, *Institutes of Elenctic Theology*, trans. G. M. Giger, 3 vols. (Phillipsburg: Presbyterian & Reformed, 1994), vol. 2, 14.XI.xxxi, p. 437.

18. Gen. 1:17; 3:19; Rom. 5:12, 19; 6:23; 1 Cor. 15:22.

19. The biblical evidence that Christ's death was deliberate on the part of both Father and Son is overwhelming (see chapter 9, sect. 2).

Bible clearly teaches that some will be saved. The second is wrong because it violates God's justice and holiness – he cannot overlook sin or sweep it under the carpet, as we shall see in more detail in the following section.

Finally, any objection to the imputation of guilt and punishment applies equally to the imputation of righteousness. If our sin cannot be imputed to Christ, then by the same reasoning his righteousness cannot be imputed to us. We must then abandon the doctrine of justification by faith, the teaching that we are counted righteous in God's sight on the basis of *Christ's* righteousness, imputed to us by faith. Without justification by faith, the only basis upon which we could stand before God on the Last Day would be our own righteousness. This inevitably leads either to despair ('I could *never* be good enough for God') or to pride ('I *am* good enough for God – well done me!'). Both of these outcomes are at variance with the Bible's teaching. The apostle Paul can assure believers that 'there is . . . now no condemnation for those who are in Christ Jesus' (Rom. 8:1), while at the same time insisting that 'boasting . . . is excluded' (Rom. 3:27). Yet this is only possible because Christ's people are united to him, share in his benefits, and are therefore justified by faith in him. Critics of penal substitution should think seriously before relinquishing this cornerstone of Christian doctrine.

## 2. 'Biblical justice is about restoring relationships, not exacting retribution'

### Objection

Some have claimed that the principle of retribution upon which penal substitution depends is immoral. Punishment, they say, should aim to achieve other objectives, such as reforming the offender or deterring others; it should not be used to exact retribution.

Paul Fiddes expresses a form of this view:

> Prominent among the reasons why human societies, or the guardians of their law, inflict penalties should be a concern to reform the offender. If penalty is to help to achieve a harmonious society striving for a common good, then it must lead to penitence in the offender, to an acknowledgement of wrongdoing and to a change of will. If a penal system can achieve this, it has done all it really needs to do. In large social groupings this aspect will always have to be mixed with other (lesser) elements such as deterrence and an upholding of the dignity of law, but within the intimate group of a family penitence will be all that is required when the parents impose discipline. What justice demands is not payment but repentance; it is finally 'satisfied'

not by any penalty in itself but by the change of heart to which penalty is intended to lead.[20]

Stephen Travis has argued at length that retribution is not a biblical idea. He summarizes the central thesis of his book *Christ and the Judgment of God* as follows: 'I argue that the judgment of God is to be seen not primarily in terms of retribution, whereby people are "paid back" according to their deeds, but in terms of relationship or non-relationship to Christ.'[21]

Tom Smail also takes the view that 'God's justice is concerned less with punishing wrong relationships than with restoring right ones'.[22] Similarly, Colin Gunton advocates a 'concept of the justice of God which . . . is . . . transformational rather than punitive or distributive'.[23]

Finally, Timothy Gorringe approaches the issue from another angle, criticizing penal substitution for legitimizing and encouraging what he regards as undesirable retributive elements in human legal systems.[24]

### Response

This objection appears, at first sight, to carry some weight. Some strands of Western society have grown increasingly hostile to the principle of retribution, and alternative conceptions of justice are in the ascendancy. This is reflected in modern views of the legal system, where the concerns of reforming the criminal, protecting society and deterring offenders dominate the discussion, and talk of criminals 'getting what they deserve' is viewed with distaste. To many people, retribution seems inherently vindictive, a kind of thinly disguised vengeance, a way of 'rationalizing the primitive urge to hit back'.[25]

---

20. Paul S. Fiddes, *Past Event and Present Salvation: The Christian Idea of Atonement* (London: Darton, Longman & Todd, 1989), p. 104.

21. Stephen H. Travis, *Christ and the Judgment of God: Divine Retribution in the New Testament* (Basingstoke: Marshall, Morgan & Scott, 1986), preface. He expresses a similar view in 'Christ as Bearer of Divine Judgement in Paul's Thought about the Atonement', in John Goldingay (ed.), *Atonement Today* (London: SPCK, 1995), pp. 21–38.

22. Smail, *Once and for All*, p. 95.

23. Colin E. Gunton, *The Actuality of Atonement: A Study of Metaphor, Rationality and the Christian Tradition* (Edinburgh: T. & T. Clark, 1988), p. 188.

24. Timothy Gorringe, *God's Just Vengeance* (Cambridge: Cambridge University Press, 1996); see e.g. pp. 102–103.

25. Derek Kidner, who himself upholds retribution, thus characterizes the view of his opponents in 'Retribution and Punishment in the Old Testament, in the Light

The suspicion that retribution is somehow fundamentally immoral runs deep in our culture. We hope to demonstrate, however, that it is an essential component in the biblical conception of justice. This is not to say that the Bible never sees punishment as corrective or restorative. Of course it does. Our point is merely that the Bible *also* upholds the necessity of the principle of retribution.

We shall proceed as follows. First, we shall outline three possible 'penal systems', that is, three different ways of construing the proper relationship between crime and punishment.[26] Secondly, we shall derive from Scripture three criteria that any penal system must satisfy in order to be judged biblical, noting that these biblical requirements coincide with our intuitive sense of what is just. Finally, we shall evaluate the three penal systems against the three biblical criteria. The retributive model is the only candidate that passes the test.

The three fundamental penal theories are distinguished by their differing views on why punishment is necessary or desirable.[27]

---

of the New Testament', *Scottish Bulletin of Evangelical Theology* 1 (1983), pp. 3–9 (p. 7).

26. Much of the analysis in this section is taken from the outstanding essay by C. S. Lewis 'The Humanitarian Theory of Punishment', in *God in the Dock* (Grand Rapids: Eerdmans, 1970), pp. 287–294 (also pub. in *Churchmen Speak* [Abingdon: Marcham Manor, 1966], pp. 39–44; and in *Churchman* 73 [1959], pp. 55–60). See also Austin Fagothey, S. J., *Right and Reason: Ethics in Theory and Practice*, 2nd edn (Rockford: Tan, 1959), pp. 418–423; Kidner, 'Retribution and Punishment'; James Rachels, 'Punishment and Desert', in H. LaFollette (ed.), *Ethics in Practice*, 2nd edn (Malden, MA: Blackwell, 2002), pp. 466–474; and Stott, *Cross of Christ*, pp. 101–102.

27. Sometimes additional categories are suggested, but they can be classified as subtypes of these three. E.g. some might suggest that punishment is necessary to protect the public or to incapacitate the criminal, perhaps by imprisonment or by imposing a regime of education or psychological treatment, so that he cannot continue to cause harm. But this is an aspect of correction, where the aim is to change the behaviour of the criminal (if only by limiting his access to victims) for the benefit of others.

Some suggest that punishment is needed only to make restitution or compensation; i.e. to repay what has been illegally taken or to make good damage that has been done. But if restitution is limited merely to restoring the situation as it was before the offence, then it is not actually a punishment at all, for the criminal is no worse off than if he had never offended in the first place (Fagothey, *Right and Reason*, p. 419). Robbing a bank and then returning the money a few weeks later becomes indistinguishable from a legitimate bank loan! If restitution seeks to go

According to the *retributive* theory, the purpose of punishment is to give a criminal what he or she deserves. People must not be allowed to do morally wrong things with impunity, and it is right therefore that offenders suffer a certain penalty.

Retribution is not equivalent to revenge. Retribution is carried out only by a properly constituted authority, whereas revenge is exacted by anyone who has both the inclination and the opportunity. Revenge is wont to be disproportionate, and thus only adds to the injustice and evil of a situation; retribution will always be fair. Revenge derives a macabre delight in the pain of an enemy, whereas retribution is motivated by the solemn demands of justice – thus God can tell us in Ezekiel 18:23 that he takes no pleasure in the death of the wicked, while assuring us in the very next verse that he will serve the death penalty as justice requires.[28] Human revenge may be considered selfish, for it seeks only its own satisfaction. Divine retribution, even if motivated by God's desire to satisfy his own sense of justice, cannot be 'selfish' in any negative sense, because it is right for God to put himself and his will at the centre of the universe in a way that would be wrong for anyone else to do.[29] Finally, those

---

beyond this (e.g. by imposing a fine considerably greater than the sum of money stolen), then it ceases to be restitution: it has actually become a punishment, and must be justified on the basis of one of the other three penal theories.

Finally, others argue that punishment should be imposed for the sake of reprobation – i.e. to express the horror of the community at a particular crime. Presumably, however, they would specify that the person punished must be guilty. This entails an expression of retributive justice, for as we shall see below only the principle of retribution establishes that penalties cannot be imposed on innocent people.

28. 'Revenge aims at the emotional pleasure one gets from hurting an enemy, retributive punishment at securing justice simply' (Fagothey, *Right and Reason*, p. 421).

29. For a human being to say 'I am the most important being in the universe' would be deluded arrogance; for God to say the same would be a simple statement of fact. It is true of course that each member of the Trinity acts selflessly towards the others. E.g. 'the Father . . . has entrusted all judgment to the Son, that all may honour the Son just as they honour the Father', while Jesus explained that 'my judgment is just, for I seek not to please myself but him who sent me' (John 5:22–23, 30). In his oneness God acts rightly for his own glory; in his threeness each person seeks to glorify the others. The underlying trinitarian theology is explained in more detail in chapter 3 and chapter 11, sect. 1.

who would refuse this distinction between retribution and revenge must reckon with Romans 12:19, where Paul discourages his readers from taking revenge into their own hands precisely because God can be trusted to bring just retribution.

According to the *deterrent* theory (sometimes called the *preventative* theory), the purpose of punishment is to discourage other people from offending. In effect, it seeks to persuade people not to commit crimes by showing what will happen to them if they do.

Finally, according to the *corrective* theory (sometimes called the *rehabilitative*, or *reformatory* theory), the purpose of punishment is to change the behaviour of the criminal, both for the benefit of the criminal himself and the rest of society. The aim is to reduce the likelihood that the criminal will repeat the offence in the future, for example by means of education or psychological treatment, and thereby to restore the relationship between the offender and the rest of society.

It is evident from these brief descriptions that those who criticize penal substitution on the grounds that biblical justice is concerned with restoring relationships, not exacting retribution, are in effect arguing that the corrective theory, and not the retributive theory, expresses the biblical view. They are correct in what they affirm but wrong in what they deny. Correction is a valid biblical reason for punishing wrongdoing. So also is deterrence, for that matter.[30] However, as we turn to the Scriptures, we shall find it impossible to exclude retribution from the picture.

What, then, are the biblical criteria against which we may assess the three penal systems outlined above?

First, the Bible teaches emphatically that *guilty* people, and *only* guilty people, should be punished. This is apparent from frequent and unambiguous statements to the effect that punishments must be determined by what offenders *deserve* (e.g. Num. 35:31; Ps. 94:2; Ezek. 16:59; Luke 23:41; Rom. 2:6).[31] There

---

30. It is unnecessary for our present purposes to justify this in more detail, since the critics of penal substitution do not deny it. In passing, we note that the principle of deterrence is found in Deut. 13:11; 17:13; 19:20; 21:21; and the principle of correction is affirmed in the numerous biblical texts where 'discipline' is presented in a positive light (Deut. 4:26; 11:2; Heb. 12:4–11; Rev. 3:19; throughout the book of Proverbs).

31. See also Lev. 26:21; Deut. 19:6; 22:26; 25:2; Judg. 20:10; 1 Sam. 26:16; Ps. 28:4; Isa. 66:6; Jer. 14:16; 17:10; 21:14; 51:6; Lam. 3:64; Zech. 1:6; Matt. 12:35–37; 13:41–42, 49–50; 25:14–46; John 5:29; Acts 25:11; Rom. 1:32; 2:5–11; 3:8; 13:1–4; 2 Cor. 5:10;

is thus an inextricable link in the Bible's teaching between wrongdoing and punishment:

> Acquitting the guilty and condemning the innocent –
>> the LORD detests them both.
> (Prov. 17:15)

Secondly, and related to this, the Bible teaches that punishment must be *proportional* to the crime. Major crimes demand firmer punishment than trivial misdemeanours. This teaching is implied by all the passages mentioned above that speak of punishments being deserved. It is also foundational to the many distinctions between the different punishments prescribed in the Old Testament law, which clearly imply that more serious offences warrant more severe punishments.[32] The same point is explicit in the teaching of Jesus (e.g. Luke 12:47–48).

Thirdly, the Bible teaches that punishments must be *equitable*, in the sense that equivalent punishments must be imposed on different people who have committed the same crime. This principle is fundamental in Scripture: 'God shows no partiality' (Rom. 2:11; cf. Deut. 10:17; 2 Chr. 19:7; Matt. 22:16; Acts 10:34–35; Gal. 2:6; Eph. 6:9; Col. 3:25; 1 Pet. 1:17).

Of course, the Bible sometimes makes quite subtle distinctions between apparently similar offences. For example, under the Old Testament law, someone would not be held responsible if he owned a normally docile bull that attacked and killed another person, but someone who owned a bull that was known to be dangerous and temperamental, and who failed to keep it securely penned, would be responsible for any injury caused (Exod. 21:28–29; cf. Exod. 21:35–36). While the offences are superficially similar (in both cases an animal

---

10:29; 11:15; Col. 3:25; Heb. 10:26–31; 1 Pet. 1:17; 2:14; 2 Pet. 3:3–7; Rev. 16:6. An analogous connection between deeds and consequences is also implied by texts that speak of rewards (e.g. Judg. 9:16; Prov. 3:27; Luke 10:7; 1 Cor. 16:18; 1 Tim. 5:18).

32. See e.g. Exod. 21–23. There are differences of opinion among Christians about precisely how the Old Testament law applies to the New Testament church. All sides agree it is a reflection of God's holy character (e.g. Rom. 7:12–16), and therefore is underpinned by certain timeless moral principles. The differences concern the extent to which the particular embodiments of these principles in the Old Testament remain binding today. The point of consensus is sufficient for the argument being made here.

caused an injury), in terms of culpability they are quite different. One is purely accidental; the other is criminally negligent. These are *relevant* differences that alter the nature and seriousness of the offence itself. The fact that a punishment is prescribed in one case and not the other does not undermine the principle of equity. But it would make no difference whether the owner were male or female, or from Judea or Samaria. These are *irrelevant* differences that do not alter the nature of the crime, and therefore equity demands that the severity of the punishment should not differ.

These three biblical elements of a penal system – guilt, proportionality and equity – accord with our instincts about what is just and right. We do not wish to overstate this point, for our instincts are not always reliable, and Scripture remains our sole and final authority. Nevertheless, the objection to penal substitution here under consideration appeals strongly to intuition, and a comprehensive reply must therefore do the same.

Our instincts tell us that the principle of *guilt* is essential. We would not tolerate a penal system that deliberately punished people who had no connection with the crime. As Fagothey puts it, 'It is immoral to punish unless the accused is guilty, no matter how much good the infliction of pain may do him or society.'[33] The principle of *proportionality* also strikes a chord with our intuitive understanding of justice. It would be intolerable to have a system of justice that administered the same penalties for dropping litter as for murder, or that prescribed death by hanging for minor speeding offences. Finally, we are quick to defend the principle of *equity*. We would think it an appalling travesty of justice if someone were to receive a harsher punishment because of the colour of her skin, or if murderers in London were hanged while perpetrators of the same crime in Birmingham were fined a few pounds. Certainly, we think it desirable that *relevant differences* between crimes result in different punishments. It is obvious that someone taken by surprise when their ordinarily placid poodle turns on the postman is less blameworthy than the owner of a Rottweiler who fails to restrain it despite a long history of hospitalized Post Office employees. We believe instinctively that the only differences that should result in different punishments are those that actually change the nature of the crime.

Having established the three criteria necessary to the biblical conception of justice (guilt, proportionality and equity), and having recognized that these components correspond with our natural intuitions about right and wrong, let us now use those criteria to assess the three penal theories outlined earlier. We begin with retribution.

---

33. Fagothey, *Right and Reason*, p. 422.

The principle of retribution guarantees that only *guilty* people are punished. Retribution is based on the premise that the appropriate authority should impose a punishment if, and only if, an offence has actually been committed. Retribution therefore ensures that no-one is punished if he or she does not *deserve* it.

Similarly, the principle of retribution also ensures a given punishment is *proportional* to its crime. It recognizes that serious crimes deserve severe punishments, whereas more trivial offences warrant milder sanctions.

Finally, the principle of retribution also safeguards the principle of *equity*, for the only factors allowed to affect the severity of a punishment are those that affect the nature of the crime. Irrelevant differences such as the race, gender or social class of the offender should have no impact on sentencing.

It is clear, therefore, that the principle of retribution secures those elements of a system of punishment both required by Scripture and in accord with our natural sense of right and wrong. Retribution may be combined with the elements of deterrence or correction, but by itself safeguards these biblical principles. Let us now consider what would happen if the principle of retribution were absent from a legal system, and penalties were guided by the principles of deterrence and/or correction alone.

A legal system based solely on deterrence would not require the *guilty* person to be punished for committing a crime. All that is necessary is that the public *thinks* the guilty person has been punished, for that would be equally effective at deterring others from committing the same offence. Moreover, it would be perfectly logical for the judiciary to punish people *whom they knew to be innocent* so long as society at large was under the impression that they were guilty. The deterrent would be just as effective. Indeed, the punishment of an innocent person would always be preferable to there being no punishment at all; for example, if the police failed to catch the perpetrator.

Moreover, a judiciary operating on the principle of deterrence might decide to punish the family members of a criminal, rather than (or as well as) the criminal himself. The knowledge that your eight-year-old daughter would be executed if you committed murder may well be a *better deterrent* than the prospect of your own execution. The chilling truth is that nothing in the principle of deterrence itself could be used to object to such a scheme.

Deterrence does little better at safeguarding the principle of proportionality. If all that really mattered were deterring people from offending, there would be no reason not to administer severe penalties for even the most trivial offences, if it was believed this increased the deterrent effect. In fact, there would be nothing in principle to prevent every crime receiving the death penalty, administered in the most painful manner possible, and (as we saw above) applied to close family members of criminals as well as the criminals themselves. So long as crime figures fall, anything goes.[34]

Finally, deterrence fails to secure the principle of equity. Reasoning from the theory of deterrence alone, the severity of the sentence imposed would have to depend on the perceived likelihood that those who heard of it would be tempted to commit the same crime. In a region where litter-dropping was widespread, offenders would be punished very severely, whereas in regions where there was an extremely low murder rate the judiciary might reasonably conclude that the occasional murder need not be punished at all, on the grounds that the rest of society do not appear to need any deterrent.

It must be emphasized that there is nothing wrong with the principle of deterrence as such. It is a perfectly biblical idea. It is abundantly clear, however, that it cannot *on its own* secure a biblical system of justice. Let us now ask whether the principle of correction fares any better.

It may seem at first sight that a correction-based penal system, even without the principle of retribution, would punish only the guilty. Yet this is not so. Suppose it became possible to identify in advance those people likely to commit a crime, perhaps by analysing their family history, social background or genetic make-up. It would not be necessary, according to the principle of correction, to wait until a crime had actually been committed. A criminal *tendency* (some evidence of a higher than average probability of future illegal activity) would suffice to justify mandatory 'correction' (punishment). It matters little how the criminal tendency reveals itself. It *might* be manifested in an actual criminal act, but it could, at least in principle, be demonstrated in any number of ways. Indeed, it would be preferable if potential criminals could be identified before any wrong were committed, a scenario explored in the film *Minority Report*. In short, a legal system operating on the principle of correction alone would seek to 'correct' anyone who, in the opinion of the social or biological 'experts', was unusually likely to commit crimes in the future, regardless of whether or not they had actually done anything wrong.

---

34. In practice, other factors will influence the optimum punishment that should be administered. E.g. W. H. Moberly has argued that the likelihood of conviction is key to the efficacy of a deterrent, and that even a very severe punishment may not be effective if conviction rates are low (*The Ethics of Punishment* [London: Faber & Faber, 1968], p. 52). A sophisticated system of deterrence would need to take account of such factors. But this is irrelevant to the point in question; we are simply pointing out that the one factor that plays no part in establishing the severity of the punishment is the seriousness of the crime.

Likewise, the principle of correction fails to safeguard the principle of proportionality. A person would have to remain in custody until the necessary educational or psychological treatment had taken effect. The seriousness of the crime itself would be immaterial. A careless driver with a bad memory who kept 'forgetting' about speed limits would, according to the principle of correction, be forcibly detained and 'treated' until his memory had improved, regardless of how long it took.

The principle of correction also fails to safeguard the principle of equity. The length of a prison sentence would depend entirely on how the criminal responded to the 'treatment'. If the punishment for a certain crime were largely educational in character, intelligent people would receive far shorter sentences than people who needed more time to understand the 'teaching', and someone who was simply unable to grasp it would never be released at all.[35]

A final criticism of correction may be made on slightly different grounds. As soon as we acknowledge that there is such a thing as final judgment, we concede at least one case where judgment cannot be corrective. There is no 'after', no second chance, no possibility of rehabilitation. Jesus himself speaks of hell as an '*eternal* fire' (Matt. 18:8; italics added).[36] Punishment that seeks to correct is too late.

It is therefore plain that a penal system based on correction alone fails to safeguard the fundamental elements of guilt, proportionality and equity required for a just, biblical penal system. Like deterrence, correction plays an important part in biblical thinking. But, isolated from the principle of retribution, it provides no protection against the most appalling injustices.

C. S. Lewis depicts the horrific consequences of a penal system detached from the principle of retribution in his famous essay 'The Humanitarian

---

35. Compare the disparity in the American legal system noted by James Rachels, which, he claims, 'has largely been shaped by the rehabilitationist ideal', and where 'an affluent white offender is likely to serve less time in prison that a black kid from the ghetto, even if they have committed the same crime' (Rachels, 'Punishment and Desert', p. 478).

36. See also Matt. 25:41, 46; Mark 9:43, 48; Heb. 6:2; Jude 1:7; Rev. 14:11; 19:3; 20:10. We believe that this language points to eternal punishment rather than annihilation, but this is not necessary to the argument. For a robust defence of hell as eternal punishment see Christopher W. Morgan and Robert A. Peterson (eds.), *Hell Under Fire* (Grand Rapids: Zondervan, 2004).

Theory of Punishment', republished most recently in *God in the Dock*.[37] 'According to the Humanitarian theory', to use Lewis's terminology, 'the only legitimate motives for punishing are the desire to deter others by example or to mend the criminal'.[38] Consequently, 'The Humanitarian theory removes from punishment the concept of desert.'[39] Such a system, Lewis argues, would put an end to justice, human dignity and human rights:

> We demand of a deterrent not whether it is just but whether it will deter. We demand of a cure not whether it is just but whether it succeeds. Thus when we cease to consider what the criminal deserves and consider only what will cure him or deter others, we have tacitly removed him from the sphere of justice altogether; instead of a person, a subject of rights, we now have a mere object, a patient, a 'case'.[40]

Someone might object that some of the worst-case scenarios envisaged above are rather fanciful. Surely no-one would seriously argue in favour of a legal system that acted in such absurd ways? Sadly, this charitable assumption is not borne out as we reflect on the catalogue of political tyranny in recent world history. But even if the scenarios are fanciful, by what principle do we instinctively judge them to be immoral? Surely it is the retributive principle, however deeply buried within our psyche, that tells us this. A penal system constructed solely on the basis of correction, deterrence or both could not lead us there. Indeed, it could avoid sanctioning these very atrocities only by failing to follow through its own principles to their logical conclusions. Perhaps the vestiges of a previous commitment to retribution would still exert a restraining influence. What is clear is that to deny the principle of retribution with absolute consistency would lead us to a grotesque world of irredeemable injustice.[41]

---

37. C. S. Lewis, 'The Humanitarian Theory of Punishment', in *God in the Dock* (Grand Rapids: Eerdmans, 1970) , pp. 287–294. Lewis's essay was also published previously in *Churchmen Speak* (Abingdon: Marcham Manor, 1966), pp. 39–44. Page references below refer to the version in *God in the Dock*.

38. Lewis, 'Humanitarian Theory of Punishment', p. 287.

39. Ibid., p. 288.

40. Ibid.

41. Incredibly, examples of such amoral views are not unknown among professional ethicists. Derek Kidner cites this example: 'With extraordinary candour, the ethicist Sir David Ross, in drawing back from the primacy of retribution in punishment, quotes Caiaphas with reluctant approval. His exact words are as follows:

These considerations also undermine Stephen Travis's claim that retribution is not a biblical idea. Travis defines retribution very narrowly, excluding any case in which the punitive consequences might be said to follow as a 'natural' consequence of the sin. This allows him to ignore a great deal of the biblical material. However, he is wrong to think that God cannot be actively involved in the 'natural' processes of his world, and that he cannot use these processes to punish sin. We address this objection, together with others that misconstrue the relationship between God's wrath and the natural order, in chapter 11, section 3.

In closing, it is necessary briefly to consider three biblical texts that might seem to undermine the retributive theory of punishment. The first is 1 Peter 3:9, where the apostle writes, 'Do not repay evil with evil or insult with insult, but with blessing.' Examination of the context reveals that this verse cannot forbid retribution per se, for in 1 Peter 2:14 it is assumed the state will punish wrongdoing. Rather the point is that individuals ought not to take revenge into their own hands. We have discussed the differences between revenge and retribution above.

Paul Fiddes claims that in Matthew 5:38–39 'Jesus . . . set aside the Old Testament law of retribution which called for a just equivalence in punishment'.[42] In fact, Jesus did no such thing. He was referring to the parts of the Old Testament law that prescribe the penalties that could be demanded from criminals by their victims (e.g. Exod. 21:18 – 22:15). The 'eye for an eye' principle was intended to prevent the uncontrolled escalation of vengeance while allowing for an appropriate retributive punishment to be imposed. It expressed the *maximum* penalty, not a mandatory one, and the law allowed the victim to demand less or to substitute an equivalent compensatory payment (e.g. Exod. 21:22, 29–30).[43] Jesus simply restated this teaching, exhorting people to show mercy in their personal relationships, and rebuking a society that had twisted the law by reinterpreting the legal maximum as the legal norm.

However, the same principle did not apply to offences committed against God either in the law of Moses or in the teaching of Jesus in the Sermon on

---

"The interests of society may sometimes be so deeply involved as to make it right . . . to punish an innocent man 'that the whole nation perish not'"' (Kidner, 'Retribution and Punishment', p. 8, citing W. D. Ross, *The Right and the Good* [Oxford University Press: Oxford, 1930], p. 64).

42. Fiddes, *Past Event and Present Salvation*, p. 103.

43. See Gordon J. Wenham, *The Book of Leviticus*, New International Commentary on the Old Testament (Grand Rapids: Eerdmans, 1979), p. 285.

the Mount. That is altogether a different case.[44] As Davies and Allison point out in their commentary on Matthew, 'What Jesus rejects is vengeance executed on a personal level. He still assumes that God, the only wise and capable judge, will, in the end, inflict fitting punishment on sinners (cf. Rom 12.14–21).'[45] To escape this judgment, both the Old and New Testaments point to the need for a substitute, one to bear our sins. Jesus introduced no change in the judicial requirements. He rather offered himself as a sacrifice to bring about the solution to them.

Finally, a superficial reading of John 8:1–11 might suggest that Jesus set aside the principle of retribution by refusing to condemn the woman caught in adultery. However, this reads into the text more than is there. Jesus' intention is merely to expose the Pharisees' malicious motives (John 8:6; cf. Exod. 23:1; Deut. 19:16–19).[46] Moreover, it would have been an abuse of the legal process for Jesus to pronounce judgment against the woman, since the man involved in the offence was absent (Exod. 23:1; Deut. 22:22–24). Finally, the fact that he actually pardoned the woman (which he, as the divine Son, is uniquely privileged to do; cf. Mark 2:7) does not imply that the penalty was dispensed with altogether. The Bible teaches that he suffered it himself at Calvary.

In summary, we have seen that, despite the aversion to the retributive principle that exists in many modern cultures, it is only this that can secure the priorities of guilt, proportionality and equity the Bible demands of any penal system. Indeed, it might be said that retribution is simply what is meant by the word 'justice' in the Bible. Neither correction nor deterrence, important as they are in biblical thinking, can do the job alone.

The objection that penal substitution must be wrong on the grounds that it implies a retributive theory of punishment is therefore turned on its head. If retribution is fundamental to the Bible's idea of justice, then a view of the atonement that takes retribution seriously is positively to be preferred.

---

44. This distinction explains why, in Num. 35:33, human courts in Israel were expressly forbidden from punishing one person for the sin of another. By contrast, it is possible and just in certain circumstances for God to do so, as we explain in chapter 10, sect. 1, where we outline the doctrine of union with Christ (see also chapter 3).

45. W. C. Davies and D. C. Allison, *A Critical and Exegetical Commentary on the Gospel According to Saint Matthew*, International Critical Commentary, vol. 1 (Edinburgh: T. & T. Clark, 1988), p. 540.

46. See D. A. Carson, *The Gospel According to John*, Pillar New Testament Commentary (Leicester: Apollos; Grand Rapids: Eerdmans, 1991), pp. 334–337.

## *Postscript*

The question might arise how believers seen by God as forensically innocent by virtue of Christ's penal substitutionary death for them should nonetheless suffer in various ways. If 'the wages of sin is death' (Rom. 6:23), and Christ has borne for believers the whole of this penalty, why do we still die? As early as the fourth century, Augustine perceived the paradox that 'absolution from sin does not entail deliverance from death, sin's punishment'.[47] And what are we to do with those Bible passages that speak of God disciplining his *children* when they sin (e.g. Heb. 12:5–11)? Does this mean that there is a punishment still outstanding, which we must pay ourselves? If so, this would seem to present serious problems for penal substitution.

The answer in both cases is that the Bible does not conceive of painful experiences that come upon *Christians* as punishment of a retributive or judicial kind. Quite the opposite. As the old hymn puts it, death, though not a good thing in itself, has become for Christians 'the gate of life immortal'.[48] Its character is transformed. Though the experience may still be intensely painful, it serves a good end.[49] Indeed, it may even be conceived as a blessing from God. The apostle Paul confessed that 'to die is gain', since it would be 'to depart and be with Christ, which is better by far' (Phil. 1:21, 23), and the prophet Isaiah saw that in death 'the righteous are taken away to be spared from evil' (Isa. 57:1).

The case of discipline is similar. Although the experience, from our perspective, may be indistinguishable from retribution, and although the biblical vocabulary is the same (both are termed 'punishment'), from the standpoint of God's *intention* they are entirely different. God's intention in retribution is to punish the guilty for the sake of his justice. It is, and will be on the Last Day, a manifestation of his wrath against those who stand rightly condemned (Rom. 1:18; 2:5). But 'there is . . . no condemnation for those who are in Christ Jesus' (Rom. 8:1). Discipline is a sign not of God's wrath but of his fatherly affection, for 'the Lord disciplines those he loves, and he punishes everyone he accepts as a son' (Heb. 12:6). In fact, discipline is precisely the *opposite* of wrath in this sense: in Romans 1:18–32 God responds in anger to people's sin by withdrawing his restraining hand and leaving them to it. By contrast, when he sees his children sinning, he may mercifully apply his restraining hand to keep them from it.

---

47. Augustine, *City of God*, bk. 13, ch. 4, p. 513.

48. 'Jesus lives! Thy terrors now', Christian F. Gellert, trans. Frances E. Cox.

49. Augustine pursues this line of argument in some detail in *City of God*, bk. 13, pp. 510–546.

We have claimed above that correction without retribution would be fundamentally unjust. That is indeed so. However, we do find the two properly separated in the specific case of God's dealing with believers.[50] Having applied the benefits of Christ's penal substitutionary death to them, thereby satisfying the requirements of his retributive justice, there is *then* no retributive character to any subsequent suffering they experience. It may be corrective, or intended for their good in some other way. Thus the apostle Paul can reflect on the prospect of violent persecution just a few verses after the reassurance that 'in *all things* God works for the good of those who love him' (Rom. 8:28; italics added; cf. v. 35).

## 3. 'Penal substitution implicitly denies that God forgives sin'

### Objection

Eleonore Stump summarizes this objection as follows: 'contrary to what it intends, [penal substitution] does not, in fact, present God as forgiving human sin. To forgive a debtor is to fail to exact all that is in justice due. But, according to [penal substitution], God does exact every bit of the debt owed him by humans; he allows none of it to go unpaid.'[51]

Stump is aware of the obvious reply to her objection; namely, that according to the doctrine of penal substitution God himself pays the debt we owe in the person of his Son, which is perfectly compatible with forgiveness. However, she finds this reply inadequate:

> The proponent of [penal substitution] might claim that God's forgiveness consists precisely in his not requiring that *we* pay the debt for sin but rather he himself paying it for us in the person of Christ. But it is hard to see what constitutes forgiveness on this claim. Suppose that Daniel owes Susan $1000 and cannot pay it, but Susan's daughter Maggie, who is Daniel's good friend, does pay Susan the whole $1000 on Daniel's behalf. Is there any sense in which Susan can be said to forgive the debt?

---

50. It seems that those who want to argue that all punishment is only corrective are in effect applying universally a paradigm appropriate only to God's covenant people, whose punishment has already been dealt with. The methodological error is apparent.

51. Eleonore Stump, 'Atonement According to Aquinas', in Thomas V. Morris (ed.), *Philosophy and the Christian Faith* (Notre Dame: University of Notre Dame Press, 1988), pp. 61–91 (p. 62).

> On the contrary, Susan has been repaid in full and has foregone none of what was owed her.[52]

She is also aware that the doctrine of the Trinity lends extra force to the case for penal substitution, for 'Christ is one in being with God the Father, so that the one paying the debt is the same as the one to whom the debt is paid.'[53] Nonetheless, she apparently remains unpersuaded that this answers her objection.

In summary, this objection claims that the emphasis in penal substitution on Christ's paying the debt we owe means that God does not actually *forgive* sinners, because in the end there is nothing to forgive.

### Response

It is hard to see why Eleonore Stump finds this objection persuasive, for she has articulated the answer herself.[54] The reason why penal substitution does not deny that God forgives sin is precisely because it is *God himself*, in the person of his Son, who pays the debt we owe.

Stump's human analogies simply cause confusion, for there is a fundamental difference between human beings and the Triune God. A human being to whom a debt is owed cannot wipe it out by 'repaying' it himself – Stump is correct to reject this as nonsensical. If Nicole lends Ben £1,000 she happens to have in her purse, and then proceeds to withdraw the same sum from her bank account and replenishes the cash in her purse, she has not *repaid* Ben's debt at all; she has simply moved it around, and he still owes her the money. Alternatively, if Rebecca pays Nicole £1,000 on Ben's behalf, there is nothing for Nicole to forgive, but Ben is still in debt – this time to Rebecca – and he must therefore pay her instead. The only way Nicole could meaningfully offer Ben forgiveness is by allowing his debt to remain unpaid. Between human beings, receiving repayment and offering forgiveness are mutually exclusive.

However, God is not like human beings.[55] As Trinity, he has both personal

---

52. Ibid., p. 62; italics original.

53. Ibid.

54. Indeed, she almost appears to concede that this answer successfully refutes the objection. For after recognizing that the doctrine of the Trinity adds extra weight to her opponents' case, she abruptly changes track to another objection altogether, without explaining why she finds this answer inadequate.

55. God the Son did become a man at the incarnation, but that is not the point at issue, for he took on a human nature without divesting himself of the trinitarian relations of his divinity, which no other human being shares.

distinction and essential oneness (see chapter 3 and chapter 11, sect. 1). He did what no human creditor could do, even in principle: he received payment by giving himself in the person of his Son to take our human nature and suffer the punishment we deserve. In this way he himself repaid the debt of all who are in Christ, paving the way for us to receive his forgiveness. Stump's criticism arises from a mistaken application of human analogies to the Triune God.

It is possible that someone may arrive at the conclusion that God offers forgiveness without requiring repayment by considering in isolation passages such as the parable of the prodigal son (Luke 15:11–32) or the woman who had her 'debt *cancelled*' by Jesus at the house of Simon the Pharisee (Luke 7:36–50). However, just because these particular passages do not spell out what needs to happen to make this forgiveness possible, we cannot conclude that atonement is superfluous. We must read them in the context of a gospel that reaches its climax as the Son of Man dies and rises again. No single episode tells the complete story, and we run into huge problems if we start inferring that something is unnecessary just because it is missing from any one particular text.[56]

This objection is further undermined by the Old Testament law, where forgiveness and atonement go hand in hand (Lev. 4:20, 26, 31, 35; 5:10, 13, 16, 18; 6:7; 19:22; Num. 15:25, 28). Moreover, the author of Psalm 130 praises the Lord that 'with you there is forgiveness' (v. 4) and then goes on to reassure his fellow Israelites that 'He himself will *redeem* Israel from all their sins' (v. 8; italics added). Pardon is on offer because a price will be paid. Surely this prophecy anticipates the coming of the Messiah, who brought, as the apostle Paul put it, 'redemption through his blood, the forgiveness of sins' (Eph. 1:7). For Stump, the language of payment is irreconcilable with forgiveness. We reply that the biblical authors seem to disagree.

## 4. 'Penal substitution does not work, for the penalty Christ suffered was not equivalent to that due to us'

### Objection
Some object to penal substitution on the grounds that the punishment suffered by Christ was simply not equivalent to that due to us. How could the death of

---

56. E.g. Matt. 11:25–27 describes the relationship between God the Father and God the Son. There is no mention of the Holy Spirit, but we would not thereby deduce his non-existence!

*one* man satisfy the penalty owed by *many* people? How could the suffering of Jesus for a few hours constitute an equivalent punishment to an eternity in hell?

Eleonore Stump voices a form of this objection:

> [Penal substitution] claims that in his suffering and death on the cross Christ paid the full penalty for all human sin so that humans would not have to pay it. And yet it also claims that the penalty for sin is everlasting damnation; but no matter what sort of agony Christ experienced in his crucifixion, it certainly was not (and was not equivalent to) everlasting punishment, if for no other reason than that Christ's suffering came to an end.[57]

### Response

The question of how one man's act can come to affect many people is addressed by the apostle Paul in Romans 5:12–21. Just as Adam, as head of humanity, brought condemnation to all who were in him, so also Christ, as head of a new humanity, brought justification that leads to life to all who were in him.

However, as we argue in chapter 10, section 2, the severity of punishment must be in proportion to the seriousness of the crime. Christ must not only suffer for many people; he must suffer an infinite punishment, for this is what our sins deserve. Jesus himself spoke of hell as a place of *everlasting* torment, 'where "their worm does not die, and the fire is not quenched"' (Mark 9:48; cf. Matt. 8:12; 13:42, 50; 22:13; 24:51; 25:30). Such a severe punishment is not arbitrary or capricious, for, as Jonathan Edwards explains, the heinousness of a crime is determined not only by the nature of the action, but also by the dignity and worth of the person offended.[58] Sin is infinitely heinous because it is directed against an infinitely holy and perfect God. This is what brought Isaiah to his knees when he saw a vision of the Lord in the heavenly temple – it was when he was confronted with the blistering holiness of 'the King, the LORD Almighty' (Isa. 6:5) that he recognized his own wretched sinfulness. The same dynamic is reflected in the intense contrition and acute remorse displayed by many other biblical characters when they realize they have sinned against God (e.g. 2 Kgs 22:11, 19; Job 42:1–6; Ps. 51; Jon. 3:6–9).

Thus the problem remains: How could Christ's suffering, which lasted only a few hours, pay an infinite price? How could an infinite punishment, infinite

---

57. Stump, 'Atonement According to Aquinas', p. 63.

58. Edwards, *Original Sin*, pp. 130–133.

pain, be borne in a finite time? The answer is that just as the heinousness of a sin is determined in part by the dignity of the person sinned against, so also the severity of a punishment is determined in part by the dignity of the one punished. Christ is the one in whom 'all the fulness of the Deity lives in bodily form' (Col. 2:9). His incarnation was an act of infinite condescension, and his blood is of infinite worth.[59] Although he was 'in very nature God', he 'made himself nothing, taking the very nature of a servant, being made in human likeness', and 'he humbled himself and became obedient to death – even death on a cross!' (Phil. 2:6–8). As Turretin puts it, 'Christ alone ought to be estimated at a higher value than all men together. The dignity of an infinite person swallows up ... all the infinities of punishment due to us.'[60] Thus Christ's suffering, though it lasted only a finite time, was infinite in value because he is infinitely worthy.

The great value of Christ's sacrificial death is implicit in 1 Peter 1:18–19, where 'the precious blood of Christ, a lamb without blemish or defect' is contrasted with 'perishable things such as silver or gold'. The eternal effects of an act of finite duration are attested in Hebrews 10:14, which proclaims that 'by one sacrifice he has made perfect *for ever* those who are being made holy' (italics added). The perpetuity of Christ's priesthood and the eternal efficacy of his work are major themes in Hebrews (e.g. 7:23–28; 9:11–15).

In summary, it is true that the punishment Christ suffered at Calvary was not identical to that due to us. Yet there can be no question of its being insufficient.

---

59. The importance of this point in articulating a doctrine of the atonement was recognized by the Synod of Dort in 1618–19. Article 3 of point 2 reads, 'The death of God's Son is the only and entirely complete sacrifice and satisfaction for sins; it is of infinite value and worth, more than sufficient to atone for the sins of the whole world' (*Ecumenical Creeds and Reformed Confessions* [Grand Rapids: CRC, 1988], p. 130. The Canons of Dort are freely available on the web in numerous locations).

60. Turretin, *Institutes*, vol. 2, 14.XI.xxx, p. 437. Finite minds, unsurprisingly, struggle to comprehend the mathematics of infinity! It might seem to us that if two people each owe an infinite debt, then together they owe 'infinity times two', and that Christ's payment of 'infinity times one' is insufficient. However, it just does not work that way; mathematically, it a nonsense to speak of 'infinity times two'. The debt of two (or more) people is still simply infinite, and the Bible attests that Christ's infinite payment is sufficient.

### 5. 'Penal substitution implies universal salvation, which is unbiblical'

#### Objection

According to some, penal substitution leads inevitably to the unbiblical idea that all people will be saved, and it must therefore be rejected. Eleonore Stump states this argument succinctly:

> [Penal substitution] maintains that Christ pays the penalty for all sin in full so that humans do not have to do so. But it is a fundamental Christian doctrine that God justly condemns some people to everlasting punishment in hell. If Christ has paid the penalty for sin completely, how is God just in demanding that some people pay the penalty again?[61]

#### Response

It is helpful to break down this argument to see exactly how it works:

(a) According to penal substitution, Jesus' death fully pays the debt of those for whom he died.
(b) Jesus died for all people.
(c) From (a) and (b) it follows that Jesus' death fully pays the debt of all people.
(d) But the Bible teaches that some people will pay their own debt in hell.
(e) From (c) and (d) it follows that God is unjust, for in hell he demands payment for a debt already paid in full by Christ. In other words, he punishes the same sins twice.
(f) This conclusion (e) is unthinkable, and so we must reject penal substitution (a) on which the whole argument rests.

The benefit of laying out the argument in this way is that it reveals a premise hidden in Stump's argument, but not stated explicitly – namely (b), the notion that Jesus died for all people. Step (f) assumes that the only way to avoid the argument that God is unjust is by jettisoning penal substitution, premise (a). However the same end could be achieved by instead rejecting premise (b).

Given that Stump's fear of attributing injustice to God can be answered *either* by denying penal substitution *or* by denying that Christ died for all, it is clear that by itself her objection does not mean penal substitution has to go. In fact, the overwhelming biblical evidence in favour of penal substitution,

---

61. Stump, 'Atonement According to Aquinas', p. 63.

presented in chapters 2 and 3, would caution strongly against this. But can we really take the other path and deny universal redemption (the idea that Christ died for all)? Is this not basic to the Bible's teaching? Many have thought not.

Perhaps the most devastating critique of universal redemption came from the pen of the great Puritan theologian John Owen. In his treatise *The Death of Death in the Death of Christ* he advances many arguments against the idea that Christ died for all. Significantly, at one point he deploys similar logic to Stump, but for him there was no question that penal substitution could be the casualty:

> If the full debt of all be paid to the utmost extent of the obligation, how comes it to pass that so many are shut up in prison to eternity, never freed from their debts? . . . If the Lord, as a just creditor, ought to cancel all obligations and surcease all suits against such as have their debts so paid, whence is it that his wrath smokes against some to all eternity?[62]

Owen believed Christ died with the intention of procuring salvation only for the elect: those whom God had determined from eternity past to save. This is known as the doctrine of *Particular Redemption*, or *Limited Atonement* (the *L* in the TULIP acrostic for the five points of Calvinism[63]). The former term is preferable, since the notion of 'limitation' is misleading and pejorative, and moreover is frequently misunderstood to mean that Jesus' death was somehow limited in its *value*. However, as Roger Nicole helpfully clarifies:

> The question is not about *the value of the death of Christ*. There is no one I know of in mainline Calvinism who would be inclined in any sense to say there are limits to the value of Christ's death. It is freely granted that what Christ suffered is so immense, in fact so infinite, that it would be amply sufficient to atone for all the sins of all the people of all ages in the whole world and in a thousand worlds besides, if these existed. It is freely granted by all parties that the work of Christ is strictly infinite in its value . . .
>
> The question is really the *design* of the atonement. The intention of God the Father in sending the Son and the intention of the Son in offering himself as a substitute are the issue. For whom did Christ die? Who were the people whom he had on his mind and in his heart as he was offering himself as a substitute for the new humanity?[64]

---

62. Owen, *Death of Death*, p. 273.

63. The others are Total Depravity, Unconditional Election, Irresistible Grace and the Preservation of the Saints.

64. Roger Nicole, *Our Sovereign Saviour: The Essence of the Reformed Faith* (Fearn: Christian Focus, 2002), pp. 58–60; italics original. See also Roger Nicole, 'The Case for

Perhaps the hardest pill to swallow in all of this is the idea that God did not will to save all. But this is already implicit in the doctrines of election and pre-destination, for which there is overwhelming biblical support.[65] Many people

---

Definite Atonement', *Bulletin of the Evangelical Theological Society* 10 (1967), pp. 199–207, which is freely available on the web at a number of locations.

65. Confusion may arise here, because the Bible does say that God 'wants all men to be saved and to come to a knowledge of the truth' (1 Tim. 2:4; cf. 2 Pet. 3:9; Ezek. 18:23). Yet at the same time it is clear that God does not elect everyone to salvation. The solution to this apparent paradox is to realize that Scripture speaks of God's will in two distinct ways. On the one hand, there is God's *moral will*, that is, what God wants or approves as revealed in his precepts and commandments. An example would be 1 Thess. 4:3, 'It is God's will that you should be sanctified: that you should avoid sexual immorality'. On the other hand, there is God's *sovereign will*. This refers to what God decides will happen in every situation everywhere in his creation, a decision he takes in secret, without always telling us or explaining his reasons. Nothing escapes his will in this sense, even our sinful actions.

This doctrine of 'two wills', though it has been scorned by some theologians (e.g. Clark H. Pinnock, *Grace Unlimited* [Minneapolis: Bethany Fellowship, 1975], p. 13), is in fact necessary to account for the death of Christ. Judas' betrayal of Christ was sinful, indeed an act inspired by Satan (Luke 22:3). Yet at the same time, Acts 2:23 makes clear that it was part of God's ordained plan. The action was contrary to God's moral will, but in accordance with his sovereign will. Brief reflection on the opening chapters of the book of Job leads to a similar distinction, and there are many more biblical passages that point this way.

Let us now apply this distinction to the question of salvation. God does want all to be saved in the moral sense. That is to say, it is an offence to him when someone fails to repent and turn in faith to his Son. But God does not want all to be saved in the sovereign sense. He does not act to bring about the salvation of all. The reason for this is that God sometimes allows something bad to happen (the death of sinner; the betrayal of his Son) to serve a higher end. The highest end of all is his glory and, strangely perhaps to our minds, it brings him more glory not to save all: against the backdrop of the fate of those without Christ, God's grace towards those in Christ is more gloriously seen, as Paul argues in Rom. 9:22–24. These matters are discussed in more detail by John Piper, 'Are There Two Wills in God?', in Thomas R. Schreiner and Bruce A. Ware (eds.), *Still Sovereign: Contemporary Perspectives on Election, Foreknowledge, and Grace* (Grand Rapids: Baker, 2000), pp. 107–131, repr. with minor changes in *The Pleasures of God*, rev. edn (Fearn: Christian Focus, 2001), pp. 313–340.

find the idea that God chose those whom he would save very difficult. It jars with our innate sense of how things should be. Moreover, many Christians vividly remember making a decision to follow Christ, and the suggestion that this choice was predetermined by the will of God seems to undercut the reality of their experience. Nonetheless, predestination is the clear and unambiguous teaching of Scripture (see e.g. John 6:37, 44; Acts 13:48; Eph. 1:4–5; Romans 8:29–30). This is one of those instances where Christ's sheep are distinguished by their willingness to follow his voice even when his words are contrary to human wisdom.[66]

Before outlining a brief defence of particular redemption, let us be clear that this was not a doctrine introduced to prop up penal substitution in the face of criticisms like Stump's. Rather, particular redemption was part of the fabric of Reformed theology in the sixteenth and seventeenth centuries,[67] and only when this was *denied* did some become uncertain about penal substitution.[68]

Let us now rehearse some of the biblical and theological arguments in favour of particular redemption.[69] First, it is not 'a doctrine without a text', as

---

66. A belief in predestination is common to the overwhelming majority of evangelical and Reformed thinkers, as well as notable Church Fathers such as Augustine. Consequently, there are many places to which the reader can turn for a fuller explanation. We would recommend in particular John M. Frame, *The Doctrine of God* (Phillipsburg: Presbyterian & Reformed, 2002), pp. 47–159, especially pp. 70–76; and Schreiner and Ware, *Still Sovereign*. Older treatments also reward careful study; e.g. John Calvin, *Institutes of the Christian Religion*, trans. F. L. Battles, 2 vols. (Philadelphia: Westminster, 1960), vol. 2, III.xxi–xxiv, pp. 920–986; Turretin, *Institutes*, vol. 1, pp. 311–430.

67. R. T. Kendall has famously argued in *Calvin and English Calvinism to 1649* (Carlisle: Paternoster, 1997, first pub. 1977) that Calvin himself did not hold to such a doctrine, but that the later Calvinists betrayed him at this point. However, Paul Helm presents a compelling case against Kendall's thesis in *Calvin and the Calvinists* (Edinburgh: Banner of Truth, 1982).

68. David P. Field, *Rigide Calvinisme in a Softer Dresse: The Moderate Presbyterianism of John Howe, 1630–1705* (Edinburgh: Rutherford House, 2004), p. 23.

69. John Owen's *Death of Death* remains the most comprehensive defence of particular redemption, but is a rather intimidating read! A much more accessible introduction may be found in Nicole, *Our Sovereign Saviour*, pp. 57–73. For a little more detail, the following may be useful: Berkhof, *Systematic Theology*, pp. 392–399; John Murray, *Redemption Accomplished and Applied* (Edinburgh: Banner of Truth, 1961; first pub. Grand Rapids: Eerdmans, 1955), pp. 59–75 (page references in our work are to the

some have claimed.[70] Passages that say Christ died specifically for his 'sheep' (John 10:11, 15), his 'friends' (John 15:13) and his 'church' (Acts 20:28; Eph. 5:25) are strongly suggestive. Moreover, Jesus says he 'lays down his life for the sheep' (John 10:11) in a context where he explicitly *excludes* some of his hearers from that group: 'you are not my sheep' (v. 26).

Another important text is Romans 8:32. The apostle Paul here assumes a doctrine of particular redemption when he reassures his hearers that, since God has already done the greatest thing for them, namely giving up his own Son, he will assuredly do the lesser thing of giving them 'all things'.[71] This could refer either to all the resources necessary to get them safely to glory (the context speaks of the unshakeable security of believers as they await their final salvation), or to the riches of their glorious inheritance itself, or quite possibly both. But, on either reading, it is plain Paul regards those for whom God gave his Son as identical with the group who will finally be saved. There can be no-one for whom Christ died who will not also receive his or her inheritance – this is Paul's very argument.[72] Christ died only for those who will be saved.

Similarly, the combination of 2 Corinthians 5:14 with Romans 6:1–14 is problematic for those who deny particular redemption. The former text teaches that all those for whom Christ died, died spiritually with him. The latter teaches that all who died with him will share in his resurrection life, which in

---

Banner of Truth edn); Turretin, *Institutes*, vol. 2, 14.XIV, pp. 455–482; and J. I. Packer, 'Saved by his Precious Blood: An Introduction to John Owen's "The Death of Death in the Death of Christ"', in *Among God's Giants: The Puritan Vision of the Christian Life* (Eastbourne: Kingsway, 1991), pp. 163–195. Packer's chapter is particularly helpful, and is freely available on the web in numerous locations.

70. See e.g. D. Broughton Knox, 'Some Aspects of the Atonement', in Tony Payne (ed.), *Selected Works*, vol. 1: *The Doctrine of God* (Kingsford: Matthias Media, 2000), pp. 253–266 (pp. 263, 266).

71. The fact that particular redemption is assumed here actually strengthens the point: particular redemption was sufficiently uncontroversial for Paul that he did not feel the need to argue for it.

72. Consider the manifold difficulties into which a doctrine of universal redemption would plunge us. We would end up with a group of people to whom God had made a guarantee in giving up his Son, but to whom God has no intention of keeping his word. We would have to modify Paul's words as follows: 'He who did not spare his own Son, but gave him up for us all – how will he not also, along with him, in some of our cases graciously give us all things.' The qualification would nullify the assurance otherwise inherent in the promise.

Romans is connected with salvation. Putting the two together, it is apparent that all for whom Christ died will enjoy salvation.[73] Universal redemption would then necessarily imply that all will be saved, which is unbiblical.

Secondly, particular redemption affirms that the Son's intention in dying to save particular people corresponds with the Father's intention to elect those people to salvation and the Spirit's intention to apply the benefits of Christ's death to those same people. By contrast, universal redemption divides the persons of the Trinity. The Son's intention to save all is in conflict with the Father's decision to choose only some, and with the Spirit's work in uniting only some to Christ by faith. Such a conflict flies in the face of orthodox trinitarian theology, particularly as revealed in the Gospel of John (see chapter 3 and chapter 11, sect. 1). It also undermines the sovereignty of the Son by implying that his will is ultimately frustrated, for the Father's decision that only some will be saved finally prevails.

Thirdly, particular redemption maintains that Christ's death does not just make salvation possible, but actually *achieves* the salvation of God's people. This is what the Scriptures teach everywhere: 'Christ redeemed us from the curse of the law' (Gal. 3:13), 'when we were God's enemies, we were reconciled to him [God] through the death of his Son' (Rom. 5:10); Christ 'has freed us from our sins by his blood' (Rev. 1:5). By contrast, universal redemption teaches that the atoning benefits of Christ's death apply equally to all, leaving only two options: either all are saved, which is unbiblical, or else something remains to be done to achieve the salvation of those who are. The cross by itself is sufficient to save no-one. J. I. Packer describes the predicament of those who would argue this way:

> If we start by affirming that God has a saving love for all, and Christ died a saving death for all, and yet balk at becoming universalists . . . let us be clear on what we have done when we have put the matter in this fashion. We have not exalted grace and the cross; we have cheapened them. We have limited the atonement far more drastically than Calvinism does, for whereas Calvinism asserts that Christ's death,

---

73. Even though the two statements come in different New Testament books, in slightly different contexts, it is nonetheless appropriate to let them mutually inform one another. In doing so, we are assuming only that the apostle Paul had a single, coherent theological system underpinning his various writings. Some would deny this, of course, and would be prepared to speak of 'contradictions' in Paul's thought. Such people escape this argument against universal redemption, but at the cost of an evangelical doctrine of Scripture.

as such, saves all whom it was meant to save, we have denied that Christ's death, as such, is sufficient to save any of them.[74]

In short, universal redemption pictures Christ's atonement as a ship with all humanity on board that drops anchor a mile or two out to sea, leaving its passengers to swim ashore; particular redemption depicts it as a lifeboat that unfailingly conveys the whole company of God's elect – 'a great multitude that no-one could count' (Rev. 7:9) – *all the way* from the storms of death and condemnation to the shelter of God's eternal kingdom.

Fourthly (although in some ways this argument is a variant on the preceding one), the logic of universal redemption runs into serious difficulty just as it tries to explain why all are not saved. Christ died for the sins of all, this it affirms. But why is his death not *effective* for all? Because not all believe, comes the reply. But unbelief is a sin like any other (cf. Heb. 3:12), and therefore Jesus' death is surely sufficient to deal with it. So why are these people not saved? At this point the proponent of universal redemption must either opt for universalism (all will be saved) or say there are sins Christ's death does not deal with.[75]

Fifthly, although some have claimed that the biblical texts that speak of Christ's death for 'all people' or 'the world' speak against particular redemption, a careful examination of these passages in their contexts shows otherwise. In many cases, the 'all' in question should be taken to mean 'all without distinction' (all *kinds* of people), and not 'all without exception' (every person who has ever lived). There are two reasons for thinking this. Firstly, in the first-century context, the idea that the gospel could extend beyond Jews to 'unclean' Gentiles was utterly revolutionary – see for example Peter's reaction to being asked to eat with Cornelius in Acts 10, or the reaction of Jesus' disciples to his conversation with a Samaritan woman in John 4. When Jesus said 'I, when I am lifted up from the earth, will draw all men to myself' (John 12:32), he almost certainly mean by 'all' that Greeks would be included, for only then can Jesus' words in verses 23–32 be understood as a reply (v. 23) to the Greeks' request (v. 21). If we think this an anticlimax relative to the idea that he meant everyone in the world, it only serves to demonstrate our distance from issues that dominated the mindset of the early Christians: for them there were few truths more earth-shattering than the inclusion of non-Jews in the people of God. Or consider Titus 2:11, where Paul says that 'the grace of God that brings

74. Packer, 'Saved by his Precious Blood', pp. 179–180.
75. Cf. Owen, *Death of Death*, pp. 173–174, 249.

salvation has appeared to all men'.[76] This is most unlikely to refer to all people without exception, since the following verses speak of the consequences of this appearing in terms that evidently apply only to Christians. Moreover, the 'all without distinction' reading makes a lot of sense in view of the preceding verses (vv. 2–10), which refer to different *types* of people in the church – older men, older women, young men, young women, slaves.

The second reason for questioning the 'all without exception' reading is that in many cases it would lead to universalism. For example, Romans 5:18 says that the result of Christ's work was 'justification that brings life for *all men*' (italics added), and 1 Corinthians 15:22 says that 'in Christ shall *all* be made alive' (italics added). Many who baulk at particular redemption nevertheless adopt (rightly) a limited reading of the word 'all' in these texts.[77] To examine every relevant passage would be far beyond the scope of this section, but these two general considerations establish that the reading proponents of particular redemption adopt is perfectly plausible in many contexts.[78]

---

76. There is some debate about exactly how this verse should be translated. Some think the 'all' modifies not 'appearing' (as in the NIV, cited above) but 'salvation'. Thus the NRSV reads, 'the grace of God has appeared, bringing salvation to all'. In this case, the 'all without exception' reading is even more problematic, for it would turn this verse into a statement of universalism.

77. Karl Barth famously argued for a universal reading of these texts, while denying that this must lead to universalism. Those who follow him in this would do well to read Oliver Crisp's devastating critique, which exposes the logical inconsistency of Barth's position (Oliver D. Crisp, 'On Barth's Denial of Universalism', *Themelios* 29.1 [autumn 2003], pp. 18–29).

78. John Owen addresses almost every text in considerable detail in *Death of Death*, pp. 316–421. 2 Pet. 2:1 does not constitute a definitive argument against particular redemption, as some have supposed. The experience of being redeemed/bought in the Old Testament meant leaving the slavery of Egypt and passing through the sea. Yet 1 Cor. 10:1–10 reminds us that some who experienced this *outwardly* did not enjoy the blessings of final salvation. Along with Heb. 6:4–6, this passage is best reconciled with those that clearly teach 'once saved always saved' (e.g. John 6:39; 10:27–29; Rom. 8:29–30, 38–39; Phil. 1:6) by saying that some who *outwardly* experienced the blessings of the Christian life were not truly born again. Thus being 'bought' in 2 Pet. 2:1 most likely refers to this outward perspective, and need not imply that those guilty of 'denying the sovereign Lord' had been *inwardly* redeemed.

Before concluding this section, we must address several arguments against particular redemption set forth in an influential essay by D. Broughton Knox. He was a faithful and godly scholar, and is held in esteem by many, but on this point we think him mistaken.

First, Knox asserts that 'the work of Christ extends uniformly to the whole of humanity'. He sets forth the following arguments in support: 'When Christ lived a life of perfect obedience to the law of God, he fulfilled the obligation which rests on all men equally, and not an obligation which the elect alone have.' Again, 'When our Lord, through his death on the cross, became a curse, he bore the curse which God threatens against all breakers of his covenant, and not the curse which is particularly applicable to the elect.'[79] But these statements do not prove what Knox thinks they prove. For while it is true that the law Christ obeyed and the curse he bore were *required* of every human being, it does not follow that Christ's obedience and curse-bearing *extend* to all. By analogy, a mother could say she paid on her son's behalf the television licence fee required of all television users in the UK and not of her son only. But this would not mean she paid it for everyone.

Secondly, Knox contends that a synthesis of penal substitution and particular redemption would imply the elect are saved at the moment of Christ's death, when the payment for the elect is made, whereas the Bible teaches that even the elect are objects of God's wrath until their *conversion* (Eph. 2:3). Knox rightly asserts that it is at the point of application to the individual believer that Christ's death becomes effective for him or her, but mistakenly assumes that the limitation as to whom it ultimately benefits must also be delayed until this point. It is quite possible for something to be effectually procured by God for specific people, without its being applied to them at that same moment. This is true, for example, of our deliverance from God's wrath on the Day of Judgment. Romans 5:8–10 teaches that this 'salvation' lies in the future, and yet nothing further needs to be done to procure it – believers have already been justified, and thus they shall certainly be saved. Knox would presumably agree with this, but this very argument ultimately defeats him. For the Bible is clear that whether or not we shall be delivered on Judgment Day is decided in advance of that day. The final deliverance is limited to those who are justified before the deliverance is applied. By analogy, it is perfectly possible for Jesus'

---

79. Knox, 'Some Aspects of the Atonement', p. 260. He gives two other arguments along the same lines: the human nature that Christ assumed was a nature shared by all, and the devil whom Jesus defeated was the enemy of all. Our reply above applies equally to these points.

death to be limited in intention as to whom it would save, in advance of those benefits being applied to them.

To put it another way, proponents of particular redemption agree with Knox that the benefits of Jesus' death are limited to the elect at the point of application – only the elect come to Jesus in faith. However, they *also* believe that the benefits of Jesus' death are limited to the elect at the point of their procurement at Calvary, on the grounds that God's intention was to save only the elect. Strangely, Knox at one point agrees that 'The intended destination of the atonement was to effect and secure the forgiveness and salvation of the elect only,'[80] yet he apparently fails to realize that this is exactly what is affirmed by the doctrine of particular redemption, which he proceeds to deny.[81]

Ironically, Knox runs into the exact reverse of the problem he puts to his opponents. If he thought them unable to explain why people are not saved prior to their conversion, then he finds himself unable to explain why Christ died prior to their conversion! If the transaction of justice occurs only at the point of *application* of redemption, as Knox suggests, then our guilt cannot

---

80. Ibid., p. 261, citing William Cunningham, *Works of William Cunningham*, vol. 3 (Edinburgh: T. & T. Clark, 1863), p. 347; see also Knox, 'Some Aspects of the Atonement', p. 262.

81. This is perhaps the most curious feature of Knox's essay. Reformed theologians have consistently stated that the particularity, or limitedness, of Christ's atoning work refers to God's particular intention to save only the elect. We have cited Roger Nicole on this point above. Similarly, Louis Berkhof writes, 'The question with which we are concerned at this point is not . . . whether the satisfaction rendered by Christ was in itself sufficient for the salvation of all men, since this is admitted by all . . . On the other hand, the question does relate to the design of the atonement. Did the Father in sending Christ, and did Christ in coming into the world, to make atonement for sin, *do this with the design or for the purpose of saving only the elect or all men?* That is the question, and that only is the question' (Berkhof, *Systematic Theology*, pp. 393–394; italics original). Or again, Francis Turretin writes, 'the question hinges upon this – not what is the nature and power of Christ's death in itself, but what was the purpose of the Father in appointing him and the intention of Christ in undergoing it' (Turretin, *Institutes*, vol. 2, 14.XIV.ix, p. 459). The question was also stated in these terms by the Synod of Dort (*Ecumenical Creeds and Reformed Confessions*, pp. 130–131, point 2, arts. 8–9). It is strange that, having affirmed God's (particular) intention to atone only for the sins of the elect, Knox goes on to deny the doctrine of particular redemption. This seems to be a contradiction.

have been imputed to Christ at the moment he died: he was punished without cause, a travesty of justice.

Particular redemption resolves these difficulties. It was the sins of the elect that were imputed to Christ, and the benefits of his redemption are applied, in due course, to those same people. Since God views things from outside time, it does not matter that the two things are not simultaneous, so long as the two sets of people (those for whom he died and those to whom he applies redemption) are identical. We know that simultaneity is not necessary, because Jesus' death works retrospectively, atoning for Old Testament believers (Rom. 3:25; Heb. 9:15), and extends also into the future, to atone for those not yet born. We know that the groups must be identical by considering what would happen if they were not. If we were to say that the sin of *all* was imputed to Christ at Calvary, but only *some* are brought to faith in him to receive the benefits of his death, then, by following Knox's trajectory, we find ourselves unwittingly impaled on the horns of Stump's dilemma: if Christ suffered for all at Calvary, why will the punishment for the same sins be paid again by some in hell?

We are conscious that this has become a rather lengthy defence of particular redemption in a book supposed to be about penal substitution! However, in theology every piece of the jigsaw is ultimately connected to everything else. In this case the confusion about penal substitution arose because some of the other pieces had been put in the wrong place. We are of course aware that many hold firmly to penal substitution but remain unpersuaded of the doctrine of particular redemption. However, we struggle to see how Stump's criticism of penal substitution could be answered from this perspective. Might it be that particular redemption deserves a second hearing? Penal substitution and particular redemption, when fitted together correctly, are quite immune to the charge of injustice Stump brings.

## 11. PENAL SUBSTITUTION AND
## OUR UNDERSTANDING OF GOD

### Introduction

Objections in this category concern the relationship between the theology of atonement and the doctrine of God. Some critics have objected that penal substitution implies a division between the persons of the Trinity. Others have objected to the idea that God's wrath is provoked by sin, either insisting that this contradicts the Bible's teaching about his love, or claiming that it misunderstands how sin and wrath are related. Finally, some critics have complained that penal substitution implies that God the Father is constrained to punish his Son by a law external to himself, when he would rather simply forgive and forget. In different ways, all of these criticisms contend that penal substitution distorts and misrepresents the biblical picture of God.

### 1. 'Penal substitution implies a division between the persons of the Trinity'

#### *Objection*
Some critics claim that penal substitution implies a division between Father and Son, setting them at odds with each other. This is unacceptable, they say, given the Bible's teaching that Father, Son and Spirit are *one* God.

According to Paul Fiddes, penal substitution depicts the Father and the Son acting independently: 'One of the problems of a theory of penal substitution is that it depends for its logic upon a strong individualisation of Father and Son as independent subjects, which makes it hard to speak of the one personal reality of a God who becomes vulnerable to love's sake within his own creation.'[1]

Green and Baker are similarly concerned about any understanding of the cross that threatens to undermine 'the oneness of purpose and activity' of the Father and the Son. In a discussion of Romans 5:8 they point out that the unity of purpose of the Father and the Son is emphasized by the apostle Paul's statement 'that *God* demonstrates his love by means of what *Christ* did'.[2] Importantly, they think this excludes the possibility of a transaction in which the Father acts upon the Son:

> In the end we find in Pauline discourse the unrelenting affirmation of the oneness of
> purpose and activity of God and God's Son in the cross. Thus any atonement
> theology that assumes, against Paul, that in the cross God did something 'to' Jesus is
> not only an affront to the Christian doctrine of the triune God but also misrepresents
> Paul's clear affirmation in Romans 5.[3]

Tom Smail claims that penal substitution undermines the unity of the persons of the Trinity. He is critical of John Stott's explanation of propitiation, where Stott concludes that 'God took his own loving initiative to appease his own righteous anger by bearing it in his own self in his own Son when he took our place and died for us'.[4] Smail responds as follows: 'What does it really mean to say "God propitiated himself"? Can the verb really have the same person for its subject and object and still retain its meaning? What is the distinction between the one who does the propitiating and the one who is propitiated?'[5]

---

1. Paul S. Fiddes, *Past Event and Present Salvation: The Christian Idea of Atonement* (London: Darton, Longman & Todd, 1989), p. 108.

2. Joel B. Green and Mark D. Baker, *Recovering the Scandal of the Cross: Atonement in New Testament and Contemporary Contexts* (Downers Grove: IVP, 2000), p. 57; italics original.

3. Ibid.

4. John R. W. Stott, *The Cross of Christ* (Leicester: IVP, 1986), p. 175; quoted in Tom Smail, *Once and for All: A Confession of the Cross* (London: Darton, Longman & Todd, 1998), p. 87.

5. Smail, *Once and for All*, p. 87.

It is inadequate, Smail continues, to posit 'a Trinitarian distinction between the Father who is propitiated and the Son who propitiates',[6] for this leaves us 'in danger . . . of making an illegitimate Trinitarian schism between the Father and the Son'.[7]

In summary, the objection is that penal substitution is in danger of severing the persons of the Trinity, either by suggesting one person did something 'to' another, or by implying they were acting independently.

### Response

We begin by addressing the claim made by Joel Green and Mark Baker that penal substitution is wrong because it 'assumes . . . that in the cross God did something "to" Jesus'.[8] It is a bizarre objection, for there is nothing wrong in principle with saying that one person of the Trinity does something 'to' another. On the contrary, as we saw in chapter 3, there are numerous biblical texts where the Father is the subject of an action (the one performing the action) of which the Son is the object (the one on whom the action is performed).

In some cases the persons of the Trinity perform the same acts towards each other. For example, the Son loves the Father and the Father loves the Son. However, this is not always the case: although the Father and the Son send the Spirit, the Spirit is never said to send the Father.

All this demonstrates that it is perfectly biblical for one person of the Trinity to perform an action upon another: no division in the Trinity is entailed. Far from being, as Green and Baker put it, 'an affront to the Christian doctrine of the triune God',[9] this kind of action is commonplace in Scripture. Indeed, to press Green and Baker's assertion to its logical conclusion would mean the Father could not *love* the Son. The absurdity is obvious.

Someone might still ask whether it is biblical for the Father to perform on the Son the particular action required by penal substitution. Certainly, the Father loves the Son, sends the Son, glorifies the Son, but is it biblical to say he *punishes* the Son? This can ultimately be answered only by examining what the Bible says on the subject, and readers are referred to chapter 2. However, some people have raised the further question of how the Father punishing the Son can be consistent with his love. This is so important that we treat it separately in the next section.

---

6. Ibid.

7. Ibid., p. 86.

8. Green and Baker, *Recovering the Scandal*, p. 57.

9. Ibid.

We turn now to the objection that propitiation is nonsensical because it makes *one person* (God) at the same time both subject and object of an action, and to a second complaint, in some ways the very converse, that penal substitution involves *two persons* (Father and Son) acting *separately*. Smail makes use of both of these arguments, as we saw, deploying the second against proponents of penal substitution just as we try to escape the first. These issues lead us into the deep waters of trinitarian theology, for we shall need to give an account of God that both keeps the persons of Father and Son distinct (so one can act on another) and at the same time safeguards their unity (so they do not act independently). A properly articulated account of the relationship between Father and Son is resistant to the critiques of penal substitution under consideration. We have already sketched such an account in chapter 3, but since Smail's criticism is quite nuanced, it will be helpful to go over some of the same ground again in a little more detail.

The first thing to be said is that there is only one God (e.g. Isa. 44:6; 1 Cor. 8:4). In many of the early church debates about the Trinity, this reality was safeguarded by speaking of a single divine 'substance' the Father, Son and Spirit share. This language is out of vogue in some circles today, and even misconstrued to refer to a fourth 'thing' that exists apart from the three divine persons. This is not at all what is meant. The divine substance 'is simply what God is'[10] – we might say that it is his 'Godness', the thing that makes the Father, Son and Spirit equally divine without implying three divinities.

Having recognized this, we can begin to think about the relationship between Father and Son. Jesus speaks of the fact that he and his Father *mutually indwell* each other: 'I am *in* the Father and the Father is *in* me' (John 14:11; italics added; see also John 10:38; 14:10, 20).[11] The technical term for this mutual indwelling is *perichoresis*, or *perichoretic union*.[12]

---

10. John M. Frame, *The Doctrine of God* (Phillipsburg: Presbyterian & Reformed, 2002), p. 700. Sometimes other terminology is used instead of 'substance' in this context, such as 'essence', or the Latin term *essentia* or the Greek term *ousia*. The jargon is a little bewildering, not least because some in the early church used the terms in different ways (a brief explanation appears in Turretin, *Institutes*, vol. 1, 3.XXIII, p. 253). Since there is little hope of a standard vocabulary emerging, it is as well to be aware of the alternatives.

11. The same applies, of course, to the relationships involving the Spirit; for simplicity we largely restrict the discussion here to the Father and the Son.

12. Sometimes theologians prefer to speak of circumcession or coinherence, or alternatively to use the Latin terms *circumincessio* or *circumcessio* (Frame, *Doctrine of God*, p. 693).

Perichoresis implies both union between the Father and the Son and distinction between them. Their union or oneness (John 10:30) is crucial. One of the horrors of polytheism is that the various supposed deities may make different or even mutually exclusive demands of people. With the Father and the Son this is avoided, not because they happen fortuitously to agree on most things, but because they *must* agree, for they are not independent, but rather one God. They share in a single divine substance, not in the sense that each has a 'piece' of it, but in the sense that, as they mutually indwell each other, each person partakes fully and equally of it.

The *distinction* between the Father and the Son is no less important. Without it, it would be nonsense to talk of a distinct 'Father' or 'Son' at all, and it would certainly be impossible for them genuinely to relate as separate persons, as the Bible plainly teaches they do. This point is clear from the many references cited in chapter 3, in which one person of the Trinity is said to act on another.

How, though, do we distinguish between the persons?[13] We must have some way of differentiating them, otherwise the Father would in effect *be* the Son, and the Son would *be* the Father, and there would be no Trinity at all. But if Son and Father are both fully divine, and moreover, if they are equal in their possession of all the divine attributes (e.g. equally holy, equally wise, equally true), what can possibly distinguish them? The answer is that they are differentiated by the asymmetry of their relationship to each other. The Father is in a relationship of fatherhood with respect to the Son, whereas the Son is in a relationship of sonship with respect to the Father. The Son is everything the Father is, except he is not the Father. The Father is everything the Son is, except he is not the Son.

Having sketched something of the nature of God in trinitarian relationship, let us now consider his actions. It is absolutely fundamental to understand that God's actions reflect his nature. God's actions are holy because he himself is holy, he always does what is good because he is good, and so on.[14] In view of this, we should expect God's triune nature to be reflected in the actions of the

---

13. It is insufficient to say that the Son is the one who took on a human nature and became man: we must have a way of distinguishing the Father and the Son in eternity, before the incarnation took place.

14. If this consistency between nature and action were not in place, we could in fact know nothing of God. Our knowledge of him comes only from how he has acted, supremely in the person of his Son, or from what he has said (and speech is an action). We trust that these things accurately reflect his nature, and therefore they do not mislead us about what he is really like.

individual persons of the Godhead, and that is precisely what we find. Both the unity and the distinction between the persons are reflected in what God does.

On the one hand, the actions of the persons reflect their unity. Consider how John 14:10, cited in part above, continues: 'Don't you believe that I am in the Father, and that the Father is in me? The words I say to you are not just my own. Rather, it is the Father, living in me, who is doing his work.' Jesus teaches that the works *he* does are at the same time the works of his *Father*, and he grounds this in their perichoretic union. An almost identical point is made in John 10:37–38. Again, Jesus testifies in John 5:19 that 'whatever the Father does, the Son also does'. There is a fundamental unity in their actions that mirrors the fundamental union of their persons.

On the other hand, the actions of the persons reflect their distinctness. While every person of the Trinity is involved in every action undertaken by one of the other persons, they are not involved *in the same way*. The asymmetrical relationships between the persons are expressed in asymmetrical involvement in their actions. To pick an example of particular relevance to penal substitution, the Bible teaches that God the Father sent the Son, and that the Son willingly obeyed the Father (see especially John 10:15–18; also John 6:38–44; 14:31; 15:10; 17:3, 8). The roles are not interchangeable.

How can we speak about the actions of the Father and the Son in such a way that we affirm both their unity and the distinction between them? We might perhaps say that the Father always acts *with* the Son, and the Son always acts *with* the Father, but this could be misunderstood to imply that both are *subjects* of every action, which as we have seen is unbiblical. We are in trouble also if we say that the Father acts *without* the Son, for this would suggest an unbiblical independence between the persons. Augustine's solution was to say that the Father's actions are *not without* the Son, and the Son's actions are *not without* the Father.[15] This captures nicely the mutual involvement of the persons without implying symmetrical involvement. Again, as we saw in chapter 3, another way to formulate the same truth is to speak of *inseparable*

15. See e.g. Augustine, *Sermon XXI, on Matt. 12:32*, in *Nicene and Post-Nicene Fathers*, ser. I, vol. 6 (Grand Rapids: Eerdmans, 1974), sect. 26, p. 327; Augustine, *Tractate XX, on John 5:19*, in *Nicene and Post-Nicene Fathers*, ser. I, vol. 7 (Grand Rapids: Eerdmans, 1974), sect. 6, p. 134. Ambrose of Milan also formulated the doctrine in this way; see e.g. *On the Holy Spirit*, in *Nicene and Post-Nicene Fathers*, ser. II, vol. 10 (Grand Rapids: Eerdmans, 1976), bk. 2, ch. 12, sects. 131, 133, pp. 131, 132.

*action*, or *inseparable operation*. Augustine also used this terminology,[16] and affirms that while the persons of the Trinity do not perform the same action in the same way, they nonetheless never act independently of each other – their respective contributions to any given activity are *inseparable*.

If this painstaking care over language seems to some to be unnecessary nit-picking, we reply that it is nothing more than an attempt to speak biblically and to avoid misunderstanding. Nor are these concerns restricted to a few theologians given to too much pontificating: all we have said is standard trinitarian theology, and enjoys a wide consensus.[17] It is not the sort of thing we tend to discuss over a cup of coffee after church, but it matters greatly.

The aim of this brief foray into trinitarian theology was to help us see how the biblical teaching about one God existing in three persons fits together. Having done so, the task of answering the trinitarian objections to penal substitution becomes relatively easy.

First, contrary to Smail's criticism, it is not meaningless to say that God the Son propitiated God the Father. It is not the same *person* who is the subject and object of the verb, for the Father and the Son are *distinct*. Secondly, the fact that the Father exacts a punishment borne by the Son does not mean the members of the Trinity are divided or act independently. Rather, they are *inseparably* engaged in two aspects of the same action. Their involvement is asymmetrical, but this is entirely apposite to the asymmetry inherent in their relationship.

In summary, it is clear there can be no successful attack on penal substitution on trinitarian grounds.

---

16. See e.g. Augustine, *Tractate XX, on John 5:19*, sect. 6, p. 134.

17. E.g. it is taught by modern Reformed writers such as John Frame (Frame, *Doctrine of God*, pp. 688–707), and modern Roman Catholics such as Thomas Weinandy (Thomas G. Weinandy, *Does God Suffer?* [Edinburgh: T. & T. Clark, 2000], pp. 116–119). Herman Bavinck gives a helpful historical outline of the development of trinitarian theology that demonstrates agreement on these matters from the Apostolic Fathers to Augustine and beyond (Herman Bavinck, *Reformed Dogmatics*, vol. 2: *God and Creation* [Grand Rapids: Baker, 2002], pp. 256–260, 279–296). Similar positions were espoused by the great Reformers (e.g. John Calvin, *Institutes of the Christian Religion*, trans. F. L. Battles, 2 vols. [Philadelphia: Westminster, 1960], vol. 1, I.xiii, pp. 120–159), the theologians of the post-Reformation era (e.g. Turretin, *Institutes*, vol. 1, pp. 253–308) and the influential medieval Catholic theologian Thomas Aquinas (Thomas Aquinas, *Summa Theologiae*, vols. 6–7 [London: Eyre & Spottiswoode, 1965], 1a, quests. 27–43).

## 2. 'Penal substitution relies on an unbiblical view of an angry God that is incompatible with his love'

### Objection

Some object to the idea that God is angry at human sin, claiming this undermines the Bible's clear teaching that God loves his world. Penal substitution, which speaks both of God's love *and* his anger, is believed to distort the biblical picture of God.

Critiques of this kind are found frequently in both popular and academic literature. For example, Tom Smail takes issue with John Stott's statement that 'God took his own loving initiative to appease his own righteous anger by bearing it in his own self in his own Son when he took our place and died for us.'[18] According to Smail, God cannot be angry and loving towards the same people at the same time. Love and anger are 'contradictory' and 'conflicting':

> [Stott's view] suggests rather that what we have here is a juxtaposition of the two divine attributes of God's wrath and God's love, so that the God who is loving sends his Son to propitiate the God who is wrathful, but how these two contradictory attributes cohere in the same divine nature is left undefined . . .
>
> Stott affirms a readjustment of attributes within God that makes his new relationship to us possible, but gives no account of how that readjustment of attributes relates to the unchanging character of God.[19]

And again, 'On the face of it the statement about God's self-propitiation is not very coherent or self-explanatory. It seems to suggest that the atonement is concerned with a manipulation of conflicting internal attributes of the divine nature in order to enable him to forgive and accept us.'[20]

Steve Chalke and Alan Mann suggest wrath is not really fundamental to God's character in the way love is. Everything about him must be viewed through the 'primary lens' of his love:

> The Bible never defines God as anger, power or judgement – in fact it never defines him as anything other than love. But more than that, it never makes assertions about his anger, power or judgement independently of his love . . .

---

18. Stott, *Cross of Christ*, p. 175; cited in Smail, *Once and for All*, p. 87.
19. Smail, *Once and for All*, p. 87.
20. Ibid., p. 88.

The fact is, however else God may have revealed himself, and in whatever way he interacts with the world he has created, everything is to be tempered, interpreted, understood and seen through the one, primary lens of God's love. We should never speak of any other attribute of God outside of the context of his love. To do so is to risk a terrible misrepresentation of his character, which in turn leads to a distortion of the gospel. Christian talk about God must always start with love and introduce the language of power only in that context.[21]

Green and Baker distance themselves from the idea of God being angry by suggesting that such language in the Bible is not to be taken literally:

Old Testament scholars today continue to debate in what sense it is appropriate to attribute anger to God in any way other than metaphorical. That is, given our limited vantage point as human beings (and so the human perspective from which the books of the Old Testament were written), perhaps we attribute 'anger' to God only because we have no language other than human language with which to comprehend God.[22]

In summary, these criticisms threaten to undermine the doctrine of penal substitution by challenging the idea that God is personally angry at human sin, particularly on the grounds that this would contradict what the Bible says about his love.

### Response

Let us affirm at the outset the glorious truth that God loves sinners. Indeed, the cross is the supreme manifestation of this: 'God demonstrates his own love for us in this: While we were still sinners, Christ died for us' (Rom. 5:8); 'This is love: not that we loved God, but that he loved us and sent his Son as an atoning sacrifice for our sins' (1 John 4:10). The apostle Paul, who saw himself as 'the worst of sinners' (1 Tim. 1:16; cf. 1 Cor. 15:9), nonetheless declared that Christ 'loved me and gave himself for me' (Gal. 2:20).

The love of God for sinful people is celebrated in what is probably the most famous verse in the Bible: 'God so loved the world that he gave his one and only Son, that whoever believes in him shall not perish but have eternal life' (John 3:16). In John's writing, the term 'world' carries negative connotations:

---

21. Steve Chalke and Alan Mann, *The Lost Message of Jesus* (Grand Rapids: Zondervan, 2003), p. 63.

22. Green and Baker, *Recovering the Scandal*, pp. 53–54.

it denotes not merely the created order, but the created order specifically in its rebellion against God (cf. John 7:7; 14:17). Therefore, as D. A. Carson notes, 'when John tells us that God loves the world (3:16), far from being an endorsement of the world, it is a testimony to the character of God. God's love is to be admired not because the world is so big but because the world is so bad.'[23] With good reason the apostle John declares that 'God is love' (1 John 4:8, 16).

Tom Smail is therefore right in his assertion 'that God's prior love for the world is the source and not the consequence of Christ's atoning death.'[24] The texts cited above establish that it was love that *motivated* God to send his Son to die; love was not somehow spontaneously generated by the atonement. Yet we would be wrong to conclude that 'prior love' precludes 'prior wrath'. Many biblical texts set both alongside each other. Only a few verses after John 3:16 we are warned that 'whoever rejects the Son will not see life, for God's wrath *remains* on him' (v. 36; italics added). The same world God loves is simultaneously under his wrath. Similarly, Ephesians 2:4 speaks of God's 'great love for us', and the preceding verse defines the 'us' as those who 'were by nature objects of wrath'.

God's love for the world is rarely denied: it is his wrath that many opponents of penal substitution wish to remove from the picture. But the testimony of Scripture is so clear that the task is impossible. We have surveyed some of the biblical teaching on God's wrath already in chapter 3. The Bible's many graphic warnings of final judgment are not restricted to the Old Testament, but occur also in the writings of the apostles and on the lips of Jesus himself. Garry Williams notes a number of examples from 'the parables when Jesus speaks of the Last Day'[25] in his contribution to *Where Wrath and Mercy Meet*:

> In Matthew 7:21–3 he warns that he will declare to some who profess his Lordship and claim to have worked in his name, 'I never knew you; go away from me, you evildoers' (v. 23). At the end of the parable of the wedding banquet he describes how the man caught without a wedding garment is thrown out of the banquet into 'outer darkness, where there will be weeping and gnashing of teeth' (Mt. 22:13). Similarly, the bridesmaids who are unprepared for the arrival of the bridegroom are shut out

23. D. A. Carson, *The Gospel According to John*, Pillar New Testament Commentary (Leicester: Apollos; Grand Rapids: Eerdmans, 1991), p. 123; see also p. 205.

24. Smail, *Once and for All*, p. 85.

25. Garry J. Williams, 'The Cross and the Punishment of Sin', in David Peterson (ed.), *Where Wrath and Mercy Meet: Proclaiming the Atonement Today* (Carlisle: Paternoster, 2001), pp. 68–99 (p. 90).

from the wedding banquet because they are unknown to the Lord (Mt. 25:1–13); the wicked slave who buried his talent in the ground is thrown 'into the outer darkness, where there will be weeping and gnashing of teeth' (25:30); and the accursed in the parable of the sheep and the goats are to 'go away' . . . into eternal punishment (25:46). Luke records that when Jesus spoke of the heavenly banquet he warned that many would try to enter and would fail, being instead told by the owner of the house, 'I do not know where you have come from; go away from me, all you evildoers!' (Lk. 13:27).[26]

Although it is uncomfortable to reflect on this subject, it is necessary, and the conclusion inescapable. These texts, and those considered in chapter 2, demonstrate that human sin provokes God's wrath. He is not merely angry at 'sin' in an abstract, impersonal sense, as if sin could be detached from its perpetrators; it is towards *sinners* that his wrath is directed.[27] It is certainly not a problem that penal substitution makes much of this; on the contrary, it is one of the doctrine's great strengths. Alone among theologies of the cross, penal substitution makes sense of this biblical theme and offers a solution equal to the problem. To construct a doctrine of the atonement without taking account of the fact that God is angry would be like building an aeroplane without reference to the fact of gravity. The biblical writers do not make this error. They recognize that the Lord Jesus who died and rose again is he 'who rescues us from the coming wrath' (1 Thess. 1:10).

A careful study of the Bible's teaching also silences the 'debate' alluded to by Joel Green and Mark Baker over whether 'it is appropriate to attribute anger to God in any way other than metaphorical'.[28] Behind this is a broader question about whether the transcendent God can ever be adequately described within the limitations of human language. Is not our understanding of words themselves governed by our finite human experience of the things they denote? Can we understand anything of God who is so beyond our experience? For example, our idea of 'light' is bound up with the fact that we have a retina connected to an optic nerve that carries electrical impulses to our brain. But God is spirit: he has no retina or optic nerve. So what does it mean to say that 'God is light'? To take an example more pertinent to the issue at hand, what would it mean to be 'angry' apart from the tension in our limbs, the quickened pulse and the specifically *human* emotions we associate with that word?

---

26. Ibid., pp. 68–99 (pp. 90–91).

27. D. A. Carson, *The Difficult Doctrine of the Love of God* (Leicester: IVP, 2000), p. 79.

28. Green and Baker, *Recovering the Scandal*, pp. 53–54.

Does God's anger have anything to do with that? Is it even analogous? What, for that matter, does it mean for God to love? Is that just a metaphor too?

The Bible does not contain merely human ideas about God; it speaks God's words about himself (e.g. 2 Tim. 3:16; 2 Pet. 1:21). God has 'accommodated' himself to human language, revealing divine truths in human terms, yet there is nothing about this process that constitutes an intrinsic barrier to under-standing.[29] Having said that, we need to take care to understand the words of Scripture correctly; we do this by looking at how they are used in their con-texts.[30] It is plain from biblical usage that the language of God's wrath refers to his personal hostility to evil, his kingly indignation at rebellion and sin. As such it is a corollary of his holiness and his Lordship. But above all, Scripture proves that God's anger is real because it often provokes him to action. The wrath of God can be no more 'metaphorical' than the mighty acts of judg-ment that flowed from it (e.g. Num. 25:1–5; 2 Sam. 6:7; 2 Kgs 24:20).[31]

We return now to Tom Smail's assertion that the love of God and the wrath of God are 'contradictory attributes'[32] and his complaint that proponents of penal substitution fail to explain how the two can 'cohere in the same divine nature'.[33] Problematically for Smail, the Bible affirms both, as we have seen. It is completely unsatisfactory to deny one or the other, and to reject the possi-bility of their coexistence is tantamount to saying the Bible contradicts itself. Nonetheless, it is still reasonable to ask exactly *how* God can be both angry and loving at the same time.

---

29. John Calvin often spoke about God's accommodating himself to our understanding (Calvin, *Institutes*, vol. 1, I.xiii.1, p. 121; II.xvi.2, p. 504; vol. 2, III.xxiv.9, p. 976; IV.i.8, p. 1022). See also Frame, *Doctrine of God*, p. 367; Herman Bavinck, *The Doctrine of God*, trans. W. Hendricksen (Edinburgh: Banner of Truth, 1977), pp. 85–88. We discuss in chapter 3 the significance of God's revelation of himself as the basis for our knowledge of him.

30. The same is true of any piece of literature: the meaning of words is ultimately determined by how they are used. See Moisés Silva, *Biblical Words and their Meaning: An Introduction to Lexical Semantics*, rev. edn (Grand Rapids: Zondervan, 1994), especially pp. 138–148.

31. For some helpful comments on the biblical use of metaphors and anthropomorphisms see John M. Frame, *The Doctrine of the Knowledge of God* (Phillipsburg: Presbyterian & Reformed, 1987), pp. 226–232; *Doctrine of God*, pp. 366–368.

32. Smail, *Once and for All*, p. 87.

33. Ibid. He is referring explicitly to Stott's articulation of the doctrine.

At the outset we must recognize that both God's anger and his love are different from ours. Perhaps we struggle to believe the two could coexist, simply because our human versions of these qualities are frequently irreconcilable. John Stott highlights the differences between God's wrath and ours with characteristic precision:

> God's wrath in the words of Leon Morris is his 'personal divine revulsion to evil' and his 'personal vigorous opposition' to it. To speak thus of God's anger is a legitimate anthropomorphism, provided that we recognize it as no more than a rough and ready parallel, since God's anger is absolutely pure, and uncontaminated by those elements which render human anger sinful. Human anger is usually arbitrary and uninhibited; divine anger is always principled and controlled. Our anger tends to be a spasmodic outburst, aroused by pique and seeking revenge; God's is a continuous, settled antagonism, aroused only by evil, and expressed in its condemnation.[34]

Similarly, God's love is very unlike ours. Human love depends on the perceived loveliness of its object, and fluctuates with our mood. God's love, by contrast, is shown towards the unlovely, and like God himself, it does not change. We speak of human love in different ways – a man's love for his wife, a child's love of ice cream, a sister's love for her brother. Similarly, the Bible speaks about God's love in several distinct ways. D. A. Carson draws attention to five:

1. The peculiar love of the Father for the Son, and of the Son for the Father.
2. God's providential love over all that he has made.
3. God's salvific stance toward his fallen world.
4. God's particular, effective, selecting love toward his elect.
5. Finally, God's love is sometimes said to be directed toward his own people in a provisional or conditional way – conditional, that is, on obedience.[35]

One does not have to agree with all the details of Carson's analysis here to appreciate the general point: God loves in ways foreign to our experience.

---

34. Stott, *Cross of Christ*, pp. 105–106, quoting Leon Morris, *The Cross in the New Testament* (Exeter: Paternoster, 1965), pp. 190–191.

35. Carson, *Love of God*, pp. 17–21. In addition to distinguishing these five biblical uses, Carson warns of the danger of imbibing the sentimentalism of our culture, and letting this, rather than the Scriptures, colour our definition of the love of God (pp. 9–17).

None of us can love in sense 1, for we are not trinitarian beings. Nor can we love in sense 2, for we neither created the world nor do we sustain it in existence. This does not mean God's love is unintelligible, for there is *some* overlap with the love we have for each other as human beings. Nevertheless, some differences remain. We cannot determine whether it is right or wrong for God to be angry with those whom he loves in the senses above simply by appealing to our own love relationships. To ask, for example, whether God's pouring out his wrath on his own Son violates love in sense 1 requires an understanding of the workings of the Trinity – we cannot hope to discover the answer within ourselves. Instead we must turn to Scripture (we consider that particular case in chapter 11, section 1).

A recognition of the fact that God loves different people in different ways goes some way to addressing Smail's concern that penal substitution implies a 'readjustment of attributes' in God when we first turn to Christ and are forgiven.[36] This is not quite correct. Penal substitution affirms that, on conversion, our status changes from rebellious outsiders to adopted children, and as a result we enter into an experience of God's *fatherly* love we did not know before (1 John 3:1). But the change occurs in us, not in God.[37] Moreover, there is no need to deny he loved us in a different sense prior to our conversion – as his creatures, and as his chosen people whom he intended to bring to faith.

Carson points out that misunderstandings about God's character sometimes arise because we consider his attributes in isolation. In particular, we have a tendency to think about God's love in isolation from his holiness, his sovereignty and his righteousness. This is a serious error. All of God's attributes are consistent with each other: his love is always holy, his holiness is always loving, and so on.[38]

Chalke and Mann misconstrue this interrelatedness when they insist that 'however else God may have revealed himself ... everything is to be

---

36. Smail, *Once and for All*, p. 87.

37. Similarly, penal substitution does not teach that a fundamental change occurs in God with respect to his holiness and justice, from which arise his wrath at sin. His justice was satisfied, but that does not make him less just. His wrath was propitiated, but that does not make him less holy. Jesus' self-sacrifice did not convert God into someone now less concerned about punishing sin. He is just as concerned that justice should be done; the difference is that he can gaze on the cross and see it has been. Penal substitution does not imply a change in God's attributes, but rather upholds their immutability.

38. See Carson, *Love of God*, especially pp. 11–14, 51–84.

tempered, interpreted, understood and seen through the *one, primary lens of God's love*.[39] This is problematic, for the primary lens readily becomes a filter that lets only certain things through. Even if God's holiness and righteousness (from which arise his wrath at sin) are allowed a place, they are seen as less important than love, or subordinate to it; the impression is given that love might somehow 'cancel out' or 'overrule' the other attributes. This will not do. God's attributes cannot be pitted against one another, neither ought one to be elevated above the others to a 'primary' position. All of God's attributes have equal significance in determining his actions. He always acts in conformity with the *whole* of his character.[40] Chalke and Mann's other significant claim, that 'The Bible . . . never makes assertions about [God's] anger, power or judgement independently of his love',[41] is plainly false, as the biblical texts cited in chapter 3 amply demonstrate. Terrifying though these texts are, they cannot be ignored. A. T. B. McGowan is quite right that Chalke and Mann do 'not attempt to justify this statement exegetically'.[42]

Having warned against drawing too close an analogy between God's love and wrath and that of human beings, it is instructive in closing to note that in certain circumstances even humans can combine both of those attributes in the same person at the same time. It is quite possible for a parent to feel angry towards a stubborn child who persists in misbehaving, without his or her love for the child ever ceasing.[43] Yet this point must not be pressed too far. Tragically some parents neglect to love their children, and others are angry with them unjustifiably. Nor is God's wrath towards humanity analogous to a parent's displeasure towards his or her child, for the judgments of hell are more than parental discipline, and God does not view unbelievers as his children. It is clear that love and anger are not always mutually exclusive in human experience, but even if they were, this would still not rule out their compatibility within the *divine* nature.

As we reach the end of this section, let us gather the threads together. We have seen that the Bible clearly teaches both that God loves his world and that

---

39. Chalke and Mann, *Lost Message of Jesus*, p. 63; italics added.

40. See Frame, *Doctrine of God*, pp. 387–401. See also A. T. B. McGowan, 'The Atonement as Penal Substitution', in A. T. B. McGowan (ed.), *Always Reforming: Explorations in Systematic Theology* (Leicester: IVP, 2006), pp. 183–210 (pp. 201–204), for a further critique of related aspects of Steve Chalke and Alan Mann's views.

41. Chalke and Mann, *Lost Message of Jesus*, p. 63.

42. McGowan, 'Atonement as Penal Substitution', p. 202.

43. For further discussion on this subject see Carson, *Love of God*, pp. 75–84.

he is angered by sin. We have seen that this 'wrath' cannot be regarded as merely metaphorical, for on occasion it provokes God to *act* in a wrathful way. Our inability to see how love and wrath cohere may be testimony simply to the fact that God is not like us; too quickly we argue from our own experience. In the Scriptures it is plain that the two can go together, just as the divine attributes of holiness, righteousness and love are perfectly consonant, none being privileged above another. It is a mistake to reject the idea that a loving God can be angry, and therefore it is wrong to reject penal substitution on the same grounds.

### 3. 'Penal substitution misunderstands the relationship between God's wrath and human sin'

#### Objection

Advocates of penal substitution claim that sin makes God angry, and for that reason he is determined to punish it. In the previous section we considered the objection that this teaching contradicts God's love. Here we respond to a different line of attack. Some argue it is incorrect to say that sin *arouses* God's wrath and *provokes* his judgment. Rather, our acts of wickedness, together with the negative consequences intrinsic to them (e.g. the feeling of emptiness that might result from promiscuous sexual activity outside marriage), *are themselves* God's judgment on sinful humanity, a manifestation of his wrath.

Joel Green and Mark Baker are among the writers who argue this way. They appeal to Romans 1:18–32 in support:

> Paul [shows] the progression from (1) the human refusal to honor God, with its consequent denial of the human vocation to live in relation to God; to (2) God's giving humanity over to its own desires – giving humanity, as it were, the life it sought apart from God; and from this to (3) human acts of wickedness – which do not arouse the wrath of God but are themselves already the consequences of its active presence.[44]

They continue, emphasizing that God does not *respond* in wrath to our sinful deeds:

> To put it pointedly, here Paul has nothing to do with an emotion-laden God who strikes out in frustration or vengeance against we who are implicated in sin. Sinful

---

44. Green and Baker, *Recovering the Scandal*, p. 55.

activity is the result of God's letting us go our own way – and this 'letting us go our own way' constitutes God's wrath. In Paul's own words, the wrath of God is revealed in God's giving humanity over to their lusts, over to their degrading passions and over to their debasement of mind (Rom 1:18, 24, 26, 28) . . . *Our sinful acts do not invite God's wrath but prove that God's wrath is already active.*[45]

Stephen Travis goes further. Claiming to build on the work of W. H. Moberly, he believes it fundamental to retribution that punishment be 'inflicted from outside'.[46] He further contends that 'God does not impose punishment retributively from outside, but allows men to experience the consequences of their refusal to live in relation to him.'[47] Accordingly, the natural consequences of sin, being intrinsic to the act itself, cannot be retributive. God is not active in punishment.

Paul Fiddes defines God's wrath as 'his active consent to the working out of . . . sin into its inevitable results',[48] insisting 'it is this Old Testament insight that the apostle Paul takes up in his portrayal of the wrath of God' in Romans chapter 1.[49] He agrees with Green, Baker and Travis that 'judgement is not a penalty imposed from *outside* human life, but a natural consequence flowing from the sin itself'.[50] He differs from them in his emphasis that God 'consents' to this 'in an *active* and personal way'.[51]

---

45. Ibid.; italics original.
46. Stephen H. Travis, *Christ and the Judgment of God: Divine Retribution in the New Testament* (Basingstoke: Marshall, Morgan & Scott, 1986), p. 3, summarizing W. H. Moberly, *The Ethics of Punishment* (London: Faber & Faber, 1968), p. 35. However, he seems not to have read Moberly with sufficient care, since Moberly concedes the possibility that a 'superhuman personal agency' (e.g. God) could 'deliberately' bring about the natural consequences of sin, in such a way that even these intrinsic consequences would be retributive (Moberly, *Ethics of Punishment*, pp. 35–36). This oversight has very serious implications for the whole of Travis's thesis (see Garry J. Williams, 'Justice, Law, and Guilt: A Paper Given at the Evangelical Alliance Symposium on Penal Substitution' [2005], http://www.eauk.org/theology/atonement/upload/garry_williams.pdf [accessed 27 March 2006], pp. 3–5).
47. Travis, *Christ and the Judgment of God*, p. 38. See also pp. 6, 39, 53.
48. Fiddes, *Past Event and Present Salvation*, p. 92.
49. Ibid., p. 93.
50. Ibid.; italics added.
51. Ibid.; italics original.

According to Fiddes, it is true to say that Christ died under the 'wrath' of God, but only in the sense that he entered into and shared the human experience of suffering the natural consequences of sin in human life. No penalty was *transferred* to Christ, paid by him in our place:

> Paul certainly has a view of the 'penal suffering' of Christ, since Christ is identified with the human situation of being under the divine penalty (understood as God's consent to the natural consequence of human sins). It would also not be entirely out of place to say that Paul conceives of Christ as a 'substitute' as well as a representative for humankind, since no human being need die the kind of death that Christ died. But these two factors do not in themselves amount to a theory of 'penal substitution', according to which atonement is achieved through a *transfer* of penalty.[52]

Or again:

> When the judgement of God is understood as his personal consent to the natural outworking of people's estrangement from God and each other, then we can think of Christ as participating in our experience of being 'accursed' without any suggestion that the Father is punishing the Son on our behalf.[53]

In summary, these criticisms challenge the idea that God's anger is provoked by human sin, and that he responds in judgment by imposing a penalty from 'outside'; rather, his anger and punishment consist *only* in the 'natural outworking' of sin in human life as he allows us to go our own way.[54]

### Response

These critics are right to affirm that God uses the natural processes of human life to judge human sin. Romans 1:18–32 teaches exactly this, as they point out. However, each of the above critics seriously misunderstands the Bible's teaching at other points.

---

52. Ibid., p. 98; italics original; see also pp. 93–99.
53. Ibid., p. 104.
54. The view that God's wrath consists only in the natural outworking of human sin is sometimes called an 'immanentist' view, in contrast to a 'transcendant' understanding, where God's active involvement is emphasized. We discuss this issue specifically in relation to the exegesis of Romans in chapter 2.

First, Green and Baker's assertion that 'our sinful acts do not invite God's wrath but prove that God's wrath is already active'[55] is unsustainable in the face of biblical texts such as Colossians 3:5–6: 'put to death . . . whatever belongs to your earthly nature: sexual immorality, impurity, lust, evil desires and greed, which is idolatry. *Because of these, the wrath of God is coming*' (italics added; see also Eph. 5:5–6). Strikingly, this list of sins that provoke God's wrath includes precisely those misdemeanours to which Romans 1 says God, in his wrath, has handed people over. The problem with Green and Baker's statement, therefore, is not what it affirms, but what it denies. It is true that the very existence of these sinful acts is a manifestation of God's wrath, as he 'takes the brakes off' and leaves us to the consequences of our rebellion against him. Yet it is also true that the resultant sins provoke his wrath further.[56] This is clearest of all from the Bible's teaching about a *future* 'day of God's wrath, when his righteous judgment will be revealed' (Rom. 2:5). It seems surprising that Green, Baker and Fiddes ignore this, given that it comes in the same letter as the text on which they build so much (Rom. 1:18–32), and only a few verses later.[57] In addition, numerous other New Testament passages pick up the Old Testament theme of the 'Day of the Lord' to teach of a future Day of Judgment (e.g. 1 Thess. 5:2–3; 2 Thess. 2:2; 2 Pet. 3:4–10).

Secondly, the strong dichotomy at the heart of Travis's thesis, between a punishment imposed by God from 'outside' normal human experience on the one hand, and the painful consequences of sin in the 'natural' processes of human life on the other, will not stand. The Bible refuses to draw such a sharp distinction between natural and supernatural, for it is God who sustains and upholds the creation at every moment of its existence.[58] God's hand is no less

---

55. Green and Baker, *Recovering the Scandal*, p. 55; original quote in italics.

56. D. A. Carson observed at the eleventh Edinburgh Dogmatics Conference (2005) that the book of Habbakuk would make no sense otherwise. The prophet, observing the injustice of Israelite society (1:3), protests that God has not yet responded as he ought. God replies that he will certainly act in judgment in the future (2:4–20). In other words, God agrees with Habakkuk that merely to hand society over to its degradation is by itself an insufficient response to human sin.

57. These authors do not explicitly deny that there will be a future day of judgment; instead, they imply that our present human experience constitutes the whole of God's judgment, leaving no room for anything else (see e.g. Fiddes, *Past Event and Present Salvation*, pp. 92–96; Green and Baker, *Recovering the Scandal*, p. 55).

58. See e.g. John M. Frame, *No Other God* (Phillipsburg: Presbyterian & Reformed, 2001), pp. 57–87.

to be discerned in the fact that lilies have petals (Matt. 6:28–30) or that sparrows die (Matt. 10:29) than in a one-off disturbance of the forces of nature such as the sun standing still for a whole day (Josh. 10:13). The same applies to cases of retribution. Ahab was killed by a stray arrow in a battle in which he chose, ill-advisedly, to take part (1 Kgs 22:34–37), and the context (especially v. 23) makes it clear that this was no less God's doing than the more obviously supernatural death of Herod, struck down by an angel of the Lord for accepting praise due to God alone (Acts 12:23). The painful 'natural' consequences of sin are just as much God's punishment as a penalty imposed from 'outside'.

Indeed, the Bible is filled with instances of God's actively judging sin, even if sometimes he works through secondary agencies or 'natural causes'. It was God who stood behind the plagues in Egypt by which the Israelites were liberated from slavery (Exod. 8:1–4, 19–21; 9:1–3, 13–18; 11:4–6; 12:29–30; see also Gen. 15:13–14). As Garry Williams notes, 'It wasn't just a good year for frogs, gnats, flies and locusts, let alone for the death of firstborn children';[59] rather, God worked decisively in human history to punish the tyrannical wickedness of Pharaoh and the Egyptians and to set his people free. On other occasions the Israelites themselves suffered God's judgment. It was God who stood behind their failure to enter the Promised Land under Moses (Ps. 95:7–11) and their defeat by the army of Ai when they finally entered under the leadership of Joshua (Josh. 7:1–12, especially vv. 1, 11–12). It was God who stood behind the numerous defeats of Israel at the hands of their enemies during the time of the Judges (Judg. 2:19–21; 3:7–8) and the numerous disasters in Israel and Judah during their decline under successive rebellious kings (1 Kgs 16:1–4; 2 Kgs 13:1–3). It was God who stood behind the destruction of the northern kingdom of Israel by Assyria (2 Kgs 17:1–23; especially vv. 1–2, 7, 18) and the final defeat and exile of the southern kingdom of Judah under the Babylonians (Jer. 30:14; 32:26–35; especially vv. 30–31; Ezra 5:12).

Moreover, God continues to stand behind the 'natural' legal processes of human society, for 'the authorities that exist have been established by God', and 'the one in authority . . . is God's servant, an agent of wrath to bring punishment on the evildoer' (Rom. 13:1, 3–4; see also 1 Pet. 2:13–14). Of course, not everyone at the time of the decline of the nation of Israel was quick to realize that God was behind it (Isa. 42:23–25), so perhaps we should not be surprised that some people fail to recognize God's sovereign control of history today. However, the Bible could hardly be clearer: in every case cited above,

---

59. Williams, 'Justice, Law, and Guilt', p. 4.

God's judgment takes the form of what we might call a 'natural' event, and yet God is acting deliberately, intentionally, to punish specific sins.

The attempts by Green, Baker and Travis to deny God's direct, personal, active involvement in the punishment of sin are really a reworking of C. H. Dodd's thesis that Paul uses the term '"the Wrath of God"... not to describe the attitude of God to man, but to describe an inevitable process of cause and effect in a moral universe'.[60] Under Dodd's leadership, the translators of the New English Bible (1961) rendered the Greek *hilastērion* (propitiation) and related words in 1 John 2:2, 4:10 and Romans 3:25 so as to obscure the point that God's anger is averted by Jesus' death.[61] Perhaps partly for this reason, Dodd's position attracted a wide following half a century ago. However, it has long since been refuted in numerous places; perhaps most notably by Leon Morris and Roger Nicole.[62] It is surprising that the many comprehensive answers to Dodd's thesis continue to be ignored in some quarters even today.

---

60. C. H. Dodd, *The Epistle of Paul to the Romans* (London: Hodder & Stoughton, 1932), p. 23. Dodd's thesis was pursued in greater detail by A. T. Hanson, *The Wrath of the Lamb* (London: SPCK, 1957). See also G. H. C. MacGregor, 'The Concept of the Wrath of God in the New Testament', *New Testament Studies* 7 (1960–61), pp. 101–109. Fiddes disavows Dodd's claim that the manifestation of God's wrath in human history is 'impersonal', but nonetheless retains the exclusive emphasis on natural process as opposed to divine intervention (Fiddes, *Past Event and Present Salvation*, p. 93).

61. Stott, *Cross of Christ*, p. 170.

62. Leon Morris, *The Apostolic Preaching of the Cross* (London: Tyndale, 1955), pp. 125–185; and *Cross in the New Testament*, pp. 189–192; Roger Nicole, 'C. H. Dodd and the Doctrine of Propitiation', *Westminster Theological Journal* 17 (1955), pp. 117–157; repr. in *Standing Forth: Collected Writings of Roger Nicole* (Fearn: Christian Focus, 2002), pp. 343–396. We summarize some of their arguments in chapter 2. See also Douglas J. Moo, *The Epistle to the Romans*, New International Commentary on the New Testament (Grand Rapids: Eerdmans, 1996), pp. 99–100; Peter T. O'Brien, *Colossians, Philemon*, Word Biblical Commentary (Nashville: Thomas Nelson, 1982), pp. 184–185; Stott, *Cross of Christ*, pp. 103–105; R. V. G. Tasker, *The Biblical Doctrine of the Wrath of God* (London: Tyndale, 1951); Leon Morris, *The Biblical Doctrine of Judgment* (London: Tyndale, 1960); Leon Morris, 'The Use of *hilaskesthai* etc. in Biblical Greek', *Expository Times* 62 (1951), pp. 227–233; Richard B. Gaffin, Jr., 'Atonement in the Pauline Corpus', in C. E. Hill and F. A. James III (eds.), *The Glory of the Atonement* (Downers Grove: IVP; Leicester: Apollos, 2004), pp. 140–162 (pp. 150–162).

Fiddes allows that God is 'actively' involved in bringing about the natural consequences of sin and that Christ experienced this 'divine penalty' during his life on earth; he denies that Christ was punished on our behalf. Yet if Christ was innocent of all sin, why did God the Father 'actively' allow him to suffer sin's penalty? Penal substitution upholds the justice of God, since it maintains that our sin was imputed to Christ by virtue of our union with him, and he was rightly punished for it (see chapter 10, sect. 1). But Fiddes denies penal substitution, so his position leads logically to two equally unpalatable options. Either God acted unjustly in 'actively' causing the innocent Lord Jesus Christ to share in penal suffering, or Christ must himself have committed some sin to justify this penalty. Both of these conclusions are plainly unbiblical.

In summary, the different facets of this objection display serious misunderstandings of the biblical teaching about God's wrath.


## 4. 'Penal substitution generates an unbiblical view of a God constrained by a law external to himself'

### Objection

Some think that penal substitution depicts God in a quandary: he longs to have fellowship with sinful people, and would be perfectly happy to forgive us freely and completely, but is forced to punish our sins by a 'law' or 'standard of justice' outside himself, over which he has no control. Penal substitution, it is claimed, implies that God the Father's hand is forced. He would be glad simply to forgive and forget, but the 'law' must be obeyed, justice must be done, and so he reluctantly punishes his Son in our place.

Joel Green and Mark Baker put it this way: 'In penal substitutionary approaches to the atonement, there is a certain sense of God's doing something he would rather not do, kill his son, but which he does do because a certain standard of justice demands he do so.'[63]

They make the same point in their criticism of Charles Hodge's exposition of penal substitution:

> Within a penal substitution model, God's ability to love and relate to humans is circumscribed by something outside of God – that is, an abstract concept of justice instructs God as to how God must behave. It could be said that Hodge presents a God who wants to be in relationship with us but is forced to deal with a problem of

---

63. Green and Baker, *Recovering the Scandal*, p. 169.

legal bookkeeping that blocks that relationship. The solution is having God the Father punish God the Son.[64]

Paul Fiddes uses Jesus' parable of the Prodigal Son (Luke 15) to bolster this objection. According to Fiddes, 'The loving father in Jesus' story is satisfied by the return of the erring son, and refuses to accept that there is any debt outstanding against him.'[65] By contrast, Fiddes likens advocates of penal substitution to 'the elder brother' in the parable, who 'wants to set a principle of retribution and compensation over the mercy of the father'.[66] Such a principle or law is then imposed upon God against his will: 'As a God of love he desires to have fellowship with his creatures, but law apparently demands that certain conditions be satisfied first.'[67] In Fiddes' view, this cannot be right, for God is under no obligation to anything outside himself: 'If God's free will is in fact the final factor, then he is also free to dispense with a satisfaction altogether.'[68]

The essence of the objection is the same in each case: according to penal substitution, the reason why God punished his Son is that he was under obligation to obey an external standard of justice, even when he would rather not do so, and this is unbiblical.

### Response

We agree with the critics that to imagine God constrained by any authority outside himself, whether a law, a standard of justice, or anything else, would be wrong. However, those who think the doctrine of penal substitution implies this have failed to understand it. The standard of justice on which basis Christ was punished in our place is not external to God, but *intrinsic* to him; it is a reflection of his own righteous, holy character. This is apparent from the giving of the law at Sinai. Immediately before Moses received the Ten Commandments, the Lord said to him, 'Now if you obey me fully and keep my covenant, then out of all nations you will be my treasured possession. Although the whole earth is mine, you will be for me a kingdom of priests and *a holy nation*' (Exod. 19:5–6; italics added).

---

64. Ibid., p. 147, referring to Charles Hodge, *Systematic Theology*, vol. 2 (London: James Clarke, 1960), ch. 7.

65. Fiddes, *Past Event and Present Salvation*, p. 101.

66. Ibid.

67. Ibid., p. 102.

68. Ibid.

In this context, the commandments that follow are to be understood as Israel's way of fulfilling their vocation to be the Lord's 'holy nation'.[69] But this 'holiness' is not to be understood as an abstract concept, external to God's own character. On the contrary, as the book of Leviticus frequently emphasizes, this holiness is a reflection of the Lord's own perfect holiness: 'be holy, *because I am holy*' (Lev. 11:44–45; italics added; see also 19:2; 20:26 and the related formulations in 20:7–8; 21:8, 15, 23; 22:2, 9, 16, 32).[70] Again, Exodus 19:5–6 makes plain that what is required is obedience to God himself ('if you obey *me* fully'; italics added) by means of the commandments, not obedience to the commandments for their own sake apart from God. 1 Peter 1:14 picks up both of these motifs, showing that they apply no less to Christians in the New Testament era. We are to be holy as the one who called us is holy (v. 15), and thereby to show our obedience as children of our heavenly Father (v. 14). God's law, then, is not external to him, but intrinsic, reflecting his own perfect righteousness and holiness. To obey God's law is to obey God.

The converse is also true. Disobedience to the law is disobedience to God himself. Sin is not a transgression of an abstract moral code: it is an affront to God's holy character. Moreover, when God punishes sin, he is not reluctantly conforming to the dictates of an arbitrary set of regulations that he would rather ignore: he is acting in conformity with his own justice and righteousness. Nowhere is this more obvious than in Romans 3:25–26, where Paul describes what God was doing when Christ suffered in our place. Christ did

---

69. Several commentators have rightly pointed out that the 'covenant' of which the Lord speaks in Exod. 19:5 refers to the covenant previously established by God with Abraham (Gen. 12:1–3; 15:18; 17:1–14), and not to the institution of an entirely new covenant. However, this does not undermine our point here, for the Mosaic laws are incorporated into this pre-existing covenant between the Lord and his people, and serve as the ethical standard for Israel after their encounter with the Lord at Sinai (W. J. Dumbrell, *Covenant and Creation: A Theology of the Old Testament Covenants* [Carlisle: Paternoster, 1984], pp. 80–90; Peter Enns, *Exodus*, New International Version Application Commentary [Grand Rapids: Zondervan, 2000], pp. 387–389; T. Fretheim, *Exodus*, Interpretation [Louisville: John Knox, 1991], pp. 208–212).

70. According to Gordon Wenham, this important phrase 'could be termed the motto of Leviticus' (Gordon J. Wenham, *The Book of Leviticus*, New International Commentary on the Old Testament [Grand Rapids: Eerdmans, 1979], p. 18; see also pp. 180–181).

not die in order to satisfy an external standard of justice, but rather to demonstrate *God's* justice – that is, the perfect righteousness of his own character:

> God presented him as a sacrifice of atonement, through faith in his blood. He did
> this to demonstrate *his justice*, because in his forbearance he had left the sins
> committed beforehand unpunished – he did it to demonstrate *his justice* at the present
> time, so as to be just and the one who justifies those who have faith in Jesus. (Rom.
> 3:25–26; italics added)

In summary, penal substitution does not imply that 'an abstract concept of justice instructs God as to how God must behave',[71] requiring him to do 'something he would rather not do, kill his son',[72] Rather, penal substitution reflects the Bible's teaching that God's law is the expression of his own righteous, holy character, and that it was in accordance with this law that Christ was punished in our place.[73]

## 5. 'Penal substitution is an impersonal, mechanistic account of the atonement'

### Objection

This criticism is similar to the previous one, though there is a slight difference. Whereas the former objected that penal substitution depicts God as *constrained* by a law external to himself, this one claims that penal substitution *excludes* God from the picture altogether. It is said to portray the atonement as a mechanistic

---

71. Green and Baker, *Recovering the Scandal*, p. 147.

72. Ibid., p. 169.

73. Garry Williams offers a similar reply to this objection, in which he also draws
   attention to an important difference between God's role as judge and the role of
   human judges in human courts (Williams, 'Cross and the Punishment of Sin',
   pp. 85–87). He points out that it would be wrong for human judges to be
   personally concerned in the laws they administer: 'the judge should sever himself
   from personal interest in the process of law' (p. 86), for personal interest from a
   human judge could lead to partiality and injustice. By contrast, it is right for
   God to be intimately and personally involved in the administration of his justice,
   precisely because it is his justice, and he is the ultimate standard of right and
   wrong.

process, where the relationship between God and humanity is sidelined, and attention is focused on impersonal categories of justice, law, sin, guilt, wrath and satisfaction as if they were nothing more than elements in a mathematical equation. This is unacceptable, for the Bible presents atonement in personal categories, focusing upon how the relationship between humanity and God can be restored.[74]

Paul Fiddes sets out the objection thus:

> All that seems to be needed in some accounts is a bare death, in order to provide
> a divine solution to the problem of human sin. Some preaching thus reduces
> the event of the cross to a factor in an equation, formulated by a divine mathematician;
> a death is needed to balance the cosmic sum, and a death is provided . . .
>
>   When the death of Jesus is presented as a legal device for satisfying a divine justice
> which has been affronted by human sin, this can easily reduce the doctrine of
> atonement to a mere formula.[75]

The Doctrine Commission of the Church of England reached a similar conclusion in their 1995 report *The Mystery of Salvation*. They criticize not just penal substitution but all juridical understandings of the atonement; that is, those where 'the model employed is provided by legal concepts'.[76] In saying this, they depart from the historic position of their denomination as expressed in *The Thirty-Nine Articles* and *The Book of Common Prayer*. The Doctrine Commission claims that 'juridical theories of the atonement have often pictured God's law, God's wrath, and human sin and guilt not as aspects of the relation between God and humanity, but as though they were actual objects or things that had somehow to be dealt with'.[77]

In short, this objection claims that penal substitution is impersonal and mechanistic, whereas the Bible depicts sin and atonement in personal, relational terms.

---

74. The outline of this objection and the response to it are indebted to Williams, 'Cross and the Punishment of Sin', pp. 81–98.

75. Fiddes, *Past Event and Present Salvation*, pp. 83–84.

76. The Doctrine Commission of the Church of England, *The Mystery of Salvation* (London: Church House, 1995), p. 210. This report also contains several of the other criticisms of penal substitution we address.

77. Ibid., p. 211.

## Response

Such is the overlap of this objection with the previous one that some of the same responses are appropriate. In particular, it is simply not true that penal substitution construes law and sin as impersonal 'objects or things that somehow had to be dealt with'.[78] For the law under which sinful human beings stand condemned before God is no abstract legal code: it is a reflection of God's perfect justice. Human sin is no mere transgression of a set of impersonal moral dictates: it is an affront to God's holiness. Penal substitution does not depict the death of the Lord Jesus as 'a factor in an equation . . . needed to balance the cosmic sum',[79] but as the loving and costly action of God in human history, to suffer in himself the personal outpouring of his own wrath at our sin.

It is worth reflecting more on penal substitution's insistence that sin must be punished, for it is often here that the charge of being impersonal or mechanistic is directed. In fact, the Bible consistently portrays God's anger at sin, and his judicial response to it, in unmistakeably personal terms. Garry Williams cites several Old Testament texts, including Psalm 66:3, Isaiah 2:10, 19–21, 6:5 and Jeremiah 4:26, to 'show that it is in a personal confrontation with God himself that sin is punished'.[80] Turning to the New Testament, he cites Revelation 6:12–17, which depicts the final judgment as a time when people will cry out 'to the mountains and the rocks, "Fall on us and hide us from the face of him who sits on the throne and from the wrath of the Lamb! For the great day of their wrath has come, and who can stand?"' (Rev. 6:16–17; cf. 14:9–10; Luke 23:28–30). Williams is surely correct that 'we must speak of the terrible *presence* of God and the Lamb appearing to judge the world'.[81]

Of course, it is true that the Bible sometimes describes punishment as *exclusion* from God's presence; for example, in the expulsion of Adam and Eve from Eden in Genesis 3, or Jesus' description of the separation that will take place on Judgment Day (e.g. Matt. 7:23; 22:13; 25:10, 30, 41, 46).[82] At first

---

78. Ibid.

79. Fiddes, *Past Event and Present Salvation*, pp. 83.

80. Williams, 'Cross and the Punishment of Sin', p. 88.

81. Ibid., p. 89; italics added.

82. It may be a mistranslation of 2 Thess. 1:9 to say that God's enemies will be 'punished with everlasting destruction and shut out from the presence of the Lord and from the majesty of his power' (NIV). The original Greek says only that the everlasting destruction will be 'from' (*apo*) the face of the Lord, which may refer to God's presence as the source of the punishment (see Charles Quarles, 'The 'APO

glance this may appear to point towards a more impersonal view of punishment – if the sentence is enacted somewhere where God is not, how can he
be directly involved? However, we cannot just sweep aside those texts cited
above that speak of punishment *in* the presence of God. Instead, exclusion
from God's presence should be understood in a qualified sense to refer to
exclusion from his loving fellowship and blessing. This not only reconciles the
two groups of biblical texts, but it also rescues us from theological nonsense,
for otherwise we would have to posit a place of punishment that did not
depend on God's sustaining work for its ongoing existence.

Taken together, these considerations suggest that 'punishment entails a
holy God directly confronting the sinner',[83] having withdrawn his fellowship
and blessing. It is a personal process. Indeed, it is even a *relational* process: 'The
relationship is one of curse rather than blessing, yet it still entails relationship.'[84] For proponents of penal substitution to speak in terms of punishment
therefore does not imply an impersonal understanding of the atonement.

Ironically, as Garry Williams points, out, 'it is often the critics of penal substitution themselves who introduce a mechanistic account of punishment'.[85]
For as we noted in chapter 11, section 3, Joel Green and Mark Baker assert that
'sinful activity is the result of God's letting us go our own way – and this
"letting us go our own way" constitutes God's wrath'.[86] God's wrath is construed here as the natural consequences of human sin *as opposed to* God's active,
personal imposition of punishment. Green and Baker thus portray punishment as an impersonal, mechanistic process.

---

of 2 Thessalonians 1:9 and the Nature of Eternal Punishment', *Westminster
Theological Journal* 59 [1997], pp. 201–211). But even if the NIV translation is correct,
it cannot mean that God is absent in every sense – see above.

83. Williams, 'Cross and the Punishment of Sin', p. 90.
84. Ibid., p. 93.
85. Ibid., p. 94.
86. Green and Baker, *Recovering the Scandal*, p. 55.

# 12. PENAL SUBSTITUTION AND THE CHRISTIAN LIFE

## Introduction

This category comprises objections that allege penal substitution has negative implications for the Christian life. Some have argued that penal substitution is entirely focused on individual sinners, and has nothing to say about the effects of sin on the rest of creation. Others complain it gives a purely 'objective' account of the cross, a distant transaction that took place 'out there' and has little to do with our everyday lives. Still others go further and argue that penal substitution has damaging pastoral consequences – it fosters an unhealthy fear of God, legitimates violence or encourages the passive acceptance of abuse.

Strictly speaking, these criticisms are not directed at penal substitution itself, but at ideas that supposedly flow from it. However, the implication in each case is that the underlying understanding of the cross must be at fault, and the objections must therefore be answered.

## 1. 'Penal substitution fails to address the issues of political and social sin and cosmic evil'

### Objection

Some criticize the doctrine of penal substitution for dealing with people individualistically and failing to address the effects of the fall on the larger structures of human society and the whole created order. Two strands of this objection can be identified. The first is that penal substitution says little about the need for, or the path to, reconciliation between nations and peoples divided by political, ethnic, economic and social barriers. The second is that penal substitution does not provide for the redemption of the whole cosmos from its fallen state.

Joel Green and Mark Baker reflect on both aspects:

> [Penal substitution] has had little voice in how we relate to one another in and outside of the church or in larger, social-ethical issues. That a central tenet of our faith might have little or nothing to say about racial reconciliation, for example, or issues of wealth and poverty, or our relationship to the cosmos, is itself a startling reality.[1]

They contend that penal substitution 'coheres so fully with the emphasis on autonomous individualism characteristic of so much of the modern middle class in the West' that a neglect to address the social problems that arise between *groups* of people is unsurprising.[2] Yet they see this as a sad indictment on the doctrine:

> A gospel that is focused on salvation for persons whose sin, or need for salvation, is understood solely or primarily in autobiographical terms can hardly be said to subvert the individualism and self-centeredness so characteristic of our social environment. A gospel that allows me to think of my relationship with God apart from the larger human family and the whole cosmos created by God – can it be said that this gospel is any gospel at all?[3]

Stuart Murray Williams raises similar concerns, alleging that 'Penal substitution fails to engage adequately with structural and systemic evil.'[4]

Martin Davie believes that penal substitution is fixated with penalties, but cares nothing for the cosmic consequences of sin. According to him, 'the

---

1. Joel B. Green and Mark D. Baker, *Recovering the Scandal of the Cross: Atonement in New Testament and Contemporary Contexts* (Downers Grove: IVP, 2000), p. 31.

2. Ibid., p. 213.

3. Ibid., pp. 213–214.

4. Stuart Murray Williams, 'Stuart Murray Williams on the Lost Message of Jesus: A Speech at the Debate on Steve Chalke's Book *The Lost Message of Jesus*', http://www.anabaptistnetwork.com/node/233 (accessed 8 February 2006).

doctrine suggests that God is not that concerned about sin as such, but only with punishment being inflicted upon sins committed. To put it simply, it suggests that God is happy as long as the *penalty* for sin is paid by someone.'[5]

Davie follows a line of argument advanced by Vernon White in *Atonement and Incarnation*.[6] White suggests that penal substitution arises out of an attempt to take seriously the 'Biblical concerns' represented by the 'Propitiatory . . . Juridical . . . [and] Substitutionary' language of Scripture. He claims, however, that these concerns are better addressed with a 'recreative' view of the atonement, rather than the 'retributivist' principles involved in penal substitution:

> If the retributivist logic is replaced by a recreative logic, these Biblical concerns surrounding the Christ event will fare better, not worse. A recreative logic actually does more justice, not less, to the wrath of God, because . . . it takes a more 'strenuous' reaction to deal with the redemption of a whole situation, compared to the limited notion of mere retributive balance, or even mere destruction.[7]

In summary, the objection is that penal substitution does not provide a sufficiently comprehensive answer to the problem of human sin, for it fails to address its effects on human society and the wider created order.

### Response

It seems this objection is often fuelled by frustration at the failure of conservative evangelicals to engage with issues in the social and political sphere. It is by no means clear, however, that this is the result of a belief in penal substitution. John Stott, one of the foremost advocates of penal substitution in recent years, has combined his convictions about the nature of the atonement with a vigorous and passionate commitment to social action. His best-selling book *Issues Facing Christians Today*[8] sought to do for the evangelical social conscience what his other bestseller, *The Cross of Christ*, did for our understanding of Jesus' death. It was Stott who founded the London Institute for Contemporary Christianity in 1982, which exists 'to equip Christians to engage biblically and relevantly with the issues they face, including Work, Capitalism,

---

5. Martin Davie, 'Dead to Sin and Alive to God', *Scottish Bulletin of Evangelical Theology* 19 (2001), pp. 158–194 (p. 174); italics original.

6. Vernon White, *Atonement and Incarnation* (Cambridge: Cambridge University Press, 1991).

7. Ibid., p. 102; cited in Davie, 'Dead to Sin', p. 174.

8. John R. W. Stott, *Issues Facing Christians Today* (London: Marshall Pickering, 1984).

Youth Culture, Media and Communication'.[9] Under Stott's chairmanship, the Lausanne Congress on World Evangelization (1974) affirmed 'that evangelism and socio-political involvement are both part of our Christian duty'.[10] Not all evangelicals would agree with Stott's precise understanding of the relationship between evangelism and social action, but it is clear, at least in the life of this man, that a belief in penal substitution does not preclude a concern for the latter. Stott's own analysis of the reason for our mislaid social conscience is that evangelicals have been 'preoccupied with the task of defending the historic biblical faith against the attacks of theological liberalism, and reacting against its "social gospel"'.[11] It does not flow from a belief in penal substitution.

Joel Green and Mark Baker are simply wrong to suggest that penal substitution 'coheres . . . fully with . . . autonomous individualism',[12] for as Garry Williams has pointed out, 'penal substitution itself relies on a *denial* of individualism'.[13] The justice of penal substitution is founded on the union between Christ and those who trust in him, such that we become a new humanity under him as the 'second Adam' (see chapter 10, sect. 1). The benefits of Jesus death can be applied to someone only as he or she relinquishes his or her autonomy and identifies with Christ. Rightly understood, therefore, penal substitution takes a significant step towards undermining the individualism of the West.

We turn now to address the supposed failure of penal substitution to deal with so-called 'structural sin': sin as it pervades the larger structures of human society – political tyrannies, exploitative business practices, ethnic conflicts and the like. It is essential to recognize that blame for all sin rests ultimately with sinful *people*, and not with the impersonal 'structures' of which they are a part. Strictly speaking, it is not 'exploitative companies' that mistreat their employees; rather, some people within the company (perhaps those at the top, who make major policy decisions) are responsible for the mistreatment of

---

9. www.licc.org.uk (accessed 14 March 2006).

10. The Lausanne Covenant, Article 5, www.lausanne.org/Brix?pageID=12891 (accessed 18 April 2006).

11. Stott, *Issues Facing Christians Today*, preface to the 1st edn.

12. Green and Baker, *Recovering the Scandal*, p. 213.

13. Garry J. Williams, 'Justice, Law, and Guilt: A Paper Given at the Evangelical Alliance Symposium on Penal Substitution' (2005), http://www.eauk.org/theology/atonement/upload/garry_williams.pdf (accessed 27 March 2006), p. 8; italics added.

others. Again, although we might refer to certain laws as 'unjust', what we mean is that those who draft and pass legislation, and perhaps also those who enforce it, are guilty of injustice. In short, it is *people* who behave morally or immorally, they alone remain responsible for their actions, and their actions affect the structures to which they belong.

Of course, complex social structures may sometimes behave as if they had a life of their own, even to the extent that we may be unable to distinguish the contributions of individual members. But ultimately no social or ethnic group, no company, no government has an existence apart from the people who comprise it. It was Nazis, not 'Nazism', that conceived, propagated and implemented the sickening plans to murder millions of Jews in the Second World War. We may be unable to disentangle the complexities of the myriad decisions taken by countless people during those dark years, and to apportion responsibility correctly, but we may be sure that the Judge of all the earth will do so without difficulty. He will not allow anyone to pass the buck to an abstract and impersonal third party, whether 'Nazism', 'the company', 'the law', 'society' or anything else.[14]

Penal substitution correctly recognizes that all sin begins with human beings, and it is this root problem that it treats. Yet in doing so, it impacts also the larger structures of society to which those individuals belong. In a 'crooked and depraved generation' God's forgiven people 'shine like stars in the universe' (Phil. 2:14–15), affecting everyone they come into contact with. It is therefore simply not true that a penal substitutionary understanding of the cross has nothing to say about 'structural sin'.[15]

Nor is it true to say that penal substitution has nothing to say about 'cosmic evil'. The key to this is recognizing that the predicament of the whole of

---

14. There is an increasing tendency among both secular and Christian commentators to speak as if social, political and economic institutions are in some sense autonomous. E.g. people sometimes speak of 'institutional racism', and Ronald J. Sider speaks of 'Structural Injustice' in *Rich Christians in an Age of Hunger: Moving from Affluence to Generosity*, new edn (Nashville: W Publishing, 1997), pp. 133–179. In some ways this language can be a helpful shorthand, but it must never be pressed to shift the focus away from the responsible individuals within those structures.

15. For further discussion of this issue see Dan Strange, 'The Many-Splendoured Cross: Atonement, Controversy, and Victory', *Foundations* (autumn 2005), pp. 5–22; Henri Blocher, '*Agnus Victor*: The Atonement as Victory and Vicarious Punishment', in John G. Stackhouse (ed.), *What Does It Mean to Be Saved?* (Grand Rapids: Baker, 2002), pp. 67–91 (especially pp. 86–91).

creation is tied to the fate of humankind, indeed, a subgroup of humankind. In Romans 8:20 the apostle Paul speaks of the creation having been 'subjected to frustration, not by its own choice, but by the will of the one who subjected it'. This is an unmistakable allusion to Genesis 3:17, where God cursed the ground in response to Adam's sin, and the whole created order suffers as a result of human rebellion. Crucially however, the liberation of the creation from this 'bondage to decay' (Rom. 8:21) is tied to the redemption of certain people.[16] Thus Paul writes that 'The creation waits in eager expectation for the sons of God to be revealed' (v. 19), and he sounds a note of glorious expectation as he continues his argument: 'the creation itself will be liberated from its bondage to decay and brought into the glorious freedom of the children of God' (v. 21). In other words, it is as Christians – 'the children of God' – are finally redeemed that the whole of creation will be made new.[17] Accordingly, by setting forth the solution to sin and guilt in individual human lives, penal substitution provides the means by which the whole cosmos will one day be transformed. As Christ endured and exhausted God's judgment in our place and thereby 'redeemed us from the curse of the law by becoming a curse for us' (Gal. 3:13), he provided also for the lifting of the curse on the whole of the created order.

Martin Davie is wrong to say penal substitution implies God is 'happy as long as the penalty for sin is paid by someone'. This is a necessary *part* of God's plan to redeem his creation from sin, for it establishes God's justice, vindicates his holiness, and demonstrates his truthfulness. But as Athanasius showed back in the fourth century, a comprehensive penal substitutionary doctrine of

---

16. This understanding is followed by many modern commentators. See e.g. Douglas J. Moo, *The Epistle to the Romans*, New International Commentary on the New Testament (Grand Rapids: Eerdmans, 1996), pp. 513–517; Thomas R. Schreiner, *Romans*, Baker Exegetical Commentary on the New Testament (Grand Rapids: Baker, 1998), pp. 432–441; N. T. Wright, *The Letter to the Romans: Introduction, Commentary and Reflections*, in *The New Interpreter's Bible*, vol. 10 (Nashville: Abingdon, 2002), pp. 393–770 (p. 597).

17. It is not that anything more has to be done to secure their redemption. Indeed, many of its benefits are already in force: 'Therefore, there is now no condemnation for those who are in Christ Jesus' (Rom. 8:1). Nonetheless, Paul explains in this chapter that we still await the consummation – 'we hope for what we do not yet have' (v. 25). The eschatological tension between 'now' and 'not yet' is perhaps best captured by the fact that we are already God's children (v. 16) and yet are somehow still awaiting our adoption (v. 23).

the atonement is the gateway to far more than this.[18] God's eternal plan includes a promise of a new creation dependent on, not an alternative to, Christ's substitutionary bearing of the curse on the old creation.[19] White goes badly astray here, for in his scheme (apparently followed by Davie) 'the retributivist logic is *replaced* by a recreative logic'.[20] But if penal substitution is abandoned, a recreative view of the atonement cannot be sustained either! The doctrinal framework with which White and Davie are operating is wholly inadequate.

In summary, penal substitution does not commit its advocates to a neglect of their social or political responsibilities, nor does it foster an unhealthy individualism. It deals with 'structural sin' inasmuch as the roots of this lie in human hearts; those who are transformed by this gospel will have an impact on society around them. Penal substitution also holds the key to the redemption of the whole created order, for as God's people are liberated from his curse, so the curse on creation will ultimately be lifted.

## 2. 'Penal substitution is an entirely objective account of the atonement, and fails to address our side of the Creator–creature relationship'

### Objection

Some object penal substitution says nothing about how the Creator–creature relationship can be restored *from our side*. Sometimes a dichotomy is drawn between so-called 'objective' views of the atonement, concerned with the impact of Christ's death on God or on evil powers, and 'subjective' accounts, concerned with its effects on us. Penal substitution is placed in the former category, since it speaks primarily of satisfying God's justice and holiness. But if the problem of sin arose because we wandered away from God, is it not we, rather than God, who most need to change? Penal substitution, it is claimed, fails to speak to this. Perhaps it is devoid of ethical implications altogether.

---

18. See further the discussion of Athanasius, *On the Incarnation* (New York: St. Vladimir's Seminary Press, 1993), in chapter 5.

19. See M. Ovey, 'The Cross, Creation and the Human Predicament', in David Peterson (ed.), *Where Wrath and Mercy Meet: Proclaiming the Atonement Today* (Carlisle: Paternoster, 2001), pp. 100–135.

20. White, *Atonement and Incarnation*, p. 102; italics added; cited in Davie, 'Dead to Sin', p. 174.

For example, Colin Greene thinks that according to penal substitution, 'the act of atonement is so objectivized that it appears to be an event or transaction whereby we are simply removed from the scene'.[21] Fiddes sets out a similar criticism in more detail, arguing that any propitiatory understanding of the atonement shares this defect:

> But we notice that 'propitiation', however sensitively it is stated, is all about dealing with the reaction of God against sin, not about the taint of sin in human life itself . . . any theory of propitiation fails to explain how one event can decisively alter the state of human personalities. Sin is a disease, a distortion of existence which alienates persons from God and from each other. A doctor might be said to 'hate' disease as God hates sin, but the first aim of medicine is to remove the disease and heal the patient, not to placate the anger of the doctor. An understanding of sacrifice as propitiation, whether it be of the ritual in ancient Israel or the death of Christ, is too objective and not subjective enough. It does not enter the actual sphere of human sin and lack of response to God, which is our present situation. Salvation must heal broken lives here and now.[22]

In particular, Fiddes levels this criticism at Anselm's view of the atonement and at the doctrine of penal substitution as articulated by John Calvin. He acknowledges that a 'subjective dimension' is often added later, but maintains that 'our subjective response of repentance and trust' is relegated firmly to a secondary position:

> They portray atonement as a transaction, or legal settlement, between God the Father and God the Son in which we are not involved, despite being the erring sinners concerned. To suggest that our debt to justice is paid . . . certainly expresses the once-for-allness of the cross of Jesus. But it does not integrate the human response to God, and the healing of the human personality here and now, into the act of atonement.
>
> Of course theories of this kind *add* our response of repentance and trust as a second stage or appendix. The subjective dimension is not entirely lacking. But it comes as a later appropriation of what has already been achieved.[23]

---

21.  Colin Greene, 'Is the Message of the Cross Good News for the Twentieth Century?', in John Goldingay (ed.), *Atonement Today* (London: SPCK, 1995), pp. 222–239 (p. 232).

22.  Paul S. Fiddes, *Past Event and Present Salvation: The Christian Idea of Atonement* (London: Darton, Longman & Todd, 1989), p. 70.

23.  Ibid., p. 99; italics original; see also p. 101.

Tom Smail makes a related objection, claiming that 'taken by itself' penal substitution attempts to deal with our guilty past without equipping us to address the future:

> By its very nature the penal model is backward rather than forward looking in its orientation. The bearing of the punishment deals with the sins of the past, but taken by itself does not say anything about how the person is brought into new and transforming relationships that will produce a new quality of life in the future.[24]

Finally, Joel Green and Mark Baker raise similar objections,[25] although they concede that 'there is nothing intrinsic to the theory of penal substitutionary atonement that leads one necessarily in these problematic directions'.[26]

In summary, this objection argues that penal substitution does not explain how the relationship between us and God can be restored *from our side*, and that it severs the close biblical link between the cross and Christian ethics.

### Response

Those who make this objection fail to recognize that penal substitution is not proposed as the only biblical facet of the atonement, and certainly not as the only implication of the death of Christ. Rather, it is one part of an interconnected web of theological themes, in which each element contributes to the whole. As in a jigsaw puzzle, the whole picture is incomplete without all of the pieces, and the individual pieces are insufficient without the whole. An individual piece can hardly be criticized for not containing the whole picture: that is simply not its job. To impugn penal substitution for saying nothing about the Christian life when it is 'taken by itself'[27] is a bit like criticizing an engine for being no good at steering a car.

We can go further. A belief in penal substitution necessarily entails a belief in certain other doctrines (the neighbouring pieces in the jigsaw, if you like), and some of these have profound ethical implications. One example of such a doctrine is 'union with Christ'. It is only by our being in union with Christ that his death brings us any benefits. Penal substitution thus implies and

---

24. Tom Smail, *Once and for All: A Confession of the Cross* (London: Darton, Longman & Todd, 1998), pp. 95–96.
25. Green and Baker, *Recovering the Scandal*, pp. 27, 31, 149.
26. Ibid., p. 31.
27. Smail, *Once and for All*, p. 95.

requires this union (see chapter 10, sect. 1). In turn, the union brings with it a moral imperative: we are *in Christ*, and therefore 'We died to sin' (Rom. 6:2) when he died. On this basis the apostle Paul exhorts his readers to 'count yourselves dead to sin' (v.11) and not to 'let sin reign in your mortal body' (v. 12). The ethical implication of putting sin to death arises from the same union with Christ by which we gain the benefits of an objectively righteous status before God.

Paul Fiddes appears to recognize this connection between doctrinal themes when he concedes that 'theories of this kind *add* our response of repentance and trust as a second stage or appendix. The subjective dimension is not entirely lacking.'[28] However, his choice of words is misleading. Proponents of penal substitution do not 'add' a subjective dimension as if the two could exist quite separately; rather, they consider them intrinsically related from the outset. Neither is it fair to speak of our subjective response as an 'appendix' as though it were considered less important. To return to the analogy of the car, one might begin describing the engine before talking about the steering wheel, but this does not mean either is much use without the other.

Perhaps the two doctrines that best explain how our relationship with God is restored *from our side* are regeneration and redemption. Regeneration has do with our being 'born again' (John 3:3; cf. Titus 3:5), being given a 'new heart' that is eager to follow God's ways, in place of our old rebellious one (Ezek. 36:26), and becoming in Christ a 'new creation' (2 Cor. 5:17). It is striking that within a few verses of each of these texts is an allusion to themes that hint at a penal substitutionary understanding of Jesus' death. Thus John 3:15 speaks of Jesus being 'lifted up', making a wordplay of his glorious exaltation and cruel elevation on a Roman cross, and thereby alluding to Isaiah 52:13 (a key text; see chapter 2). More explicit in the background are the events of Numbers 21:4–9, which Jesus refers to directly, and that tell of how God's people needed deliverance from a fatal curse brought on them as a result of his anger at their sin. Titus 3:4–7 links regeneration to God's mercy (his not punishing sinners as they deserve) and to salvation. Ezekiel 36 connects the idea of a new start with God's cleansing from past sins, and in the wider context of the book, the chapter is set against the backdrop of God's anger at a nation whom he had sent into exile because of their idolatrous ways. 2 Corinthians 5:21 contains the extraordinary statement that Christ was 'made sin', meaning he bore our sins as he died on the cross. In summary,

---

28. Fiddes, *Past Event and Present Salvation*, p. 99; italics original.

regeneration is repeatedly found side by side with penal substitutionary themes in Scripture.

The same is true of redemption, the glorious truth that Christ has paid a price to set us free from our old life of wickedness in order that we might belong to God and live to serve him (e.g. 1 Cor. 6:20; Titus 2:14; 1 Pet. 1:18). The ethical implications are obvious – why would we want to continue to live in slavery now we have been liberated to serve God? But the point we wish to draw attention to here is that redemption is closely tied to penal substitution. The defining use of the word in the Old Testament relates to God's deliverance of his people from slavery in Egypt at the time of the exodus, in order that they might be free to serve him (e.g. Exod. 6:6–8). Yet, as we saw in chapter 2, this happened by way of the Passover, a sacrificial death by which God's people were spared not from the wrath of the Egyptians, but from the wrath of God himself. Redemption by the blood of a lamb prefigured the death of Jesus, who by his penal suffering would similarly avert the wrath of God and thereby secure redemption for his people (Rom. 3:24–25).

In fact, we do not even have to travel via other connected doctrines (although that is a valid route) in order to encounter subjective implications of penal substitution. A response in us is called forth by penal substitution itself. For just as a right recognition of the objective horror of our sin in the sight of a holy God ought to lead to an intense subjective reaction of fear before him, so also the objective propitiatory achievement of the cross in turning aside God's righteous wrath ought to have a correspondingly direct, subjective impact on our assurance and confidence before God. We may sometimes find it hard to connect head and heart in this way, but the fault lies with us, not with the doctrine of penal substitution.

Similarly, Tom Smail's criticism that 'the penal model is backward rather than forward looking in its orientation' misses the point.[29] For it is by addressing our objectively guilty status before God that penal substitution liberates us from the subjective feelings of bondage to sin and guilt, and allows us to face the future with new eyes.

Of course, it might be possible in theory to present the Christian faith in a way that fails to draw out its ethical implications, or even to imply that penal substitution is all there is to say. This would be a terrible distortion, and we are glad we have been unable to find any published examples. Moreover, we are determined not to become the first; the whole of chapter 4 is devoted to exploring the practical implications of penal substitution for the Christian life.

---

29. Smail, *Once and for All*, p. 95.

In summary, the doctrine of penal substitution carries necessary ethical implications when placed in its correct theological context, and an objective understanding of the atonement is in many ways the pathway to a renewed spiritual life, not a barrier to it.

## 3. 'Penal substitution causes people to live in fear of God'

### *Objection*

This objection to penal substitution takes the previous one a stage further. Rather than complaining that penal substitution has nothing to say about important aspects of the Christian life, it contends that penal substitution has negative pastoral consequences, generating a picture of an angry God and causing people to live in fear of him. Tom Smail warns of this danger:

> If the fact that 'the Father himself loves you' (John 16:27) is not continually underlined and emphasized, we shall be in danger . . . of encouraging people to hide behind the coat tails of a loving Jesus to shield them from the anger of a vengeful God. That is blasphemy against the Father and devastating in its pastoral effects on people.[30]

Green and Baker conclude that such damaging pastoral effects have proved inescapable, despite the best efforts of advocates of penal substitution to guard against such a warped view of God:

> Of course, many proponents of penal substitution recognize that God is not foremost an angry God who desires to punish humans, and they attempt to explain that God is foremost a merciful God, a God of love, even though the penal substitutionary model of the atonement would lead one to think otherwise. Unfortunately, trying to nuance the meaning of this model in the pages of a theology book has not proven sufficient to protect people in the pew from the damaging effects of the image of God this model communicates and seems to demand. Tragically, many Christians (and former believers) still live in fear of a God who seems so intent on punishing, and much less willing to forgive, than folks we encounter in day-to-day life.[31]

---

30. Ibid., pp. 85–86.

31. Green and Baker, *Recovering the Scandal*, pp. 202–203. See also pp. 220–221.

## Response

There are several possible lines of response here. One is simply to say that the Bible writers, and even Jesus himself, seem rather less wary of the dangers than Smail, Green and Baker. Ought we to reprimand Jesus for the damaging pastoral consequences of the following words? 'I tell you, my friends, do not be afraid of those who kill the body and after that can do no more. But I will show you whom you should fear: Fear him who, after the killing of the body, has power to throw you into hell. Yes, I tell you, fear him' (Luke 12:4–5). Strikingly, Jesus was addressing his disciples at this point, not his opponents. And these words of warning come side by side with the most tender words of comfort: 'Are not five sparrows sold for two pennies? Yet not one of them is forgotten by God. Indeed, the very hairs of your head are all numbered. Don't be afraid; you are worth more than many sparrows' (vv. 6–7).

In fact, fear of God is viewed positively throughout the Scriptures (e.g. Ps. 34:7, 9; Prov. 1:7; 1 Pet. 1:17; Rev. 14:7). Conversely, the *failure* to fear God is a terrible indictment (e.g. Ps. 36:1; Jer. 5:20–25). One of the most dramatic passages is Acts 5:1–11, where God punishes Ananias and his wife Sapphira, striking them both dead; twice we are told that 'great fear seized' those who heard about it (vv. 5, 11). We instinctively think of this as a negative outcome, but the narrative demonstrates otherwise – 'more and more men and women believed in the Lord and were added to their number' (v. 14).[32] Rightly understood, the fear of the Lord is a good thing, and the Lord esteems the one who 'trembles' at his word (Isa. 66:2).

But what about 1 John 4:18? The apostle John seems much closer to Green and Baker's position when he says, 'There is no fear in love. But perfect love drives out fear, because fear has to do with punishment. The one who fears is not made perfect in love.' Matthew Henry's commentary is helpful at this point:

> We must here distinguish, I judge, between fear and being afraid; or, in this case, between the fear of God and being afraid of him. The fear of God is often mentioned and commanded as the substance of religion (1 Pet. 2:17; Rev. 14:7); and so it imports the high regard and veneration we have for God and his authority and government. Such fear is consistent with love, yea, with perfect love, as being in the angels themselves. But then there is a being afraid of God, which arises from a sense of guilt . . . fear here may be rendered *dread; There is no dread in love.*[33]

---

32. We are grateful to Greg Haslam of Westminster Chapel, London, for this insight.

33. *Matthew Henry's Commentary on the Whole Bible*, vol. 6 (Peabody, MA: Henrickson, 1991), p. 876; italics original.

In other words, the apostle John is telling us we need not be afraid of God in the sense that we dread his wrath. But why not, given that the Bible warns of it so often? The answer is because of the doctrine of penal substitution! In the very same chapter of his letter, John explains that God 'sent his Son as an atoning sacrifice [more literally, 'a propitiation'] for our sins' (1 John 4:10). It is because the Lord Jesus Christ bore God's wrath in our place that we need not dread him.

We have no wish to trivialize the plight of those Christians whose tortured consciences are unable to find liberation from the feeling that God's face is set toward them with a permanent scowl. Many of us have felt the occasional restlessness that comes from a lack of assurance before God, and there are some who experience this as a daily reality. Green and Baker are right to draw our attention to this distressing pastoral problem. Ironically, however, critics of penal substitution may be among those responsible for bringing it about. For a lingering fear of God may actually arise from a *neglect* of penal substitution. It is impossible to expunge from the pages of Scripture the fact that our sin arouses God's righteous wrath against us. The only ultimate hope for salvation is Christ's substitutionary bearing of this penalty at Calvary. Christians who spend time reflecting on the Bible will inevitably be convinced of the horror of our sin before God, and of his fearful wrath against sinners. If they then turn to Christian theologians or preachers and find the doctrine of penal substitution ignored, opposed or denied, is it any wonder they are left with a troubled conscience? For if God's holy wrath was not endured by Christ in our place, it remains upon us. It is tragic that some Christians live in dread of God's anger, but in view of the recent criticisms of penal substitution, it is unsurprising.

In closing, we must address Smail's image of a loving Jesus placating the wrath of an irascible Father. This is a grotesque caricature of penal substitution. Jesus was not acting against the will of his Father in his self-offering on the cross. On the contrary, the will of the Father and of the Son coincided perfectly – God the Father gave his Son; God the Son gave himself: '*God* was reconciling the world to himself *in Christ*, not counting men's sins against them' (2 Cor. 5:19; italics added). Both Father and Son show their love towards us in the same act. This is the great climax of Paul's argument in Romans 8:

> He who did not spare his own Son, but gave him up for us all – how will he not also, along with him, graciously give us all things? Who will bring any charge against those whom God has chosen? It is God who justifies . . . I am convinced that neither death nor life, neither angels nor demons, neither the present nor the future, nor any powers, neither height nor depth, nor anything else in all creation, will be able to

separate us from the love of God that is in Christ Jesus our Lord. (Rom. 8:32–33, 38–39)

It is vital to recognize that the love of God the *Father* is shown by the death of his Son, for this is a key step on the journey towards assurance of salvation in Christ and confidence before God. A right understanding of penal substitution does not entail 'encouraging people to hide behind the coat tails of a loving Jesus to shield them from the anger of a vengeful God',[34] but rather delights in the immeasurable love of God, that he should give his precious Son, the Lord Jesus Christ, to die in our place. Far from being the cause of many pastoral problems, penal substitution is frequently the cure.

## 4. 'Penal substitution legitimates violence and encourages the passive acceptance of unjust suffering'

### Objection
This criticism entails two related claims: first, that penal substitution serves to legitimate oppression and violence; and secondly, that it encourages the victims of violence to accept abuse passively. Joanne Carlson Brown and Rebecca Parker raise both criticisms in their contribution to *Christianity, Patriarchy, and Abuse*, a collection of essays edited by Joanne Carlson Brown and Carole R. Bohn. Women and children, they claim, may feel compelled to endure violence without protest, and parents may feel justified in abusing their children:

> The imitator of Christ, which every faithful person is exhorted to be, can find herself choosing to endure suffering because she has become convinced that through her pain another whom she loves will escape pain. The disciple's role is to suffer in the place of others, as Jesus suffered for us all. But this glorification of suffering as salvific, held before us daily in the image of Jesus hanging from the cross, encourages women who are being abused to be more concerned about their victimizer than about themselves. Children who are abused are forced most keenly to face the conflict between the claims of a parent who professes love and the inner self which protests violation . . . when parents have an image of a God righteously demanding the total obedience of 'his' son – even obedience to death – what will prevent the parent from engaging in divinely sanctioned child abuse? The image of God the

---

34. Smail, *Once and for All*, p. 86.

father demanding and carrying out the suffering and death of his own son has sustained a culture of abuse and led to the abandonment of victims of abuse and oppression.[35]

Joel Green and Mark Baker raise similar concerns. Like Brown and Parker, they are alarmed at the possible implications of penal substitution:

> For others, atonement theology represents an even more startling drama in which God takes on the role of the sadist inflicting punishment, while Jesus, in his role as masochist, readily embraces suffering. From this perspective, it is only a small step from the crucifixion of Jesus to the legitimation of unjust human suffering or the idealization of the victim. As bewildering as this view might seem, the fact remains that the popular model of penal substitution is represented in songs and sermons in ways that lend themselves to such a reading.[36]

In summary, this objection claims that penal substitution justifies the perpetration and passive acceptance of violent abuse, by setting forth as an example the image of a Father inflicting suffering upon his Son.

### Response

We begin with the charge that penal substitution serves to legitimate oppression and violence. This is a serious charge. The oppression of women and children is offensive enough, but more appalling still is the thought that some might twist the gospel of Christ to provide an ostensible justification for such depravity. This would be an unspeakable perversion of the Christian faith. It must be said, however, that such a distortion of the gospel does not appear to be widespread in mainstream Christian writing. In fact, we have been unable to locate a single example. If this sadistic misappropriation of the gospel exists at all, it seems not to have a wide following.[37]

---

35. Joanne Carlson Brown and Rebecca Parker, 'For God So Loved the World?', in Joanne Carlson Brown and Carole R. Bohn (eds.), *Christianity, Patriarchy, and Abuse: A Feminist Critique* (New York: Pilgrim, 1989), pp. 1–30 (pp. 8–9).

36. Green and Baker, *Recovering the Scandal*, p. 30; see also p. 149. Green and Baker note (pp. 91–92, 171–183) that these criticisms are often made by feminist theologians, and refer to Darby Kathleen Ray, *Deceiving the Devil: Atonement, Abuse and Ransom* (Cleveland: Pilgrim, 1998); and Brown and Bohn, *Christianity, Patriarchy and Abuse*.

37. On the contrary, numerous proponents of penal substitution have written extensively on the implications of the gospel for the Christian life, and their

Moreover, it is only by a horrific misunderstanding of penal substitution that someone could conclude that such violence is acceptable. The argument would have to proceed on the assumption that we should imitate God the Father in what he did at the cross. But, as we saw in our discussion of retributive violence (chapter 9, sect. 3), this is precisely what the Bible says we should not do. An abuser may say God exacts retributive punishment and he, the abuser, therefore has the right to do so, but Romans 12:17–19 says that God will exact retributive punishment and individuals must therefore *not* do so.[38] The Bible does not set forth God's judgment as an example for us to follow; on the contrary, it is something to avoid. Penal substitution simply cannot be deployed to sanction human violence.

The troubling thing about the way in which the above criticisms are expressed is that they make no distinction between God's holy and righteous punishment of our sin in Christ at Calvary and the vindictive and godless atrocities of men and women. We should be careful before insinuating that penal substitution makes the Father a sadist and the Son a masochist, lest we find that we have committed blasphemy in the service of rhetorical points-scoring.

It is certainly true that those who put Jesus to death were guilty of appalling brutality. For their unjust acts of violence they are condemned (e.g. Acts 3:13–15; 7:51–53). It is also true, however, that God justly worked through those same actions for his good purposes (Acts 2:23; 4:27–28). It is unfortunate that, in an otherwise helpful book, Paul Wells attributes entirely to the human agents the violence Jesus suffered, emphasizing God as victim rather than perpetrator.[39] Scripture will not allow us to do this, for it insists, 'it was the LORD's will to crush him [Jesus] and cause him to suffer' (Isa. 53:10). Indeed, as Jesus himself contemplated his own death he recalled the Lord's promise to Zechariah that '*I* will strike the shepherd' (Mark 14:27; italics added; cf. Zech. 13:7). Yet this is not vindictive or capricious of God, but a perfectly holy demonstration of justice (Rom. 3:25–26). We consider these issues in more detail in our response to the claim that penal substitution makes God the Father guilty of child abuse (chapter 9, sect. 2).

---

conclusions bear no resemblance at all to the menacing picture depicted above. See e.g. J. C. Ryle, *Holiness* (Welwyn: Evangelical Press, 1979; first pub. 1879); Stott, *Issues Facing Christians Today*; John R. W. Stott, *The Cross of Christ* (Leicester: IVP, 1986); Vaughan Roberts, *Distinctives* (Carlisle: OM, 2000).

38. Williams, 'Justice, Law, and Guilt', pp. 2–3.

39. Paul Wells, *Cross Words: The Biblical Doctrine of the Atonement* (Fearn: Christian Focus, 2006), pp. 81–92.

Let us now turn to the second charge, that penal substitution encourages the passive acceptance of abuse among victims. In fact, this supposed difficulty pertains not to penal substitution but to the so-called 'exemplary theory' of the atonement: the idea that Christ's death provides an example for us to follow. As we have emphasized before, we do not see the different facets of the Bible's teaching on the cross as mutually exclusive, and indeed we would affirm that the exemplary theory is taught in Scripture, particularly in 1 Peter. We address the concern here not because a defence of penal substitution requires it, but because it is an important pastoral issue in its own right.

Let us consider 1 Peter 2:18–25, where Jesus' submission to his persecutors is set forth explicitly as a model for others who suffer unjustly. Note first that Peter does not commend unjust suffering as a good thing in itself. His intention is to show oppressed Christians how to respond to persecution when it arises, not to encourage them to seek it as an intrinsic good. Thus he does not commend the perpetrators of injustice, nor does his teaching entail 'the legitimation of unjust human suffering or the idealization of the victim'.[40]

Secondly, the immediately preceding paragraph of Peter's letter teaches that those who are in a position to change unjust social systems must do so. Peter highlights the role of political authorities 'to punish those who do wrong and to commend those who do right' (1 Pet. 2:14).[41] In other words, one function of governments is to stamp out injustices like those spoken of in 1 Peter 2:18–25.

The point at issue in 1 Peter is how we should respond in a situation where we cannot escape injustice. Peter assures his readers that their patient endurance 'is commendable before God' (1 Pet. 2:21). To take up our cross and follow in the path of our Saviour is a privilege and a blessing (4:12–16; cf. Mark 8:34).

In summary, penal substitution justifies neither the perpetration nor the passive acceptance of violence. Jesus' submissiveness as he went to his death is commended in the New Testament, and hardly constitutes a valid objection to penal substitution.

---

40. Green and Baker, *Recovering the Scandal*, p. 30.

41. Paul similarly teaches that 'the governing authorities . . . have been established by God' (Rom. 13:1) for the same purpose.

# 13. A FINAL WORD

## Introduction

Our aim in Part Two of this book has been to discuss all the current species of objection to the biblical doctrine of penal substitution. These criticisms may resurface in different guises, but we hope our responses have been sufficiently broad ranging to address future variants also.

Before we finish, we need to deal with two objections of a different kind to those discussed above. They are distinguished not by their content, but by their style. More common in conversation than in print, they are heard fairly frequently. We could hardly finish without mentioning them.

## 'The Vague Objection'

The first might be called 'The Vague Objection'. The Vague Objection insinuates that there are problems with penal substitution – theological problems, moral problems, sociological problems or whatever – without actually saying what they are. In fact, the less specific this objection is, the more force it has. It needs only to hint at the nature of the difficulty, to sow a seed of doubt in the hearers' minds.

The Vague Objection is most damaging when deployed by someone with a reputation for theological expertise, and is therefore often heard in universities or in debates between theologians. The tendency is to defer to the greater knowledge of the speaker, despite the fact that he or she has not actually produced an argument for the position taken.

This objection is flexible: it can take numerous forms. For example, 'There are all sorts of theological problems with penal substitution'; 'Penal substitution causes all manner of difficulties for the doctrine of the Trinity'; 'Penal substitution tends to be associated with other troublesome theological positions'; 'Many theologians, including some evangelicals, find penal substitution problematic.' The combination of imprecision, complexity and the presumed wisdom of the speaker is so intimidating that many Christians will feel compelled to lay down arms. It is tempting to surrender to the critic simply on the basis of the fleeting glimpse granted us of deep thoughts too profound to argue with.

This objection is in fact a naked exercise of power. It is a form of intellectual intimidation that says, in effect, 'You should believe this because I say so.' It is easy to see why it is rarely found in print, for in the cold light of day it looks less formidable. If a critic of penal substitution does not state his or her own position, and does not spell out exactly what he or she thinks is wrong with penal substitution, nor *why* it is wrong, and if he or she fails to answer any counter-objections adequately, the objection has no force at all. We should of course listen carefully and patiently, but there is no reason to be intimidated, and still less reason to abandon cherished articles of faith on the basis of what is said.

## 'The Emotional Objection'

The second attack is best described as 'The Emotional Objection'. The use of emotive language is legitimate when used to communicate the force of a reasoned argument – Jesus used it in this way (e.g. Matt. 5:29–30), as did the apostle Paul, who spoke of the fate of those without Christ 'with tears' (Phil. 3:18). But The Emotional Objection is different. The Emotional Objection deploys forceful langue in the *absence* of a reasoned argument, rather than as a climax to it. Its effect is to overwhelm the hearer, and to make calm, level-headed evaluation of the ideas on the table almost impossible. We find ourselves agreeing, not because we have been persuaded, but because we have been swept along by the emotional tide. At worst, we have simply been manipulated. Those who indulge in this kind of argument do not merely put the rhetorical cart before the logical horse; they unhitch the cart completely, take it to the top of a steep hill, give it a firm shove, and watch with satisfaction as the pedestrians are scattered into the hedge-rows.[1]

At its worst, The Emotional Objection does three things. First, it raises the temperature so that otherwise easily refutable criticisms of penal substitution seem weightier than they are. Secondly, it acts as a vehicle for all kinds of mis-understandings of the doctrine. Thirdly, and most destructively of all, it gen-erates a kind of guilt by association: it insinuates connections with various unpleasant notions but fails formally to demonstrate them.

Consider this extract from Steve Chalke and Alan Mann's book *The Lost Message of Jesus*:

> John's Gospel famously declares, 'God loved the people of this world so much that he gave his only Son' (John 3:16). How then, have we come to believe that at the cross this God of love suddenly decides to vent his anger and wrath on his own Son?
>
> The fact is that the cross isn't a form of cosmic child abuse – a vengeful Father, punishing his Son for an offence he has not even committed. Understandably, both people inside and outside of the Church have found this twisted version of events morally dubious and a huge barrier to faith. Deeper than that, however, is that such a concept stands in total contradiction to the statement 'God is love'. If the cross is a personal act of violence perpetrated by God towards humankind but borne by his Son, then it makes a mockery of Jesus' own teaching to love your enemies and to refuse to repay evil with evil.[2]

This example has it all. First, penal substitution is criticized, but in vague and unspecified terms; it is said to contradict the Christian teaching about God's love, but we are not told exactly how; it is said to be 'morally dubious', but we are not told why; it is said to contradict the Sermon on the Mount, but there is no careful exegesis to enable us to assess this claim. Secondly, penal substi-tution is misrepresented. Whoever said that God's decision to punish his Son was 'sudden', as if to imply that it was a capricious outburst of rage? Certainly no proponent of penal substitution we have read. Was the penal suffering of the cross not carefully planned, even prophesied in Isaiah 53 many centuries

---

1. We realize that in this section we too have become emotional and rhetorically forceful. However, we have sought also to make clear the reasoned argument that underpins our attempt to persuade.
2. Steve Chalke and Alan Mann, *The Lost Message of Jesus* (Grand Rapids: Zondervan, 2003), pp. 182–183.

before the event? Thirdly, there is the ultimate example of guilt by association. Penal substitution is portrayed as 'a form of cosmic child abuse'. This sticks in the mind, tugging at the conscience, for there are few crimes more despicable than violence towards an innocent, defenceless child.

The fact is that none of it is true. Nowhere in Chalke and Mann's book do they even attempt to argue that it is true. The above quotation amounts to a form of verbal bullying, a scare tactic calculated to coerce people into abandoning long-held beliefs out of fear of being associated with something nasty.

### Conclusion

The Vague Objection and The Emotional Objection have several differences. The former can be deployed only by an acknowledged expert, the latter, by anyone; the former works by underhand manipulation, the latter by brute force. But they share a common feature. Neither engages in a reasoned, logical discussion of the issue at hand: they substitute intimidation for the hard work involved in thinking about the teaching of Scripture.

The apostle Paul warns sternly, 'Even if we or an angel from heaven should preach a gospel other than the one we preached to you, let him be eternally condemned!' (Gal. 1:8). We have not enjoyed the encounter with 'other gospels', but as we have read them we have been increasingly convinced of the need to reply. We would rejoice if some of those whose positions we have criticized would turn from them and embrace the glorious truth that our Lord Jesus Christ 'bore our sins in his body on the tree, so that we might die to sins and live for righteousness' (1 Pet. 2:24).

# APPENDIX: A PERSONAL NOTE TO PREACHERS

## Introduction

We hope and pray that this book will meet the needs of a wide range of people. In closing, we want to highlight an issue especially relevant to those involved in teaching the Bible to others, which it seemed wise to deal with separately. We particularly have in mind full-time pastors and preachers, but the issues may well be relevant to people involved in other teaching ministries.

In the course of research for this book, we have encountered a large number of criticisms of the doctrine of penal substitution itself; these we have tried to address in Part Two. However, we have also come across criticisms of the way in which penal substitution has been *taught*, particularly with respect to some favourite illustrations used by preachers. For example, Tom Smail recalls an analogy taken from a court of law:

> The illustration . . . of the judge who pronounces sentence on the criminal and then divests himself of his robe, comes down from his judgement seat and says 'I will bear this punishment in your place' is, in terms of justice, a quite scandalous story

and any legal system that allowed such a thing to happen would be an unjust system.[1]

Joel Green and Mark Baker cite another example:

> Similarly, some of us may remember hearing the more gruesome story that compares God to a railroad switchman who sees that his son has wandered onto the main track just as a passenger train is hurtling toward him. If the man throws the switch, his son will live, but the train will crash into freight cars parked on the siding, and many people will die. The father opts to leave the switch open and kill his son instead of killing the people on the train.[2]

Both of these extracts come from critiques of penal substitution that reflect serious misunderstandings of the doctrine, and we have argued in this book that a carefully nuanced statement of the biblical doctrine entirely answers them. However, in fairness we must acknowledge that *these illustrations of penal substitution* are open to criticism, and it is easy to see how they might in some circumstances generate misunderstandings of the biblical doctrine. In a recent article defending penal substitution Garry Williams concurs: 'in agreement with Professor Green we must absolutely reject the ludicrous railroad illustration where the father switches the points to rescue his passengers and in so doing kills his wandering son'.[3]

Paul Weston, in a contribution to a book defending penal substitution, gives another example of an illustration open to misunderstanding. He recounts the horrifying story from the book *Miracle on the River Kwai*, often heard in evangelistic sermons:

> An innocent soldier steps forward to be punished in place of his fellow prisoners on account of some missing tools. Though innocent, he takes responsibility for the tools, and is immediately butchered at the end of an array of rifle-butts, while his fellow internees are allowed to go back to their huts, spared and profoundly moved

---

1. Tom Smail, *Once and for All: A Confession of the Cross* (London: Darton, Longman & Todd, 1998), p. 97.
2. Joel B. Green and Mark D. Baker, *Recovering the Scandal of the Cross: Atonement in New Testament and Contemporary Contexts* (Downers Grove: IVP, 2000), p. 141.
3. Garry J. Williams, 'Justice, Law, and Guilt: A Paper Given at the Evangelical Alliance Symposium on Penal Substitution' (2005), http://www.eauk.org/theology/atonement/upload/garry_williams.pdf (accessed 27 March 2006), p. 6.

by their colleague's act of self-sacrifice. But, as events turn out, the missing tools are later re-counted and none is found to be missing.[4]

Weston acknowledges, 'This story may be profoundly moving as an example of supreme self-sacrifice'[5], but points out some significant shortcomings:

> God the Father is pictured as a sadistic camp guard screaming for vengeance on charges that turn out to be entirely false; Jesus the Son is represented as an innocent bystander unwittingly caught up in the drama but motivated on impulse to sacrifice himself at the hands of the enemy (God the Father by implication); and the resulting bloodbath is portrayed not only as a senseless waste of human life, but also as a complete travesty of justice.[6]

D. A. Carson, another advocate of penal substitution, notes the misunderstanding inherent in the 'judge' illustration criticized by Smail. He explains the problem in more detail:

> In certain crucial ways, human law courts, whether contemporary or ancient Hebrew courts, are merely analogical models and cannot highlight one or two crucial distinctions that are necessarily operative when the judge is God. In particular, both the contemporary judge and the judge of the Hebrew law court is an administrator of a system. To take the contemporary court: in no sense has the criminal legally offended the judge . . . the crime has been 'against the state' or 'against the people' or 'against the laws of the land.' In such a system, for the administrator of the system, the judge, to take the criminal's place would be profoundly unjust; it would be a perversion of the justice required by the system, of which the judge is the sworn administrator. But when God is the judge, the offense is always and necessarily against him. He is never the administrator of a system external to himself; he is the offended party as well as the impartial judge. To force the categories of merely human courts onto these uniquely divine realities is bound to lead to distortion.[7]

---

4. Paul Weston, 'Proclaiming Christ Crucified Today: Some Reflections on John's Gospel', in David Peterson (ed.), *Where Wrath and Mercy Meet: Proclaiming the Atonement Today* (Carlisle: Paternoster, 2001), pp. 136–162 (p. 148).

5. Ibid.

6. Ibid.

7. D. A. Carson, 'Atonement in Romans 3:21–26: "God Presented Him as a Propitiation"', in C. E. Hill and F. A. James III (eds.), *The Glory of the Atonement* (Downers Grove: IVP; Leicester: Apollas, 2004), pp. 119–139 (p. 132).

## Exploring the problem

Weston and Carson's observations shed light on why illustrations sometimes work well, and why they sometimes mislead. An illustration works well when it corresponds closely to the biblical idea it seeks to explain. Translating an unfamiliar concept into everyday terms can bring clarity and perhaps also a certain vividness and immediacy. It brings our world and the Bible's world together, and puts us and our lives into the picture. However, illustrations never correspond to reality at *every* point, and it is at the points of difference that they may mislead. In the case of the story from *Miracle on the River Kwai*, the key point of similarity is the extraordinary, self-sacrificial love of the soldier who died, which powerfully illustrates the love of Christ for his people. The important points of difference are between the callous sadism of the camp guard and the love of God the Father, the injustice of the soldier's death and the justice of the cross, the senselessness of the soldier's death and the wisdom of the cross.

Let us reflect on the illustrations Smail, Green and Baker cite. The story of the judge in the courtroom is a good illustration of the fact that God graciously takes action to save guilty, sinful men and women from the punishment we deserve for our sin. However, as Carson points out, the problem is that the judge (representing God) does not act justly in doing so. Instead, he violates justice by unilaterally letting the criminal off the hook. There would be a public outcry if a judge in a human court acted like this, and rightly so. This contrasts starkly with Paul's emphasis in Romans 3:25–26 that the atonement is a *demonstration* of God's justice, not an infringement of it. In fact, this particular difficulty with the story stems from a deeper problem; namely, that the law does not reflect the character and will of the judge. Instead, it stands outside him, constraining him, and he therefore needs to find a way around it in order to spare the criminal from punishment. By contrast, the law by which all humanity stands justly condemned before God is a flawless reflection of his holy being, which perfectly expresses his own character.

The story of the railway switchman illustrates the substitutionary nature of Christ's death, but gives a distorted portrayal of God's will and God's law. The switchman (representing God the Father) is compelled to make a choice between two distinctly unpalatable options, and the decision is forced upon him by the pressure of unforeseen circumstances. His son is an unfortunate, passive victim who has landed himself and his father in this dreadful situation by sheer carelessness, and he does not willingly consent to die. This contrasts starkly with the biblical picture of the cross as part of God's eternal plan, devised before the creation of the world to glorify the Son; of the Father as the one who deliberately chose to send his Son into the world; of the Son as the willing, determined, self-giving Saviour of his people. As Garry Williams concludes, 'The son has no idea of what is going on, and presumably should not have been standing around on a railway track in the first place. Let me be clear: this illustration is a total travesty of penal substitution.'[8]

## Addressing the problem

At this point, we may be tempted to throw up our hands in frustration and concede defeat. The fact is that no illustration is perfect, if by 'perfect' we mean it corresponds with reality at every point. Does that mean every illustration is invalid? Does it mean every sermon that uses illustrations is doomed to mislead at the very points we are making the most effort to be clear? Should we abandon illustrations altogether?

Of course we should not. After all, the Bible is filled with illustrations. The fact that an illustration does not correspond with reality at every point does not mean it will *always* mislead; merely that it ought to be used to illustrate only those aspects of reality with which it does correspond. To take an example, consider Isaiah 53:7, with its brief illustration of the ministry of the Servant of the Lord:

> He was oppressed and afflicted,
>     yet he did not open his mouth;
> he was led like a lamb to the slaughter,
>     and as a sheep before her shearers is silent,
>     so he did not open his mouth.

This text compares the Servant to a sheep standing silently, meekly, submissively before its shearers. It is true there are major differences between the scene depicted here and the biblical doctrine of the atonement, for the sheep is essentially passive, whereas Christ determinedly chose to go to the cross; sin, law and justice are not mentioned, whereas these are essential elements of the work of Christ; no beneficiary is explicitly involved, whereas Christ died *for us*, to reconcile us to God. However, Isaiah does not use this illustration to illustrate the will of the Messiah, the justice and law of God, or the sin and salvation of humanity. In the context, Isaiah uses it simply to shed light on the silence and submissiveness of the Servant throughout oppression and

---

8. Williams, 'Justice, Law, and Guilt', p. 6.

affliction as he is led to his death, and brings these aspects of the Servant's ministry to life in a striking way.

The criticisms cited above therefore do not mean we must abandon our illustrations altogether. We just need to take care not to press them too far, or to use them to illustrate the wrong things. To repeat: it is the points at which they fail to correspond to reality that are liable to mislead. The risk of this is increased when we are attempting to explain something complicated, for no single analogy will be up to the job. There is no illustration that can capture the whole doctrine of penal substitution without obscuring important subtleties. And even if we choose (wisely) to illustrate just one aspect of it, we must take care we do not inadvertently distort other closely related themes. For example, some illustrations of God's love distort his justice, as in the case of the judge cited above.

The solution, then, is not to abandon illustrations in preaching, but to make sure we use them carefully, and in particular to ensure they do not extend beyond their rightful limits. To avoid being misunderstood, we need to consider the specific strengths and weaknesses of any given illustration: what it captures well, and where it might fail. The following seven questions may help:

1. *Does the illustration deny the active, consenting involvement of the Father and the Son?* Are their wills directly opposed to each other? Is the Son merely a passive participant, or an unwilling victim, exercising no consent at all? Is the Father a coercive or manipulative figure, acting against the wishes of the Son, or even without his knowledge? According to the Bible, both Father and Son actively consent to their saving work; any other representation undermines the doctrine of the Trinity.

2. *Does the illustration imply a conflict between God's law and God's will?* Is the law pictured as an external restriction on God's will? Is God 'hemmed in' by the law in such a way that he is forced to look for a loophole? Is there a suggestion that the law is bad, or that the proposed punishment is unjust? According to the Bible, God's law is perfect, a flawless reflection of his character and his will.

3. *Does the illustration imply that God's action in averting our punishment is unjust?* Does God violate the spirit, if not the letter, of the law? This problem often arises as a consequence of the previous one, for if God's will conflicts with his law he will inevitably be forced to try to find a way around it. According to the Bible, the atonement is a demonstration and vindication of God's justice, not a violation of it.

4. *Does the illustration imply a conflict between God's wrath and God's will?* Is God's wrath pictured as something impersonal, outside himself, which he

struggles to control? The Bible depicts God's wrath as his personal, settled, holy response to human sin.

5. *Does the illustration imply a conflict between God's attributes?* Do the demands of God's justice and holiness conflict with those of his love? Does his love 'overcome' his wrath? Some illustrations implicitly cast God's justice or wrath in a negative light and allow it to be swamped by something else (normally his love), whereas the Bible teaches that all God's actions are carried out in accordance with all his attributes, and that the cross is as much a manifestation of God's justice, wrath and holiness as of his love.

6. *Does the illustration imply that God did not foreordain Christ's atoning work?* Is the cross conceived as God's solution to an unforeseen dilemma, or purely as his response to the pressure of urgent circumstances? Is God taken by surprise and forced to act precipitately? According to Scripture, the cross is the climax of God's eternal plan of salvation, conceived before the creation of the world.

7. *Does the illustration imply that no-one actually benefits from God's saving work?* Is the atonement conceived purely as a transaction between Father and Son, with no implications for sinful humanity? According to Scripture, the cross saved sinners as well as glorifying God.

Some of our illustrations may be so seriously flawed they are best avoided altogether. One such example is the story of a tribal chief who is confronted with the news that a member of the tribe has committed a crime against the tribal law. He insists that the usual punishment be inflicted (a public beating), whereupon the messenger nervously informs his leader that the offender is none other than the chief's own son. The chief insists the punishment must stand, but after his son is tied to a stake the chief stands behind him, embracing him and absorbing the pain of the blows himself.

This moving tale has all of the problems of the episode recounted above involving the judge – it makes a mockery of justice because the man responsible for administering the law exploits an unjust loophole in the system with the result that the guilty man is *not* punished, and it portrays the law as standing against the will of the judge, rather than perfectly reflecting it. But there is an even more serious problem: the *son* commits the crime, and the *father* is punished! The intention is presumably to illustrate God's love for us by the analogy with the chief's love for his son. However, once the illustration is detached from the context in which it is told, fatal confusion could easily arise. There is little to stop the chief's son from being identified with God's Son, and the chief with God the Father. The story would then cause disastrous misunderstanding, because Christ is depicted not as an innocent, self-giving Saviour but as a wicked criminal, and it is God the Father who suffers, not the incarnate Lord Jesus. Obviously, no preacher would ever deliberately represent the cross in this way, but the verbal coincidence is unfortunate, to put it mildly. Such misunderstanding is all the more likely if this story is used in evangelistic contexts, where the hearers have little prior understanding of the gospel. In view of the potential seriousness of this confusion, this story should be abandoned altogether.

In closing, let us reiterate that an illustration is not useless just because it fails to convey everything perfectly, or scores less than 100% on the checklist above. Isaiah's illustration of the silent sheep would be a very poor illustration of the *whole* of the doctrine of the atonement, but Isaiah does not use it that way. Vividly, movingly, he captures a single aspect of the Servant's character that Jesus so wonderfully fulfilled. As Peter, an eye-witness of the events that first Good Friday, later recalled, 'When they hurled their insults at him, he did not retaliate; when he suffered, he made no threats. Instead, he entrusted himself to him who judges justly' (1 Pet. 2:23). Not a sound from the perfect Lamb of God, as he humbly submitted to his Father's will. Praise him.

# BIBLIOGRAPHY

ALAND, B., K. ALAND, J. KARAVIDOPOULOS, C. M. MARTINI and B. M. METZGER
(eds.), *The Greek New Testament*, 4th edn (Stuttgart: Deutsche Biblegesellschaft, 2001).

ALEXANDER, T. D., 'The Passover Sacrifice', in Roger T. Beckwith and Martin J. Selman
(eds.), *Sacrifice in the Bible* (Carlisle: Paternoster; Grand Rapids: Baker, 1995), pp. 1–24.

AMBROSE of MILAN, *Flight from the World*, in *The Fathers of the Church*, vol. 65, trans. M. P.
McHugh (Washington, DC: Catholic University of America Press, 1972), pp. 281–323.

—, *On the Holy Spirit*, in *Nicene and Post-Nicene Fathers*, ser. II, vol. 10 (Grand Rapids:
Eerdmans, 1976).

AQUINAS, THOMAS, *Summa Theologiae* (London: Eyre & Spottiswoode, 1965).

ATHANASIUS, *Against the Arians*, in *Nicene and Post-Nicene Fathers*, ser. II, vol. 4 (Grand
Rapids: Eerdmans, repr. 1975).

—, *Defence of the Nicene Definitions*, in *Nicene and Post-Nicene Fathers*, ser. II, vol. 4 (Grand
Rapids: Eerdmans, repr. 1975).

—, *On the Incarnation* (New York: St. Vladimir's Seminary Press, 1993).

AUGUSTINE, *Against Faustus*, in *Nicene and Post-Nicene Fathers*, ser. I, vol. 4 (Grand Rapids:
Eerdmans, 1974).

—, *City of God*, trans. Henry Bettenson (London: Penguin, 1984).

—, *On the Trinity*, in *Nicene and Post-Nicene Fathers*, ser. I, vol. 3 (Grand Rapids: Eerdmans,
1956).

—, *Sermon XXI, on Matthew 12:32*, in *Nicene and Post-Nicene Fathers*, ser. I, vol. 6 (Grand
Rapids: Eerdmans, 1974).

AUGUSTINE, *Tractate XX, on John 5:19*, in *Nicene and Post-Nicene Fathers*, ser. I, vol. 7 (Grand Rapids: Eerdmans, 1974).

AULÉN, GUSTAV, Christus Victor: *An Historical Study of the Three Main Types of the Idea of the Atonement*, trans. A. G. Herbert (London: SPCK, 1945; first pub. 1931).

—, *The Faith of the Christian Church* (Philadelphia: Muhlenberg, 1948).

BALMER, R., *Encyclopedia of Evangelicalism* (Louisville: Westminster John Knox, 2002).

BAUER, WALTER, *A Greek-English Lexicon of the New Testament and Other Early Christian Literature*, 3rd edn, rev. and ed. F. W. Danker (Chicago: University of Chicago Press, 2000).

BAVINCK, HERMAN, *Reformed Dogmatics*, vol. 2: *God and Creation* (Grand Rapids: Baker, 2002).

—, *The Doctrine of God*, trans. W. Hendricksen (Edinburgh: Banner of Truth, 1977).

BERKHOF, LOUIS, *Systematic Theology* (London: Banner of Truth, 1959; first pub. 1941).

BETHUNE-BAKER, J. F., *An Introduction to the Early History of Christian Doctrine* (London: Methuen, 1903; repr. 1933).

BLOCHER, HENRI, '*Agnus Victor*: The Atonement as Victory and Vicarious Punishment', in John G. Stackhouse (ed.), *What Does It Mean to Be Saved?* (Grand Rapids: Baker, 2002), pp. 67–91.

—, 'Biblical Metaphors and the Doctrine of the Atonement', *Journal of the Evangelical Theological Society* 47 (2004), pp. 629–645.

—, 'Everlasting Punishment and the Problem of Evil', in N. M. De S. Cameron (ed.), *Universalism and the Doctrine of Hell* (Carlisle: Paternoster; Grand Rapids: Baker, 1992), pp. 283–312.

—, *Evil and the Cross: Christian Thought and the Problem of Evil*, trans. D. G. Preston (Leicester: Apollos, 1990).

—, 'The Sacrifice of Christ: The Current Theological Situation', *European Journal of Theology* 8.1 (1999), pp. 23–36.

BOLT, PETER G., *The Cross from a Distance: Atonement in Mark's Gospel*, New Studies in Biblical Theology 18 (Downers Grove: IVP; Leicester: Apollos, 2004).

BOWDEN, J., *Who's Who in Theology* (London: SCM, 1990).

BROCK, RITA NAKASHIMA, 'And a Little Child Will Lead Us: Christology and Child Abuse', in Joanne Carlson Brown and Carole R. Bohn (eds.), *Christianity, Patriarchy and Abuse: A Feminist Critique* (New York: Pilgrim, 1989), pp. 42–61.

BROWN, JOANNE CARLSON and CAROLE R. BOHN (eds.), *Christianity, Patriarchy and Abuse: A Feminist Critique* (New York: Pilgrim, 1989).

BROWN, JOANNE CARLSON and REBECCA PARKER, 'For God So Loved the World?', in Joanne Carlson Brown and Carole R. Bohn (eds.), *Christianity, Patriarchy, and Abuse: A Feminist Critique* (New York: Pilgrim, 1989), pp. 1–30.

BROWN, RAYMOND E., *The Gospel According to John*, Anchor Bible (London: Geoffrey Chapman, 1966).

BRUCE, F. F., *The Canon of Scripture* (Downers Grove: IVP, 1988).

—, *The Epistle to the Galatians*, New International Greek Testament Commentary (Exeter: Paternoster, 1982).

BÜCHSEL, F., 'Hilaskomai, hilasmos', in G. Kittel (ed.), *Theological Dictionary of the New Testament*, vol. 3 (Grand Rapids: Eerdmans, 1965), pp. 301–318.

BUNYAN, JOHN, *The Pilgrim's Progress* (Oxford: Oxford University Press; this version first pub. 1966).

BUSHNELL, HORACE, *The Vicarious Sacrifice* (London: Alexander Strahan, 1866).

CALVIN, JOHN, *Institutes of the Christian Religion*, trans. F. L. Battles, 2 vols. (Philadelphia: Westminster, 1960).

—, *The Epistles of Paul to the Romans and Thessalonians*, trans. Ross Mackenzie, eds. David W. Torrance and Thomas F. Torrance (Grand Rapids: Eerdmans, 1995).

CAMPBELL, JOHN MCLEOD, *The Nature of the Atonement* (Cambridge: Macmillan, 1856).

CAREY, P. W. and J. T. LIENHARD (eds.), *Biographical Dictionary of Christian Theologians* (Peabody: Hendrickson, 2002).

CARROLL, JOHN T. and JOEL B. GREEN, with ROBERT E. VAN VOORST, JOEL MARCUS and DONALD SENIOR, C. P., *The Death of Jesus in Early Christianity* (Peabody: Hendrickson, 1995).

CARSON, D. A., 'Atonement in Romans 3:21–26', in C. E. Hill and F. A. James III (eds.), *The Glory of the Atonement* (Downers Grove: IVP; Leicester: Apollos, 2004), pp. 119–139.

—, *Becoming Conversant with the Emerging Church: Understanding a Movement and Its Implications* (Grand Rapids: Zondervan, 2005).

—, *Divine Sovereignty and Human Responsibility: Biblical Perspectives in Tension* (London: Marshall, Morgan & Scott, 1981).

—, *Exegetical Fallacies* (Grand Rapids: Baker, 1984).

—, *How Long, O Lord?* (Leicester: IVP, 1990).

—, *Matthew: Chapters 1 through 12*, Expositor's Bible Commentary (Grand Rapids: Zondervan, 1995).

—, *The Difficult Doctrine of the Love of God* (Leicester: IVP, 2000).

—, *The Gospel According to John*, Pillar New Testament Commentary (Leicester: Apollos; Grand Rapids: Eerdmans, 1991).

CARSON, D. A., P. T. O'BRIEN and M. A. SEIFRID (eds.), *Justification and Variegated Nomism*, vol. 1: *The Complexities of Second Temple Judaism* (Tübingen: Mohr Siebeck; Grand Rapids: Baker, 2001).

—, *Justification and Variegated Nomism*, vol. 2: *The Paradoxes of Paul* (Tübingen: Mohr Siebeck; Grand Rapids: Baker, 2004).

CHALKE, STEVE, 'Cross Purposes', *Christianity* (September 2004), pp. 44–48.

CHALKE, STEVE and ALAN MANN, *The Lost Message of Jesus* (Grand Rapids: Zondervan, 2003).

CHILDS, BREVARD S., *Isaiah*, Old Testament Library (Louisville: Westminster John Knox, 2001).

*Christian Hymns* (Bryntirion, Bridgend: Evangelical Movement of Wales, 1977).

CHRYSOSTOM, JOHN, *Homilies on Second Corinthians*, in *Nicene and Post-Nicene Fathers*, ser. I, vol. 12 (Grand Rapids: Eerdmans, repr. 1969).

COOPER, BEN, *Just Love: Why God Must Punish Sin* (London: Good Book, 2005).

—, *Must God Punish Sin?* (London: Latimer Trust, 2005).

CRANFIELD, C. E. B., *A Critical and Exegetical Commentary on the Epistle to the Romans*, vol. 1, International Critical Commentary (Edinburgh: T. & T. Clark, 1975).

CRISP, OLIVER D., 'On Barth's Denial of Universalism', *Themelios* 29.1 (autumn 2003), pp. 18–29.

—, 'On the Theological Pedigree of Jonathan Edwards's Doctrine of Imputation', *Scottish Journal of Theology* 56 (2003), pp. 308–327.

CUNNINGHAM, WILLIAM, *Works of William Cunningham*, vol. 3 (Edinburgh: T. & T. Clark, 1863).

CYRIL OF ALEXANDRIA, *De adoratione et cultu in spiritu et veritate*, iii, 100–102, in J. P. Migne (ed.), *Patrologiae Cursus Completus: Series Graeca*, vol. 68 (Paris, 1857–).

DAS, A. ANDREW, *Paul, the Law, and the Covenant* (Peabody: Hendrickson, 2001).

DAVIE, MARTIN, 'Dead to Sin and Alive to God', *Scottish Bulletin of Evangelical Theology* 19 (2001), pp. 158–194.

DAVIES, W. C. and D. C. ALLISON, *A Critical and Exegetical Commentary on the Gospel According to Saint Matthew*, International Critical Commentary, vol. 1 (Edinburgh: T. & T. Clark, 1988).

DENNEY, JAMES, *The Death of Christ* (London: Hodder & Stoughton, 1902).

DIMOCK, N., *The Death of Christ*, 2nd edn (London: Elliot Stock, 1903).

DOCTRINE COMMISSION OF THE CHURCH OF ENGLAND, *The Mystery of Salvation* (London: Church House, 1995).

DODD, C. H., '*Hilaskesthai*, its Cognates, Derivatives and Synonyms, in the Septuagint', *Journal of Theological Studies* 32 (1931), pp. 352–360.

—, *The Epistle of Paul to the Romans* (London: Hodder & Stoughton, 1932).

—, *The Johannine Epistles* (London: Hodder & Stoughton, 1946).

DUMBRELL, W. J., *Covenant and Creation: A Theology of the Old Testament Covenants* (Carlisle: Paternoster, 1984).

DUNN, JAMES D. G., *The Epistle to the Galatians*, Black's New Testament Commentaries (London: A. & C. Black, 1993).

—, *The Theology of Paul the Apostle* (Grand Rapids: Eerdmans, 1998).

*Ecumenical Creeds and Reformed Confessions* (Grand Rapids: Eerdmans: CRC, 1988).

EDWARDS, JONATHAN, 'Concerning the Necessity and Reasonableness of the Christian Doctrine of Satisfaction for Sin', in *The Works of Jonathan Edwards*, vol. 2 (Edinburgh: Banner of Truth, repr. 1986), pp. 565–578.

—, *The Great Christian Doctrine of Original Sin Defended*, in C. A. Holbrook (ed.), *The Works of Jonathan Edwards*, vol. 3, corrected edn (Yale: Yale University Press, 1997), pp. 102–437.

EHRHARDT, A. A. T., *The Framework of the New Testament Stories* (Manchester: Manchester University Press, 1964).

ENNS, PETER, *Exodus*, New International Version Application Commentary (Grand Rapids: Zondervan, 2000).

EUSEBIUS OF CAESAREA, *Proof of the Gospel*, trans. and ed. W. J. Ferrar (London: SPCK; New York: Macmillan, 1920).

*Evangelical Alliance Atonement Symposium Statement*, 8 July 2005, www.eauk.org/theology/atonement/atonement-statement.cfm (accessed 21 April 2006).

*Evangelical Belief: An Explanation of the Doctrinal Basis of the Inter-Varsity Fellowship*, 4th edn (London: IVP, 1973).

FAGOTHEY, AUSTIN, S. J., *Right and Reason: Ethics in Theory and Practice*, 2nd edn (Rockford: Tan, 1959).

FAHLBUSH, E. et al. (eds.), *The Encyclopedia of Christianity* (Grand Rapids: Eerdmans; Leiden: Brill, 1999).

FERGUSON, E. (ed.), *Encyclopedia of Early Christianity* (Chicago: St. James, 1990).

FIDDES, PAUL S., *Past Event and Present Salvation: The Christian Idea of Atonement* (London: Darton, Longman & Todd, 1989).

FIELD, DAVID P., *Rigide Calvinisme in a Softer Dresse: The Moderate Presbyterianism of John Howe, 1630–1705* (Edinburgh: Rutherford House, 2004).

FRAME, JOHN M., *No Other God* (Phillipsburg: Presbyterian & Reformed, 2001).

—, *The Doctrine of God* (Phillipsburg: Presbyterian & Reformed, 2002).

—, *The Doctrine of the Knowledge of God* (Phillipsburg: Presbyterian & Reformed, 1987).

FRANCE, R. T., 'Chronological Aspects of "Gospel Harmony"', *Vox Evangelica* 16 (1986), pp. 33–59.

—, *The Gospel According to Matthew: An Introduction and Commentary*, Tyndale New Testament Commentaries (Leicester: IVP, 1985).

—, 'The Servant of the Lord in the Teaching of Jesus', *Tyndale Bulletin* 19 (1968), pp. 26–52.

FRETHEIM, T., *Exodus*, Interpretation (Louisville: John Knox, 1991).

GAFFIN, RICHARD B., JR., 'Atonement in the Pauline Corpus', in C. E. Hill and F. A. James III (eds.), *The Glory of the Atonement* (Downers Grove: IVP; Leicester: Apollos, 2004), pp. 140–162.

—, *Resurrection and Redemption: A Study in Paul's Soteriology*, 2nd edn (Phillipsburg: Presbyterian & Reformed, 1987).

GATHERCOLE, SIMON J., 'Justified by Faith, Justified by His Blood: The Evidence of Romans 3:21–4:25', in D. A. Carson, P. T. O'Brien and M. A. Seifrid (eds.) *Justification and Variegated Nomism*, vol. 2: *The Paradoxes of Paul* (Tübingen: Mohr Siebeck; Grand Rapids: Baker, 2004), pp. 147–184.

—, *Where Is Boasting? Early Jewish Soteriology and Paul's Response in Romans 1–5* (Grand Rapids: Eerdmans, 2002).

GELASIUS OF CYZICUS, *Church History*, ii, 24, in *Die Griechischen Christlichen Schriftsteller der ersten drei Jahrhunderte* (Leipzig: Preussische Akademie der Wissenschaften, 1897–).

GIRARD, RENÉ, *The Scapegoat* (Baltimore: Johns Hopkins University Press, 1986).

—, *Things Hidden since the Foundation of the World*, trans. Stephen Bann and Michael Metteer (Stanford: Stanford University Press, 1987).

—, *Violence and the Sacred* (Baltimore: Johns Hopkins University Press, 1977).

GOLDINGAY, JOHN (ed.) *Atonement Today* (London: SPCK, 1995).

—, 'Old Testament Sacrifice and the Death of Christ', in John Goldingay (ed.), *Atonement Today* (London: SPCK, 1995), pp. 3–20.

—, 'Your Iniquities Have Made a Separation between You and Your God', in John Goldingay (ed.), *Atonement Today* (London: SPCK, 1995), pp. 39–53.

GOLIGHER, LIAM, *The Jesus Gospel: Recovering the Lost Message* (Milton Keynes: Authentic Media, 2006).

GORRINGE, TIMOTHY, *God's Just Vengeance: Crime, Violence and the Rhetoric of Salvation* (Cambridge: Cambridge University Press, 1996).

GREEN, JOEL B. and MARK D. BAKER, *Recovering the Scandal of the Cross: Atonement in New Testament and Contemporary Contexts* (Downers Grove: IVP, 2000).

GREENE, COLIN, 'Is the Message of the Cross Good News for the Twentieth Century?', in John Goldingay (ed.), *Atonement Today* (London: SPCK, 1995), pp. 222–239.

GREGORY OF NAZIANZUS, *The Fourth Theological Oration*, in *Nicene and Post-Nicene Fathers*, ser. II, vol. 7 (Grand Rapids: Eerdmans, repr. 1974).

GREGORY THE GREAT, *Morals on the Book of Job*, vol. 1 (Oxford: John Henry Parker, 1844).

GRENSTED, L. W., *A Short History of the Doctrine of the Atonement* (Manchester: Manchester University Press; London: Longmans, Green, 1920).

GROVES, J. ALAN, 'Atonement in Isaiah 53', in C. E. Hill and F. A. James III (eds.), *The Glory of the Atonement* (Downers Grove: IVP; Leicester: Apollos, 2004), pp. 61–89.

GRUDEM, WAYNE, *Systematic Theology: An Introduction to Biblical Doctrine* (Leicester: IVP, 1994).

GUNTON, COLIN E., *The Actuality of Atonement: A Study of Metaphor, Rationality and the Christian Tradition* (Edinburgh: T. & T. Clark, 1988).

HANSON, A. T., *The Wrath of the Lamb* (London: SPCK, 1957).

HARTLEY, J. E., *Leviticus*, Word Biblical Commentary (Dallas: Word, 1992).

HELM, PAUL, *Calvin and the Calvinists* (Edinburgh: Banner of Truth, 1982).

HENRY, MATTHEW, *Matthew Henry's Commentary on the Whole Bible*, vol. 6 (Peabody, MA: Henrickson, 1991).

HILARY OF POITIERS, *Homily on Psalm 53 (54)*, in *Nicene and Post-Nicene Fathers*, ser. II, vol. 9 (Grand Rapids: Eerdmans, repr. 1976).

—, *On the Trinity*, in *Nicene and Post-Nicene Fathers*, ser. II, vol. 9 (Grand Rapids: Eerdmans, 1976), pp. 40–233.

HILL, CHARLES E. and FRANK A. JAMES III (eds.), *The Glory of the Atonement: Biblical, Historical and Practical Perspectives* (Downers Grove: IVP; Leicester: Apollos, 2004).

HIPPOLYTUS, *The Refutation of All Heresies*, in *The Ante-Nicene Fathers*, vol. 5 (Grand Rapids: Eerdmans, 1968).

HODGE, CHARLES, *Systematic Theology*, vol. 2 (London: James Clarke, 1960).

HOFIUS, OTFRIED, 'The Fourth Servant Song in the New Testament Letters', in B. Janowski and P. Stuhlmacher (eds.), *The Suffering Servant: Isaiah 53 in Jewish and Christian Sources*, trans. Daniel P. Bailey (Grand Rapids: Eerdmans, 2004), pp. 163–188.

HOLMES, M. W., *The Apostolic Fathers: Greek Texts with English Translation* (Grand Rapids: Baker, 1999).

HOOKER, MORNA D., 'Did the Use of Isaiah 53 to Interpret His Mission Begin with Jesus?', in William H. Bellinger, Jr., and William R. Farmer (eds.), *Jesus and the Suffering Servant* (Harrisburg: Trinity Press International, 1998), pp. 88–103.

—, *Jesus and the Servant: The Influence of the Servant Concept of Deutero-Isaiah in the New Testament* (London: SPCK, 1959).

INSTONE-BREWER, D., *Techniques and Assumptions in Jewish Exegesis before 70 CE*, Texte und Studien zum Antiken Judentum 30 (Tübingen: Mohr Siebeck, 1992).

IRENAEUS, *Against Heresies*, in *The Ante-Nicene Fathers*, vol. 1 (Grand Rapids: Eerdmans, 1973).

JACKSON, S. M. (ed.), *The New Schaff-Herzogg Encyclopedia of Religious Knowledge* (New York: Funk & Wagnalls, 1910).

JANOWSKI, B. and P. Stuhlmacher (eds.), *The Suffering Servant: Isaiah 53 in Jewish and Christian Sources*, trans. Daniel P. Bailey (Grand Rapids: Eerdmans, 2004).

JOHNSON, D. (ed.), *A Brief History of the International Fellowship of Evangelical Students* (Lausanne: International Fellowship of Evangelical Students, 1964).

KAMINSKY JOEL S., *Corporate Responsibility in the Hebrew Bible*, Journal for the Study of the Old Testament Supplement Series 196 (Sheffield: Sheffield Academic Press, 1995).

KENDALL, R. T., *Calvin and English Calvinism to 1649* (Carlisle: Paternoster, 1997; first pub. 1977).

KEYES, R., 'The Idol Factory', in O. Guinness and J. Seel (eds.), *Breaking with the Idols of Our Age* (Chicago: Moody, 1992), pp. 29–48.

KIDNER, DEREK, 'Retribution and Punishment in the Old Testament, in the Light of the New Testament', *Scottish Bulletin of Evangelical Theology* 1 (1983), pp. 3–9.

KNOX, D. BROUGHTON, 'Some Aspects of the Atonement', in Tony Payne (ed.), *Selected Works*, vol. 1: *The Doctrine of God* (Kingsford: Matthias Media, 2000), pp. 253–266.

KOEHLER, LUDWIG and WALTER BAUMGARTNER, *The Hebrew and Aramaic Lexicon of the Old Testament*, Study Edn, vol. 1 (Leiden: Brill, 2001).

LANE, TONY, *The Lion Book of Christian Thought* (Oxford: Lion, 1984).

LANE, WILLIAM L., *The Gospel of Mark*, New International Commentary on the New Testament (Grand Rapids: Eerdmans, 1974).

LARSEN, T. (ed.), *Biographical Dictionary of Evangelicals* (Leicester: IVP, 2003).

LEWIS, C. S., 'The Humanitarian Theory of Punishment', in *God in the Dock* (Grand
Rapids: Eerdmans, 1970), pp. 287–294; also pub. in *Churchmen Speak* (Abingdon:
Marcham Manor, 1966), pp. 39–44; and in *Churchman* 73 (1959), pp. 55–60.

—, *The Lion, the Witch and the Wardrobe* (London: Fontana, 1980; first pub. 1950).

LLOYD-JONES, D. M., *Romans: An Exposition of Chapters 3:20–4:25, Atonement and Justification*
(London: Banner of Truth, 1970).

LUTHER, MARTIN, *A Commentary on St Paul's Epistle to the Galatians* (London: James
Clarke, 1953).

—, *The Freedom of a Christian*, in *Three Treatises*, trans. W. A. Lambert, rev. H. J. Grimm
(Philadelphia: Fortress, 1970).

MACGREGOR, G. H. C., 'The Concept of the Wrath of God in the New Testament',
*New Testament Studies* 7 (1960–61), pp. 101–109.

MANN, ALAN, *Atonement for a 'Sinless' Society: Engaging with an Emerging Culture* (Milton
Keynes: Paternoster, 2005).

MARCUS, JOEL, 'The Old Testament and the Death of Jesus: The Role of Scripture in
the Gospel Passion Narratives', in John T. Carroll and Joel B. Green (eds.), *The Death
of Jesus in Early Christianity* (Peabody: Hendrickson, 1995), pp. 205–233.

MARTYR, JUSTIN, *Dialogue with Trypho, a Jew*, in *Ante-Nicene Fathers*, vol. 1 (Grand Rapids:
Eerdmans, repr. 1969), pp. 194–270.

MCCARTNEY, DAN G., 'Atonement in James, Peter and Jude', in Charles E. Hill and
Frank A. James III (eds.), *The Glory of the Atonement: Biblical Historical and Practical
Perspectives* (Downers Grove: IVP; Leicester: Apollos, 2004), pp. 176–189.

MCCORMICK, PATRICK, *Sin as Addiction* (New York: Paulist Press, 1989).

MCGOWAN, A. T. B., 'The Atonement as Penal Substitution', in A. T. B. McGowan (ed.),
*Always Reforming: Explorations in Systematic Theology* (Leicester: Apollos, 2006),
pp. 183–210.

MCKNIGHT, SCOT, *Jesus and His Death: Historiography, the Historical Jesus, and Atonement
Theory* (Waco: Baylor University Press, 2005).

MCLAREN, BRIAN D., *The Story We Find Ourselves in: Further Adventures of a New Kind of
Christian* (San Francisco: Jossey-Bass, 2003).

MEYNELL, MARK, *Cross Examined: The Life-Changing Power of the Death of Jesus* (Leicester:
IVP, 2001).

MICHAELS, J. RAMSEY, *1 Peter*, Word Biblical Commentary (Waco: Word, 1988).

MOBERLY, R. C., *Atonement and Personality* (London: John Murray, 1901).

MOBERLY, W. H., *The Ethics of Punishment* (London: Faber & Faber, 1968).

MOO, DOUGLAS J., 'Israel and the Law in Romans 5–11: Interaction with the New
Perspective', in D. A. Carson, P. T. O'Brien and M. A. Seifrid (eds.), *Justification and
Variegated Nomism*, vol. 2: *The Paradoxes of Paul* (Tübingen: Mohr Siebeck; Grand
Rapids: Baker, 2004), pp. 185–216.

—, *The Epistle to the Romans*, New International Commentary on the New Testament (Grand Rapids: Eerdmans, 1996).

—, 'The Problem of *Sensus Plenior*', in D. A. Carson and John D. Woodbridge (eds.), *Hermeneutics, Authority, and Canon* (Grand Rapids: Baker, 1995), pp. 175–211.

MORGAN, CHRISTOPHER W. and ROBERT A. PETERSON, (eds.), *Hell Under Fire* (Grand Rapids: Zondervan, 2004).

MORRIS, LEON, *Glory in the Cross: A Study in Atonement* (London: Hodder & Stoughton, 1966).

—, *The Apostolic Preaching of the Cross* (London: Tyndale, 1955).

—, *The Atonement: Its Meaning and Significance* (Leicester: IVP, 1983).

—, *The Biblical Doctrine of Judgment* (London: Tyndale, 1960).

—, *The Cross in the New Testament* (Exeter: Paternoster, 1965).

—, *The Cross of Jesus* (Grand Rapids: Eerdmans; Exeter: Paternoster, 1988).

—, 'The Use of *hilaskesthai* etc. in Biblical Greek', *Expository Times* 62 (1951), pp. 227–233.

MOULTON, J. H. and G. MILLIGAN, *The Vocabulary of the Greek Testament, Illustrated from the Papyri and Other Non-Literary Sources* (London: Hodder & Stoughton, 1930).

MURRAY, JOHN, *Redemption Accomplished and Applied* (Edinburgh: Banner of Truth, 1961; first pub. Grand Rapids: Eerdmans, 1955).

—, *The Imputation of Adam's Sin* (Grand Rapids: Eerdmans, 1959; repr. Phillipsburg: Presbyterian & Reformed, 1992).

NICOLE, EMILE, 'Atonement in the Pentateuch', in C. E. Hill and F. A. James III (eds.), *The Glory of the Atonement* (Downers Grove: IVP; Leicester: Apollos, 2004), pp. 35–50.

NICOLE, ROGER, 'C. H. Dodd and the Doctrine of Propitiation', *Westminster Theological Journal* 17 (1955), pp. 117–157; repr. in *Standing Forth: Collected Writings of Roger Nicole* (Fearn: Christian Focus, 2002), pp. 343–396.

—, '*Hilaskesthai* Revisited', *Evangelical Quarterly* 49 (1977), pp. 173–177.

—, 'James I. Packer's Contribution to the Doctrine of the Inerrancy of Scripture', in D. Lewis and A. McGrath (eds.), *Doing Theology for the People of God* (Leicester: Apollos, 1996).

—, *Our Sovereign Saviour: The Essence of the Reformed Faith* (Fearn: Christian Focus, 2002).

—, 'Postscript on Penal Substitution', in Charles E. Hill and Frank A. James III (eds.), *The Glory of the Atonement: Biblical Historical and Practical Perspectives* (Downers Grove: IVP; Leicester: Apollos, 2004), pp. 445–452.

—, *Standing Forth: Collected Writings of Roger Nicole* (Fearn: Christian Focus, 2002).

—, 'The Case for Definite Atonement', *Bulletin of the Evangelical Theological Society* 10 (1967), pp. 199–207.

O'BRIEN, PETER T., *Colossians, Philemon*, Word Biblical Commentary (Nashville: Thomas Nelson, 1982).

—, *The Letter to the Ephesians*, Pillar New Testament Commentary (Leicester: Apollos; Grand Rapids: Eerdmans, 1999).

—, 'Was Paul a Covenantal Nomist?', in D. A. Carson, Peter T. O'Brien and Mark A. Seifrid (eds.), *Justification and Variegated Nomism*, vol. 2: *The Paradoxes of Paul* (Tübingen: Mohr Siebeck; Grand Rapids: Baker, 2004), pp. 249–296.

*On the Other Side: The Report of the Evangelical Alliance's Commission on Evangelism* (London: Scripture Union, 1968).

ORLINSKY, H. M., 'The So-Called "Servant of the Lord" and "Suffering Servant" in Second Isaiah", in H. M. Orlinsky and N. H. Snaith (eds.), *Studies on the Second Part of the Book of Isaiah*, Supplements to Vetus Testamentum 14 (Leiden: Brill, 1976), pp. 1–133.

OSWALT, J. N., *The Book of Isaiah, Chapters 40–66*, New International Commentary on the Old Testament (Grand Rapids: Eerdmans, 1998).

OVEY, M., 'The Cross, Creation and the Human Predicament', in David Peterson (ed.), *Where Wrath and Mercy Meet: Proclaiming the Atonement Today* (Carlisle: Paternoster, 2001), pp. 100–135.

OWEN, JOHN, *A Dissertation on Divine Justice*, in William H. Goold (ed.), *The Works of John Owen*, vol. 10 (London: Banner of Truth, repr. 1967), pp. 481–624.

—, *The Death of Death in the Death of Christ* (London: Banner of Truth, 1959); also in William H. Goold (ed.), *The Works of John Owen*, vol. 10 (London: Banner of Truth, repr. 1967), pp. 139–421.

PACKER, J. I., *'Fundamentalism' and the Word of God* (Leicester: IVP, 1958; repr. 1996).

—, *Knowing God* (London: Hodder & Stoughton, 1973; 2nd edn 1993).

—, 'Saved by his Precious Blood: An Introduction to John Owen's "The Death of Death in the Death of Christ"', in *Among God's Giants: The Puritan Vision of the Christian Life* (Eastbourne: Kingsway, 1991), pp. 163–195; also pub. as 'Introductory Essay', in John Owen, *The Death of Death in the Death of Christ* (London: Banner of Truth, 1959), pp. 1–25.

—, 'What Did the Cross Achieve? The Logic of Penal Substitution', *Tyndale Bulletin* 25 (1974), pp. 3–45; also pub. as *What Did the Cross Achieve? The Logic of Penal Substitution* (Leicester: Theological Students' Fellowship); and as 'What Did the Cross Achieve? The Logic of Penal Substitution', in *Celebrating the Saving Work of God: Collected Shorter Writings of J. I. Packer* (Carlisle: Paternoster, 1998), pp. 85–123.

PARSONS, MIKEAL C., 'Isaiah 53 in Acts 8: A Reply to Professor Morna Hooker', in William H. Bellinger, Jr., and William R. Farmer (eds.), *Jesus and the Suffering Servant* (Harrisburg: Trinity Press International, 1998), pp. 104–119.

PAYNE, D. F., 'Baal', in *The New Bible Dictionary*, 3rd edn (Leicester: IVP, 1996), p. 108.

PETERSON, DAVID, 'Atonement in the New Testament', in David Peterson (ed.), *Where Wrath and Mercy Meet: Proclaiming the Atonement Today* (Carlisle: Paternoster, 2001), pp. 26–67.

—, 'Atonement in the Old Testament', in David Peterson (ed.), *Where Wrath and Mercy Meet: Proclaiming the Atonement Today* (Carlisle: Paternoster, 2001), pp. 1–25.

—(ed.), *Where Wrath and Mercy Meet: Proclaiming the Atonement Today* (Carlisle: Paternoster, 2001).

PINNOCK, CLARK H., *Grace Unlimited* (Minneapolis: Bethany Fellowship, 1975).

PIPER, JOHN, 'Are There Two Wills in God?', in Thomas R. Schreiner and Bruce A. Ware (eds.), *Still Sovereign: Contemporary Perspectives on Election, Foreknowledge, and Grace* (Grand Rapids: Baker, 2000), pp. 107–131; repr. with minor changes in *The Pleasures of God*, rev. edn (Fearn: Christian Focus, 2001), pp. 313–340.

—, *Counted Righteous in Christ: Should we Abandon the Imputation of Christ's Righteousness?* (Leicester: IVP, 2003).

—, *The Passion of Jesus Christ: Fifty Reasons Why He Came to Die* (Wheaton: Crossway, 2004).

—, *The Pleasures of God*, rev. edn (Fearn: Christian Focus, 2001).

QUARLES, CHARLES, 'The 'APO of 2 Thessalonians 1:9 and the Nature of Eternal Punishment', *Westminster Theological Journal* 59 (1997), pp. 201–211.

RACHELS, JAMES, 'Punishment and Desert', in H. LaFollette (ed.), *Ethics in Practice*, 2nd edn (Malden, MA: Blackwell, 2002), pp. 466–474.

RANDALL, I. and D. HILBORN, *One Body in Christ: The History and Significance of the Evangelical Alliance* (Carlisle: Paternoster, 2001).

RAY, DARBY KATHLEEN, *Deceiving the Devil: Atonement, Abuse and Ransom* (Cleveland: Pilgrim, 1998).

REYMOND, ROBERT L., *The Lamb of God: The Bible's Unfolding Revelation of Sacrifice* (Fearn: Christian Focus, 2006).

ROBERTS, VAUGHAN, *Distinctives* (Carlisle: OM, 2000).

ROSS, W. D., *The Right and the Good* (Oxford: Oxford University Press, 1930).

RYLE, J. C., *Christian Leaders of the 18th Century* (London: Banner of Truth, repr. 1997).

—, *Holiness* (Welwyn: Evangelical Press, 1979; first pub. 1879).

SANDERS, E. P., *Paul and Palestinian Judaism* (Philadelphia: Fortress, 1977).

SAPP, DAVID A., 'The LXX, 1QIsa, and MT Versions of Isaiah 53 and the Christian Doctrine of Atonement', in William H. Bellinger, Jr., and William R. Farmer (eds.), *Jesus and the Suffering Servant* (Harrisburg: Trinity Press International, 1998), pp. 170–192.

SCHAEFFER, FRANCIS, *The Finished Work of Christ* (Leicester: IVP, 1998).

—, *The God Who Is There*, in *Trilogy* (Leicester: IVP, 1990), pp. 1–202.

SCHREINER, THOMAS R., *Romans*, Baker Exegetical Commentary on the New Testament (Grand Rapids: Baker, 1998).

—, 'The Penal Substitution View', in *Four Views of the Atonement* (Downers Grove: IVP, 2006), pp. 67–98.

—, *The Law and Its Fulfillment: A Pauline Theology of Law* (Grand Rapids: Baker, 1993).

SCHREINER, THOMAS R. and BRUCE A. WARE (eds.), *Still Sovereign: Contemporary Perspectives on Election, Foreknowledge, and Grace* (Grand Rapids: Baker, 2000).

SEIFRID, MARK A., 'Paul's Use of Righteousness Language against its Hellenistic Background', in D. A. Carson, Peter T. O'Brien and Mark A. Seifrid (eds.), *Justification*

*and Variegated Nomism*, vol. 2: *The Paradoxes of Paul* (Tübingen: Mohr Siebeck; Grand
  Rapids: Baker, 2004), pp. 39–74.

SHAW, IAN J., 'Justice Divine is Satisfied: The Early Methodists and Penal Substitution',
  *Foundations* (autumn 2005), pp. 23–27.

SHAW, IAN J. and BRIAN H. EDWARDS, *The Divine Substitute: The Atonement in the Bible and
  History* (Leominster: Day One, 2006).

SHEDD, WILLIAM G. T., *Dogmatic Theology* (New York: Charles Scribner's Sons, 1889).

SIDER, RONALD J., *Rich Christians in an Age of Hunger: Moving from Affluence to Generosity*,
  new edn (Nashville: W Publishing, 1997).

SILVA, MOISÉS, *Biblical Words and Their Meaning: An Introduction to Lexical Semantics*, rev. edn
  (Grand Rapids: Zondervan, 1994).

—, 'Faith Versus Works of Law in Galatians', in D. A. Carson, Peter T. O'Brien and
  Mark A. Seifrid (eds.), *Justification and Variegated Nomism*, vol. 2: *The Paradoxes of Paul*
  (Tübingen: Mohr Siebeck; Grand Rapids: Baker, 2004), pp. 217–248.

SMAIL, TOM, 'Can One Man Die for the People?', in John Goldingay (ed.), *Atonement
  Today* (London: SPCK, 1995), pp. 73–92.

SMAIL, TOM, *Once and for All: A Confession of the Cross* (London: Darton, Longman &
  Todd, 1998).

SOCINUS, FAUSTUS, *De Iesu Christo Servatore*, in *Opera Omnia*, vols. 1–2 of *Bibliotheca
  Fratrum Polonorum Quos Unitarios Vocant*, 8 vols. (Irenopoli: post 1656).

SOPHOCLES, E. A., *Greek Lexicon of the Roman and Byzantine Periods from B.C. 146 to A. D.
  1100* (Whitefish, MO: Kessinger, 2004).

SPIECKERMANN, HERMANN, 'The Conception and Prehistory of the Idea of Vicarious
  Suffering in the Old Testament', in B. Janowski and P. Stuhlmacher (eds.), *The Suffering
  Servant: Isaiah 53 in Jewish and Christian Sources*, trans. Daniel P. Bailey (Grand Rapids:
  Eerdmans, 2004), pp. 1–15.

SPURGEON, C. H., 'Our Suffering Substitute: A Sermon on 1 Peter 3:18', originally pub.
  in *The Sword and The Trowel Magazine* (1895),
  http://www.members.aol.com/pilgrimpub/substute.htm (accessed 20 February
  2006).

—, 'Sin Laid on Jesus', Sermon no. 694 in *The Metropolitan Tabernacle Pulpit: Sermons
  Preached and Revised by C. H. Spurgeon during the Year 1866*, vol. 12 (London: Passmore &
  Alabaster, 1896), pp. 313–324.

—, 'The Blood of Sprinking (part 1)', Sermon no. 1888 in *The Metropolitan Tabernacle
  Pulpit: Sermons Preached and Revised by C. H. Spurgeon during the Year 1886*, vol. 32 (London:
  Passmore & Alabaster), pp. 121–132.

STIBBS, ALAN M., *The Meaning of the Word 'Blood' in Scripture* (London: Tyndale, 1948).

STOTT, JOHN R. W., *Issues Facing Christians Today*, rev. edn (London: Marshall Pickering,
  1990; first pub. 1984).

—, *The Cross of Christ* (Leicester: IVP, 1986).

STRANGE, DAN, 'The Many-Splendoured Cross: Atonement, Controversy, and Victory', *Foundations* (autumn 2005), pp. 5–22.

STUMP, ELEONORE, 'Atonement According to Aquinas', in Thomas V. Morris (ed.), *Philosophy and the Christian Faith* (Notre Dame: University of Notre Dame Press, 1988), pp. 61–91.

SYKES, STEPHEN W., 'Outline of a Theology of Sacrifice', in Stephen W. Sykes (ed.), *Sacrifice and Redemption: Durham Essays in Theology* (Cambridge: Cambridge University Press, 1991), pp. 282–298.

—, *The Story of Atonement* (London: Darton, Longman & Todd, 1997).

TASKER, R. V. G., *The Biblical Doctrine of the Wrath of God* (London: Tyndale, 1951).

TERTULLIAN, *Against Praxeas*, in *The Ante-Nicene Fathers*, vol. 3 (Grand Rapids: Eerdmans, 1968), pp. 597–627.

—, *On Idolatry*, in *The Ante-Nicene Fathers*, vol. 3 (Grand Rapids: Eerdmans, 1968), pp. 61–76.

THIELMAN, FRANK, 'The Atonement', in Scott J. Hafemann and Paul R. House (eds.), *Central Themes in Biblical Theology: Mapping Unity in Diversity* (Nottingham: Apollos, 2007).

THOMSON, A., *John Owen: Prince of Puritans* (Fearn: Christian Focus, 1996).

TRAVIS, STEPHEN H., *Christ and the Judgment of God: Divine Retribution in the New Testament* (Basingstoke: Marshall, Morgan & Scott, 1986).

—, 'Christ as Bearer of Divine Judgement in Paul's Thought about the Atonement', in John Goldingay (ed.), *Atonement Today* (London: SPCK, 1995), pp. 21–38.

TURRETIN, FRANCIS, *Institutes of Elenctic Theology*, trans. G. M. Giger, 3 vols. (Phillipsburg: Presbyterian & Reformed, 1994).

—, *The Atonement of Christ*, trans. J. R. Willson (Grand Rapids: Baker, 1978).

VOS, GEERHARDUS, *Biblical Theology: Old and New Testaments* (Grand Rapids: Eerdmans, 1948).

WACE, H. and W. C. PIERCY (eds.), *Dictionary of Christian Biography* (London: John Murray, 1911).

WALSH, M. (ed.), *Dictionary of Christian Biography* (London: Continuum, 2001).

WALTKE, BRUCE K. 'Atonement in Psalm 51', in C. E. Hill and F. A. James III (eds.), *The Glory of the Atonement* (Downers Grove: IVP; Leicester: Apollos, 2004), pp. 51–60.

WEAVER, J. DENNEY, *The Nonviolent Atonement* (Grand Rapids: Eerdmans, 2001).

WEINANDY, THOMAS G., *Does God Suffer?* (Edinburgh: T. & T. Clark, 2000).

WELLS, PAUL, *Cross Words: The Biblical Doctrine of the Atonement* (Fearn: Christian Focus, 2006).

WENHAM, GORDON J., *Genesis 1–15*, Word Biblical Commentary (Nashville: Thomas Nelson, 1987).

—, *The Book of Leviticus*, New International Commentary on the Old Testament (Grand Rapids: Eerdmans, 1979).

WESLEY, JOHN, *Explanatory Notes Upon the New Testament* (London: Epworth, 1976).

WESTERHOLM, STEPHEN, *Perspectives Old and New on Paul: The 'Lutheran' Paul and His Critics* (Grand Rapids: Eerdmans, 2004).

WESTON, PAUL, 'Proclaiming Christ Crucified Today: Some Reflections on John's Gospel', in David Peterson (ed.), *Where Wrath and Mercy Meet: Proclaiming the Atonement Today* (Carlisle: Paternoster, 2001), pp. 136–162.

WHITE, VERNON, *Atonement and Incarnation* (Cambridge: Cambridge University Press, 1991).

WHITEFIELD, GEORGE, *Select Sermons of George Whitefield* (Edinburgh: Banner of Truth, 1958).

—, 'Sermons Preached by the Rev. George Whitefield in the High Church-Yard, Glasgow', in D. MacFarlan, *The Revivals of the Eighteenth Century* (Wheaton: Richard Owen Roberts, 1980).

WHYBRAY, R. N., *Isaiah 40–66*, New Century Bible (London: Oliphants, 1975).

WHYBRAY, R. N., *Thanksgiving for a Liberated Prophet: An Interpretation of Isaiah Chapter 53*, Journal for the Study of the Old Testament Supplement Series 4 (Sheffield: JSOT Press, 1978).

WILLIAMS, GARRY J., 'A Critical Exposition of Hugo Grotius's Doctrine of the Atonement in *De Satisfactione Christi*' (unpub. doctoral thesis, University of Oxford, 1999).

—, 'Justice, Law, and Guilt', paper given at the Evangelical Alliance Symposium on Penal Substitution (2005), http://www.eauk.org/theology/atonement/upload/garry_williams.pdf (accessed 27 March 2006), forthcoming in *Journal of the Evangelical Theological Society*.

—, 'The Cross and the Punishment of Sin', in David Peterson (ed.), *Where Wrath and Mercy Meet: Proclaiming the Atonement Today* (Carlisle: Paternoster, 2001), pp. 68–99.

WILLIAMS, STUART MURRAY, 'Penal Substitution and the Myth of Redemptive Violence', paper given at the Evangelical Alliance Symposium on Penal Substitution (2005), http://www.eauk.org/theology/atonement/upload/stuartmurraywilliams.pdf (accessed 8 February 2006).

—, 'Stuart Murray Williams on the Lost Message of Jesus: A Speech at the Debate on Steve Chalke's Book *The Lost Message of Jesus*', http://www.anabaptistnetwork.com/node/233 (accessed 8 February 2006).

WINK, WALTER, *Engaging the Powers: Discernment and Resistance in a World of Domination* (Minneapolis: Fortress, 1992).

WRIGHT, N. T., 'New Exodus, New Inheritance: The Narrative Substructure of Romans 3–8', in Sven K. Soderlund and N. T. Wright (eds.), *Romans and the People of God* (Grand Rapids: Eerdmans, 1999), pp. 26–35.

—, *Paul for Everyone: Galatians and Thessalonians* (London: SPCK, 2002).

—, *The Climax of the Covenant: Christ and the Law in Pauline Theology* (Minneapolis: Fortress, 1993).

—, *The Letter to the Romans: Introduction, Commentary and Reflections*, in *The New Interpreter's Bible*, vol. 10 (Nashville: Abingdon, 2002), pp. 393–770.

—, *The New Testament and the People of God* (London: SPCK, 1992).

ZIMMERLI, W., 'Zur Vorgeschichte von Jes 53', in *Studien zur alttestamentlichen Theologie und Prophetie* (Munich: Kaiser, 1974).

Much of the material dating from the early church may be downloaded from www.piercedforourtransgressions.com.

# INDEX OF NAMES

Particularly significant references are in **bold**.

# INDEX OF SUBJECTS

Particularly significant references are in **bold**.

# INDEX OF BIBLICAL REFERENCES

Particularly significant references are in **bold**.